The Roman amphitheatre in Pula

Buzara, a typical Dalmatian dish,
shellfish in tomato sauce

The bustling harbour of Makarska

The church of
St Donat in Zadar

HOW TO USE THIS GUIDE

The detailed information and tips given in this guide will help you to get the most out of your visit to Croatia. *Introducing Croatia* maps the country and sets it in its historical and cultural context. The six sections, one dedicated to Zagreb, describe the main sights using maps, photographs and illustrations. In Istria, Kvarner and part of Dalmatia, two languages are spoken (Croatian and Italian) and two place names may refer to the same town. Where both names are officially recognized, the Croatian name is given first, then the Italian in brackets. Restaurant and hotel recommendations can be found in the section *Travellers' Needs*, together with information about shopping and entertainment. The *Survival Guide* has tips on everything from transport to making a phone call, as well as other practical matters.

CROATIA AREA BY AREA

Croatia has been divided into six main areas, each one identified by its own colour code. On the inside front cover is a general map of the country showing these six areas. All the most interesting places to visit are located on the *Regional Map* in each chapter.

Each area can be easily identified by its colour-coded thumb tab.

1 Introduction
This section describes the character and history of each area, highlighting its development over the centuries and what it has to offer the visitor today.

2 Regional Map
This shows the road network and provides an illustrated overview of the whole region. The most interesting places to visit are numbered, and there are useful tips on getting around the region by car and public transport.

3 Detailed Information
All the important towns and other places to visit are described individually. They are listed in order and follow the numbering shown on the Regional Map. Detailed information is given about the most important sights.

The Visitors' Checklist
provides practical information
about transport, opening times,
events and the closing dates of
places of particular interest.

**4 Detailed Information
on Each Sight**
*The main attractions are listed
for each place. A map shows
the main towns, villages and
beaches on the larger islands.*

5 Main Towns
*All the main towns have an
individual section where the
museums, monuments and
other places of interest are listed.
All the sights of major interest
are located on the town map.*

The town map shows
the main roads, stations,
car parking areas and
tourist offices.

6 Street-by-Street Map
*This gives a bird's-eye view
of the key areas of interest in
the main towns and cities with
photographs and captions
describing the sights.*

7 Croatia's Top Sights
*These are given two full
pages. There are cutaways or
reconstructions of historic
buildings, maps of national
parks with information about
trails and facilities available,
and there are floorplans of the
major museums. There are also
photographs of the main sights.*

Stars indicate the sights
that no visitor should miss.

INTRODUCING CROATIA

DISCOVERING CROATIA

With over 4,800 km (3,000 miles) of Mediterranean coastline and 1,185 islands, Croatia is one of Europe's leading holiday playgrounds. Close to the beaches there are picturesque ancient ports and excellent restaurants with sea views.

Mosaic of Christ from Poreč

But there is more to Croatia than just the coast. Inland lie the cultural hot spots of Zagreb and Varaždin, as well as a varied countryside dotted with castles, spa-towns and nature parks. These pages pinpoint Croatia's main attractions and highlights.

ISTRIA AND THE KVARNER AREA

- Beautiful old port towns
- Imperial Opatija
- Plitvice Lakes National Park
- The Island of Rab

Istrian port towns are notable for their stout walls, church towers, and medieval houses tumbling down steep, cobbled alleys to picturesque harbours. Prettiest is **Rovinj** *(see p56)*, but **Poreč** *(see pp53–5)* with its 6th-century **Euphrasian Basilica** and **Pula** *(see pp60–3)* with its 1st-century **Roman Amphitheatre** have the star attractions. The best way to enjoy **Opatija** *(see p67)* is by checking into one of the grand 19th-century seafront promenade hotels – originally built as holiday villas for the Austrian imperial elite; the crystal chandeliers, grand halls of stuccoed columns, elegant parks and formal gardens, contrast sharply

Holidaymakers on the white sand beach at Makarska, Dalmatia

with the more Italianate Istria. Arguably the greatest natural wonder in Croatia is the **Plitvice Lakes National Park** *(see pp86–7)*. A whole day of lakes, cliffs, forests and falls will leave you both awe-struck and coolly refreshed. Serious bathers should seek out the secluded, sandy beach of Lopar on the island of **Rab** *(see pp82–3)*, one of the most exquisite islands in Kvarner Bay.

DALMATIA

- Carefree island hopping
- Great seafood restaurants
- Beaches aplenty
- Coastal capitals of antiquity

Frequent ferry services make Dalmatia's archipelago of islands easily accessible to visitors: see lavender-scented **Hvar** *(see pp126–7)*; medieval **Korčula** *(see pp132–5)* prettily fortified by the Venetians; and unspoilt, pine-covered **Mljet** *(see pp136–7)*, with its quiet coves and picturesque lakeside monastery. The most

expensive region of Croatia, Dalmatia offers one of its finest treats – dining al fresco on a terrace looking over the sea. Swimming in the cool, clean water is also a delight, and you soon learn the art of finding a flat, warm rock to lie on and how to cross a stretch of sharp pebbles. The walk round the walls at **Dubrovnik** *(see pp140–7)* above the mosaic of orange-tiled roofs is amazing, as is **Diocletian's Palace** in **Split** *(see pp118–123)*, a repository brimful of Roman, Renaissance and Baroque architecture. Quaint **Trogir**, *(see pp112–5)* an historic town on an island, also cannot fail to charm.

ZAGREB

- Sophisticated nightlife
- Enchanting Upper Town
- Cathedrals and churches
- Galleries and museums

Having emerged from the historical shadow of Belgrade, Croatia's capital city, Zagreb now resounds again with all

The picturesque old Roman port of Rovinj, Istria

◁ *Noon at Koločep* 1931 by Jerollm Miše

its old self-confidence. At night the city comes out to play in Croatia's classiest choice of bars, clubs, casinos, restaurants, theatres and concert venues. The **Upper Town** *(see pp151–7)*, with its cosy medieval alleyways, churches, funicular railway and fine views, is clearly the loveliest part of Zagreb. At the city's heart stands the **Cathedral of the Assumption of the Blessed Virgin Mary** *(see p150)* with its Neo-Gothic spires. Enjoy too the array of galleries and museums, especially the **Gallery of Old Masters** *(see pp162–3)*, and the **Meštrović Atelier** *(see p156)* devoted to the most renowned Croatian artist.

The Cathedral of the Assumption of the Virgin Mary in Zagreb

CENTRAL CROATIA

- **Fairytale Samobor**
- **Country houses and castles**
- **Lonjsko Polje Nature Park**

The least visited part of the country, Central Croatia nonetheless holds several gems. Just west of Zagreb, up in forested hills typical of the region, lies **Samobor** *(see p170)*. With trim, pastel houses, wooden bridges and a pretty trout stream, this showcase village also offers 13th-century ruins, great walks and family-run restaurants with local specialities. Try local sausages with smoked mustard followed by *kremšnita* custard pastries. Near Zagreb, the **country houses** *(see pp172–3)*

Black Stork, Lonjsko Polje Nature Park

The imposing Veliki Tabor castle in the Northern Counties

of the Croatian aristocracy dot the landscape, while further away in **Sisak**, **Ogulin** and **Hrvatska Kostajnica** *(see pp174–5)*, great castles bear witness to the area's turbulent history. For nature, head southeast to **Lonjsko Polje Nature Park** *(see p176)*, home to Posavina horses, Turopolje spotted pigs and black storks; and smoke-house cottages.

SLAVONIA AND BARANJA

- **Kopački Rit Nature Park**
- **Beautiful Osijek**
- **The rural charm of Topolje**

The flat, fertile plains of Slavonia contain **Kopački Rit Nature Park** *(see pp194–5)*, a wetland extravaganza of animal, fish and bird species that is best explored by boat. Stroll along the Drava at **Osijek** *(see pp190–3)* or enjoy a summer's evening swim in the river, hot from admiring the Baroque architecture of the city's 18th-century centre, the **Tvrđa** *(see pp191–3)*. See the Hungarian influenced farmhouses in the charming countryside around **Topolje** *(see p189)*, many garlanded with drying chilli peppers. In much of the area the painful consequences of war are all too obvious, but as the rebuilding shows, the astonishing resilience of the human spirit is also much in evidence.

THE NORTHERN COUNTIES

- **Baroque Varaždin**
- **Dramatic castles**
- **Historic spa-towns**

Linked by winding country roads through green rolling hills, the Northern Counties are best visited by hire-car from **Varaždin** *(see pp202–3)*. Once the capital of Croatia, 12th-century Varaždin may have a medieval castle and town hall but the atmospheric charm of its cobbles, pretty churches, and outdoor cafés is pure Austrian Baroque. The 14th-century castle **Veliki Tabor** *(see p210)* looks good from the outside, but the century older **Trakošćan** *(see pp206–7)*, overlooking a lake, is more impressive. Nestled in a lush green forest, **Varaždinske Toplice** *(see p213)* is a Roman spa-town that should not be missed.

Chilli peppers drying in the sun in Topolje, Baranja

Putting Croatia on the Map

Covering an area of 56,542 sq km (21,825 sq miles),
Croatia has a population of approximately 4,290,600
with an average of 76 inhabitants per square
kilometre. Since the break-up of the former
Yugoslavia, and Croatian independence, the country
has been bordered by Slovenia, Hungary, Bosnia-
Herzegovina and the two now independent republics
of Serbia, and Montenegro. It is not a large country,
but it has a wide variety of natural and man-made
environments. From a topographical point of view the
country is made up of three types of terrain. Much is
mountainous, with peaks up to 2,000 m (6,560 ft) high,
mostly covered with forest and pasture. The vast
Pannonian Plain lies between the rivers Drava, Sava
and the Danube. Coastal Croatia is nearly 600 km
(372 miles) long, but over 2,000 km (1,242 miles) long
when the indented coastline is taken into account, and
twice that when the hundreds of islands are included.

A U S T

LJUBLJANA

SLOVENIA

Verona

Venice

Trieste

Rijeka

Pazin

Poreč/
Parenzo

Rovinj/
Rovigno

Pula/
Pola

Labin

Krk

Cres

Cres

Rab

Senj

Otočac

Gospić

Bologna

Lošinj

Veli Lošinj

Pag

Pag

Zadar

ITALY

ADRIATIC

Dugi Otok

Florence

S. MARINO

Ancona

Kornat

SEA

Pescara

Satellite view of Croatia

CROATIA AND EUROPE

FINLAND
ATLANTIC
NORWAY
SWEDEN
ESTONIA
LATVIA
UNITED KINGDOM
DENMARK
LITHUANIA
IRELAND
RUSSIA
THE NETHERLANDS
BELORUSSIA
BELGIUM GERMANY POLAND
ATLANTIC OCEAN
LUXEMBOURG
CZECH REPUBLIC
UKRAINE
FRANCE
SLOVAKIA
SWITZERLAND
AUSTRIA
HUNGARY
SLOVENIA Zagreb
ROMANIA
PORTUGAL
ANDORRA
BOSNIA HERZEGOVINA SERBIA
MONTENEGRO BULGARIA
SPAIN
CORSICA
CROATIA
ALBANIA
SARDINIA
ITALY
GREECE

MOROCCO ALGERIA TUNISIA

Győr
E60
E65
E59
E84
HUNGARY
E66
Lake Balaton
Čakovec
Varaždin
A4
Koprivnica
ZAGREB
Bjelovar
SERBIA
Drava
Čazma
Virovitica
E70
Daruvar
Našice
Osijek
A5
Sisak
Kutina
A3
Vukovar
Glina
Sava
Požega
Đakovo
Novi Sad
Nova Gradiška
Vinkovci
Slavonski Brod
4
Danube

Banja Luka
E761
E73
BOSNIA
HERZEGOVINA
E761
Knin
E71
E760
E73
Šibenik
Sinj
SARAJEVO
A1
Split
Brač
Šolta
Hvar
Hvar
E65
Mostar
Korčula
A10
Opuzen
Lastovo
A1
Mljet National Park
Dubrovnik
Bari

KEY

✈	International airport
⛴	Ferry terminal
▬	Motorway
▬	Major road
▪ ▪	Under construction
—	Railway line
–·–	International border
---	Ferry route

0 kilometres   75

0 miles   50

A PORTRAIT OF CROATIA

Croatia forms a meeting point between the Mediterranean and central Europe, and between the Alps and the Pannonian Plain. Its relatively small territory is made up of a wide variety of landscapes. A stunningly beautiful country, it has re-emerged from the difficult years of conflict and regained its role as a popular holiday destination.

Croatia seceded from the Federal Socialist Republic of Yugoslavia in 1990, following the first free elections since World War II. However, the brutal conflict that quickly followed had disastrous effects on the economy and led to the damage and destruction of many historic monuments and treasures. The United Nations administered disputed territories until 1995, and the last region, Eastern Slavonia, was returned to Croatian administration only in January 1998.

The national flag of Croatia

The resolution of the conflict recreated a country which had lost its autonomy long ago in 1102, when Croatian nobles handed the vacant crown to King Koloman. Under Koloman, Croatia became part of Hungary and remained so for 900 years, until 1918. At the end of World War I, Croatia declared independence but, under pressure from greater powers, agreed to become part of the kingdom of Yugoslavia. From the ruins of the Habsburg empire emerged Yugoslavia: a new state of Serbs, Croatians and Slovenes.

Few people live in the steep mountainous areas and as a result the forests of this region, among the most beautiful in southern Europe, are unspoilt. The coast and larger islands are more densely populated and the income from tourism is important to many. The political upheavals of the last decade of the 20th century have caused a shifting of the population and many Serbs have moved away.

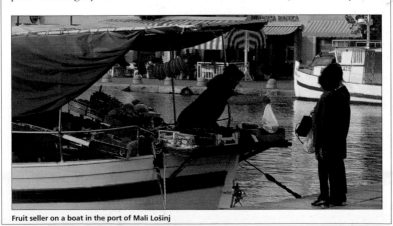

Fruit seller on a boat in the port of Mali Lošinj

◁ People strolling along Krešimirova ulica in the busy centre of Split

Fisherman mending his nets in the port of Fažana

POPULATION

According to a census carried out in 2011, Croatia has a population of 4,290,612. Compared with the census of 2001, this is a decrease of nearly 150,000 in the population. These figures, a reflection of the upheavals of the 1990s, reduce the numbers to the population levels of 1968. Two different factors were responsible for these changes. Firstly, the departure of thousands of Serbians (partially offset by the return of Croatians resident in other parts of former Yugoslavia), and secondly, the emigration of many young people in search of work in other countries in Europe, America or Australia.

The tragic events of the 1990s have also altered the distribution of the population, emptying villages and concentrating populations in large urban centres. Changes to the size of many towns and cities, the result of enlarging their territorial boundaries, make detailed analysis difficult, particularly with regard to Zagreb, Rijeka, Split, Osijek and Zadar.

Woman in the typical costume of Konavle

ECONOMY

Manufacturing industries are concentrated in the larger cities and employ 20 per cent of the population. The service industry is being overhauled and provides employment for an increasing number of workers, mainly in the tourist sector, which has recovered after a decade of recession and neglect: 7 per cent of the population is employed in this area.

Demand for fresh fish to supply the tourist resorts means that the fishing industry has revived and mussel farming has also expanded, in particular along the Limski Channel and around Ston. The privatization of much agricultural land, and the introduction of modern machinery and the rationalization of crops, have reduced the number of farm workers. However, the production of fruit and wine grapes has recovered, and overall quality is improving significantly.

The urgent need to rebuild public and privately-owned buildings damaged during the conflict in the 1990s and the ever-increasing demand for tourist facilities keeps the numbers employed in the building trade high: 7 per cent of the workforce is involved in the construction industry. However, in spite of an improved standard of living for most of the population, unemployment is still high. Croatia hopes to resolve most of its employment problems by joining the European Union, and by providing land, energy and labour at competitive costs. The building of a modern road network with the construction of new motorways, the modernization of the railways and plans to improve the ports will also help to alleviate high unemployment levels.

TRADITIONS AND CUSTOMS

Since the rebirth of the Croatian state, all kinds of traditional festivals have reappeared. These festivals, ceremonies or games commemorate historical, religious and military events. Some festivals are expressions of primitive or ancient faith, and mix Christianity with ancient pagan rites, others are linked to the religious calendar. Traditional costumes and jewellery, carefully preserved by the older generation, are worn on these occasions. The materials may sometimes be new but the designs stay faithfully traditional.

Other expressions of popular culture are the rites linked to the rhythms of farming: harvesting, bringing flocks down from the mountains, felling trees. The Feast of St Blaise, the patron saint of Dubrovnik, is magnificent. People from local and surrounding parishes gather, dressed in splendid costumes and displaying ancient banners in honour of the saint. Even the communists were unable to suppress this tradition. Another spectacular festivity is the Olympics of Ancient Sports in Brođanci, when young people parade in gold-embroidered costumes, followed by groups of musicians. Other important events are the Festival of the Bumbari in Vodnjan with its donkey race, the

One of many religious events in Split

Folk Festival in Đakovo and the Moreška and Kumpanija festivals in Korčula, commemorating battles against the Ottoman Turks.

LANGUAGE

The attempt to fuse the Croatian and Serbian languages lasted more than a century, but in 1991 the official language of Croatia became Croatian, and this is now part of the constitution. The language has always been a fundamental part of Croatian identity, even under foreign domination. The people continue to use three basic dialects, štokavski in southern and eastern Croatia, čakavski in Istria and parts of Dalmatia, and kajkavski in Zagreb and the north. A dialect similar to Venetian is spoken along the coast.

RELIGION

Religious feeling has always been important to Croatians. Religion was relegated to a secondary role during the communist period but the great sanctuaries are once again centres of spirituality. In the 2001 census, over 90 per cent declared they were Christian (88 per cent Catholic, 4 per cent Orthodox), with a Muslim minority, mostly Bosnians, and a Protestant minority, mostly Hungarians. The Orthodox community has shrunk due to the fall in the number of Serbians.

The lively centre of Split, a popular meeting place

The Landscape and Wildlife of Croatia

A wide variety of landscapes can be found in Croatia, from wild uninhabited craggy gorges to steep river valleys and a stunningly beautiful indented coastline stretching into the lower Adriatic, dotted with hundreds of islands. A plateau stretches from the Istrian peninsula towards Gorski Kotar and ends in the hilly vine-growing region of Zagorje. The geological formations produced by the porous limestone terrain called karst are found in Gorski Kotar and continue to nearby Istria and the Velebit mountains, where the combination of wind, rain and rock has created strange shapes called *kukovi*. Nicknames and legends have been created by folklore for these rock formations, and for the thousands of rocky islands off the coast, remnants of an ancient mountain chain.

Seagull perched on a rocky outcrop near the island of Pag

MOUNTAINS

Mountains form 40 per cent of Croatia and rise to nearly 2,000 m (6,560 ft) high. The higher land is given over to sheep farming and the breeding of livestock. The forests are mixed, with pine, fir, chestnut and beech, depending on altitude and microclimate. The wildlife includes bears, wolves, wild boar, lynxes, badgers, foxes, roebucks and chamois. Forestry management aims to control deforestation.

The forests *are a precious resource in Croatia. Thick vegetation covers more than 30 per cent of the country.*

The chamois *was thought to have disappeared from Croatia but there are now a dozen or so animals originating from Slovenia.*

THE PLAIN

The plain is bordered by wide rivers which also define Croatia's borders for much of their length. The vast Pannonian Plain is the breadbasket of Croatia. Maize, wheat, soya and tobacco are grown here and at the fringes are vine-covered hills. At one time there were forests here, dominated by the Slavonian oak, much sought-after in Europe for the quality of its wood. A few isolated remnants of these forests can still be seen.

The oak of Slavonia, *famous since ancient times, was used to build most of the ships in the Venetian and Dubrovnik fleets, because of its extraordinary strength.*

The Croatian plain *is one of the most fertile areas in Europe. Some agricultural produce is exported.*

NATIONAL PARKS

Croatia began protecting wildlife areas of particular importance in 1949 by setting up the Plitvice Lakes National Park on the Lika plateau. A few years later, the Risnjak National Park was founded north of Rijeka, then in 1985 the Krka National Park north of Šibenik. The Paklenica National Park, at the heart of the Velebit mountain chain, dates from 1949. In 1978 it was declared a world biosphere reserve by UNESCO and later included on the list of World Heritage Sites. It is home to over 2,400 species of plant. There are four national parks in the Adriatic: the Mljet National Park, founded in 1960, the Kornati National Park (1980), the Brijuni National Park (1983) and the North Velebit National Park (1999). There are also nature reserves, oases, biotopes (environments characterized by particular conditions) and two marshes: Kopački Rit and Lonjsko Polje. In 2008, Stari Grad Plain on the island of Hvar was declared a UNESCO World Heritage Site.

Risnjak National Park with its thick forests of fir and beech

THE COAST

The coast's appearance is determined by the extent of its exposure to the fierce, northeast bora wind. Mediterranean flora flourishes on the sheltered side, with olives, lemon trees and vines. Low-growing vines are cultivated along the central part of the coast and on some of the islands, sheltered from the wind by stone walls. Two common plants along the coast and on the islands are lavender, particularly on Hvar, and broom.

The marine life *is extraordinarily varied, with a wide range of species including sea-horses.*

Broom *is a common sight in Croatia. In spring, it bears bright yellow flowers.*

LAKES AND RIVERS

The lakes of Croatia are not large, but some are truly spectacular, as for example those of Plitvice and those formed by the River Krka. The rivers are another of Croatia's valuable resources. The Danube, Drava, Sava and Kupa are all navigable and form international transport routes (although traffic is currently partly interrupted). The rivers abound with a variety of fish and are a big attraction for fishing enthusiasts.

Waterlilies *are in flower in late spring, particularly in Lonjsko Polje and Kopački Rit.*

Storks *live near the rivers as well as in protected nature reserves in Croatia. The wetlands make an ideal habitat for the rare black stork.*

Art and Artists in Croatia

For centuries Croatian art has combined elements from
eastern and western Europe. The coast was ruled by Venice
for 400 years, and between the Middle Ages and the 17th
century, Croatia was in regular contact with the other side of
the Adriatic. Italian artists came to the islands to work, and
the Dalmatians crossed the sea and brought Romanesque,
Gothic and Renaissance styles back to their country. After
the expulsion of the Turks at the end of the 17th century,
many churches were rebuilt in the Baroque style, and
acquired rich ornamentation. The 20th century saw the
advent of Naive painting, an important artistic trend, and
sculptor Ivan Meštrović was confirmed as Croatia's
most famous contemporary artist *(see p157)*.

Maria Banac, sculpture
by Ivan Meštrović

SCULPTURE

The art of sculpture in
Croatia has ancient origins
and may have been inspired
by the local stone, used to
construct some of the most
important Roman monu-
ments in Pula and Split,
which became models for
future generations of
Adriatic sculptors.

Sculpture and stone
carving reached the height of
expression with the
Romanesque style. Dating
from this time are the
cathedral doors of Trogir and
Split, the rose windows of
Zadar and Rab, the capitals
in the cloisters in Dubrovnik
and Zadar, and much church
statuary. The technical skills
of the Renaissance period
are documented in Šibenik
cathedral, with masterpieces
by Juraj Dalmatinac, Nikola
Firentinac and Andrija Aleši.

The stonemasons should
also be remembered,
particularly those of Korčula.
Decades of skilled work
went into Korčula cathedral
and the masons' work can
be seen in hundreds of other
towns and cities in Croatia.

Sculpture again reached a
peak in the 20th century
with Ivan Meštrović, the
chief figure in a group of
great artists which included
Antun Augustinčić.

ANDRIJA BUVINA

All that is known of this
sculptor is that he was born

**Wooden panel by Andrija Buvina
in Split cathedral**

in Split and lived in the 13th
century. The great door of
the cathedral of his native
city is testament to his skill.
This masterpiece from 1214
consists of 28 wooden panels depicting the life of
Christ, and uses simple lines
allied to a wealth of detail.

MASTER RADOVAN

The sculptor Master Radovan
was of Dalmatian origin and
lived in the 13th century. His
name appears on the door of

**The door of the cathedral of Trogir
by Master Radovan**

the cathedral in Trogir,
which he started in about
1240 and which was later
completed by other artists.
This complex masterpiece
has columns, arches,
sculpted relief figures and
rich decoration. It is possible
to discern scenes from the
life of Christ such as the
Annunciation, the Flight to
Egypt, and the Martyrdom
on Golgotha, while other
sculptures represent the
months of the year. The
artist's expressive skill is
revealed in the figures of
Adam and Eve in particular.

JURAJ DALMATINAC

Juraj Dalmatinac, also known
as Giorgio Orsini, was an
ambassador for Dalmatian
art, which was
greatly
influenced by
Venice. The
artist was born
in Zadar in
about 1400 and
died in 1475.
He was active
in Dalmatia
and in Italy as
a sculptor and
an architect.

**Face by
Dalmatinac in
the cathedral
of Šibenik**

The cathedral of St James in
Šibenik *(see pp108–9)*, to
which he contributed, is
regarded as one of the
masterpieces of the Croatian
Renaissance. Dalmatinac
sculpted the faces on the
upper part of the base of the
apses and also the statues of
Adam and Eve at either side
of the Door of Lions.

ARTISTS

Painting in Croatia cannot boast a history equal to that of sculpture since it was only after contact with the Venetian school at the end of the 16th century that Croatian painting emerged in Istria and Dalmatia. The monasteries and cathedrals commissioned Venetian masters to make altarpieces and in emulating these models the great artists of Dubrovnik developed.

In the late 17th–18th centuries, the Baroque style predominated in inland Croatia in architecture as well as art. Baroque originated in German-speaking areas and inspired local artists; the Austrian artist Ivan Ranger *(see p206)* was a key figure. Interest in religious paintings then dwindled, and in the 19th century, young artists were inspired by pan-European culture. In the 1930s and 40s Naive Art developed.

Polyptych by Lovro Dobričević in the church of St Mary of Dance

VINCENT OD KASTVA

One of the most expressive cycles of frescoes in Istria bears the signature of this Istrian painter, Vincent od Kastva (Vincenzo da Castua), who lived in the 15th century. The frescoes are hidden away in the small church of St Mary (Sv. Marija na Škriljinah) in Beram. The brightly coloured frescoes, on the side walls and the inside façade, were painted in about 1471 with assistants and have a primitive but vigorous style. The *Life of Christ and the Virgin* has figures of saints; the best-known work is the *Dance of Death*, where Death, holding a scythe, punishes sinners, here represented by all the most powerful

people on earth (from the pope to lords of the manor).

LOVRO DOBRIČEVIĆ

Little is known of Lovro Marinov Dobričević (Lorenzo De Boninis), pupil of Paolo Veneziano, who lived in the 15th century and is regarded as one of the most significant exponents of the Dubrovnik school. Two of his great works are in Dubrovnik: the *Baptism of Christ* (c.1448) is in the Dominican Museum and the polyptych *Virgin, Christ and the Saints Julian and Nicholas* (1465) is in the church of St Mary of Dance (Sv. Marije na Dančama).

JULIJE KLOVIĆ

Julije Klović (Giulio Clovio) was one of the most famous Renaissance miniaturists. A native of Croatia (he was born in Grižane in 1498), his most significant works are found outside the country. The painter developed his craft in Venice, and was then summoned to work in Rome, Mantua, Perugia and numerous monasteries. He died in Rome in 1578.

Miniature by Klović

Dance of Death **by Vincent od Kastva**

THE HLEBINE SCHOOL

Krsto Hegedušić (1901–75), Expressionist painter and later a Naive artist, founded a group of artists called Zemlja ("Earth"). He encouraged the work of two amateur painters from the village of Hlebine, near Koprivnica: Ivan Generalić and Franjo Mraz, who depicted their local world on glass and canvas in fresh, vivid style. Together with Mirko Virius they founded the Hlebine school which flourished from 1930 to the beginning of World War

Woodcutters **by Generalić, Museum of Naive Art, Zagreb**

II. Many other painters, including Ivan Večenaj, Dragan Gaži, Franjo Filipović and Josip Generalić, followed their ideas, concentrating on depicting the lives of outcasts, the poor, and working folk. The Hlebine school became a world-wide phenomenon with the 1952 Venice Biennale and exhibitions in Brazil and Brussels. Naive works are on show at the Hlebine Gallery in Koprivnica and the Museum of Naive Art in Zagreb.

Architecture in Croatia

Croatian architecture, like its art, has also been influenced by Croatia's position in Europe. Secular and religious buildings display a fusion of elements from nearby Italy and Germany and other forms originating in the Byzantine or Slavic worlds. This blending of influences was first noticeable in the time of the Romans and still continues today. Some styles became particularly important: for example the impressive cathedrals of the Adriatic coast, the legacy of many centuries of Venetian rule. In inland Croatia Baroque architecture prevails, characterized by exuberant decoration and expansive forms.

The Byzantine Euphrasian Basilica in Poreč

PRE-ROMANESQUE AND ROMANESQUE

True Croatian architecture begins with pre-Romanesque and dates back to the time of Duke Branimir (879–92), who created the first state of Croatia. Contact with the Byzantine world influenced the look of religious buildings in Istria and Dalmatia but some decorative elements reveal the first signs of Romanesque: small churches with irregular ground-plans appear in areas inhabited by Croatian tribes. The founding of Šibenik (1066) saw the first Romanesque buildings, introduced by the Cistercians. The style spread and remained popular until the end of the 16th century, and three-aisle cathedrals with apses were built as well as monasteries with cloisters, public buildings, town halls and loggias.

The church of the Holy Cross in Nin (see p100), *one of the most interesting examples of the pre-Romanesque, known as the world's smallest cathedral, was built in the 9th century. It has a Greek cross ground-plan with three apses. It is positioned to ensure that the sun's rays fall in pre-planned positions on the floor and act as a clock.*

The façade consists of vertical and horizontal lines: the upper order is decorated with blind arcades and rose windows.

The cathedral of St Anastasia in Zadar (see p94), *founded in the 9th century but rebuilt in the 12th–13th, shows the links between Croatian and Italian Romanesque, particularly in the façade, similar to churches found in Pisa and Lucca in Italy.*

Romanesque rose window

The arched main door, richly decorated

GOTHIC

The Gothic style, more than any other in Croatia, is lasting evidence of the long rule of the Venetians along the Istrian and Dalmatian coasts. It developed following the Venetian conquest of the Adriatic coast (1420) and is a fundamental expression of the close contact that was established. Venetian Gothic not only influenced the design of Dalmatian and Istrian churches but also mansions in Pula, Rab, Pag, Zadar, Šibenik and Split.

The door with an ogival arch is decorated with thin spiral columns and has two lions on the corbel.

Rose window

Façade of the Town Hall in Split

The cathedral of St Mark in Korčula (see p132) *is of Romanesque origins – the bell tower is evidence of this. The façade shows similarities with churches in Puglia in southern Italy. Gothic elements include the pointed arches over the entrance door, which was the work of Bonino of Milan.*

RENAISSANCE

The Renaissance style was only able to develop in those parts of the country which did not fall under Turkish rule. The most important architects and artists of the time were Juraj Dalmatinac *(see p20)*, Nikola Firentinac and Andrija Aleši, who worked mainly along the Adriatic coast. They were all involved in the construction of churches and public buildings. The cathedral of St James in Šibenik *(see pp108–9)* became a model for the churches of St Stephen in Hvar, St Mary in Zadar and St Saviour in Dubrovnik. Renaissance buildings also appeared in the north of Croatia, both in the form of private residences (Varaždin and Čakovec) and castles (Trakošćan and Veliki Tabor).

The second storey, with windows and a statue of the city's patron saint, St Blaise, in the centre, was a later addition.

The windows in Venetian Gothic symbolize the ties between Dubrovnik and Venice.

Sponza Palace in Dubrovnik (see p144) *has both Gothic and Renaissance elements, a reflection of the time it took to build. It was begun in 1312 (the beautiful Gothic windows on the first floor date from this period) and remodelled in 1516–22, when the Renaissance arcaded loggia on the ground floor was added.*

BAROQUE

This was the style that characterized the legitimization of Christian worship in Croatia after the expulsion of the Turks at the end of the 17th century. The signs of Ottoman rule were eradicated and architects, mainly of German extraction, constructed public and private buildings, enriching them with ornate decorations equal to those of the churches, castles and sanctuaries. The most notable examples of the Baroque style can be found in Varaždin, Požega, Osijek, Križevci, Ludbreg and Krapina.

Vojković-Oršić-Rauch Palace, *now home of the Croatian Historical Museum (see p158), is one of many fine Baroque buildings in Zagreb. The façade and interior have the sumptuous decorations of the time with elegant columns, scalloped windows and a decorated tympanum.*

MODERNISM

By the 19th century Zagreb had become the centre of political and cultural life in Croatia, which gave it a prominent role as leader in the architectural field. Much experimentation took place in the following century in the capital, inspired first by the Viennese Secession style and later by Modernism. The church of St Blaise and Villa Krauss are interesting examples of the latter style.

The Neo-Renaissance Mimara Museum in Zagreb

This typically elegant building is functional and symmetrical

The decorations in Secession style are stylized and not figurative.

On the façade are sculptures and bas reliefs by the Croatian artists Robert Frangeš-Mihanović and Rudolf Valdec.

The former National and University Library *in the centre of Marulić Square in Zagreb was designed by a local architect, Rudolf Lubinsky. It is regarded as the most significant work in the Secession style in Croatia.*

CROATIA THROUGH THE YEAR

The upheavals of the decade from 1991–2000 inevitably affected the calendar of events which characterizes the cultural life of Croatia. However, concerts, theatre seasons and sporting events have now largely been resumed along with religious festivals and events linked to local traditions. The different stages in the agricultural year, such as the grape

Typical costume of Pag

harvest, the threshing, fishing or hunting seasons, are also marked. In addition, every town celebrates its patron saint's day and the "town's day", which is linked to episodes in the town's history. Zagreb offers a rich calendar of cultural events all through the year, while the festivals in the towns and villages along the coast are generally held during the summer season.

SPRING

The arrival of spring in Croatia coincides with a series of important dates in the religious calendar. Spring brings warmer weather and also sees the beginning of a series of festivals and events which continue throughout the summer. Catholic churches are especially busy around Easter time, with its associated rituals.

Procession during Holy Week on the island of Korčula

MARCH

Holy Week *(Easter)*. On Korčula Easter is celebrated with processions of brotherhoods performing mystery plays and singing.

APRIL

Musical Biennial of Zagreb *(Apr)*. Annual festival of modern music.

St George's Day, Senj *(23 Apr)*.
St Vincenca's Day, Korčula *(28 Apr)*. The Kumpanjija dance which commemorates an ancient battle between enemy armies is performed. At the finale local girls in costume dance in a circle.

MAY

Croatian Wine Exhibition, Kutjevo *(May)*. Displays of Croatian wines plus a folk-lore and music programme.
Days of Hvar Theatre, Hvar *(May)*. Annual celebration of Croatian literature and theatre, as well as scientific themes and presentations by scientists from other countries.
Regatta Rovinj–Pesaro–Rovinj, Rovinj.
Meeting of Puppet Theatres, Osijek *(early May)*. Performances of professional and amateur puppet theatre companies.
Tournament of Rab *(9 May)*. Parade of costumed riders with crossbows.
Festival of the Small Theatre, Rijeka *(first half of May)*. Groups from all over Europe participate.
Josip Štolcer Slavenski Memorial, Čakovec *(first half of May)*. Musical festival dedicated to the great 20th-century Croatian composer.
Festival of Croatian Tambour Music, Osijek *(mid-May)*. Festival of ancient music with period instruments, including the tambour.

Festival of Amateur Film and Video, Požega *(end May)*. Screenings of short amateur films and videos.

SUMMER

As this is the season when most tourists visit Croatia, particularly Istria and Dalmatia, this is also the period when the calendar of events is busiest. There are festivals dedicated to music, theatre and dance, as well as many traditional festivals. The folk festivals held throughout the summer are particularly colourful events.

JUNE

Dance Week, Zagreb *(May/ Jun)*. International festival of dance, movement and mime, organized in collaboration with European associations.
Music events, Pula *(all summer)*. Various events in the Roman amphitheatre.
Festival of Satire, Zagreb *(Jun)*. International festival celebrating the satirical.

The festival of Brodsko Kolo, Slavonski Brod

AVERAGE DAILY HOURS OF SUNSHINE

Sunshine
The Dalmatian coast is one of the sunniest parts of Europe, and the island of Hvar holds the record with its 2,700 hours of sun a year. The summers along the coast are hot and dry, while the inland areas have a continental climate with hot summers and cold winters.

Đakovački Vezovi, a folklore and embroidery festival in Đakovo

Brodsko Kolo, Slavonski Brod *(mid-Jun)*. Displays of folk dancing in costume, shows and exhibitions of regional produce.

Summer of Margherita, Bakar *(last week of Jun)*. Concerts and performances in the čakavski dialect.

International Children's Festival, Šibenik *(end Jun–beginning Jul)*. Festival dedicated to the creativity of the very young. Music, dance, theatre and film.

Summer Festival, Hvar *(Jun–Sep)*. A fun festival of music, theatre, folklore and dancing.

JULY

Festival klapa, Omiš *(Jul)*. Celebration of traditional Dalmatian songs performed by groups of five to ten men.

Rapska fjera, Rab *(Jul)*. For three days the town of Rab is returned to medieval times, with craft displays, preparation of traditional dishes and an archery tournament.

Đakovački Vezovi, Đakovo *(first week of Jul)*. Folklore displays and exhibition of local embroidery.

St Theodore's Day, Korčula *(29 Jul)*. The Moreška, a dance re-enacting a battle between Christians and Muslims.

International Tennis Tournament, Umag *(end Jul)*.

International Folklore Festival, Zagreb *(end Jul)*. Croatian music and dance with international guests.

Pag Carnival, Pag *(end Jul)*. Traditional dancing, kolo, and various shows with the local people in traditional costumes.

International Jazz Festival, Grožnjan *(Jul–Aug)*. International jazz artists participate in this festival in the picturesque Istrian town of Grožnjan.

Labin Art Republic, Labin *(Jul–Aug)*. Classical concerts, folk music.

Music Festival, Zadar *(beginning Jul–beginning Aug)*. Church, theatre and instrumental music.

Osor Music Festival, Osor *(mid-Jul–mid-Aug)*. Chamber music.

Split Summer *(mid-Jul–mid-Aug)*. A programme of opera, concerts, dance, theatre and performances of the first plays written in the Croatian language.

International Festival of Theatre, Pula *(mid-Jul–mid-Aug)*. Multimedia festival with the participation of other European groups.

Dubrovnik Summer Festival, Dubrovnik *(mid-Jul–end Aug)*. The oldest international festival in Croatia: music, theatre, folklore, ballet, with performers from many countries.

Krk Summer Festival, Krk *(mid-Jul–end Aug)*. Music and prose, concerts, ballet, performances by young artists and folklore.

Concerts in the Basilica of Euphrasius, Poreč *(Jul–mid Sep)*. Performances of church and secular music given by Croatian and European musicians.

The Moreška dance, St Theodore's Day, Korčula

AVERAGE MONTHLY RAINFALL

Rainfall
Rain is sparse along the coast, particularly in summer, when there is often the threat of drought. However, in the mountains, rain and snow are plentiful. In northeastern parts of the country there may be summer thunderstorms. Winter brings snow.

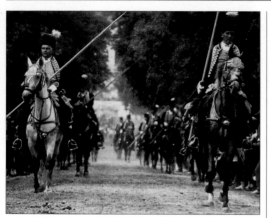
Costumed jousters on horseback during the folk festival, Sinj

AUGUST

Summer Carnival, Novi Vinodolski *(Aug)*.
Festival of the Bumbari, Vodnjan *(2nd Sat in Aug)*. "Bumbari" is what the local people call themselves. A folk festival in costume with an unusual donkey race and the preparation of *crostoli*, cakes of Venetian origin.
Baljanska Noć, Bale *(first Sun in Aug)*. Festival of the city.
Trka na prstenac, Barban *(3rd weekend in Aug)*. Jousting tournament, dating back as far as 1696.
Sinjska Alka, Sinj *(beginning Aug)*. Folklore festival commemorating victory over the Turks, with jousting competitions for horse riders. Parades, dancing, folk music and displays of regional produce.
St Roch's Day, Žrnovo and Postrana (on Korčula) *(16*

Aug). Events include the Mostra, a traditional sword dance. At one time the festivities ended with the sacrifice of an ox.
Olympics of Ancient Sports, Brođanci *(last Sun in Aug)*. Folk festival with traditional costumes and musicians playing in the streets.
Mediterranean Sculptors' Symposium, Labin *(Aug–Sep)*. A meeting place for sculptors from all over the world since the 1960s.

Festival of Vinkovačke Jeseni, Vinkovci

AUTUMN

Visiting Croatia in this season means there are fewer crowds, even along the busy Adriatic coast. However this season also offers an unexpectedly rich and varied calendar of events. Many of the events are cultural but there are also several festivals celebrating wine and food – offering an ideal opportunity to discover some of the local produce of this country.

SEPTEMBER

Festival of the Golden Strings of Slavonia, Požega *(Sep)*. Festival of folk and modern music using the traditional Slavonian instrument the *tamburica*.
Lace Exhibition, Lepoglava *(Sep)*. Exhibition of traditional hand-made lace, still made according to ancient methods.
Week of Kajkavian Culture, Krapina *(Sep)*. Festival of Kajkavian poetry, folk music and painting.
International Doll Festival, Zagreb *(beginning Sep)*.
Grape Festival, Buje *(3rd weekend in Sep)*.
Vinkovačke Jeseni, Vinkovci *(Sep–Oct)*. Festival of music and folk traditions. Parades in costume.
Baroque Evenings in Varaždin, Varaždin Cathedral *(second half of Sep–first half of Oct)*. Festival of

AVERAGE MONTHLY TEMPERATURE

Temperature
The climate in Croatia is typically Mediterranean along the coast, with mild winters and hot, dry summers. Inland the climate is continental with hot summers and cold winters. The mountainous areas have an alpine climate.

Baroque music with the participation of top Croatian and European musicians.

OCTOBER

Dora Pejačević Memorial, Našice *(Oct)*. Music festival commemorating this composer, with concerts, performances by artists and competitions.
Bela Nedeja, Kastav *(first Sun in Oct)*. Wine festival.
Marunada, Lovran *(mid-Oct)*. Chestnut festival.
Triennial of Ceramics, Zagreb *(mid-Oct–mid-Nov)*. Ceramics festival.

NOVEMBER

St Martin's Day, Dugo Selo, Samobor, Sv. Ivan Zelina, Velika Gorica, Zagreb County *(Nov)*. A traditional wine festival that celebrates the period when the must is turned into wine.

The Town's Day, Lipik *(4 Nov)*. Traditional festival celebrating the town.

WINTER

The cold makes itself felt throughout Croatia, with the temperatures in Zagreb and Slavonia dropping well below freezing point and the cold bora wind sweeping across Istria and Dalmatia. But Croatians still love to go out and enjoy themselves and attend cultural events.

DECEMBER

The Town's Day, Osijek *(2 Dec)*. Celebration of Osijek's main feast day with music and dancing.

JANUARY

International Competition for Young Pianists, Osijek *(second half of Jan)*. For young musicians under 21.
Feast of St Blaise, Dubrovnik *(end Jan or early Feb)*. Processions celebrating town's saint.

FEBRUARY

Shrovetide Sezona, Kraljevica. Traditional masked ball.
Carnival of Rijeka, Rijeka. Colourful parade in elaborate costumes.
Carnival of the Riviera, Opatija.
International Violin Competition (Vaclav Huml), Zagreb *(first half of Feb)*. For violinists under 30.
Carnival, Lastovo.

Costume at the Carnival of Lastovo

CROATIAN HOLIDAYS

New Year's Day 1 Jan
Epiphany 6 Jan
Easter Sunday and Monday Mar or Apr
Labour Day 1 May
Corpus Christi May or Jun
Anti-Fascist Victory Day 22 Jun
Statehood Day 25 Jun
Victory and National Thanksgiving Day 5 Aug
Assumption Day 15 Aug
Independence Day 8 Oct
All Saints' Day 1 Nov
Christmas 25 Dec
Boxing Day 26 Dec

A Baroque music ensemble playing in the cathedral, Varaždin

THE HISTORY OF CROATIA

*S*ituated between eastern and western Europe, Croatia has long been a land of passage but also a point of contact between different worlds and cultures. Diverse events and cultural influences have all contributed to the country's history. Croatia is particularly proud of its close ties to the West; for more than a century, parts of the country struggled to free themselves from harsh Turkish domination. The history of Croatia goes back almost as far as man's first appearance on earth.

Clay vase found in Vučedol, 2800–2500 BC

PREHISTORY

Early in the 19th century ancient human remains were found at Krapina in the north of Croatia. Dating from the Neander-thal period, "Krapina man" places human presence in Croatia in the middle-Palaeolithic. Other traces of prehistoric cultures have been found in Croatia. The richest site is probably Vučedol, near Vukovar, where the Neolithic "Vučedol Dove" *(see p188)* was found.

THE ILLYRIANS

Around 1200 BC, tribes of Indo-European origin settled on the Pannonian Plain, the larger islands and along the coast. The tribes had different names (Istrians, Liburnians, Dalmatians, Japods) depending on where they settled, but the area was known under one name, Illyria. They traded amber and had dealings with other Mediterranean people and northern European traders. Traces of ancient walls on some hilltops confirm their presence.

THE CELTS

In the 4th century BC, the Celts began to search for new lands when Gaul became over-populated. Some tribes followed the River Danube to the present-day Bohemia, some went as far as the Greek border. In the same period the Greeks founded fortified colonies on some Dalmatian islands including Vis and Hvar and in the area of Trogir and Salona. Greek historians claim the Celts fought against Alexander the Great in 335 BC on the southern banks of the Danube. A century later, they attacked Delphi and on their return stopped at the Paludes Volcae, an area between the rivers Sava, Drava and Danube. These people were called Scordisci and mixed with the Illyrians. The Celts and Illyrians were defeated by the Romans in the 2nd century BC. After a number of rebellions, some people were expelled, but those remaining adopted their conquerors' customs and became thoroughly Roman.

TIMELINE

50,000–30,000 BC Homo sapiens neanderthalensis lives at Krapina	*Krapina man, dating from the middle-Palaeolithic*	**1200 BC** Illyrian settlement in the Balkans	**279 BC** Celts, now settled in the Balkans, defeat the Greeks
6500 BC	**3500 BC**	**500 BC**	
6000–2500 BC Neolithic: sites of Danilo, Hvar, Butmir	**2200-1800 BC** Aeneolithic: sites of Lasinje and Vučedol	*Bronze cap 7th–6th centuries BC*	**390 BC** Dionysius the Elder of Syracuse captures the island of Vis and founds an administrative post

◁ St Paul and St Blaise, patron saint of Dubrovnik, in a triptych by Nikola Božidarević

THE ROMAN CONQUEST

The Romans conquered Croatia at different times and in different ways. First, they wanted to put an end to attacks on their merchant ships, which were falling into the hands of the Liburnians or the Dalmatians,

Symbol of the Roman Empire, Sisak

so they subdued the coastal towns by landing Roman legions transported by the fleet. The first battle took place in 229 BC, when Teuta, the queen of the Illyrians, put to death a Roman ambassador who had tried to persuade her to put an end to the acts of piracy. Roman revenge was fierce and the towns of Epidaurum, Lissa and Pharos were attacked, conquered and forced to pay taxes to Rome. However, despite promises to the contrary, acts of piracy continued and Rome decided to deploy its legions based in Aquileia, east of Venice, a fortified town founded in 181 BC.

The legions succeeded in subduing Istria, a process completed by 177 BC. Twenty years later Publius Scipio Nasica inflicted the first defeat on the Dalmatians at Delminium and again on the Dalmatians and the Japods who inhabited the area of the delta of the River Neretva. In 107 BC the Romans defeated the Scordisci and the Illyrians and conquered the town of Segestica (Sisak). In 87 BC another war broke out between the Romans and the Illyrians which lasted for three years and was won by the Romans. In 48 BC the Illyrians sided with Pompey in the fight against Caesar, providing ships and men. Pompey's defeat also at first appeared to be the decisive defeat of the Illyrians. However, many Illyrians, still determined to fight, fled to inland forests not occupied by the Romans. A few decades later, in 6 AD, the Illyrian people staged their greatest united rebellion yet, under the command of Batone. The first battles were won by the Illyrians who soon began to march towards Italy. After three further years of war, the Romans managed to get the better of Batone's exhausted, famished army, thanks to better military organization.

Over the years that followed, Caesar Augustus made the Balkans part of the Roman Empire. After a military campaign waged by Tiberius and completed in AD 12, the Illyrian defences were dismantled and cities were founded, linked by roads wide enough for marching armies. The inhabitants became Roman citizens and were allowed to stand for public office. Indeed, Illyria produced several emperors, including Septimius Severus, Aurelian, Claudius II, Probus, Valens, Valentinian and, perhaps most famous of all, Diocletian.

ROMAN ROADS

The roads were the first great public works built by the Romans. They allowed them to move legions quickly

The Tabula Peutingeriana showing Roman roads

TIMELINE

229 BC The Roman army destroys Illyrian forts, subdues the Greek colonies of Lissa and Pharos and forces Illyrians to pay taxes

107 BC Decisive Roman victory over the Scordisci who are driven from the region; Rome owes the victory to Quintus Minucius Rufus

300 BC   **200 BC**   **100 BC**

177 BC The Roman fleet is attacked by Istrians; Rome sends an army which defeats them and drives them out

One of the many Roman fragments from the city of Sisak

119 BC The Dalmatian Lucius Metellus defeats the Scordisci and Dalmatian tribes near Segestica (Sisak); Romans settle in Salona and begin work on the Via Gabina from Salona to Andretium

and in fact the Roman road network remained the principal means of communication in this part of the Balkans for many centuries.

Two important arteries led from Aquileia: one towards the Istrian peninsula to Pula, the other in the direction of Aemona (Ljubljana). The main communication link in Dalmatia began in Aenona (Nin), went on to Zadar and continued, connecting Scardona (Skradin), Tragurium (Trogir), Salona, Narona, Epidaurum (Cavtat) and finally Catarum (Kotor). Other roads branched off inland from this coastal road: the busiest was that from Salona which went towards present-day Bosnia, through Klis and Sinj, near the town of Aequum (Čitluk). Another road followed the river Narenta (Neretva) to Sirmium, the present-day Sremska Mitrovica, which would become one of the capitals of the Roman Empire.

The inland roads were no less important: these followed the rivers Sava, Drava and the Danube. In the centre of Pannonia, one town which grew in importance was Siscia (Sisak), from which roads led towards Andautonia (Šćitarjevo), Mursa (Osijek), Cuccium (Ilok), Marsonia (Vinkovci) and the thermal spas of Aquae Salissae (Daruvar), Aquae Valissae (Lipik) and Aquae Iasae (Varaždinske Toplice), which were used by the emperors.

Relief in the Baths in Varaždinske Toplice

Pula in Roman times, in an engraving from 1819

the existing Illyrian towns on the main islands and along the coast were turned into Roman towns. The main towns were Senia (Senj), Aenona (Nin), Jadera (Zadar), Delminium (now a village east of Salona with few remains), Promona (a village near Makarska, with parts of the Roman walls), Burnum (the remains of the ancient town are near Kistanje along the road between Knin and Benkovac), Blandona (which no longer exists, near the lake of Vrana), Scardona (today Skradin), Narona (at the mouth of the Neretva near Vid), Tragurium (Trogir) and lastly, Salona (near Split). The towns had walls, forums, triumphal arches and aqueducts, the remains of which can often still be seen. The best-preserved aqueduct, built to serve Salona, was extended by Diocletian as far as Split and is, for the most part, still in use.

The principal Roman monuments remaining today in Croatia are in Pula, with its magnificent Roman amphitheatre *(see pp62–63)*, and in Split, site of the extraordinary Palace of Diocletian *(see pp120–121)*.

FOUNDING OF TOWNS

The Romans initially founded the Istrian towns of Poreč, Rovinj and Pula, which became a place of great importance in the 2nd century. Later

AD 6–9 Augustus conquers all of Pannonia and begins construction of forts along the rivers; later the region becomes part of the Roman Empire with the name Provincia Pannoniae

AD 1   **100**

AD 12 Final defeat of the Illyrians. In Rome Tiberius celebrates his triumph with a solemn procession, at the front of which is Batone, chief of the rebels, now a prisoner

A statue of Emperor Augustus

271 Aurelian defines the border of the Empire as the Danube, unable to defeat the Dacians who live along the river

200

284 Diocletian becomes emperor; some years later work begins on the palace in Split, to which he retires in 304

Aerial view of the Roman ruins of the ancient city of Salona, destroyed in 614

THE BARBARIAN INVASIONS AND THE CRISIS OF THE ROMAN EMPIRE

In 378, after a century of relative peace, the Goths invaded Pannonia and then turned towards Italy. From that time, and for the entire 5th century, the Balkans were attacked by the Huns, Vandals, Visigoths and Longobards which finally caused the fall of the Roman empire in 476.

THE AVARS AND SLAVS IN THE BALKANS

The beginning of the 6th century saw invasion by the Avars, who were followed by other Slavic tribes. Those Roman inhabitants who did not manage to flee to the mountains or the islands were captured and sold as slaves. In 582 the Avars conquered and destroyed Sirmium (Sremska Mitrovica), one of the ancient capitals of the Roman Empire. Later they also subdued other nomadic tribes and organized a powerful army to

conquer Constantinople, but they were defeated by the Byzantines. Some of the troops returned to the Asiatic steppes, while others settled between the Danube and Tisza rivers, leaving the field clear for the Slavs who occupied Moravia and Bohemia to push southwards and towards the Adriatic, conquering all the Roman cities and destroying Salona (614). The Slavs settled in the countryside or in what remained of the sacked cities. These people cultivated the land and bred livestock and formed extended family groups *(županija)* with a *župan* at the head of each.

THE BULGARS AND THE BYZANTINE RECONQUEST

The Slavs' expansion to the south was halted by the Bulgars, a people of Turkish origin, who settled along the final stretch of the Danube. After the fall of the Western Empire, Byzantium attempted to reconquer

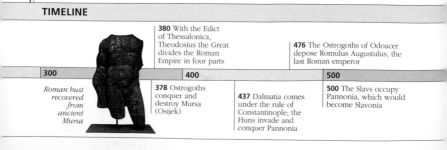

TIMELINE

380 With the Edict of Thessalonica, Theodosius the Great divides the Roman Empire in four parts

476 The Ostrogoths of Odoacer depose Romulus Augustulus, the last Roman emperor

| 300 | 400 | 500 |

Roman bust recovered from ancient Mursa

378 Ostrogoths conquer and destroy Mursa (Osijek)

437 Dalmatia comes under the rule of Constantinople; the Huns invade and conquer Pannonia

500 The Slavs occupy Pannonia, which would become Slavonia the Balkans and inflicted various defeats on the Slavs, while at the same time trying to make them part of the empire. The Byzantine fleet was able to move the army rapidly and in this way Greece, part of Macedonia and the Dalmatian islands and cities were retaken. Inland areas remained in Slav possession.

Foundations of one of the churches in Biskupija

THE CROATS
At the beginning of the 7th century, perhaps summoned by the Byzantine emperor Heraclius, the Croats, a Slavic people possibly from what is now Iran, settled in upper Pannonia and Dalmatia, mixing with the native Roman people or refugees from the interior. In the inland regions, in the 8th and 9th centuries, the Croats set up territorial bases, while the coastal cities and the islands were governed by Byzantine officials with a fleet based in Zadar. In the 9th century, the Croats established a fledgling state in a hilly area now called Biskupija on the Dalmatian plateau, far from the Byzantine-controlled coast and away from central Croatia, subject to the Franks. Several churches were built here and the small settlement was named Pet Crikvah. Recent archaeological digs have unearthed the foundations of religious buildings. The finds are now in Split and Knin.

Dalmatia. The area was divided into counties which were entrusted to loyal nobles or bishops. The Aquileian patriarch assumed particular importance for these lands when, in the 9th century, he sent monks and priests from Byzantium to spread the gospel and convert the Croats to Christianity. Among the priests were Cyril and Methodius, who devised Glagolitic script to spread the word in a language intelligible to the Slavs *(see pp34–5)*.

THE FIRST CROATIAN TOWNS
During the 8th and early 9th centuries, the first Croatian towns were built next to the Byzantine-governed towns. Many (Dubrovnik, Zadar, Split and Trogir) were inhabited by people of mainly Roman origin. Biograd was founded near Zadar, and the town of Knin was repopulated by Croats under Prince Višeslav. Later, the town of Šibenik was founded. In Pannonia, the Roman town of Siscia (now Sisak) and the town of Mursa (Osijek) were revived by Prince Vojnomir.

THE FRANKS
Towards the end of the 8th century, the Franks led by Charlemagne succeeded in conquering what is now northern Croatia, Bohemia, Istria, Slovenia and part of

The baptismal font of Prince Višeslav, found near Nin

Cyril and Methodius

The two key figures in the process of converting the Slav population to Christianity were the brothers Cyril (827–69) and Methodius (815–85). They were the sons of a Byzantine army officer and were born in Thessalonica, where they learnt several languages, including Slavic. The city, at that time Byzantine territory, was one of the most cosmopolitan in the Mediterranean. Initially, the two brothers took up different careers, but both eventually became monks. In 863 Emperor Michael III of Byzantium sent the two brothers to Moravia to spread the Slavonic (rather than Latin) liturgy among the people. The two men devised the Glagolitic alphabet to represent the Slav tongue, and translated religious texts. Croatian priests, especially along the coast, adopted Glagolitic and texts survive in a number of places. Glagolitic was a forerunner of Cyrillic script, named after Cyril.

The priests, Cyril and Methodius among them, were received in Rome by the pope with great solemnity.

Methodius *followed an administrative and military career, later entering a monastery. In 869 he was invited to Prague as the Archbishop of Moravia and Pannonia and the papal delegate to the Slav population. Here he undertook evangelical work, and completed the translation of the Bible into Slavonic.*

The Glagolitic alphabet *is composed of 40 letters, arranged in a sequence based on the Greek alphabet. Extra signs were added to represent particular sounds in the Slavic language, which are not found in Greek.*

Methodius and his brother presented the pope with the relics of St Clement, the fourth Roman pope, who had died in the Crimea in the year 102.

The Croat population's acceptance *of Christianity soon became evident in the country's artworks and crafts. The working of stone and gold was already a traditional craft, but was now used for sacred objects. A primitive representation of the figure of Christ can be seen in this small cross from Zadar, dating from the 9th century.*

*The use of **Glagolitic script** spread among the Slavonic clergy. Although banned from Roman-controlled territories, it was used for centuries in more far-flung monasteries.*

Cyril and Methodius became patron saints of mainland Europe in 1979. Many churches, centres of religious studies, university institutions and libraries, including that of Bulgaria, are dedicated to Cyril, often with Methodius.

Cyril, whose real name was Constantine (he changed his name in Rome when he became a monk), dedicated himself to humanist studies. He was a teacher of philosophy and later responsible for the Library of Byzantium, becoming famous for his work. He died in Rome in 869.

CYRIL AND METHODIUS IN ROME

In 867, the two brothers were invited to Rome by Pope Hadrian II. Convinced by their cause, the pope approved the use of Slavonic language in liturgy. After his return to Moravia, Methodius had to face the hostility of the Aquileia patriarch and the Archbishop of Salzburg who wanted to reserve the Slavs' conversion to Christianity for priests of German origin. Methodius was arrested, tortured and only freed 15 months later after intervention by Pope John VIII.

TIMELINE

863 King Rastislav invites Cyril and Methodius to Moravia to help convert the local population to Christianity

869 Cyril, sick, retires to a monastery in Rome where he dies shortly after. Methodius is nominated Archbishop of Pannonia and Moravia and the papal delegate to the Slav population. Methodius moves to Prague

893 Glagolitic is altered, introducing Greek characters: the new Cyrillic alphabet spreads among Serbs, Macedonians and Russians.

| 860 | 870 | 880 | 890 |

866 Cyril and Methodius translate the Gospel and sacred texts into Slavonic and devise Glagolitic script. Slavonic liturgy is introduced to Bohemia

867 Cyril and Methodius are invited to Rome by Pope Hadrian II, who agrees to the use of Slavonic in liturgy

Mosaic on the tomb of Cyril

885 Pope Stephen V forbids the use of the Slavonic language in liturgy

THE HUNGARIANS

The situation in the Balkans seemed stable enough towards the end of the 9th century. However, Hungarians from the Urals came to Europe and, under the leadership of King Arpad, settled along the middle stretches of the Danube and in the valleys of Transylvania, forcing out the Slavs and other tribes. They carried out military raids in Italy and Austria but were defeated in 955 by Emperor Otto I at Lechenfeld, on the plain near Ljubljana, and were forced to retreat to what are today the borders of Hungary and Transylvania. This Hungarian invasion was the last great invasion of the first millennium.

Statue of the alleged first Croat king, Tomislav

THE KINGDOM OF THE CROATS

In the meantime, in 845, under Prince Trpimir, the Croats obtained a tacit autonomy from the Franks and formed a state which also controlled part of Dalmatia. This was recognized by the pope while Duke Branimir (879–92) was its leader. Prince Tomislav was allegedly crowned king in 925 and his death, in 928, was followed by years of anarchy until King Petar Krešimir IV (1058–74) came to power and united Croatia. Krešimir also

Relief of King Zvonimir in the baptistry of St John in Split

conquered the islands of Dalmatia. In 1054, with the schism of the Roman and Byzantine churches, Croatia sided with Rome. After the death of Petar Krešimir IV, his successor Zvonimir, who had married the sister of the Hungarian king Ladislaus, was crowned king by Pope Gregory VII and declared himself subject to Rome. The Croat nobles refused to participate in the war against the Turks and killed Zvonimir in 1089.

THE UNION WITH HUNGARY

Claiming the right of succession, Koloman (1102–1116), the Hungarian king, came to power after Ladislaus. He conquered Croatia and was crowned king of Dalmatia and Croatia. In 1102 an agreement united the two states under one dynasty. A Croatian parliament (Sabor) was set up, to be ruled by a royally appointed Ban (governor), and the state was divided into counties governed by Croatian and Hungarian nobles. In the following century, to deal with the Tartar raids, King Bela IV reorganized the state into two parts (Croatia and Slavonia), each ruled by a Ban. New cities were founded and some were granted the privileges of a free city.

THE ROYAL FREE CITIES

These cities, defended by walls, moats and towers, were built mainly in Pannonia and the northern counties. Varaždin, founded at this time, became one of the area's busiest trading centres and, for a long period, the seat of the Sabor. The

TIMELINE

896 Hungarians settle between the Tisza and the Danube	**901** Prince Tomislav defeats the Hungarians and forces them beyond the Sava. He obtains from Byzantium the authority to administer the cities of Dalmatia	**956** Branimir, prince of Croatia, rebels against the Byzantines. He obtains the title of king of Croatia with the pope's blessing	
850	**900**	**950**	**1000**
899 Hungarians enter the Balkans and destroy the cities of the Croats, who seek refuge in Dalmatia		**930** The Byzantines renew the union with the coastal towns and cities who pay taxes to the emperor	**1000** Venice's first armed naval expedition against pirates near mouth of Neretva river; towns on islands and coast of Istria and Dalmatia declare allegiance to Venice
		925 Tomislav allegedly becomes king of the Croats with the pope's blessing	

The Golden Bull of 1242 declaring Zagreb (Gradec) a Free Royal City

cities which emerged from the ruins of old Roman towns were fortified: as in Križevci, proclaimed a royal city in 1252, Koprivnica, declared a free town in 1356, and Ludbreg, which became a free town in 1320 and played an important role in the region's defences. The lower stretch of the Drava was strengthened, with a rebuilt Sisak and, further south, a new Slavonski Brod. Zagreb became a free royal city in 1242; Vukovar became a free town in 1231. Thanks to tax advantages and non-subjection to feudal lords, these towns prospered and attracted foreign merchants and artisans.

THE DEFENCES

King Bela IV built forts in strategic positions which were directly dependent on royal power or granted to the great feudal lords. Impressive ruins remain of these forts, including the famous one of Ružica near Orahovica in Slavonia. Samobor, in central Croatia, was enlarged and given a fort, as were Klis, Knin and Sinj in Dalmatia. Several noble families were also given the task of building and manning forts, as was the case with the Bribir counts, who moved to Zrin (taking the name of Zrinski). This intense programme strengthened a state which was threatened on many sides: after the danger of the Tartars had passed, threat of a Turkish invasion loomed.

VENICE, ISTRIA AND DALMATIA

The Adriatic coast fared differently; its fate was linked to that of Venice. Much of Istria belonged to the Aquileian patriarchate, which held civil and ecclesiastical jurisdiction. From the year 1000, many coastal towns had agreements of mutual assistance with Venice, which had a powerful fleet for defence against attacks by pirates. Venice needed the Istrian cities, which often had fortified ports, for mooring their merchant fleets which plied the Croatian coast on their expeditions to the East. In the 13th century, some cities asked to come under Venetian rule for defence reasons, a process which in most cases took place peacefully. In Zadar, however, this was not the case and two warring factions forced Venice to employ crusaders on their way to the Holy Land to subdue the city (1202). In 1204 Zadar surrendered, and a year later Venice also conquered Istria and the city of Dubrovnik.

The taking of Zadar by the Venetians depicted by Andrea Vicentino

1058 King Krešimir enlarges his kingdom by uniting Croatia and conquering the Dalmatian islands

1102 The Hungarian king, Koloman, successor to Ladislaus, is crowned king of Croatia and Dalmatia

Royal coin of Slavonia from 1200

1202 To repay the debt to Venice the crusaders undertake to conquer Zadar which falls after long resistance

1050   1100   1150   1200

1091 Ladislaus, king of Hungary, brother of Zvonimir's widow, unites Croatia and the Hungarian kingdom

1222 With the Golden Bull the king of Hungary, Andrew II, guarantees the rights of the Croatian nobility, surrendering some of his power to the aristocracy

1075 Zvonimir is crowned king of Croatia by Pope Gregory VII

THE REPUBLIC OF RAGUSA

The story of the city of Dubrovnik, for a long time known as Ragusa, takes up an entire chapter in Croatia's history. The city was founded by exiles from Epidaurum which had been

The Republic of Ragusa in a contemporary illustration

destroyed by the Avars. It became an important trading port thanks to its central position in the Adriatic, and its safe mooring. In 1205, it came under Venetian rule. This lasted for 150 years and resulted in the city's current appearance. In 1358, Hungary's Louis I of Anjou defeated the Venetians and reunited the Croatian territories, but in 1382 Ragusa bought its freedom by means of a treaty with the king of Hungary. It became an independent republic and flourished as a great power and a thriving spiritual and cultural centre. In 1808, Napoleon Bonaparte's troops entered the city and the republic came to an end.

TURKISH DOMINATION

The Kingdom of Hungary went through a long period of dynastic crisis when the house of Arpad died out after the death of Andrew III in 1301. There were numerous contenders for the crown, provoking fierce battles until 1308 when Charles Robert of Anjou, of the Neapolitan royal family, came to the throne. Under the Angevin dynasty, with Matthias Corvinus (1458–90), the Hungarian-Croatian kingdom enjoyed long periods of prosperity, competing with Venice for possession of the coast and Adriatic islands. However,

a Turkish invasion was imminent and after the battle of Kosovo Polje in 1389, the Turks conquered nearby Bosnia and part of Serbia. In 1463, the Sultan Mohammed II began to invade Croatia from Bosnia. The Croatian army was defeated in 1493 at the battle of Krbavsko Polje. In the Battle of Mohács, on 29 August 1526, the Hungarian king, Louis II, died without heirs, leaving the way clear for the Turks of Suleyman II the Magnificent to conquer almost all of Croatia and much of Hungary.

Ottoman army in the Battle of Mohács

TIMELINE

View of Osijek at the time of liberation from the Turks in 1687

VENICE AND THE PURCHASE
OF DALMATIA

The wars with Venice over coastal Dalmatia continued until 1409 when Ladislaus of Anjou, the King of Naples, renounced all rights over Dalmatia and sold it for 100,000 gold ducats to Venice. The towns and islands stayed under Venetian rule from 1409 until 1797, when Venice surrendered to Napoleon. As well as the territories purchased by Venice, other towns wanted to become Venetian possessions. They were given a great deal of autonomy by Venice, whose principal interest was in the security of the ports and their defence, building the ramparts which today characterize these towns. During the wars of the early 18th century, Venice conquered the whole of Dalmatia, except for Dubrovnik, then an independent republic, and a small stretch of coast, extending its borders to the Velebit passes, which still separate Croatia from Bosnia-Herzegovina today.

Fran Krsto Frankopan, beheaded in 1671

TIES WITH
THE HABSBURGS

In 1527, Croatian and Hungarian nobles granted what remained of the kingdom to Archduke Ferdinand of Habsburg, who then concentrated all power in the court, depriving the nobility of control of the cities and border areas. In 1578, he established the Military Frontier *(Vojna Krajina)* which was administered by the military governor of Vienna. This was to serve as a buffer zone against the advancing Turks. To populate this frontier, Serb, Morlach and Bosnian refugees were brought in and integrated with the military garrisons. For some decades there was a truce, then the Turkish offensive against Vienna resumed, but the Turks were pushed back, first in 1664 and again in 1683. The slow retreat of the "infidels" from Croatia began at this point. Croatia was liberated ten years later, while Bosnia remained under the Turks. The liberated areas became border lands and remained so until 1881. Vienna's heavy taxation and centralized rule caused discontent, but a plan to detach Croatia from Hungary and Vienna, in 1670 by some of Croatia's most influential families (including the Frankopans and Zrinskis) *(see p177)*, resulted in the beheading of Ban Petar Zrinski and Fran Krsto Frankopan and the other two rebel leaders in 1671, halting any attempt at revolt.

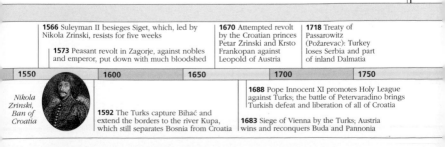

1566 Suleyman II besieges Siget, which, led by Nikola Zrinski, resists for five weeks

1573 Peasant revolt in Zagorje, against nobles and emperor, put down with much bloodshed

1670 Attempted revolt by the Croatian princes Petar Zrinski and Krsto Frankopan against Leopold of Austria

1718 Treaty of Passarowitz (Požarevac): Turkey loses Serbia and part of inland Dalmatia

1550 | 1600 | 1650 | 1700 | 1750

Nikola Zrinski, Ban of Croatia

1592 The Turks capture Bihać and extend the borders to the river Kupa, which still separates Bosnia from Croatia

1688 Pope Innocent XI promotes Holy League against Turks; the battle of Petervaradino brings Turkish defeat and liberation of all of Croatia

1683 Siege of Vienna by the Turks; Austria wins and reconquers Buda and Pannonia

Drawing showing the Congress of Vienna

THE KINGDOM OF THE ILLYRIAN PROVINCES

The Napoleonic wars also affected Croatia, where the Kingdom of Illyrian Provinces was established in 1809, governed by the French marshal, Marmont. This relatively short period (five years) saw the introduction of important economic and legal reforms which left a deep impression on Croatian culture. With the mood of growing nationalism in Europe, people felt inspired to rebuild a united state. However, at the Congress of Vienna (1815), Croatia supported the expansionist aspirations of Austria, which annexed all the Istrian and Dalmatian territories which had belonged to Venice, and the Republic of Dubrovnik.

THE ILLYRIAN MOVEMENT

Croatian aspirations were apparent in movements which also influenced and politicized the newly emerging working class, a product of early industrialization. The origins of this nationalist trend can be dated to the 1834 writings of Ljudevit Gaj (1809–72),

Ban Josip Jelačić, a Croatian national hero

known as "the Illyrian". Moving against this trend, however, was the expansion of Hungary, which tried to extend its influence in frontier zones by imposing the use of the Magyar language in administrative affairs and schools. In the former Venetian territories on the other hand, a pro-Italian nationalism, with ideas of unification, was spreading among the middle classes in the Dalmatian and Istrian cities. The Austrian government opposed all these movements and continued to govern without compromise. Indeed, they tried to introduce the teaching of German in schools. Any possible unification of Croatian territories was blocked by maintaining the *Krajina*, the military border, and by customs barriers between the various areas. Major public works, the expansion of the ports of Rijeka and Pula, which became a base for the Austrian fleet, and a renewed road network were all made to promote Austrian interests.

FROM THE REVOLT OF 1848 TO AUSTRO-HUNGARIAN REIGN

After 1847, when the Sabor (parliament) of Zagreb managed to proclaim Croatian as the official language and abolished feudalism, the revolt of the Hungarian people and the hopes aroused by the Italian revolution in 1848 also involved Croatian political movements. The failure to understand the Hungarian rebels and ambiguous Austrian policy forced the Ban, Josip Jelačić, into war against Hungary, now ruled by

TIMELINE

1809 Napoleon Bonaparte founds kingdom of Illyrian Provinces

Napoleon Bonaparte

1830 Ljudevit Gaj publishes *Essential Rules of Croatian-Slavic Spelling*, introducing to the script the signs missing from the Latin alphabet

Ljudevit Gaj, head of the Croatian national revival

| 1800 | 1810 | 1820 | 1830 | 1840 | 1850 |

1815 Treaty of Vienna: Austria is allotted all the territories of the Republic of Venice

1832 Janko Drašković publishes *Dissertation* against Hungarian and Austrian supremacy, introduces idea of Illyria as the "mother" of Croats

1847 The Illyrian Movement gains majority in Croatian Parliament and proclaims Croat the official language

1848–50 Hungarian uprising against Austria: Vienna abolishes local autonomy, dissolves the Sabor and makes German the official language rebels. The Austrian monarchy was saved but then became, if anything, even more keen on centralization. In 1867, Franz Joseph, the Austrian emperor, modified the structure of the state and established the Austro-Hungarian empire. Hungary was granted autonomy and a corridor to the sea. Rijeka and the hinterland became part of the Magyar state. However, under pressure from the Sabor, in 1868 the Austrian emperor granted Croatia the status of "a nation with territory within the Austro-Hungarian Empire", and Zagreb became its cultural and political centre. In 1863 the bishop of Đakovo, Josip Juraj Strossmayer, founded the Croatian Academy of the Arts and Sciences and the University (1874), the first in the Balkans.

Bishop Josip Juraj Strossmayer, founder of the University of Zagreb

Political contention continued to develop along different lines. Some people dreamed of a confederation of states within the Habsburg monarchy, others felt that the moment had come to unite the Slav peoples in one state, and lastly, others felt it was time for Croatian independence.

Tension increased in 1878 when Bosnia and Herzegovina came under Austrian rule, sparking reaction from the Kingdom of Serbia, which had been established in 1882 after the expulsion of the Turks. The Serbian ruling classes aspired to unify the southern Slavs and intended to extend their territories towards Dalmatia and Slavonia, which they regarded as Serbian land. In the last decade of the 19th century a political battle developed in Dalmatia and Istria. It formed between a movement supported by the bourgeoisie in the cities formerly under Venetian rule which pushed for autonomy, and other groups which aimed at a union with Serbia. Austria, which as always took advantage of these internal controversies, did not concede any form of autonomy.

WORLD WAR I

In 1914, with the assassination of Archduke Franz Ferdinand in Sarajevo, World War I broke out which caused the dissolution of the Habsburg Empire. Croatians paid dearly for their involvement in the war, as did many other countries, but finally the Croatian population was able to free itself from foreign rule.

Flag of the Hungarian-Croatian Imperial regiment

1860 Austrian emperor reinstates the Sabor

1881 Vienna dissolves the *Vojna Krajina* and those areas are part of the Croatian state again

1904 Antun and Stjepan Radić found the People's Peasant Party

1914 Assassination in Sarajevo and World War I begins

1860	1870	1880	1890	1900	1910

1868 Birth of United Kingdom of Croatia and Slovenia supported by Emperor Franz Joseph

Emperor Franz Joseph

1908 Austria annexes Bosnia and Herzegovina

1912 Slavko Cuvaj proclaimed Ban of Croatia, dissolves the Sabor and abolishes the Constitution

Assassination of King Alexander in Marseilles (1934)

FROM THE STATE OF SLOVENES, CROATS AND SERBS TO THE KINGDOM OF YUGOSLAVIA

Croatia proclaimed independence in 1918, but a few months later agreed to be part of a state formed by Slovenes and Serbs under the Serbian dynasty of Karađorđević. The Treaty of Rapallo (1920) allotted Istria, Zadar, the islands of Cres, Lošinj, Lastovo and Palagruža to Italy, followed in 1924 by Rijeka. The discontent of Croatians led many citizens to join the People's Peasant Party, led by Stjepan Radić until he was shot and fatally wounded in parliament in Belgrade in 1928. The revolts which broke out in Croatia were repressed and in 1929 King Alexander abolished the constitution and then established the Kingdom of Yugoslavia. The assassination of the king in Marseilles (1934) by the Ustaše (Croatian fascists), led by Ante Pavelić, increased tension and in an attempt to suppress the uprising and placate the discontented, in 1939 the government of Belgrade established the Banovina of Croatia within the Kingdom of Yugoslavia. However, a few days later World War II began.

WORLD WAR II

Initially, Yugoslavia supported the Axis, but a military revolt removed the king of Yugoslavia, and the country was then invaded by Nazi troops. A kingdom of Croatia was established, which was to be governed by Aimone of Savoy, but in reality it was an independent state led by Pavelić. Italy took control of the islands and cities of the Dalmatian coast. Resistance gained ground in all of Yugoslavia led by the Communist Party and its chief, Marshal Tito: from 1941 to 1945 Croatia was bloodied by war and internal conflicts which caused hundreds of thousands of deaths.

MARSHAL TITO

At the end of the war the state of Yugoslavia was reunited, and regained land granted to Italy after World War I *(see p49)*, as well as the area of Prekomurje and a part of Baranja, which were both Hungarian at the time.

In 1948, the break between the Yugoslav Communist Party and the Soviet Union led Marshal

Tito with his wife and son in a photo from 1927

TIMELINE

1920	1930	1940	1950	1960	19

1919 Treaty of Paris: a country of Slovenes, Croats and Serbs is created, which later becomes the kingdom of Yugoslavia

1934 King Alexander is killed in Marseilles; his cousin Paul takes power

1948 Yugoslavia breaks away from Soviet influence and begins policy of non-alignment

1929 King Alexander Karađorđević proclaims a dictatorship. Croat Ante Pavelić founds terrorist organization of Ustaše to fight the Serbs

1939–41 World War II: Yugoslavia is conquered and divided, and Croatia nominally becomes a kingdom under Aimone of Savoy

1947–48 Exodus of nearly all the Italians from Istria and Dalmatia

1945 The Yugoslav Federal state is founded

Tito to employ a policy of mediation and neutrality between the opposing international factions of the Cold War. Tito held together the country's various ethnic groups (with great difficulty) and these ties showed signs of strain after he died in 1980. The reform of the constitution, aimed at weakening Serbia's dominance over the other states, did not alter the resentment of the Croats and Slovenes who sought support for opposition to the regime in religion and nationalism.

Ivo Josipović, elected president in 2010

THE DISSOLUTION OF THE SOCIALIST REPUBLIC OF YUGOSLAVIA

The fall of the Berlin Wall (November 1989) and the break-up of the Soviet Union at the end of 1991 convinced the governments of Slovenia, Croatia (under its first president, Franjo Tuđman) and Macedonia that they should dissolve federal ties and proclaim independence, after a referendum which was won by a wide margin by the secessionists (May 1991). However, a Serb faction, supported by the Yugoslav People's Army (JNA) from Belgrade, stirred up rebellion and war broke out. In Slovenia the war lasted only ten days, but the battle in Croatia was prolonged. Under the pretext of defending the Serbs, parts of Slavonia and Baranja were occupied by the JNA, and in Krajina the Serbian Republic of Krajina was created with Knin as its capital. A fifth of Croatia fell to Serb soldiers, and the city of Dubrovnik was held under a seven-month siege.

THE INDEPENDENT STATE OF CROATIA

Five years later the land occupied by the Serbs was liberated by the Croatian army and the Erdut Agreement (1995) sanctioned reunification, although the disputed territories (Slavonia and Krajina) were overseen by the UN until 1998.

Croatia joined the World Trade Organization and elections held in December 2000 voted in a coalition of democratic parties. As a result steps were taken for Croatia's entry into the European Union. In March 2002, the Italian bank, UniCredito, bought the important Croatian bank, the Zagrebačka Bank, bringing it into the European circuit. However, in 2005, after failing to hand over an indicted general, Croatia was accused of not co-operating fully with the international war crimes tribunal at the Hague and negotiations for entry to the EU stalled. Soon after, the general was captured and talks resumed. Croatia was given EU applicant status with entry to the European Union in July 2013.

Bombed houses in Vukovar during the war of 1991–95

1980	1990	2000	2010	2020
1980 President Tito dies and conflict between the various nationalities begins	**1998** The restitution of Slavonia and Krajina reunites a now free Croatia	**2000** On 7 February Stipe Mesić is elected President of the Republic	**2009** The accession of Croatia to NATO	
1991 Slovenia and Croatia abandon Republic, Croatian land inhabited by Serbs is occupied by Yugoslav People's Army: war between Serbia and Croatia begins		**1995** Erdut Agreement: Slavonia and Krajina are administered by the United Nations	**2010** Ivo Josipović elected President	

CROATIA
AREA BY AREA

Croatia at a Glance

Croatia is a fascinating country with great ethnic, historical and architectural diversity as well as varied topography. The north had close ties with the former Austrian empire, and the bell towers alongside 19th-century Baroque churches and buildings have a Viennese look. The eastern side marks the start of the Hungarian plain with broad rivers and houses with overhanging roofs. The Adriatic coast is quite different, with its indented coastline fringed with lovely islands. The coastal cities reflect the centuries-old Venetian culture with churches, monasteries, palaces and forts testifying to the brilliance of the late Middle Ages and the greatness of the Renaissance period.

St Mark's Square (pp154–5), *with its Gothic church of the same name, is the heart of the Gornji Grad district in Zagreb and the city's oldest square.*

Euphrasian Basilica *in Poreč (pp54–5) has marvellous mosaics, some of the best preserved examples of Byzantine art in Croatia.*

ISTRIA AND THE KVARNER AREA (pp48–87)

ZAGREB (pp148)

CENTRAL CROATIA (pp166–79)

Amphitheatre, Pula (pp62–63)

Plitvice Lakes National Park (pp86–7) *is one of nature's natural wonders with 16 lakes surrounded by woods. The cascading waterfalls create an impressive display of light and colour.*

DALMATIA (pp88–147)

Kornati National Park (pp98–9) *is made up of over 150 islands with underwater caves and sheltered coves. The park covers an area of about 300 sq km (115 sq miles) and is surrounded by clear seas. These wooded, rocky islands present an unforgettable sight.*

ADRIATIC SEA

◁ Typical cultivated landscape in the north of Croatia

Zagorje (pp200–1), west of Varaždin, towards the border with Slovenia, is a fascinating area with vine-covered hills, thermal spa towns and castles.

THE NORTHERN COUNTIES *(pp198–215)*

0 kilometres 50

0 miles 50

Kopački Rit Park (pp194–5) is an oasis of great ornithological interest. In spring and summer the Danube overflows, transforming this area into a large lake attracting more than 200 bird species.

SLAVONIA AND BARANJA *(pp180–97)*

Lonjsko Polje Nature Park *(p176)*

The Palace of Diocletian in Split (pp120–1) was built by Emperor Diocletian at the end of the 3rd century. The city of Split grew up in and around it. Almost in its original state, it is the largest Roman building in the Adriatic.

The Tvrđa in Osijek (pp192–3), the fortified nucleus of the city, has 18th-century military buildings. Initially Roman, then Hungarian, Turkish and lastly Austrian, the city retains traces of most of these diverse cultures.

The City of Dubrovnik (pp140–7) is situated on the coast. It is surrounded by fortifications begun in the 8th century and enlarged over the years.

ISTRIA AND THE KVARNER AREA

The Istrian peninsula, nestling at the northern end of the Adriatic Sea, and the islands that tumble down the Kvarner gulf are some of the most sought-after holiday destinations in Europe. The coast is spectacular and the towns and cities are fascinating. Three National Parks: the Brijuni Islands, the Plitvice Lakes and Risnjak preserve the natural charm of the area.

Until 1000 BC, the region was inhabited by Illyrians. From 42 BC Istria became part of the Roman empire, when the Province of Dalmatia was founded. Cities were built along the coast and on the islands, and many traces of Roman presence remain. Pula has a well-preserved amphitheatre dating back to the 1st century, the sixth largest arena of its kind in the world.

Mosaic in the Euphrasian Basilica in Poreč

With the fall of the western Roman empire, much of the eastern Adriatic coast came under the control of Byzantium. The intricate, well-preserved golden mosaics of the 6th-century basilica of St Euphrasius in Poreč survive from that time.

In 1420 the area came under Venetian rule, a situation which was to last until 1797, when Napoleon dissolved the Venetian Republic. Nearly 400 years of Venetian rule are recorded by 15th-century open air loggias, elegant bell towers and buildings with Venetian-Gothic windows, built by wealthy merchants.

With the Treaty of Vienna in 1815, Austria-Hungary extended its domain to include Venetian lands. Rijeka developed into an industrial port under Austro-Hungarian rule and is still today a hub for Croatian shipping. Close by in Opatija the Habsburgs built elegant villas and planted lush gardens for their winter holidays.

In 1918 Istria briefly became part of the new kingdom of Serbs, Croats and Slovenes, which subsequently became Yugoslavia in the same year.

Many Istrian towns have two official names, an Italian and a Croatian, a legacy from 1920, when Istria was given to Italy as a reward for having joined the Allies in World War I. During World War II, the region became a stronghold for Italian partisans. After 1943, most of Istria was given back to Yugoslavia.

The Roman amphitheatre at Pula, one of the best preserved Roman theatres in the world

◁ View of the shoreline, Rab

Exploring Istria and the Kvarner Area

Istria is a triangular peninsula, traditionally divided into three areas. White Istria is a central plateau of karst or limestone with sparse areas of oak, pine and ash trees; grey Istria consists of a strip of eroded limestone with rich soil, used for vines and olive trees; and red Istria is a plateau furrowed by the rivers Mirna and Raša, farmed for cereals and vegetables. The most popular destinations in Istria are Poreč, Rovinj, Pula and the Brijuni National Park. The Kvarner area includes the city of Rijeka and the coastline as far as Jablanac. Woods cover the northern hinterland, with the Risnjak National Park to the north, and the Plitvice Lakes National Park to the southeast. The islands of Krk, Cres, Lošinj and Rab are delightful places to explore. Many of the towns on the coast have an Italianate appearance.

The cathedral of St Mary the Great on the island of Rab

GETTING AROUND

The roads are good; there is a motorway linking Rijeka to Zagreb, as well as from Pula to the border with Slovenia. The larger islands can be reached by tourist and local ferries and there are frequent sailings in the summer season – these take cars also. Buses link all the main towns and there's a bus that runs from Pula to Trieste, while trains link Rijeka and Zagreb, with connections to the south of Croatia.

For additional map symbols see back flap

SIGHTS AT A GLANCE

Bakar ㉙
Bale (Valle) ➐
Barban ⑫
Brijuni National Park pp58–9 ➓
Buje (Buie) ➊
Cres ㉕
Crikvenica ㉛
Fažana (Fasana) ➒
Gračišće ⑮
Kastav ㉓
Kraljevica (Porto Re) ㉚
Krk ㉘
Labin ⑰
Lošinj (Lussino) ㉖
Lovran ⑳
Mošćenice ⑲
Novigrad (Cittanova) ➌
Novi Vinodolski ㉜
Opatija ㉒

Pazin ⑭
Pićan ⑯
Plitvice Lakes National Park pp86–7 ㉟
Plomin ⑱
Poreč (Parenzo) pp53–5 ➍
Pula (Pola) pp60–63 ⑪
Rab pp82–83 ㉞
Rijeka pp70–71 ㉔
Risnjak National Park pp74–5 ㉗
Rovinj (Rovigno) ➏
Senj ㉝
Svetvinčenat ⑬
Umag (Umago) ➋
Vodnjan (Dignano) ➑
Vrsar (Orsera) ➎

Tour

Tour of the Fortified Towns ㉑

LOCATOR MAP

KEY

▬▬	Two lane motorway
▬	Major road
═══	Minor road
▪ ▪	Motorway under construction
▭	Main railway
▬	County border
▬▬	International border
- - -	Ferry route
△	Summit

The rocky coastline near Rovinj

SEE ALSO

- *Where to Stay* pp222–26

- *Where to Eat* pp240–42

Façade of the church of St Servelus, Buje

Buje (Buie) ❶

Map A2. 🏘 6,000. ✈ Pula, 70 km (43 miles) S. 🚌 from Pula, Rijeka, Kopar, Trieste, Padova, Zagreb, Rovinj, Poreč. ℹ Istarska 2, (052) 773 353. 🍇 Grape festival (3rd weekend Sep). **www**.coloursofistria.com

On an isolated hill, among flourishing vineyards, stands Buje, the ancient Roman settlement of Bullea. Formerly a Frankish feudal village, in 1102 it became part of the Patriarchate of Aquileia and in 1412 the town came under Venetian rule.

The town still retains the outline of the ancient walled castle and has kept its original medieval layout, with narrow alleys and lanes leading to the main square. The cathedral of **St Servelus** (Sv. Servol) and its Aquileian bell tower stand here. The church was built in the 16th century over the remains of a Roman temple, of which a few columns and pieces survive.

Inside the church are wooden statues from the 14th and 15th centuries *(Madonna with Child* and *St Barbara)*, sculptures representing St Servelus and St Sebastian (1737) by Giovanni Marchiori, and an organ by Gaetano Callido (1725–1813).

A 15th-century Venetian Gothic palace and a 16th-century loggia with a frescoed façade also face the square.

Outside the walls is the church of **St Mary** (Sv. Marija), erected in the 15th century: a wooden statue of

the Virgin and a *Pietà* are from the same period. Some of the paintings of biblical scenes are by Gasparo della Vecchia (early 18th century).

The **Civic Museum** houses some interesting handicrafts and pieces made by local craftsmen.

🏛 **Civic Museum**
Trg Josipa Broza Tita 6. **Tel** (052) 773 075. 🕐 Jul & Aug: 9am–1pm, 5–9pm Mon–Sat; Sep–Jun: by appt.

Environs
Perched on a hilltop, 8 km (5 miles) south-east of Buje, is the medieval town of **Grožnjan** (Grisignana).

The town was first documented in 1102 when it became the property of the patriarch of Aquileia. In 1358 the Venetians bought the town from Baron Reiffenberg and since that time it has been the administrative and military centre of the surrounding area. A tower, some parts of the walls and two doors are all that remain of the old town.

Within the walls are a 16th-century loggia, in the main square, and the Baroque church of St Vitus and St Modest. The church has splendid altars and an impressive marble choir.

After World War II, the majority of the inhabitants, nearly all of them Italian, abandoned the town. In 1965, however, it was declared a

15th-century polyptych, church of St Mary, Umag

"City of Artists". Contemporary artists work and exhibit their art in the various local galleries and workshops.

Umag (Umago) ❷

Map A2. 🏘 13,000. ✈ Pula, 83 km (51 miles). 🚌 Joakima Rakovca bb, (060) 381 381. ℹ Trgovačka 6, (052) 741 363. 🍇 Feast of St Pilgrim (weekend nearest 23 May); International tennis tournament (end Jul); concerts in summer. **www**.coloursofistria.com

This town is located on a narrow peninsula which frames a small bay. It was founded by the Romans and given the name of Umacus. In 1268, it became an important port when it passed into Venetian hands. Later, in the 14th century, a wall and towers were built, some of which still remain.

The town still has many 15th- and 16th-century stone houses, some with ornate Gothic windows.

On the left outer wall of the 18th-century church of **St Mary** (Sv. Marija) is a relief of St Pilgrim and the fortified town of Umag, and inside the church is a 15th-century Venetian-school polyptych.

Today Umag is a busy seaside resort with numerous hotels. It has become known for its well-equipped sports centres and major tennis tournaments are held here.

View of the ancient wall and port of Umag

Boats in the harbour at Poreč

Novigrad (Cittanova) ❸

Map A2. 🏠 *4,000.* ✈ *Pula, 60 km (37 miles).* 🚉 *Pazin, 41 km (25 miles).* 🛈 *Mandrač 29a, (052) 757 075.* 🎭 *GnamGnam Fest: Novigrad Scallop Evening (first Fri in Jun), Patron saint's day, St Pelagius (weekend nearest 28 Aug).* **www**.novigrad-cittanova.hr

Originally a Greek colony and later a Roman one called Aemonia, Novigrad stands at the mouth of the River Mirna. In the Byzantine period (6th century) when it was enlarged, it was called "New Town" (Neopolis). From the early Middle Ages until 1831 it was an episcopal seat. In 1277 it passed into Venetian hands and oak from Motovun Forest was shipped to Venetian dockyards.

In the 13th century the town was walled for defence, but it was unable to withstand a Turkish attack in 1687 and the town was partially destroyed along with many works of art.

Evidence of the Venetian period can be seen on the façades of the houses in the narrow lanes which lead to the main square (Veliki Trg). An 18th-century loggia stands here. Of the early Christian basilica of **St Pelagius** (Sv. Pelagij), rebuilt in the 16th century, only the Romanesque crypt from the 11th-century remains. In the present-day Baroque church are paintings from the Venetian school of the 18th century. Evidence of the Roman and medieval periods can be seen in the museum housed in the Urizzi Palace.

Poreč (Parenzo) ❹

Map A2. 🏠 *11,000.* ✈ *Pula, 53 km (33 miles).* 🚉 *Pazin, 32 km (20 miles).* 🚌 *Ulica K Hoguesa 2, (060) 333 111.* 🛈 *Local: Zagrebačka 9, (052) 451 458;* **Regional:** *Pionirska 1, (052) 452 797.* 🎭 *Season of classical music (at St Euphrasius) and jazz festival (both Jul–Aug).* **www**.to-porec.com

Poreč was a Roman town (Colonia Julia Parentium) which, after centuries of splendour, was sacked by the Goths and fell into decline. In 539 it was conquered by the Byzantines, who founded a bishopric around the year 800. The town then became part of the kingdom of the Franks, who gave it to the Patriarchate of Aquileia. In 1267 it was the first Istrian town to choose Venetian rule, and the town acquired a Venetian look as palaces, squares and religious buildings were built.

In 1354 it was destroyed by the Genoese and later, plague, pirates and a long war greatly reduced the population. During Austrian domination it became the seat of the Istrian parliament and an important shipyard.

The old centre shelters on a narrow peninsula protected by rocks and the island of St Nicholas. Despite being a popular base for visitors to Istria, the old town has

remained intact and Poreč invariably wins an annual award for "best-kept town".

The layout is based on the original Roman network, with a main road (Decumanus) and another main road at right angles (Cardo). The main monuments of the town line these roads.

Along the Decumanus stand many Gothic houses. At the easternmost point is the Baroque Sinčić Palace (18th century), which houses the **Poreč Museum** (Zavičajni Muzej Poreštine). It is dedicated to Roman and early Christian archaeology; an ethnographic section illustrates daily life in the Poreč region. Nearby in St Maurus Street (Sv. Mauro) is the House of Two Saints, all that is left of the abbey of St Cassius (12th century), with two Romanesque figures on the façade. To the west, the Decumanus leads to Trg Marafor, once the site of the forum, with houses from the 12th and 13th centuries and the remains of a pre-Roman temple.

North of the square is the church of **St Francis** (Sv. Frane, 12th–14th centuries), altered in the Baroque period. To the east is the parish house with an ornate Romanesque façade. From here there is a passage that leads to the 6th-century Euphrasian Basilica, which has marvellous Byzantine mosaics *(see pp54–5).*

Archaeological exhibit in the Poreč Museum

🏛 **Poreč Museum**
Sinčić Palace, Dekumanska 9.
Tel *(052) 431 585.* ⬤ *for restoration.*

A typical trefoil window in Venetian Gothic style, Poreč

Poreč: Euphrasian Basilica
Eufrazijeva Bazilika

A mosaic in the apse

This 6th-century church, a Byzantine masterpiece, is decorated with splendid mosaics on a gold background. The Euphrasian Basilica was built for Bishop Euphrasius between 539 and 553, by enlarging the existing 4th-century Oratory of St Maurus Martyr. Some of the original floor mosaics still survive. Over the centuries the building has undergone numerous alterations. In December 1997 the basilica was added to the UNESCO World Heritage List. Classical concerts are held in the church in July and August.

★ **Ciborium**
Dominating the presbytery is a beautiful 13th-century ciborium, supported by four marble columns. The canopy is decorated with mosaics.

★ **Apse Mosaics**
Mosaics from the 6th century cover the apse. On the triumphal arch are Christ and the Apostles (above), on the vault, the Virgin enthroned with Child and two Angels, to the left St Maurus, Bishop Euphrasius with a model of the basilica, and Deacon Claud with his son.

Remains of a 4th-century mosaic floor from the Oratory of St Maurus are in the garden.

Sacristy and the Votive Chapel
Past the sacristy's left wall is a triple-apsed chapel with a mosaic floor from the 6th century. Here lie the remains of the saints Maurus and Eleuterius.

STAR FEATURES

★ Apse Mosaics

★ Ciborium

For hotels and restaurants in this region see pp222–6 and pp240–42

Interior
The entrance leads to a large basilica with a central nave and two side aisles. The 18 Greek marble columns have carved capitals featuring animals, some of Byzantine origin and others Romanesque. All bear the monogram of Euphrasius.

VISITORS' CHECKLIST

Eufrazijeva ulica 22. *Tel (052) 429 030.* ☐ call ahead for opening times.

Baptistry
This octagonal building dates from the 6th century. In the centre is a baptismal font and there are also fragments of mosaics; to the rear rises a 16th-century bell tower.

Atrium
This has a roughly square portico with two columns on each side. Tombstones and a variety of archaeological finds dating from the medieval period are displayed in this area.

The Bishop's Residence, a triple-aisled building dating from the 6th century, now houses several paintings by Antonio da Bassano, a polyptych by Antonio Vivarini and a painting by Palma il Giovane.

The church of St Anthony in
Vrsar, built in the 17th century

Vrsar (Orsera) ❺

Map A3. 🏛 *2,200*. ✈ *Pula, 41 km
(25 miles)*. 🚉 *Pazin, 42 km (26
miles)*. 🛈 *Rade Končara 46, (052)
441 187*. 🎭 *International sculpture
school, Montraker quarry (end Aug,
early Sep); classical music concerts
(summer)*. **www**.infovrsar.com

The remains of a villa,
a quarry and the foundations
of an early Christian building
all provide evidence that
Romans once settled here. In
documents preceding 1000
AD, this village is mentioned
as the feudal territory of the
bishop of Poreč, who owned
a fortified summer residence
here. Until 1778 it remained
under the protection of the
bishop and then came under
Venetian rule.

The town had an outer wall
and towers which have now
almost disappeared except for
the Sea Gate. Near the gate is
the church of **St Mary** (Sv.
Marija) from the 10th century,
one of the most important
Romanesque monuments in
Istria. Inside are frescoes
which are among the oldest
in the region and a mosaic
floor with floral motifs.

The town is dominated by
the 18th-century **Vergottini
Castle**, built by restructuring
the bishop's former residence.
Near the Romanesque gate in
the medieval wall is the small
church of **St Anthony**, built in
the 17th century with an
open portico.

Environs

Just outside Vrsar lies
Koversada, Europe's largest
naturist resort.

To the south of Vrsar,
towards Rovinj, is the **Limski**

Channel, now a marine
reserve. The channel is 9 km
(5 miles) long, and 600 m
(1,970 ft) wide with steep
sides, perforated by limestone
caves which have been lived
in from time to time since the
Neolithic Age. In the early
11th century, one of the caves
was the home of the hermit
St Romualdo, who founded
the monastery of St Michael
near Kloštar.

Many of the restaurants in
the area offer the oysters and
mussels farmed in the channel.

Fishermen on the Limski Channel

Rovinj (Rovigno) ❻

Map A3. 🏛 *13,000*. ✈ *Pula, 40 km
(25 miles)*. 🚉 *Pula*. 🚌 *Trg na Lokvi,
(060) 333 111*. 🛈 *Obala P Budičina
12, (052) 811 566*. 🎭 *Grisia,
International art exhibition (2nd Sun
in Aug); Patron St Euphemia's day (16
Sep)*. **www**.tzgrovinj.hr

Rovinj was originally an
island port built by the
Romans. In 1763, Rovinj was
joined to the coast by filling
in the channel dividing the
island from the mainland,
creating a peninsula.

Initially ruled by the
Byzantines and the Franks,
from 1283 until 1797 the town
was under Venetian control.
The remains of a wall dating

back to the Middle Ages can
still be seen.

In the square in front of the
pier is Balbi's Arch (1680), an
ancient city gate, as well as a
late-Renaissance clock tower.
The Califfi Palace, dating from
1680, is now the **Heritage
Museum**, housing 18th-century
art from the Venetian school
and works by modern
Croatian artists.

In the roads branching off
the square are Baroque and
Renaissance buildings. The
backs of many of these face
the sea. The **cathedral**,
dedicated to St Euphemia
(Sv. Eufemije) dominates the
town. Originating in early
Christian times, it was rebuilt
in 1736. The saint's remains
are preserved in a Roman
sarcophagus in the apse on
the right of the three-aisle
church. The adjacent bell
tower is 62 m (200 ft) high
(the highest in Istria), and
was modelled on that of
San Marco in Venice. It is
crowned by a copper statue
of St Euphemia.

In the east of the city is the
13th-century **Baptistry of the
Holy Trinity** (Sv. Trojstvo).

Along the waterfront is the
Institute of Marine Biology. It
was founded in the late 19th
century and has an aquarium.
Nearby, Red Island (Crveni
otok), is in fact two islands
linked by an embankment.

South of the town is Zlatni
Rt, a park planted with
cedars, pines and cypresses.

🏛 **Heritage Museum**
Trg M Tita 11. **Tel** *(052) 816 720,
830 650*. ◻ *summer: 10am–2pm,
6–10pm Tue–Fri, 10am–2pm, 7–
10pm Sat–Sun; winter: 10am–1pm
Tue–Sat*. **www**.muzej-rovinj.com

The port of Rovinj, dominated by the cathedral

The church of St Elizabeth inside the walls of Bale

Bale (Valle) **❼**

Map A3. 🏠 *900.* 🛫 *Pula, 10 km (17 miles).* 🚉 *Pula, 25 km (15 miles).* 🚌 *Trg palih Boraca.* 🛈 *Rovinjska 1, (052) 824 391.* 🎭 *Night of Bale, Baljanska Noć (first Sun in Aug); Castrum Vallis, art exhibition (Jul & Aug).* **www**.bale-valle.hr

On a hill of limestone, the Illyrians constructed a fort which dominated the surrounding countryside. The Romans also built a *castrum* (Castrum Vallis) on the same site, which was renovated when the place became a feudal estate of the Patriarchate of Aquileia. During Venetian rule, which began in 1332, the town grew in size and acquired its present layout of an elliptical wall with towers enclosing two parallel rows of houses. Interesting buildings include the Gothic-Venetian Magistrates' Court with coats of arms on the portico, the loggia, and the Gothic-Renaissance **Castle** dating from the 15th century, a residence for the Soardo Bembo family. Under one of the two side towers is a gate leading to the old town.

The church of **St Elizabeth** (Pohođenje Blažene Djevice Marije), of Romanesque origins, was reconstructed in the 16th century and again in the 19th. The church contains a splendid Romanesque crucifix, a sarcophagus, a polyptych and a crypt with a marble Renaissance altar.

There are two other churches in Bale. One dates from the 14th century and is dedicated to St Anthony; the other, dedicated to the Holy Spirit, was built in the 15th century.

Vodnjan (Dignano) **❽**

Map A3. 🏠 *4,000.* 🛫 *Pula, 11 km (7 miles).* 🚉 *Ulica Željeznička, (052) 511 538.* 🛈 *Narodni trg 3, (052) 511 700.* 🎭 *Bumbari, a festival in costume based on the name given to the town's inhabitants (2nd Sat in Aug).*

The town of Vodnjan stands on a hill among vineyards and olive groves. At one time it was an Illyrian fort and later, a Roman military post known as Vicus Atinianus. From 1331 until 1797 the town was under Venetian rule.

The old part of town still has various buildings in Venetian-Gothic style, including the Bettica Palace and the 18th-century church of **St Blaise** (Sv. Blaž). In the church are some splendid statues and about 20 paintings from the 17th to 19th centuries, as well as a *Last Supper* by G Contarini (1598) and an *Encounter of Saints* attributed to Palma il Vecchio.

Seven rooms of the church are given over to religious art (730 pieces): vestments, china and silver reliquaries, statues and paintings, and a fine polyptych by Paolo Veneziano from 1351 (*Portrait of the Blessed Leon Bembo*). There are also six mummies of saints, which have survived miraculously without being embalmed. The most revered is that of St Nicolosia.

🔒 **St Blaise**
Župni trg. **Tel** *(052) 511 420.*
◻ *by appt.* **Collection of Religious Art Tel** *(052) 511 420.*
◻ *by appt.*

Fažana (Fasana) **❾**

Map A3. 🏠 *2,800.* 🛫 *Pula, 8 km (5 miles).* 🚉 *Vodnjan, 5 km (3 miles).* 🚢 *to the Brijuni Islands.* 🛈 *43. Istarske divizije 8, (052) 383 727.* **www**.infofazana.hr

This small town is known mainly as the embarkation point for the islands of the Brijuni National Park (*see pp58–9*). Its ancient name, Vasianum, derives from the production of oil and wine amphorae during the Roman period. Facing the sea is the church of **SS Cosmas and Damian** (Sv. Kuzma i Damjan), which was founded in the 11th century and has undergone various reconstructions. Inside is a painting by Jurai Ventura of *The Last Supper* (1578), and in the sacristy are remains of frescoes by Italian artists from Friuli dating from the 15th–16th centuries.

To the side of the church is a seven-storey bell tower with an octagonal spire. The church of **Our Lady of Carmel** from the late 14th century has Gothic frescoes by unknown artists and a 17th-century loggia. Nearby is the church of **St Elys** from the 6th century, with a stone doorway and blind-arch windows, which preserves its Byzantine appearance from the 8th–9th centuries.

Thanks to the growth in numbers of visitors heading for the Brijuni Islands, the town has grown and new facilities have been built.

The façade of the church of SS Cosmas and Damian in Fažana

Brijuni National Park ❿
Nacionalni Park Brijuni

The Brijuni Archipelago is made up of 14 islands and was declared a national park in 1983. The two largest islands have been inhabited since the Palaeolithic era. In Roman times there were aristocratic villas and later religious communities. The islands were abandoned in 1630 because of malaria, but people returned in the following century to work the stone quarries. In the late 19th century, the islands were bought by the Tyrolean industrialist Paul Kupelwieser. After World War II they were used as a summer residence by Marshal Tito, and were visited by heads of state. Visitors are only allowed on the two main islands, Veli Brijun and Mali Brijun.

The Fort of Mali Brijun is situated on the second largest island in the archipelago. The Austro-Hungarian fort was built at the end of the 19th century.

SV. MARKO

GAZ

OBLJAK

MALI BRIJUN
LESSER BRIJUN

SUPIN

SUPINIĆ

Aerial View of the Brijuni Islands
The islands are covered with lush vegetation, much of it undisturbed by human habitation.

Barban •

GALIJA

GRUNJ

Safari Park
Tito introduced many species of exotic animal, including zebra. Many were gifts from visiting heads of state.

VANGA

VRSAR

Native Animals
Numerous indigenous animals also live freely in the park: fallow deer, moufflon, roedeer, hares, peacocks and about 200 species of wild bird.

KEY

▬	Minor road
⛴	Ferry
🚊	Electric train
ℹ	Tourist information
⌂	Archaeological site

Ancient Trees
Hundreds of different plant species from all over the world were planted on Brijun. Many of the trees, like this ancient olive, are now fully mature and are regarded as living monuments.

VISITORS' CHECKLIST

Map A3. 🚢 *from Fažana.*
Brijuni National Park 🛈 *(052) 525 883; 525 882. Individuals and groups must book on an excursion, which includes the boat crossing. Bicycles can be hired.* 🔓 *always, but access limited to crossing times.*
***Tel** (052) 525 882.* 🎫 🚻 ♿
📷 www.brijuni.hr

The museum, opened in 1955, contains cultural and archaeological finds from the island.

In the area around Brijuni harbour hotels and a golf course have been built.

Roman Villa
Excavations have unearthed the foundations of a Roman villa, its calidarium (hot room) and a frigidarium (cold room). A large room where the family met for banquets and ceremonies is decorated with mosaics.

VELIKI BRIJUN
GREATER BRIJUN

Brijuni

PUSTI

0 metres	800
0 yards	800

Rt Ploče

The Tegetthoff Fortress is a ruined Austrian defence system which was built in the 19th century.

The White Villa (Bijela Vila) dates from the Venetian period. It was restored in 1721. This was Tito's summer residence and was used for receptions and political meetings.

Byzantine Castrum
On the western coast, in the gulf of Dobrika, are the ruins of a complex of buildings dating from the Byzantine era (539–778), with towers and walls for defence.

…eda

Pula (Pola) ⓫

Vase, Archaeological Museum

Pula is well-known for its magnificent monuments from the Roman era, when it was a colony known as Pietas Julia. It became an episcopal seat in 425 and still has the foundations of some 5th-century religious buildings. It was destroyed by the Ostrogoths, but flourished again when it became the main base for the Byzantine fleet in the 6th and 7th centuries: the cathedral and church of St Mary of Formosa date from this time. In 1150 it came under Venetian rule, but by the mid-17th century the population had declined to 300. Revitalized in 1856 when Austria made it the base for its fleet, it is still one of the most important naval bases in Croatia. Today, Pula is a university town and, with Pazin (see pp64–5), the administrative centre of Istria.

The cathedral's interior, a combination of styles and periods

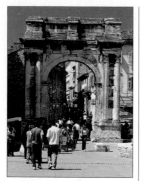

Arch of the Sergii, 1st century BC

⋔ Arch of the Sergii
Slavoluk obitelji Sergijevaca
Ulica Sergijevaca.
The arch was erected in the 1st century BC on the orders of Salvia Postuma Sergia, to honour three brothers who held important positions in the Roman Empire. The arch is small with fluted columns, a winged victory and Corinthian capitals. Its frieze has a bas-relief depicting a chariot pulled by horses.
Next door is a bar named Uliks ("Ulysses"), in memory of James Joyce, who lived here for six months in 1904.

⛪ Church of St Mary of Formosa
Kapela Marije Formoze
Maksimilijanova ulica. ◐ to public.
A small Byzantine church, built on a Greek cross plan, this was once a chapel, part of the large Basilica of St Mary of Formosa. Inside are remains of mosaics from the 6th century.

⛪ Church of St Francis
Sv. Frane
Uspon B. Lupetine 5.
◯ Jun–Sep: 10am–1pm, 4–8pm; Oct–May: for mass.
Built at the same time as the adjacent monastery in the late 13th century, this church has a fine doorway with a Gothic rose window. The interior is a single nave with three apses; on the main altar is a splendid wooden 15th-century polyptych by the Emilian school. Various exhibits from the Imperial Roman era can be seen in the monastery cloisters.

⋔ Temple of Romae and Augustus
Augustov hram
Forum. **Tel** (052) 218 603. ◯ May: 9am–9pm Mon–Fri; Jun–Aug: 9am–10pm Mon–Fri, 9am–3pm Sat & Sun; Sep–Apr: by appt. 🖼
Built in the 1st century AD, this temple stands in the square which was once the site of the Roman forum. It is a splendid example of

Temple of Romae and Augustus, a jewel of Roman architecture

Roman architecture, built on simple lines, with six plain columns and beautiful carved capitals.

⛪ Cathedral
Katedrala
Trg Sv. Tome 2. ◯ Jun–Sep: 10am–1pm, 4–8pm; Oct–May: for mass.
The cathedral, dedicated to the Blessed Virgin Mary, was founded in the 5th century after Pula became an episcopal seat. Its present appearance dates back only as far as the 17th century. However, parts of the walls, some of the capitals and the windows are from the original building. On the right is a doorway from 1456, while the bell tower, which was built by 1707, contains stone blocks from the amphitheatre.

⛪ Church of St Nicholas
Sv. Nikola
Castropola 39. ◯ for mass.
ℹ (052) 212 987 (Tourist office).
This church dates from the 6th century but was partially rebuilt in the 10th century. Towards the end of the 15th century it was assigned to the Orthodox community. Inside are some fine icons from the 15th and 16th centuries.

⛫ Castle and Historical Museum of Istria
Povijesni Muzej Istre
Gradinski uspon 6. **Tel** (052) 211 566. ◯ Jun–Sep: 8am–9pm daily; Oct–May: 9am–5pm daily. 🖼
This star-shaped castle with four bastions houses the Historical Museum of Istria

and was built by the Venetians in the 14th century on the ruins of the Roman Capitol in the city centre. The walls linking the four towers offer splendid views over the city. Nearby are the remains of a 2nd-century theatre.

🏛 Archaeological Museum of Istria
Arheološki Muzej Istre
Carrarina 3. **Tel** (052) 351 301.
⬜ May–Sep: 9am–8pm Mon–Fri, 10am–3pm Sat & Sun; Oct–Apr: 9am–3pm Mon–Fri.
🈂 🎫 (by appt) ♿
www.ami-pula.hr
This museum is housed in the former German school, within a park which is reached from the Twin Gate. On display are finds from Pula, with collections from the Prehistoric era to the Middle Ages. On

Headless Statue, Archaeological Museum

the ground floor are architectural remains, mosaics, altars and other exhibits from antiquity to medieval times.

The rooms on the first floor contain exhibits from the Neolithic to the Roman era. Three rooms on the second floor are dedicated to Roman antiquity (including a headless female statue found at Nesactium, near Pula). Two rooms have exhibits from the late-Classical to medieval periods. Of particular interest are pieces from Slavic tombs dating from the 7th to 12th centuries.

⋒ Twin Gate
Dvojna vrata
Carrarina.
The gate, from the 2nd–3rd centuries, has two arches with an ornate frieze. Nearby are parts of the wall which once encircled the city.

VISITORS' CHECKLIST

Map A3. 🏘 60,000. ✈ 8 km (5 miles), (052) 530 105. ⛴ Jadroagent (052) 210 431. 🚉 (052) 541 722. 🚌 43. istarske divizije, (060) 304 090. ℹ **Tourist office**, Forum 3, (052) 219 197. 🎭 Music events in Arena, Pula Amphitheatre (summer), Croatian Film Festival (summer). **www**.pulainfo.hr

⋒ Gate of Hercules
Herculova vrata
Carrarina.
South of the Archaeological Museum stands the single-arched Gate of Hercules. Built in the 1st century BC, it is the oldest and best preserved Roman monument in the city. At the top of the arch is a carving of the head of Hercules with a club.

⋒ Amphitheatre
See pp62–3.

PULA TOWN CENTRE

Train Station 200 m (220 yards)
Bus Station 250 m (275 yards)

Harbour

⑪ Amphitheatre

Cathedral ⑤
⑥ Church of St Nicholas
⑧ Twin Gate
Theatre
⑨ Archaeological Museum of Istria
Town Hall
④ Temple of Romae and Augustus
FORUM
Roman Mosaic
⑦
③ Church of St Francis
Castle and Historical Museum of Istria
⑩ Gate of Hercules
② Church of St Mary of Formosa
① Arch of the Sergii
Market

KOLODVORSKA · FLANJIPEKA · SCALIEROVA · ISTARSKA · AMFITEATARSKA · DOBRICEVA · EPULONOVA · ZADARSKA · ZAGREBAČKA · VERONSKA · GIARDINI · SERGIJEVACA · ANTICOVA · NARODNI TRG · MATKA LAGINJE · DOBRILINA · ARSENALSKA · CASTROPOLA · KANDLEROVA · RIVA · SV. TEODORA · SV. IVANA · CARRARINA · FLACIUSOVA · OZARKA · MAKSIMIJANOVA · CASTROPOLA

0 metres 200
0 yards 200

Key to Symbols see back flap

Pula Amphitheatre
Amfiteatar

The elliptical arena in Pula is one of the six largest Roman amphitheatres existing today. Originally a small amphitheatre built here by Claudius, it was enlarged by Vespasian in AD 79 for gladiator fights. The amphitheatre could hold 23,000 spectators and had about 20 entrances. It remained intact until the 15th century when some of the stone was used to construct the castle and other buildings in the city. It was restored, first by the French governor of the Illyrian provinces, General Marmont, and again more recently when it was adapted for musical events. It can seat 5,000 spectators and is a venue for concerts ranging from opera to rock as well as for an annual film festival.

View of the amphitheatre today

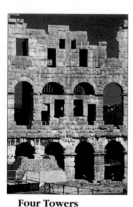

Four Towers

The roofs of the towers were designed to collect the scented water that was sprayed onto the stalls. It is also thought that there was a structure capable of supporting large awnings as protection from the sun and rain.

Amphitheatre Wall

The well-preserved external wall of the amphitheatre has three floors on the side facing the sea, and two on the opposite side, because it was constructed on an incline. At its highest point, the external wall measures 29.40 m (96 ft).

Interior of the Amphitheatre
*When first built, the broad tiers could seat an audience
of 23,000 people. Shows of every kind were performed,
including naval battles. Today, during the summer
season, operas, ballets and plays are put on here.*

VISITORS' CHECKLIST

Flavijevska ulica.
***Tel** (052) 219 028.*
⬛ *call ahead for opening
hours.* 🅿 ♿ *limited access.*

The various corridors
which led to the seats
allowed spectators to find
their places efficiently.

RECONSTRUCTION

The main floor of the
arena, 67.75 m (222 ft)
long and 41.05 m (135 ft)
wide, was originally
framed by iron railings to
separate spectators from
the performance. Between
the tiers of seats and the
railings there was a space,
3m (10 ft) wide, reserved
for staff. Along the main
axis, under the arena,
were underground
corridors which were used
by the gladiators and
cages for animals. The
animals were kept here
before being sent into
the stadium.

Today the southwest
tower is one of the
entrances.

Arches
*The first two floors have
72 arches, the third has
64 large rectangular
openings. The arches lit
the internal corridors
which enabled spectators
to move from one sector
of the amphitheatre
to another.*

Underground Area
*Many archaeological finds
from the amphitheatre and
other Roman buildings are
kept in the underground
passages, where there were
once cages and prisons.*

Barban ⑫

Map B3. 🏛 *250.* ✈ *Pula, 28 km (17 miles).* 🚌 *Pula.* 🚢 *from Pula.*
ℹ *Barban 69, (052) 567 420.*
🎪 *Trka na prstenac, Tournament of the Ring (3rd weekend in Aug).*
www.barban.hr

A free town in the late Middle Ages, in the 13th century Barban came under the rule of the county of Pazin, and from 1516 until 1797 it was part of Venetian territory. It was granted to the Loredan family in 1535, and many buildings acquired their current Venetian look.

Church of the Annunciation, Svetvinčenat

The town still has some medieval fortifications which now incorporate several Renaissance buildings.

The church of **St Nicholas** (Sv. Nikola) faces the square, which is reached through the Great Gate (Vela Vrata). The church has five marble Gothic altars and many Venetian paintings (16th–18th centuries), one attributed to the Italian artist Padovanino.

In the same square is the Loredan Palace from 1606 and, towards the Small Gate (Mala Vrata), the Town Hall dating from 1555.

Outside the Great Gate is the 14th-century church of St **Anthony** (Sv. Antun), with some frescoes from the 15th century. In 1976, the Tournament of the Ring was revived and costumed lancers on horses participate in this traditional annual event.

🏛 **St Nicholas**
Tel *(052) 567 173.* ⬭ *by appt.*

Svetvinčenat ⑬

Map A3. 🏛 *300.* 🚌 *Pazin.* 🚢 *from Pula.* ℹ **Local:** *Svetvinčenat 20, (052) 560 349.* **Regional:** *Pionirska 1, Poreč, (052) 452 797.*
www.tz-svetvincenat.hr

This walled village was built in the 10th century on a small hill around a much restructured fort. The main square is one of the most beautiful in Istria. Many of the main buildings in the village are found here, including the 15th-century church of the Annunciation which contains two paintings by Palma il Giovane and an Annunciation by Giuseppe Porto-Salviati.

The **Castle** dates from the 13th century and is one of the best preserved in the region. It belonged to the Venetian families of Castropola, the Morosini and the Grimani. In 1589, the Grimani commissioned the architect Scamozzi to convert one of the square towers into a residence for the Venetian governors, the other into a prison. High walls connecting the other two round towers enclose a large internal courtyard. This is reached through the citadel's only gate, which at one time had a drawbridge. The town's coat of arms and that of the Grimani family can also be seen here.

The town's name derives from the Romanesque church and cemetery of St **Vincent** (Sv. Vinčenat), whose walls were frescoed by an unknown 15th-century artist.

🏛 **St Vincent**
Cemetery. **Tel** *(052) 560 004.* ⬭ *by appt.*

Environs

About 10 km (6 miles) away are the ruins of **Dvigrad** (Duecastelli), an atmospheric, abandoned walled village, surrounded by lush vegetation.

Around 1000 AD, two castles were built on neighbouring hills and were later enclosed by an oval wall. A village of 200 inhabitants grew up inside the wall around the basilica of St Sophia, built between the 11th and 12th centuries. Although attacked and burnt by the Genoese in the 14th century during the war with Venice, the village soon recovered. In the 17th century, sacking by the Uskoks *(see p81)* and a malaria epidemic depopulated the village. It has not been inhabited since then.

Reconstruction of a room in the Ethnographic Museum, Pazin

Pazin ⑭

Map B2. 🏛 *5,300.* 🚌 *(052) 624 310.* 🚢 *(060) 306 040.* ℹ *Franine i Jurine 14, (052) 622 460.* **www**.tzpazin.hr

The town of Pazin originated in the 9th century as a fort and stands on a cliff 130 m (426 ft) high. One side of the cliff falls away to an abyss, which is 100 m (328 ft) deep and about 20 m (65 ft) wide, and is said to have inspired Dante's description of the Gateway to Hell in *Inferno.*

In the 14th century, Pazin passed into the hands of the Habsburgs, who granted it to the Montecuccoli family.

The imposing, overgrown ruins of Dvigrad

They maintained ownership of the castle after the end of the feudal regime.

The castle's present layout dates from the 16th century. The tower is reached through a doorway in the façade made in 1786. Since 1962 it has housed the **Ethnographic Museum of Istria** (Etnografski muzej Istre). In 1996 the **Civic Museum** was set up, with weaponry and finds from the castle on display.

The church of the **Visitation of the Blessed Virgin Mary** (Pohođenje Blažene Djevice Marije) and its 15th-century monastery were cultural centres for the area.

🏛 **Ethnographic Museum of Istria**
Castle, Trg Istarskog razvoda 1275, no 1. **Tel** (052) 622 220. ⬜ 10am–6pm Tue–Sun. 🏢 📷 www.emi.hr

🏛 **Civic Museum**
Castle, Trg Istarskog razvoda 1275, no 1. **Tel** (052) 623 054. ⬜ Apr–Oct: 10am–6pm Tue–Sun (Jul & Aug daily); Nov–Mar: 10am–3pm Tue–Thu, 11am–4pm Fri, 10am–4pm Sat & Sun. 🏢 📷

Gračišće ⓯

Map B2. 🏠 470. 🚉 Pazin, 7 km (4 miles). 🚌 only during school year; contact Pazin (060) 306 040. ℹ Franine i Jurine 14, Pazin, (052) 622 460.

The small village of Gračišće stands on a hill among woods and vineyards. At one time this was a strong military garrison, which stood on the borders of the Venetian Republic and the Habsburg empire. The town has some interesting buildings, such as the 15th-century **Salamon Palace** and to the side, the **Bishop's Chapel** (both in Venetian Gothic style) where the bishop of Pićan spent the summer.

The church of **St Mary** (Sv. Marije) was consecrated in 1425 and has a characteristic barrel vault and several frescoes. The Romanesque church of **St Euphemia** (Sv. Fumija) was rebuilt in the 16th century and still has a wooden crucifix from the 14th century. The loggia near the main gate dates from 1549.

The picturesque town of Pićan, once a bishop's see

Pićan ⓰

Map B2. 🏠 316. 🚉 only during school year; contact Pazin (060) 306 040. ℹ Franine i Jurine 14, Pazin, (052) 622 460.

Known as Petena under the Romans, Pićan stands on a hilltop 350m (1,150 ft) high. It was a bishop's see from the 7th century to 1788, and has some intriguing medieval buildings. Inside the medieval walls is a cathedral dedicated to St Nicephorus, built in the 14th century, and rebuilt in the early 18th century after an earthquake. The story of the Christian martyr Nicephorus is shown in a painting by Valentin Metzinger (1699–1759) in the cathedral. The Romanesque church of St Michael (Sv. Mihovil) in the cemetery has early 15th-century frescoes.

Labin ⓱

Map B3. 🏠 12,400. 🚌 Ulica 2, marta, (060) 333 888. ℹ Aldo Negri 20, (052) 855 560. 🎵 Classical music concerts (Jul–Aug). www.rabac-labin.com

The old part of Labin is made up of the medieval part inside the walls, and the part from the Venetian period around Tito Square (Titov Trg). Here stand the 19th-century Town Hall, a 17th-century bastion, a loggia (1550) and the St Flora gate (1587) with a Lion of St Mark.

The Gothic **Church of the Blessed Mary's Birth** (Rođenje Marijino), built in the late 14th century, stands in a street leading to the square called Stari Trg. A rose window

decorates the façade and inside are works by Venetian artists of the 16th and 17th centuries, including a painting by Palma il Giovane.

In the same square lies the Magistrates' Court (1555), near Scampicchio Palace and the early 18th-century Baroque Battiala Lazzarini Palace, now the **Town Museum** with Roman and medieval finds, and a lifelike reconstruction of a coal mine. Labin was Croatia's most important coal mining town until the mines were closed down in 1999. In 1921, in opposition to rising Fascism in Italy, 2,000 coal-miners set up the Labin Republic, a socialist mini-state that barely lasted a month.

🏛 **Town Museum**
Ulica 1 Maja 6. **Tel** (052) 852 477. ⬜ Jun–Sep: 10am–1pm, 6–8pm Mon–Fri, 10am–1pm Sat; Oct–May: 7am–3pm Mon–Fri.

Environs
About 4 km (2 miles) from Labin lies the popular seaside resort of Rabac.

Stepped road and ancient buildings, Labin

Detail of the altar in the church of St George the Younger, Plomin

Plomin ⑱

Map B3. 🏠 140. ✈ Pula, 54 km (34 miles). 🚉 Rijeka, 55 km (34 miles). 🛈 Vozilići 66, Vozilići; (052) 880 155; **Regional:** Pionirska 1, Poreč, (052) 452 797.

An ancient fortified town once stood here on the site of the Roman town Flanona, which was destroyed by the Avars in the 6th century. It was rebuilt after 1000 AD and took on its present look in the 13th century after it had become Venetian territory. Plomin, built on a sheer cliff 168 m (550 ft) above the bay of the same name, was once densely populated.

Houses take up nearly all the space inside the walls (from the 13th–14th centuries and only partially preserved). Worn, narrow roads climb towards the centre, where the 11th-century Romanesque church of **St George the Elder** (Sv. Juraj Stari) stands. Inside is a tablet in Glagolitic script (*see p35*) also dating from the 11th century, one of the oldest Glagolitic documents in Croatia.

The church of the **Blessed Virgin Mary** (Crkva Blažene Djevice Marije) also contains treasures of artistic merit. The church was consecrated in 1474, but was greatly altered in the 18th century. There are three Baroque altars in carved, painted wood and a rich church treasury. A fresco by Albert, a German painter, was found on the wall during restoration work.

Mošćenice ⑲

Map B2. 🏠 330. ✈ Rijeka, 53 km (33 miles), on the island of Krk. 🚉 Rijeka. 🛈 Aleja Slatina bb, Mošćenička Draga, (051) 739 166. **www**.tz-moscenicka.hr

This small village was founded by the Liburnians on a small hilltop. The structure of the medieval town is still evident, with houses pressed against the walls, narrow streets, small alleys and courtyards. There are lovely views over the Kvarner Gulf from the village.

In the main square is the church of **St Andrew** (Sv. Andrije), a building of medieval origin which was rebuilt in the Baroque style in the 17th century. Inside are some statues by the Paduan sculptor Jacopo Contieri. Just outside the walls are the small church of St Sebastian from the 16th century, and the 17th-century church of St Bartholomew.

The history of the area is documented in the **Ethnographic Museum** (Etnografski Muzej).

Statue by Contieri, church of St Andrew, Mošćenice

🏛 Ethnographic Museum
Tel (051) 737 551.
🕐 summer: 9am–1pm, 6–9pm daily; winter: 11am–3pm daily.
⬤ Jan & Feb.

Environs
A series of steps leads down to Mošćenićka Draga (2 km/1 mile), where there is a large pebble beach.

Lovran ⑳

Map B2. 🏠 4,050. ✈ Rijeka, 50 km (31 miles, island of Krk). 🚉 Rijeka, 20 km (13 miles). 🚌 Opatija, 6 km (4 miles). 🛈 Trg Slobode 1, (051) 291 740. 🎭 Asparagus Festival (Apr); Cherry Days (Jun); Marunada, chestnut festival (mid-Oct). **www**.tz-lovran.hr

The town of Lovran (whose name derives from the laurel trees which are common throughout the area) extends along the coast until it meets the long seafront at Opatija (*see p67*). The old part of the town is situated on a small peninsula along the coast. The houses in the ancient fortified town lean against the enclosing walls, of which only a very few parts and sections remain: just a tower and the Stubica Gate. In the main square, as well as a medieval tower there are several houses with Venetian Gothic façades and also the church of **St George** (Sv. Juraj), built in the 12th century and rebuilt in the Baroque period, along with a Romanesque bell tower. Inside the church, on the vault and the arch of the apse are some late-Gothic frescoes (1470–79) depicting the life of Christ and several saints. A building with a figure of St George stands in the main square and is worth a visit.

Along the coastal promenade, which extends between Lovran and the

Old mill at the Ethnographic Museum, Mošćenice

For hotels and restaurants in this region see pp222–6 and pp240–42

The Villa Angiolina in Opatija, surrounded by a splendid park

village of Ika, stand several beautiful early 20th-century Secessionist villas *(see p23)*, surrounded by lush gardens.

🔒 **St George**
🕐 Jul & Aug: 7–9:30pm Mon, Wed & Fri.

Tour of the Fortified Towns ㉑

See pp68–9.

Opatija ㉒

Map B2. 👥 *13,000.* ✈ *Rijeka, 40 km (25 miles), island of Krk.* 🚌 *Rijeka.* 🚊 *Rijeka.* 🛈 **Local:** *Nazorova 3, (051) 271 710;* **Regional:** *Nikole Tesle 2, (051) 272 988.* 🎭 *Carnival of the Riviera (Feb); Summer Festival (May–Sep); "Kaisernacht" (Jul); Liburnia Jazz Festival (Jul); Chocolate Festival (Dec).* **www**.opatija-tourism.hr

The tourist resort of Opatija takes its name from a 14th-century Benedictine abbey, around which a village was built. On the site of the monastery now stands the church of St James (Sv. Jakov), built in 1506 and enlarged in 1937.

Tourist interest began to grow in around 1845 when a nobleman from Rijeka, Iginio Scarpa, built the grand **Villa Angiolina** here. The villa is surrounded by a large park and became the first hotel.

A few years later the Austrian Empress Maria Anna stayed here and her visit was immediately followed by visits from other court dignitaries. More luxury hotels and villas were then built and the small town became a fashionable turn-of-the-century resort. Tourism in Opatija was given a boost by the construction of the railway line which linked Austria with Rijeka, with a tram line to Opatija.

The Emperor Franz Joseph also stayed at a hotel here, often for long periods during the winter in order to enjoy the mild climate of the area. Today the coast is still lined with luxury late-19th-century hotels and villas surrounded by parks and gardens. However, it is no longer the height of fashion, although older visitors are drawn by its comparative tranquillity.

Kastav ㉓

Map B2. 👥 *10,470.* ✈ *Rijeka, 20 km (12 miles), island of Krk.* 🚌 *Rijeka, 11 km (7 miles).* 🚊 *Rijeka, 11 km (7 miles).* 🛈 *Matka Laginje 5, (051) 691 425.* 🎭 *Bela Nedeja, wine festival (first Sun in Oct).* **www**.kastav-touristinfo.hr

On a hill a short distance from Rijeka is the town of Kastav, which originated in the early Middle Ages. The castle was the residence of the local lord of the manor until the 16th century, and later the home of the Austrian governor. In Lokvina square stand the church of St Anthony of the Desert, which dates from the 15th century, and a loggia from 1571, restored in 1815. By the water trough a plaque recalls the drowning in 1666 of Captain Morelli, guilty of imposing excessive taxes.

The harbour at Opatija, once a great favourite with the Habsburg royals

Tour of the Fortified Towns ㉑

Message box for denunciations

The villages and towns of Istria were all fortified. The first people to build walls were the Histri (an Illyrian tribe), who put up defences on the hilltops where they settled. There are 136 such fortified towns in Istria. Many were abandoned, but evidence in some shows continuous occupation from 1000 BC up to the present day. The walls were reinforced in Roman times and rebuilt in the late Middle Ages, then enlarged when the towns came under Austrian or Venetian rule. Documents written in the ancient Glagolitic script can be seen on a detour.

Hum ③
This small village is protected by an oval wall, reinforced by the Venetians. The church of St Jerome has splendid 12th-century Byzantine frescoes.

Buzet ④
An Illyrian fort and a Roman fortification (Pinquentum), Buzet belonged to the Venetians from 1420 onwards. They rebuilt the town wall with a Large Gate and a Small Gate (16th century). Today Buzet is known for its truffles.

Istarske Toplice

Livade

Račice

↓ *PAZIN*

Draguć ⑤
Medieval walls form the backs of the houses in this village. Ramparts were built by the Venetians after 1420. The 14th-century church of St Roch has a series of frescoes, including a Journey of the Magi.

KEY

▬▬	Tour route
▪ ▪	Trail of the Glagolitics
---	Other roads
🛈	Tourist information
🔆	Viewpoint

Motovun ⑥
This medieval town stands on a hill dominating the valley. The old town is still encircled by an original 13th–14th-century wall. Later, a second wall was built around the suburbs. An internal gate, under a 15th-century tower, leads from the Lower Town to the Upper Town.

Roč ②

The wall around Roč was built by the Patriarchate of Aquileia in the 14th century. Towers were added in the 1500s. Roč was an important centre for Glagolitic writing and in the 1200s the alphabet was carved on a wall in the church of St Anthony Abbot. The Romanesque church of St Roch contains two fresco cycles.

TIPS FOR WALKERS

Departure point: Boljun. *Distance:* 77 km (48 miles) one way. *Stopping-off points:* **Motovun** Restaurant MCotić, (052) 681 758; **Hum** Humska Konoba, (052) 660 005 (restaurant); **Buzet** Šetalište Vladimira Gortana 9, (052) 662 867 (restaurant). **Buzet** Trg Fontana 7, (052) 662 343. **Poreč** Istria Tourist Board, Pionirska 1, Poreč, (052) 880 088.

0 kilometres   3

0 miles   3

Boljun ①

The village still has some of its medieval walls, the 16th-century ramparts, a tower and a water trough from 1697. The grain store, loggia and the Romanesque church of SS Cosmas and Damian are on the main road. Gothic paintings can be seen in the 14th-century church of St Peter.

Ročko Polje

Lupoglav

Dolenja Vas

Vranja

OPATIJA

PAZIN

THE TRAIL OF GLAGOLITIC DOCUMENTS

The "Glagolitic Alley" (Aleja Glagoljaša) winds between Roč and Hum. It is 7 km (4 miles) long and was created from 1977 to 1985 to commemorate this ancient Slavic script. Along the way are 11 significant Glagolitic documents recalling events and people who contributed to the spread of the writing, invented in the 9th century by the saints Cyril and Methodius to translate the scriptures *(see pp34–5)* into Slavonic.

Glagolitic document in stone on the trail to Roč

Rijeka ㉔

Founded by the Liburnians and conquered by the Celts, this town became a Roman city called Tarsatica. Over the centuries it frequently changed hands, and finally came under the rule of the Habsburgs. In 1719, to develop its maritime role, Ferdinand of Habsburg declared Rijeka a free port. The city became part of the kingdom of Hungary in 1870 and its economic importance continued to grow. Together with shipyards and industry, Rijeka is one of Croatia's main ports and a key rail and road junction. In February and March each year, Rijeka hosts Croatia's largest carnival celebrations.

Local handicraft (see p252)

The Korzo, a pedestrian avenue with 19th-century buildings

Exploring Rijeka

Over recent decades, the city has expanded, somewhat chaotically, along the coast and into the surrounding hills. However, its Central European atmosphere is still preserved in the majestic 19th-century buildings along the Korzo and the Riva, two broad avenues south of the Old Town (Stari Grad), built on land reclaimed from the sea. The Korzo is the heart of the city, lined with cafés, bars, restaurants and shops.

🔒 Church of the Capuchins
Kapucinska crkva
Kapucinske stube 5. *Tel (051) 335 233.* ☐ 7am–noon, 4–8pm.
North of Žabica Square (Trg Žabica) is the Capuchin Church, built between 1904 and 1923. The church is also known as the Madonna of Lourdes, because it was built on the 50th anniversary of the miracle of Lourdes.

🔒 Church of St Nicholas
Sv. Nikola
Ignacija Henkea 2. *Tel (051) 335 399.* ☐ 8am–1pm & 6–6:40pm daily.
The church of St Nicholas, built by the Orthodox community in 1790, contains fine icons from Vojvodina, Serbia.

🏛 Civic Tower
Gradski Toranj
About halfway along the Korzo is the Civic Tower. The tower is the result of alterations made to the gate of the Old Town from the 15th century. It was erected in the 18th century and the clock *(Pod Urom)* was also added. In 1890 the dome was built. An imposing building, it is decorated with coats of arms, including those of the city and the Habsburgs, and busts of the emperors Leopold I and Charles VI.

Detail of the Civic Tower

🏛 Town Hall
Municipij
Trg Riječke Rezolucije.
In 1883, the 14th-century Augustinian monastery was turned into the Town Hall. It takes up three sides of the square and is now used as offices.

🔒 Roman Arch
Stara Vrata
Trg Ivana Koblera.
In an alley leading from the north side of the square are the remains of a Roman arch, which was probably a gate to the city. It is a simple stone structure. Nearby, excavations have unearthed the foundations of a perimeter wall from the Roman period.

🔒 Church of the Assumption
Crkva Uznesenja Blažene Djevice Marije
Pavla Rittera Vitezovića 3. *Tel (051) 214 177.* ☐ 8am–noon, 4–6pm.
The Church of the Assumption, once a cathedral, preserves little of its original 13th-century aspect. It was renovated in the Baroque style in 1695 and altered in 1726 with Rococo details, and a 16th-century rose window was inserted. Inside, the altars, some paintings and the chancel are from the Baroque period. The bell tower bears the date of its construction (1377); the upper part is in Gothic style.

🔒 Cathedral of St Vitus
Katedrala Sv. Vida
Trg Grivica. *Tel (051) 330 879.* ☐ 7am–noon, 4:30–7pm.
The church of St Vitus, patron saint of the city, is now the cathedral. This large Baroque church was built between 1638 and 1742 by the Jesuits. Baroque altars, and a Gothic crucifix from the 13th century adorn the interior.

🏛 Maritime and Historical Museum of Coastal Croatia
Pomorski i Povijesni Muzej Hrvatskog Primorja
Muzejski trg 1/1. *Tel (051) 213 578.* ☐ 9am–8pm Tue–Fri, 9am–1pm Sat. 🎫
This is the oldest museum in Rijeka, founded in 1876, but

Gothic crucifix in the cathedral of St Vitus

71

since 1955 housed in the Governor's Palace built in 1896. The history of navigation is told through the collections of model ships, weapons and seafaring equipment from the 17th and 18th centuries. There are also rich archaeological collections from prehistory to the Middle Ages, displays of prints, furniture, paintings and an ethnographic collection.

The altar of Our Lady of Trsat, with a copy of the painting of the Virgin

🏛 Our Lady of Trsat
Gospa Trsatska

Frankopanski trg. *Tel (051) 452 900.* ⏺ daily.
On the opposite bank of the Rječina river, above the centre of Rijeka, is Trsat. At the top of the 561 steps from Tito Square (Titov trg) is the Sanctuary of Our Lady of Trsat. The church and Franciscan monastery were built in 1453 by Martin Frankopan on the site of a 12th-century church. It was in this church, from 1291 to 1294, that parts of the Holy House of Mary of Nazareth were preserved before being transferred to

Loreto in Italy. To compensate the local people for this loss, in 1367 Pope Urban V donated to them a *Virgin with Child*, painted by St Luke, a copy of which now stands on the main altar.

The sanctuary was visited by soldiers and sailors who left votive gifts, now kept in a chapel next to the cloisters. The church was remodelled in 1864 but retained the triumphal arch, the marble altar which sits underneath the painting of the Virgin, and tombs of the Frankopan family.

VISITORS' CHECKLIST

Map B2. 🏘 130,000. ✈ Krk, (051) 842 132. 🚉 Krešimirova ulica, (060) 333 444. 🚌 Trg Žabica 1, (060) 302 010. 🚢 Riva, (051) 212 696; Adriatica d.o.o.: Verdijeva 6, (051) 214 511; Jadrolinija Riječki lukobran bb, (051) 211 444. 🛈 Korzo 14, (051) 335 882. 🎭 Rijeka's Summer Nights (Jun–Jul), Rijeka Carnival (Feb–Mar). **www**.tz-rijeka.hr

🏛 Trsat Castle
Gradina Trsat

Ulica Zrinskog. *Tel (051) 217 714.* ⏺ summer: 8am–8pm; winter: 9am–5pm.
The Sanctuary of Our Lady leads to a castle built by the Romans to defend Tarsatica, parts of which still survive. In the 13th century, Trsat was owned by the Frankopans, who built another castle on the same site. In the 19th century it was bought and renovated by an Austrian general, Laval Nugent, who was buried here. There are fine views from the site over the Kvarner gulf.

RIJEKA TOWN CENTRE

Cathedral of St Vitus ⑦
Church of the Assumption ⑥
Church of the Capuchins ①
Church of St Nicholas ②
Civic Tower ③
Marine and Historical
Museum of Coastal Croatia ⑧
Roman Arch ⑤
Town Hall ④

Key to Symbols see back flap

Cres ㉕

The narrow island of Cres is 65 km (40 miles) long. In the north, a colony of native griffon vultures, protected by law since 1986, nests on a plateau swept by the dry, cold bora wind. The south is milder and olives and vines are grown. A single road travels from the north of Cres to the south of Lošinj, linking the islands by a bridge. Tourism focuses on just a few villages such as Cres, Osor, Martinšćica and Valun.

Dry-stone walls and olive groves overlooking the town of Cres

Cres Town

Cres nestles in a bay sheltered by the hill behind. The town became important when the bishopric and governor's seat were transferred here from Osor.

The walls and the three gates with stone arches give the town a Venetian feel, and the church of Our Lady of the Snow has paintings by artists from the Venetian school. The 16th-century Town Hall, or Loggia, is now a fruit and vegetable market.

The old port is a lively place, bustling with fishermen and visitors. The Town Gate, a clock tower and several Renaissance buildings face the port. The church of St Isidore (the patron saint), dates from the 12th century.

Osor

Until the mid-15th century this was the main town on the island, with a port and a bishopric. It later declined and the capital was moved to

VISITORS' CHECKLIST

Map B3. 🚶 3,200. 🚢 (051) 211 444. **Cres** 🚹 Cons 10, (051) 571 535. **Osor** 🚹 (051) 231 547. www.tzg-cres.hr

Cres. Today the entire town is a museum, with Bronze Age remains and some splendid monuments, making it a centre of great artistic interest.

The beautiful 15th-century cathedral of the Assumption was completed in 1497 and is built of honey-coloured stone. The façade has an arched tympanum above a doorway with a relief of the Virgin Mary. Inside the church there is a painting of SS Nicholas and Gaudentius on the altar.

The Cres Museum (Creski muzej) occupies the Town Hall and has stone inscriptions and interesting finds from the Illyrian and Roman periods, and the early Middle Ages. The façade of the Bishop's Palace (second half of the 15th century) bears coats of arms of the bishops and nobles of the island and the interior is richly decorated. Some walls, foundations and mosaics are all that remain of the church of St Peter.

🏛 Cres Museum
Creski muzej
Petris-Arsan Palace, Ribarska 7. **Tel** (051) 571 127. ⬤ for restoration. Temporary exhibitions mid-Jun–mid-Jul: 10am–noon, 7–10pm; mid-Jul–mid-Aug: 9–11am, 8–11pm; mid-Aug–mid-Jun: 10am–noon, 6–9pm. ⬤ Mon.

KEY

▬	Minor road
▬	Scenic road
🚢	Ferry
🚹	Tourist information
🏖	Beach with facilities
🌤	Viewpoint

0 kilometres   8

0 miles   8

Door of the Gothic church of Our Lady of the Snow, Cres

Lošinj (Lussino) ㉖

The island of Lošinj has a mild climate and sub-tropical vegetation with maritime pines, palms, oleanders and citrus trees. The main town, Mali Lošinj, was founded in the 12th century, when 12 Croat families landed here. The most famous beach is at Čikat bay, southwest of Mali Lošinj. It is 30 km (19 miles) long and a popular place for water sports.

Interior of the church of St Anthony Abbot, Veli Lošinj

Mali Lošinj
This pretty town, which, like Cres, belonged to Venice for many centuries, has many buildings from the 18th and 19th centuries, when maritime activity was at its height. The oldest part of the town lies around the 18th-century church of St Mary. Large hotel complexes just outside the town cater for package holiday-makers.

Veli Lošinj
Quieter than Mali Lošinj, this is a lovely town with villas hidden among the vegetation. The church of St Anthony Abbot (Sv. Antun Pustinjak) was built in the 18th century on the site of a smaller 15th-century church. It has a rich store of paintings, including examples by Bartolomeo Vivarini (1430–90), Bernardo Strozzi (1581–1644) and Francesco Hayez (1791–1882). The Baroque style is much in evidence on the seven altars.

There is a splendid view of the town and the coastline from the 16th-century tower of the Uskoks (see p81).

Environs
The island of **Susak** is renowned for its unusual geology: a 10-m (33-ft) layer of sand covering a calcareous platform. Vines grow well on this soil and all the islanders have vineyards; their wealth is measured by the number of vines they own. The vines, grown on terraces and protected by cane wind-breaks, are further sheltered by dry-stone walls which are typical of the islands and the coastline of the upper Adriatic. The picturesque, brightly coloured women's costumes are famous. They are made by the islanders during the winter months and shown off at festivals.

The island of **Ilovik**, south of Lošinj, covers an area of nearly 6 sq km (2.3 sq miles) and is home to about 170 people, most of whom live in the village of Ilovik on the northeast coast. Vines, olives, fruit and flowers grow well in this mild climate. Nearby is the uninhabited island of Sv. Petar, where there are the ruins of a Venetian fortress and a Benedictine Abbey with a church and monastery. Prehistoric and Roman finds (mosaics, coins and other objects) have been discovered on Susak and Ilovik.

Unije is the largest of the lesser islands. It is hilly with little vegetation and a steep rocky coast on the eastern side, but there is a more accessible coast on the western side. The village is built around the church of St Andrew and its bell tower can be seen from a distance. The islanders tend to make their living from market gardening or fishing.

KEY

— Minor road

= Path

Ferry

Airport

Tourist information

Beach with facilities

Viewpoint

VISITORS' CHECKLIST

Map B3. 8,500. Mali Lošinj ⓘ Riva Lošinjskih Kapetana 29, (051) 231 547, 231 884. (051) 231 765. Veli Lošinj ⓘ (051) 231 547. Unije ⓘ (051) 231 547. For Susak and Ilovik, contact the Tourist Office at Mali Lošinj. www.tz-malilosinj.hr

Overlooking the fishing harbour of Mali Lošinj

For hotels and restaurants in this region see pp222–6 and pp240–42

Risnjak National Park: The Leska Trail ㉗
Nacionalni Park Risnjak

The vast Gorski Kotor plateau, which separates Croatia from Slovenia, begins north of Rijeka. Part of the area has been declared a national park in order to protect the forests and natural environment and the ecological balance of the area. The park, set up in 1953, originally covered an area of 32 sq km (12 sq miles), but it is now double that size, most of it made up of forests and grass-lands with many karst (limestone) features. The climatic conditions, caused by the territory's particular exposure and altitude, are very varied and about 30 different plant communities have been identified. The Leska trail was set up in 1993, and 23 information panels inform visitors about various aspects of this area.

■ Park area
■ The Leska trail

Silver Fir Forest ⑧
The silver fir, in great demand for boat building, has disappeared from many woods in Croatia; here it mingles with beech trees.

Chasm ⑦
Cold air from the chasm and the damp subsoil of this rocky fissure make the flora of great interest: plants which normally only grow at the higher altitudes of the park can be found here.

Feed Troughs ⑥
Feed troughs are set up here in winter to provide food for all the animals in the park.

Hranilište

⑥

685

⑦

Osmatačnica

⑨

690   *Klada*

Gmajna

MARKOV BRLOG

686

Observatory ⑨
From this viewing platform the behaviour of animals such as bears, foxes, lynxes, martens and wild cats can be observed in the woods. There are also many birds, both non-migratory and birds of passage. Towards evening at certain times of the year, eagles, hawks and crows can also be seen.

707

⑫

⑩

Leska

⑪

Cultivating the Countryside ⑩
Only one house is inhabited in the village of Leska. It is used from spring to autumn by farmers, who come to grow potatoes, peas and beans on specially built terraces.

Springs ⑪
Water flows under the layers of impervious rock and springs are created where the water emerges.

Tree Trunks ⑫
Fungi thrive in the cracks of old tree trunks providing a source of food for insects too.

Beech and Fir Forests ⑤
The trail goes through woods of fir and beech trees; many of the trees are very large. The undergrowth consists of hazelnut, bilberry and elder bushes.

Mountain Meadows ④
The areas which were deforested for agriculture or grazing land for animals are now mountain meadows. In late spring they explode with the varied colours of heather, purple moor grass, fescue and other grasses.

Conservation of Trees ①
The protection of the older, larger plant species was one of the reasons the reserve was set up. Within the park are examples of enormous ancient beech, silver and spruce fir trees, and also some rarer trees, such as the mountain elm and maple.

CRNI LUG

| 0 metres | 200 |
| 0 yards | 200 |

Storm Damage ②
When strong winds blow down old or sick trees, they are left where they fall as they provide suitable growing conditions for microorganisms such as fungi.

KEY

▬ Pedestrian trail

= Other roads

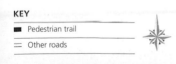

Karst Sinkholes ③
A karst sinkhole is a funnel-shaped hollow in the land. This feature is caused by water erosion of the rock and is characteristic of limestone areas.

Krk ㉘

Part of the Frankopan castle

This is the largest of the Adriatic islands, with an area of 409 sq km (158 sq miles). A bridge links the island to the mainland, built to provide good connections to the island's international airport. Along the eastern coast the island looks almost ghostly, its white rocks swept by the bora wind. Inland and on the more protected western coast, there is rich, lush vegetation.

VISITORS' CHECKLIST

Map B3. 🏘 17,860. ✈ (051) 842 040. ⛴ Valbiska: (051) 863 170. **Island of Krk** 🚹 Trg Sv. Kvirina 1, (051) 221 359. **Town of Krk** 🚹 Vela placa 1, (051) 221 414. **Baška** ⛴ (051) 856 821. 🚹 Kralja Zvonimira 114, (051) 856 817. **Njivice** 🚹 Ribarska Obala 10, (051) 846 243. **www**.krk.hr

The crystal-clear waters surrounding the island of Krk

Krk was first inhabited by the Liburnians, followed by the Romans, who founded Curicum (the present-day Krk) and Fulfinum. Traces of walls, baths and villas with floor mosaics still remain.

In the 6th century it came under Croatian rule and after the Frankish and Byzantine occupation it became part of the possessions of Venice. It was then granted to Dujam I, founder of the Frankopan family, and from 1480 to 1797 it was directly ruled by Venice.

Krk was a centre for Glagolitic script and the Baška Tablet, now in the Croatian Academy of Arts and Sciences in Zagreb, was found on the island.

Krk Town

The town of Krk developed in the Middle Ages on the site of the Roman town of Curicum. The wall and three Venetian city gates are still visible: the City Gate with a guard tower called Kamplin, the Sea Gate (Pisana) and the Upper Gate. Facing the main square are Renaissance-era buildings and in the area of the Roman baths is the cathedral of **Our Lady of the**

Assumption, dating from the 1100s but modified since. The three-aisle church has a façade of light-coloured stone. Inside are four paintings (1706) by Cristoforo Tasca, and a fine wooden Baroque pulpit.

The treasury is in the adjacent Romanesque church of **St Quirinus** which houses the **Diocesan Museum**. This contains works from the cathedral and other churches on the island, including the silver Frankopan altarpiece depicting the *Virgin Mary in Glory* and a polyptych (1350) by Paolo Veneziano.

Behind the cathedral stands the Frankopan castle with four square towers from 1191, and a round tower from the Venetian period. Inside the walls are churches dedicated to Our Lady of Health and St Francis. The latter has an engraved wooden pulpit.

Omišalj

Omišalj lies on a headland near the site of Roman Fulfinum. The village (Castrum Musculum in the Middle Ages) was enclosed by walls, some of which

KEY

━ Major road

━ Minor road

━ Scenic route

⛴ Ferry

✈ Airport

🚹 Tourist information

🏖 Beach with facilities

Map locations: Rijeka, Omišalj, Rudine, Njivice, Klimno, Malinska, Šilo, Porat, Glavotok, Šepići, Vrbnik, Košljun, Valbiska, Krk, Punat, Jurandvor, Baška, Stara Baška, KRK

0 kilometres 8

0 miles 8

◁ **Red-tiled roofs of the town of Krk**

survive. There is a square with a 17th-century Venetian loggia, the church of St Helen with reproductions of Glagolitic script, and the Romanesque church of Assumption of St Mary (Uznesenja Marijina) (13th century) with a dome, bell tower and 16th-century choir, and a 15th-century triptych by Jacobello del Fiore.

Glagolitic inscription and rose window, Assumption of Mary, Omišalj

Baška

Stara Baška (Old Baška) is opposite Omišalj. Baška (New Baška) is on the coast and is a popular tourist resort with a beautiful beach, 2 km (1 mile) long, and clear sea. The church of the Holy Trinity (1723) stands in a small square; inside is a fine *Last Supper* by Palma il Giovane.

Behind Baška, around a castle destroyed in the 11th century, is Stari grad, with the Romanesque church of St John, rebuilt in 1723.

In the church of St Lucy in Jurandvor, a short distance from Baška, is a copy of the Baška Tablet (the original is in Zagreb), the oldest document in Croatia written in Glagolitic script in 1100.

Košljun

Since 1447 a Franciscan monastery has stood on this small island. In the cloisters are stone inscriptions from the Roman and medieval eras and the library has over 20,000 Glagolitic documents. In the church is a polyptych by Girolamo di Santacroce (1535) and a *Last Judgment* by Ughetti. The treasury and many sacred objects are in the church of St Bernard.

Bakar ㉙

Map B2. 🏘 *1,600.* 🚆 *Primorje 39, (051) 761 111.* 🎭 *Margareta's Summer, concerts, sports events and shows in the čakavski dialect (Jun–Aug).* **www**.tz-bakar.hr

The demolition of a refinery and a coke plant has brought visitors back to this village, which was once a popular destination for people attracted to the landscape of the area and curious about the phenomena of the fresh-water springs. These springs originate in underground sources and flow out to the coast.

The **Frankopan Castle** and surrounding fishing village are also worth a visit. The village stands on the site of the Roman Volcera. From the 13th century until 1577 it belonged to the Frankopans who, in 1530, built a triangular-shaped castle. It is still well-preserved with high windows which were salvaged when it was transformed into a palace for the Šubić-Zrinski family who lived in the property after the Frankopans.

The parish church of St Andrew the Apostle has a painting of the *Holy Trinity* by Girolamo da Santacroce and a Crucifix from the 14th century. Evidence of the past is preserved in the **Civic Museum** which has many tombstones and sculptures dating from the Roman and early Middle Ages. Bakar keeps its naval traditions alive thanks to the prestigious Maritime Academy, which was founded in 1849.

The internal courtyard in the Frankopan castle, Kraljevica

Kraljevica ㉚

Map B2. 🏘 *4,600.* 🚆 *Rijeka.* 🚌 *(051) 282 078.* 🚆 *Rovina bb, (051) 282 078.* 🎭 *Shrovetide Sezona, traditional masked ball (carnival).*

A well-known tourist resort on the mainland, Kraljevica is linked to the island of Krk by a long bridge which also connects with Rijeka airport (on Krk). In the old town (Stari Grad) is a castle, built in the 16th century by the family of the counts of Šubić-Zrinski. The castle walls also shelter the small church of St Nicholas.

A village inhabited by families from the fortress of Hreljin developed around the castle. In the new district (Novi Grad), on a small promontory above the sea, is a castle built by the Frankopan family in 1650 in the late-Renaissance style. It has a square ground-plan with four round towers. It was turned into a magnificent palace in the middle of the 18th century.

In 1728, the Austrian emperor Charles VI began to create a sizeable port here, at the end of a road that went from Karlovac to the sea.

The Frankopan castle in Bakar, dominating the village

Crikvenica ③

Map B2. 🏘 5,800. ✈ Rijeka, 16 km (10 miles), island of Krk. 🚌 Nike Veljačića 3, (051) 781 333. 🚏 Trg Stjepana Radića 3, (051) 784 101. 🎭 Trade fair of Croatian products (Jul); Town festival (Aug).
www.rivieracrikvenica.com

A Roman staging post called Ad Turres existed here at one time, with a port for trading in timber. In 1412 Nikola Frankopan (whose name derives from the noble Roman family of the Frangipani) built a castle here. It was later donated to the Pauline order, who set up a church, monastery and school. In the 16th century a wall and a round tower were built and, in 1659, the church was enlarged by adding a nave. The town, now a popular tourist resort, takes its name from the monastery. At the beginning of the 19th century, the Pauline order was dissolved and in 1893 the ancient monastery was turned into the Hotel Kaštel (see p222).

The town has a long gravel beach and is one of the most popular tourist resorts along this stretch of coast. Thanks to its position, protected from the winds by the Velebit mountains, it enjoys a mild climate with dry summers and warm winters.

Gate of the former Pauline monastery, now a hotel, in Crikvenica

The altar in the church of SS Philip and James, Novi Vinodolski

Novi Vinodolski ③

Map B3. 🏘 4,000. ✈ Rijeka, 28 km (17 miles), island of Krk. 🚌 Rijeka, 49 km (30 miles). 🚏 Ulica Kralja Tomislava 6, (051) 791 171. 🎭 Patron saints' day, Philip and James (May); Novi Vinodolski summer carnival (1st weekend Jul).
www.tz-novi-vinodolski.hr

The old town, built on a hill overlooking the Vinodol valley, holds an important place in Croatian history. On 6 January 1288, in the castle built by the Frankopan dukes, the Vinodol Codex, one of the oldest legislative Croatian texts in Glagolitic script (see pp34–5), was produced. The document is now in the National Library in Zagreb. It was signed by the representatives of nine communes, and established rules for the ownership and use of local land.

In 1988, the 700th anniversary of the Vinodol Codex, a fountain created by the sculptor Dorijan Sokolić was placed in the central square of Novi. The fountain bears the names of the places which participated in drawing up the laws.

The town is also remembered for the stratagem used by Bishop Kristofor to

Costume in the castle of Novi Vinodolski

save the troops defeated by the Turks: the horses' shoes were put on backwards so as to foil their pursuers. Having reached the safety of Vinodol Castle, the bishop gave thanks by rebuilding the church of **SS Philip and James** (Sveti Filip i Jakov). He was buried here in 1499. The church, decorated in the 17th century in the Baroque style, has a magnificent altar from that period. The side altar has a Gothic Virgin Mary from the 15th century.

The 13th-century **Frankopan Castle**, which has been restored, is now a museum, with exhibits from the Roman and medieval periods and a rich, varied collection of traditional folk costumes.

Senj ③

Map C3. 🏘 8,000. ✈ Rijeka, 52 km (32 miles); Island of Krk. 🚌 Obala Kralja Zvonimira 8, (060) 394 394. 🚏 Stara cesta 2, (053) 881 068. 🎭 Feast of St George (23 Apr).
www.tz-senj.hr

The cold wind known as the bora of Senj blows through a pass in the Velebit chain of mountains, making the town the chilliest place in the Adriatic. People have long been aware of it, yet despite this notoriety, Senj has always been inhabited, first by the Illyrians, then by the Romans who first created a port at Senia.

THE USKOKS

In 1526, shortly before the Battle of Mohács, numbers of Christians from the hinterland fled to the safer coastal cities to escape the Turks. The refugees were called "Uskoks" ("the ones who jumped in") and their main desire was to fight those who had taken their land; and they carried out a highly successful guerrilla war. Initially they were organized by Venice around the fortress of Klis, from which they attacked the Turk-occupied land. In 1537 the Turks conquered Klis. Some Uskoks went to Primošten, but the main nucleus settled in Senj, under the rule of the Habsburgs, who encouraged them to procure fast boats in order to plunder the heavy Venetian ships. When Austria also slowed down operations against the Turks, the Uskoks took up piracy and started sacking coastal towns. At the end of the war between Venice and the Ottoman empire in 1617, the emperor was forced to remove the Uskoks from the coast and they and their families were transported to the west of Zagreb, to the Žumberak mountains.

Relief in the Museum of the Uskoks, Senj

This became a bishopric in 1169 and an important trading port for the transport of timber. After 1000 AD it was granted to the Templar Knights. It then passed to the Frankopans, and finally came under the direct rule of the King of Hungary. As defence against the Turks, the Habsburgs established the first station of the Military Frontier *(Vojna Krajina)* here. This stronghold had a powerful outer wall which is now only partly preserved.

After the Battle of Mohács in 1526, many Uskoks from Sinj and Klis came to Senj, and were co-opted by the local Austrian governor in the fight against the Turks. Their presence is recorded in **Nehaj Castle**, a fortress built on a square plan, constructed in 1553–8 by the Uskok captain, Ivan Lenković, on a hill a short distance from the town. It was positioned so as to sight approaching ships. The well laid-out **Museum of the Uskoks** is on the first floor of the fort, and has an excellent view over the bay.

In the southern part of the wide bay is the main square, called Cilnica. Facing the square is the Frankopan palace, built in 1340 and altered in the 19th century. There are also large salt warehouses, and, further in, the **Cathedral of St Mary** (Sv. Marija), built

Nehaj Castle, dominating the town of Senj

in the 13th century and altered in the Baroque period. It has tombstones with Renaissance reliefs and Baroque works, including an altar decorated with four marble statues.

A short distance from the square is the Vukasović Palace which houses the **Civic Museum** (Gradski Muzej Senj), a museum of local history. The palace was once the residence of an Uskok captain. Flanking the roads of the town and in the Small Square (Mala Placa), also known as Campuzia, are Renaissance buildings such as the Town Hall with its splendid loggia.

Nearby is the Leon tower (Leonova kula), dedicated to Pope Leo X, and the small, pretty church of St Mary.

Environs

The small village of **Jablanac** lies 37 km (23 miles) south of Senj. This bustling place is also a departure point for ferries to the island of Rab, and a good starting point for visiting the Velebit massif.

Jablanac is a well-preserved town and worth an unhurried visit. It was a county seat and its representatives met in the medieval castle. The castle was built by the Ban (governor) Stjepan Šubić, as was the church and its cemetery, both known from documents from 1251. The castle is now in ruins.

To the east of Jablanac is the Sjeverni Velebit National Park (Nacionalni park Sjeverni Velebit) where there is an interesting **Botanical Garden** (Botanički Vrt) founded in 1966 on the slopes of Mount Zavižan at an altitude of 1,576 m (5,169 ft).

Jablanac, south of Senj, departure point for the island of Rab

Rab 🄴

A window in the Prince's Palace in Rab town

The island of Rab lies parallel to the Velebit massif, creating a channel which was much dreaded by sailors because it forms a tunnel for the cold, dry bora wind which makes this part of the coast rocky and barren. The opposite, western side of the island is protected from the wind and the climate is mild. Here the landscape is much greener and maquis alternates with woods of pine, oak and holm oak. The Romans knew the island by the name of Arba, or Scadurna, and, after its conquest, built a settlement on the site of the present-day town of Rab. This island is a popular holiday destination with its sandy beaches, rocky coves and mild climate.

Rab Town

The main town, Rab, which gives its name to the island, became a bishopric in the early Christian period and was inhabited by Slavic people in the 6th century. After it had been conquered by the Franks, it was administered by Venice and a treaty of mutual defence was agreed upon which lasted until 1000 AD. Rab was at times under the rule of the Hungarian kings until 1409, when it became Venetian territory. Venice ruled the island until 1797.

View of Rab with its four bell towers

The town, famous for its four bell towers which make it look like a ship with four masts, has some lovely Venetian architecture. Along the three main streets are fine aristocratic buildings with Romanesque doorways, such as the Nimira, Tudorin, Kukulić, Galzigna and Cassio Palaces. The ancient medieval walls that encircled the Old Town on the southern point of the peninsula were destroyed, and in the 15th century a wall was built which also enclosed the New Town, called Varoš. Part of this wall is well-preserved, particularly the stretch facing the bay of St Euphemia.

🏛 Loggia
Ulica Srednja, Rab.
Where the main road, Srednja ulica, widens out, there is a beautiful Venetian loggia, built in 1506 in Renaissance style, and a granary *(fondak)*. To the left is the Sea Gate (Morska Vrata), a tower from the 14th century. Through the gate is the town square.

🏛 Prince's Palace
Knežev Dvor
Trg Municipium Arba, Rab. *Tel (051) 724 064.* ⬚ *call for opening times.*
The port and the town square are the heart of Rab, and this is also where the Prince's Palace was built in the 13th century in the Romanesque style. It was later enlarged in the Gothic style and then rebuilt in the Renaissance style. It has Venetian Gothic windows and Renaissance mullioned windows. In the courtyard are some Roman and medieval remains.

🄰 Monastery and Church of St Andrew
Sv. Andrija
Ulica Ivana Rabljanina, Rab.
This small Romanesque church is annexed to a Benedictine convent founded in 1118. The bell tower, the oldest in Rab, is from the following century. The belfry has trefoil windows.

🄰 Cathedral of St Mary the Great
Katedrala Sv. Marija Velika
Ulica Ivana Rabljanina, Rab.
This splendid Romanesque building was consecrated by Pope Alexander III in 1177. The façade has alternating layers of pink and white stone and above the portal is a sculpted *Deposition* by Petar Trogiranin dating from 1514. The three-aisle interior, divided by columns, has a beautiful baptismal font made by the same sculptor in 1497, and a polyptych by Paolo Veneziano (1350) on the altar.

In the presbytery is a splendid altar canopy with marble columns and on the main altar, surrounded by an ornate wooden choir, is a reliquary from the 12th century with the remains of St Christopher.

The 13th-century bell tower stands 70 m (230 ft) away from the cathedral. It is the tallest of all the bell towers on the island.

The Sea Gate, one of the ways into the town of Rab

The bell tower of the Cathedral of St Mary the Great

For hotels and restaurants in this region see pp222–6 and pp240–42

🔒 Chapel of St Anthony of Padua

Sv. Antun

Ulica Ribara, Rab.

The small church of St Anthony, dating from 1675, is a good example of religious Baroque architecture. Inside is a marble inlaid altar and a 17th-century painting from the Venetian school.

🔒 Franciscan Convent of St Anthony Abbot

Sv. Antun Opat

Rab. **Tel** (051) 724 064. ☐ call for opening times.

The church and convent of St Anthony Abbot stand behind the cathedral at the end of the promontory. This convent, built for a closed order of nuns, was founded in 1497 by the noblewoman Magdalena Budrišić.

🔒 Church of St Francis

Sv. Frane

Park Komrčar, Rab.

The church dates from 1491 and stands to the north of the the town in Komrčar Park. It is a blend of Gothic and Renaissance and has an original façade with three sculpted shells.

The altar in the Renaissance church of St Justine in Rab

🔒 Convent and Church of St Justine

Sv. Justine

Gornja Ulica, Rab. **Tel** (051) 724 064. ☐ call for opening times.

The convent and church were consecrated in 1578, and were intended for nuns from non-noble families. The bell tower with its onion dome dates from 1672. The church now houses a Museum of Holy Art, with the crucifix of King Koloman from 1112, and the reliquary of St Christopher (12th century), protector of

the town. Also on display are paintings and panels, including a polyptych by Paolo Veneziano (1350), Gospels and illuminated books in Glagolitic script.

Kampor

Kampor lies at the end of a long bay (Kamporska Draga) and has preserved its stone houses and terraces of olives and vines. Many private holiday houses have sprung up around the village.

The Franciscan convent of St Euphemia, with a small adjacent Romanesque church, is near the church of St Bernard. The church contains two panels by Bartolomeo and Antonio Vivarini, a Byzantine panel (14th century) and other works. In the cloister there are various tombs and the sarcophagus of Magdalena Budrišić, the noblewoman who founded the convent of St Anthony Abbot in Rab.

Lopar

The village of Lopar is at the end of a rocky peninsula. It is a popular spot thanks to the sandy beaches fringed by pinewoods and the leisure facilities on offer (tennis, football and mini-golf).

KEY

— Major road
— Minor road
⛴ Ferry
🛈 Tourist information
🏖 Beach with facilities
🔆 Viewpoint

Polyptych by the Vivarini, church of St Bernard, Kampor

One of the spectacular waterfalls at the Plitvice Lakes ▷

Plitvice Lakes National Park ㉟
Nacionalni Park Plitvička Jezera

The Plitvice Lakes National Park, located in the heart of
Croatia, was founded in 1949. This area of 300
sq km (115 sq miles), covered in lakes and forest, has
been part of the UNESCO World Heritage list since
1979. It is particularly known for its spectacular
waterfalls. There are 16 lakes within the park and
visitors can move around by following the paths along
the shores or by using footbridges. Shuttle buses take
people to the starting points of the trails and to the
hotels in the park. The largest lake can be
toured by electric boat. There are
no towns or villages in the
reserve, only hotels.

A hut by the lake shore

The bird life is extremely varied:
160 species have been record-
ed, including the eagle, marsh
harrier, peregrine falcon, hoo-
poe, kingfisher, heron, little
owl, and tawny owl.

Proščansko
jezero

Ciginovac

Okrugljak

Labudovac

STUBICA

Galovac

Gradinsko
jezero

Footbridges
*Numerous footbridges and
rowing boats enable visitors to
get from one shore of a lake to
another and are a lovely way
to get in and explore the fir,
pine and beech forests.*

PRIJEKA
KO

Gliborita
draga

Dense forests alongside the
waters are home to some of
the largest European species
of animal, including wolves,
lynxes, foxes, wild boar,
roebucks, wild cats, otters
and badgers.

Velika
Poljana

Entrance 2   ZAD

0 metres	500
0 yards	500

Flora

The park flora is very varied, from waterlilies on the lakes to forests of gigantic trees. There is also a rich undergrowth of shrubs, a source of food for wildlife.

VISITORS' CHECKLIST

Map C3.
🛈 (053) 751 014, 751 015.
⏰ summer: 8am–sunset daily;
winter: 9am–sunset daily.
♿ limited access.
www.np-plitvicka-jezera.hr

Along the banks of the River Korana, into which the lakes drain, are a few shepherds' huts and several sawmills, which are run on hydraulic power. The river flows between steep cliffs in a spectacular natural landscape.

Plitvice

Draga Matijaševac

KARLOVAC

Jezero Kozjak

Milanovac

Gavanovac

KARLOVAC

🛈

P
Entrance 1

M E D V E D A K

E71

The park vehicles, shuttle buses, take visitors around the area on special routes.

Waterfalls

It is possible to follow signposted routes, which lead to viewpoints for watching the rushing waters as they cascade from the lake above.

KEY

▬	Major road
▬	Route for park vehicles
▪▪	Footpath
---	Boat route
🚤	Electric boat
🛈	Tourist information
P	Parking

DALMATIA

Dalmatia is the most visited region of Croatia. Although tourism collapsed in the 1990s because of the war, visitors are again flocking to the rocky coastline and sandy beaches, the deserted islands and the splendid cities of this Adriatic region. As a consequence of relationships and trade with Italy, an Adriatic culture developed here which has given Dalmatia an Italianate feel.

In the 1st century BC, after two centuries of war, the Romans managed to conquer the Dalmatian and Liburnian tribes and integrate them into their system. For over three centuries the region enjoyed a period of prosperity which was eventually brought to an end by the arrival of peoples from Asia, including the Slavs in the 7th century.

The Lion of St Mark on the Land Gate in Zadar

In 915, after a long period of wars and unrest, the first Croatian kings founded a new state, blessed by papal authority. New public and religious buildings, walls and town halls were built, the arts began to flourish, and trading with the Italian coast increased. This was a period of great cultural vitality, which survived the collapse of the Croatian state and its integration into the Kingdom of Hungary in the 12th century. In 1409, after a long series of conflicts, the Hungarian king sold the islands and many of the coastal cities to Venice. In the 16th century, there followed a second flowering of the arts, and the sculptors, architects, painters, writers and scholars of this period laid the foundations for the future development of Croatian culture, art and literature.

In late spring, when the Jadranska Magistrala coast road has yet to be invaded by heavy summer traffic, this must be one of the loveliest parts of Europe. From Karlobag the road winds along the edge of the Velebit mountain chain and the Dalmatian and the Biokovo plateaux. Seawards is the long, lunar-surfaced island of Pag and further along are the islands around Zadar, those around Split, and finally the lovely island of Mljet, set in an azure sea. Behind are hillsides covered in vineyards and maquis vegetation, dominated by the bright yellow flowers of broom.

View of the city of Šibenik with the white dome of the Cathedral of St James

◁ Lavender flowering on the island of Hvar

Exploring Dalmatia

To the north is Zadar, with its exceptional monuments, and the islands of the Zadar archipelago, the southern part of which is designated the Kornati National Park. The road travels on to Šibenik, with its perfectly preserved old town centre and splendid cathedral, and Trogir, an architectural jewel. The ruins of the Roman town of Salona are just outside the city of Split, which developed within the Palace of Emperor Diocletian. The coastal road turns inland to cross the delta of the Neretva and reaches Ston, a point of access to the peninsula of Pelješac. Finally, on a rocky spur stands the medieval city of Dubrovnik, now a UNESCO World Heritage Site.

Bell tower of the cathedral, Zadar

KEY

▬▬	Motorway
▬▬	Major road
▭▭▭	Minor road
▬ ▬	Under construction
▬▬	Main railway
▬▬	County border
▬▬	International border
- - -	Ferry route
▲	Summit

GETTING AROUND

The most comfortable way of visiting Dalmatia is by car, which allows you to stop when and where you like. Traffic is always heavier during the summer holiday months. Cities and towns are not directly connected by railway, but buses are frequent and run between almost all the towns. The main coastal towns and the more important islands are linked by frequent ferry connections (see pp278–79). Yachts can be hired for cruising along the coast (see p258).

0 kilometres   30

0 miles   30

The imposing 15th-century Minčeta Tower in Dubrovnik

LOCATOR MAP

SIGHTS AT A GLANCE

The island of Dugi Otok, in the Zadar Archipelago

SEE ALSO

• *Where to Stay* pp226–30

• *Where to Eat* pp243–6

Zadar ①

Originally Illyrians inhabited this narrow peninsula, but its present layout dates back to Roman rule, when the straight roads and forum were built. It became an important *municipium*, and a port for the trading of timber and wine. In the Middle Ages it was the main base for the Byzantine fleet. Venice and the king of Hungary fought over Zadar in the 12th–13th centuries but in 1409, King Ladislaus of Hungary sold his Dalmatian islands and cities to Venice for 100,000 ducats. Zadar became Zara and enjoyed a spell of prosperity; churches and palaces were built. After World War I, Zadar was ceded to Italy by the Treaty of Rapallo, but many Italians left after the forming of Yugoslavia in 1947. Zadar was repeatedly bombed during World War II and suffered considerable damage.

The Sea Gate, rebuilt from a Roman arch

The medieval tower, Bablja Kula, with part of the ancient wall

🏛 Land Gate and Walls
Kopnena Vrata

The Land Gate was built in 1543 by the great Veronese architect Michele Sanmicheli as the entrance to the city. The gate has a large central aperture and two smaller openings at the sides, divided by four white stone pilasters supporting four half-columns.

Above the main gate is a relief of St Chrysogonus on horseback and the lion of St Mark, symbol of Venetian rule. Beyond the gate are a few remains of the ancient walls, the former Venetian arsenal, and Liberation Square (Zoranićev trg or Trg Petra Zoranića) with a Roman column in the centre.

On one side of the square stands the medieval tower of Bablja Kula. At the base are five fountains (Trg Pet Bunara), which once supplied water to the city of Zadar.

🛡 Church of St Simeon
Sv. Šime

Trg Petra Zoranića 7. *Tel (023) 211 705.* ☐ 8:30am–noon Mon–Sat.
Originally constructed in Romanesque style, the church was rebuilt after 1632 to house the remains of the saint, which are kept in a silver reliquary. This impressive work is nearly 2m (6 ft) long and was made between 1377 and 1380 by Francesco da Milano and bears reliefs showing scenes of St Simeon's life.

🛡 Museum of Ancient Glass
Muzej antičkog stakla

Poljana Zemaljskog odbora 1. *Tel (023) 363 831.* ☐ summer: 9am–9pm daily; winter: 9am–4pm Mon–Fri. ⊠ www.mas-zadar.hr
Housed in the restored Cosmacendi Palace, this museum displays a large number of Ancient Roman glass objects found on archaeological sites in Zadar and its surroundings.

🏛 People's Square
Narodni trg

The Town Hall, which was built in 1934, faces the square, as does the Renaissance City Loggia (Gradska loža) built by Michele Sanmicheli in 1565 as the city courts. It is now used for exhibitions.

Nearby, the 16th-century Town Guard Palace houses the Ethnographic Museum, with collections of costumes and objects from the entire county.

🏛 Sea Gate
Vrata Sv. Krševana

This complex construction is the result of rebuilding work carried out by Michele Sanmicheli in 1573 on a Roman arch dedicated to the Sergi family. On the seaward side is the lion of St Mark and a memorial stone recalling the Battle of Lepanto (1571). On the inner side of the gate is a stone commemorating Pope Alexander III's visit in 1177.

🛡 Church of St Chrysogonus
Sv. Krševan

Poljana Pape Aleksandra III.
⊙ Closed for restoration.
Prior to AD 1000 a church and monastery were built by Benedictines on the site of the Roman market. While the church, rebuilt in 1175, has survived with few alterations, the monastery was destroyed in World War II. At the height of the monastery's splendour it possessed a rich library and a *scriptorium*, famous for its transcribed and illuminated

The apse of the church of St Chrysogonus

works. The three-aisle church, divided by columns (salvaged from a previous building), has a simple Romanesque appearance, except for the Baroque main altar with statues of Zadar's four patron saints: Chrysogonus, Zoilus, Simeon and Anastasia. The apse is the best-preserved part, with some 13th-century frescoes and a Romanesque crucifix on the altar.

🏛 Archaeological Museum
Arheološki Muzej

Trg opatice Čike 1. *Tel* (023) 250 516. ☐ Jan–Mar: 9am–1pm Mon–Sat; Apr, May & Oct: 9am–3pm Mon–Sat; Jun–Sep: 9am–9pm daily; Nov & Dec: 9am–2pm Mon–Sat. 🖾 🖾 by appt. 🚻

This museum is housed in a building near the old Roman Forum. Its collection contains objects that date from prehistory all the way to recent times, and come from the entire Zadar area and the islands. Of particular interest is glass from the Roman period and the early Christian and medieval liturgical objects.

The beautiful Renaissance façade of the church of St Mary

🔒 Church of St Mary and Museum of Sacred Art
Sv. Marija i Zlato i Srebro Zadra

Trg opatice Čike 1. *Tel* (023) 250 496. ☐ summer: 10am–1pm, 6–8pm Mon–Sat, 10am–noon Sun; winter: 10am–12.30pm, 5–6.30pm Mon–Sat. 🖾 🖾 🗲 🚻

On one side of the square called Poljana pape Ivana Pavla II stands a tall, Romanesque bell tower, built

Sculpture, Museum of Sacred Art

for King Koloman in 1105, and the church of St Mary. The church, built in 1066, has undergone various alterations and now has a Renaissance façade. The three-aisle interior has a large women's gallery; the stuccowork is from 1744. The former monastery next door is now the Museum of Sacred Art: on the ground floor are gold pieces; on the upper floor are paintings and statues, including a fine polyptych by Vittore Carpaccio (1487).

ZADAR TOWN CENTRE

0 metres   300
0 yards   300

Key to Symbols *see back flap*

🚇 Forum

The main square of the ancient Roman city of Jadera was built between the 1st century BC and the 3rd century. The Forum, 90 m (295 ft) long and 45 m (147 ft) wide, was bordered on three sides by porticoes with marble columns. In the present square, Poljana pape Ivana Pavla II, are the foundations of public buildings, including a meeting hall, some of the original paving, several *tabernae* (rectangular-shaped trading areas) and a monumental pillar, used in the Middle Ages as a "pillar of shame".

The Romanesque façade of the Cathedral of St Anastasia

🔓 Cathedral of St Anastasia
Katedrala Sv. Stošije

Forum. *Tel (023) 251 708.*

⬤ *8am–noon, 5–7pm daily.*

The magnificent cathedral of St Anastasia also stands on the site of the Forum. It was founded by the Byzantines in the 9th century and rebuilt in the Romanesque style in the 12–13th centuries. It has a rectangular ground-plan with a large semicircular apse. The harmonious façade with three doors, completed in 1324, is divided in half horizontally with the upper part characterized by arches and columns and two splendid rose windows. The main window is Romanesque and the other is Gothic.

Rose window, St Anastasia

The three-aisle interior is divided by two rows of columns and pilasters which support the high arcades. At the sides of the raised presbytery are engraved wooden choir stalls, the work of the Venetian Matteo Moronzoni (early 15th century). The ciborium with four Corinthian columns is decorated with different motifs (1332). Underneath is a small sarcophagus containing the remains of St Anastasia, dating from the 9th century.

The right-hand altar inside the Cathedral of St Anastasia

The altars are mostly Baroque; on one there is a lovely painting by Palma il Giovane. In the right-hand nave is an imposing Baroque altar dedicated to the Holy Sacrament; just beyond is the hexagonal baptistry.

🚇 Sea Organ and Greeting to the Sun

Designed by architect Nikola Basic, this musical instrument is built into the quayside. Under white stone steps are a set of pipes which produce musical chords naturally as waves push air up through the pipes. Next to it is another installation by the same architect called Greeting to the Sun, consisting of 300 glass plates that produce interesting light effects.

PLAN OF THE CATHEDRAL OF ST ANASTASIA

KEY

① Altar of the Holy Sacrament
② Baptistry
③ Roman pilaster
④ Sacristy
⑤ Choir stalls
⑥ Main altar and ciborium
⑦ Bishop's chair
⑧ Chapel of St Anastasia
⑨ Souls of Purgatory altar
⑩ Bell tower

0 metres 15
0 yards 15

Zadar: Church of St Donat
Sv. Donat

The Church of the Holy Trinity, which later took the name of its founder Bishop Donat, is one of the finest examples of Byzantine architecture in Dalmatia. It was built in the early 9th century on the paving stones of the former Roman Forum and has a circular ground-plan with three circular apses. Inside is a women's gallery which goes all the way around the church and creates an upper storey. St Donat has not been used as a church since 1797, but because of the good acoustics, concerts are often held here.

VISITORS' CHECKLIST

Forum. ▪ (023) 250 516.
◻ Apr, May & Oct: 9am–5pm daily; Jun–Sep: 9am–9pm daily; Nov–Mar: by appt. 🖉

Exterior
The church is built of honey-coloured Dalmatian stone, much of which came from the old Roman Forum.

Dome
The cylindrical-conical dome rises in the centre of the church to a height of 27 m (88 ft).

One of the three apses with blind arches. At one time the altar was situated in the central apse.

The Women's Gallery
The interior of the church has a matroneum, or women's gallery, supported by six pilasters and two Roman columns which border the circular nave and divide the structure into two floors.

The internal walls are completely bare. Probably the original decorations, frescoes or mosaics, have been lost.

Roman Fragments
Stones from the Roman Forum were used for the paving; other Roman material is visible in the walls, entrance and gallery.

Zadar Archipelago ❷

Crucifix in SS Cosmas and Damian, Pašman

The Zadar Archipelago is made up of more than 300 islands surrounded by crystal-clear waters. The larger islands are covered in Mediterranean scrub and olive trees. The archipelago is what remains of a mountain chain which once ran parallel to the Velebit mountains, but which is now almost submerged. Only about a dozen of the islands are inhabited, and the small communities live by fishing, farming and rearing animals. There are a few hotels on the larger islands closer to Zadar, and private accommodation can be found on all the others. Daily ferry services link Zadar with the main islands.

Dugi Otok, the largest island in the Zadar archipelago

Dugi Otok

Covering an area of 124 sq km (48 sq miles), this is the largest island in the archipelago. The inhabitants live in about ten villages. Fishing and farming takes place in the northern part of the island and on the flatter areas of the island, while the southern, hillier terrain is given over to sheep farming. The western coast is steep and desolate but beaches and bays punctuate the eastern coast.

Proximity to Zadar means that since Roman times it has been a popular place for the city nobles to build holiday villas. In the Renaissance period more summer residences were built here, particularly in **Sali**. This is the largest town and port on the island and there are some houses in the flamboyant Gothic style. The Renaissance church of St Mary has some paintings from the same period by Juraj Čulinović.

The fishing village of Božava, at the island's northernmost point, is also a popular yacht marina. It has a small church, dedicated to St Nicholas, which dates from the 10th century. Inside the church a sculpture depicts Arab saints.

The long bay of Telašćica, to the south, is a natural harbour and was once used by the Venetian fleet. One side ends in a sheer cliff and the other in thick pine woods. This area is being reforested after a disastrous fire in 1995. The southern part of the island is part of the Kornati National Park (see pp98–9).

Ugljan

This lush, green island is 22 km (13 miles) long and covers an area of 50 sq km (19 sq miles). It has a population of 7,600 and the small villages lie along the eastern coast of the island. In the main village, Ugljan, is the Franciscan monastery of St Jerome, built in the 15th century. It has a pretty cloister and the library contains numerous works written in Glagolitic script.

A more newly built village is **Preko**, where the wealthier citizens of Zadar own villas. There are also rooms in private houses available for renting. The village is dominated by the large Venetian fortress of St Michael which stands on a hill 265 m (869 ft) high. A bridge links the island to Pašman.

View from the fortress of St Michael, Preko

OLIB

SILBA

SESTRUNJE
Sestrunj

IST
MOLAT
Zapuntel
Brgulje • Molat

ŠKARDA
Ist

PREMUDA
Premuda

Veli Rat • Božava • Drag

DUGI OTOK

0 kilometres 10

0 miles 10

The Monastery of SS Cosmas and Damian in Pašman

Pašman

This wild, unspoilt island has a population of 3,500, who live in villages on the coast facing the mainland. There are fewer tourists than on Ugljan. The western side is given over to vineyards, while the eastern part has thick maquis right down to the coastline, where there are also some pebble beaches.

South of **Pašman**, a fishing village and the main centre on the island, is **Tkon**, an embarkation point for ferries. On Mount Čokovac, north of Tkon, is the Benedictine **Monastery of SS Cosmas and Damian** (Sv. Kuzma i Damjan). Built in 1125, it became a centre of Glagolitic culture and has a well-stocked library with Glagolitic texts. In the 15th century the church and monastery were rebuilt in the Gothic style when they were taken over by the Franciscan order. The church (14th–15th century) has some good sculptures, including a painted crucifix.

Premuda

This island covers an area of 9 sq km (3 sq miles) and has fewer than 100 inhabitants, all of whom live in the village of Premuda. It is the most isolated of the islands in the archipelago. There are no hotels but visitors can find rooms in private houses.

In Italy, the island is remembered for a naval battle between Italy and Austria which took place on 10 June 1918 during World War I.

The island has beautiful beaches and thick pine woods, and as there are no private cars it is also very peaceful. There are several weekly connections to Zadar.

Molat

The three villages on Molat support several hundred people, who depend on fishing and farming. There are two ports, Zapuntel, the main ferry port, and Brgulje, which is used when the main port is inaccessible.

For centuries the island belonged to Venice, which fostered the establishment of a community of monks and local people, who set about re-establishing the woods which had disappeared with over-exploitation. An intense reforestation programme has been under way to aid with this.

The church of St Andrew is all that remains of the monastery. There are no hotels on the island but accommodation can be found in private houses in Molat, Zapuntel and Brgulje. There are many coves along the low, jagged coastline.

VISITORS' CHECKLIST

Map B–C4. 🚢 *Harbour master's office: (023) 254 888; Jadrolinija: (023) 254 800.*
Zadar 🛈 *Sv. Leopolda Mandića 1, (023) 315 316.*
www.zadar.hr
Dugi Otok 🛈 *Obala P. Lorinija bb, Sali, (023) 377 094.*
www.dugiotok.hr
Ugljan 🛈 *Ugljan, (023) 288 011.* **www**.ugljan.hr

Olib

About 700 people live here in the village of Olib, where buildings include several 16th-century houses and a tower. The church of St Anastasia is from the same period and was once part of a monastery. In the parsonage are manuscripts and sacred books written in Glagolitic, as well as many stone remains, which confirm the presence of a community here in Roman times. The sea is delightful, and rocky cliffs alternate with coves and sandy beaches. Rooms can be found in private houses.

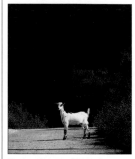

Goat on the peaceful island of Olib

Kukljica · Pašman
Ugljan · 110 · 110 · Banj · Nevidane · Tkon
Preko
UGLJAN
IŽ · PAŠMAN
Veli Iž · Mali
109 · Sali

KEY

🚍	Minor road
=	Path
🚢	Ferry
🛈	Tourist information
🏖	Beach with facilities
☀	Viewpoint

Kornati National Park ❸

Nacionalni Park Kornati

In 1980 the southern part of the Zadar Archipelago was declared a national park. The name Kornati derives from the name of the main island in the group, Kornat. The park was set up to protect the waters, to allow all kinds of marine life to flourish, and to stop people building on the islands. The park is 36 km (22 miles) in length and 6 km (4 miles) wide and is made up of 89 islands of white stone. Nearly all the islands are uninhabited and have little or no vegetation. The islands are surrounded by clear blue sea, with jagged coastlines, hidden coves and underwater caves.

One of the few houses on the Kornati Islands

Exploring Kornati National Park

The Kornati Islands were the peaks of a mountain chain about 20,000 years ago. When this area was part of the Roman empire, the main islands were holiday resorts, popular with the prosperous inhabitants of Zadar. Beautiful Roman villas with mosaic floors as well as fishponds and baths were built.

During the long period under Venetian rule the islands, which were then covered with rich vegetation, were used as a base for the Venetian fleet. At present the Kornati Islands belong to the inhabitants of Murter, to the east, who bought them around the end of the 19th century to use as grazing for sheep and goats.

The islands are bare and arid and are characterized by steep cliffs, stony ground and sinkholes typical of a karst (limestone) landscape. Sheep farming has impoverished the flora of these islands. In fact, the vegetation disappeared when the shepherds of Murter cut down the trees and burnt the scrub in order to grow grass for their livestock, which were left here to graze freely from spring to autumn. Dry-stone walls were built between the plots of land to form pens for the animals.

On some of the islands near the coast there are small cottages. Each has a stable at the side with an outdoor hearth for making cheese. Many also have a small jetty.

The Kornati Islands have become a popular destination for scuba divers and sailors. The marine life is varied with around 350 plant species and 300 animals. Fishing is prohibited throughout the entire Kornati National Park.

Besides dozens of rocky outcrops, the islands of Kornat, Levrnaka, Piškera, Lavsa, Kasela, Mana and Katina make up the park, as well as the southern part of Dugi Otok (see p96), with the bay of Telašćica the only wooded area. The best way to visit is by sailing boat, and there are organized day trips from Murter, Zadar, Biograd, Vodice, Primošten and Rogoznica.

Aerial view of the Kornati Islands

DUGI OTOK
Sali
Telašćica
Mala Proversa
KATINA
SVRŠATA
KORNAT
Lučica
Vrulje
MANA
PI

KEY

═══ Path

—— Borders of the park

▣ Ferry

▣ Beach with facilities

☼ Viewpoint

0 kilometres 10

0 miles 10

The steep chalk cliffs on the island of Kornat

Kornat

The island of Kornat is the
largest island in the park.
There is a small medieval
church dedicated to the
Virgin Mary here. There is
also a look-out tower with the
Venetian name of Toreta
dating from the 6th century,
an example of Byzantine
military architecture. Near the
old village of Vrulje, the main
village in the archipelago, is
Vela Ploča, where there is a
spectacular chalk cliff leaning
at a 40-degree angle over the
sea, measuring 200 m (656 ft)
long and 150 m (492 ft) high.

Mala Proversa

At Mala Proversa, the straits
which divide Dugi Otok from
the island of **Katina**, it is

possible to see some
interesting Roman remains:
the ruins of a villa, a fishpond
and a huge tank for water,
which was distributed to
the villa's rooms. The few
mosaics found here are now
in the Archaeological Museum
in Zadar *(see p93)*.

Lavsa

This island with its pretty
bays and coves is a popular
tourist destination. The ruins
of a partly submerged wall
are all that remain of an
ancient Roman salt works.

Piškera

There are also traces of
Roman presence in Piškera.
Once there was a village here
with about 50 houses, a

warehouse for fish and a
tower for the tax collector.
The houses and tower are
now almost all in ruins.
However, the church from
1560 is still standing.

Svršata

On the small island of Svršata
there are two walls that go
down to the sea and continue
into the water, where they
join up with another wall. It is
thought that this square tank
was a Roman construction for
keeping fish fresh.

Mana

The island of Mana is famous
for its semicircular cliffs.
Spray from the waves
breaking on the cliffs can
reach up to a height of 40 m
(131 ft). On top of the cliffs
are the ruins of a Greek-style
fishing village, built for the
film *The Raging Sea* in 1961.

THE KORNATI ISLANDS BY BOAT

The archipelago of the
Kornati Islands is a real
paradise for sailors. These
are beautiful islands where
the only sounds are those
of the sea and the wind.
There is only one small
port, Piškera, which is
open from Easter (March
or April) to October;
electricity and fresh water
are rationed. The natural
beauty of the area makes
sailing here unforgettable.

A typical island of white rock, bare of vegetation

LAVSA SMOKVICA KURBA VELA

Kornati National Park, a
paradise for sailing

Nin

Map C4. 🏠 1,500. ✈ Zadar, 24 km (15 miles). 🚆 Zadar, 17 km (11 miles). 🚌 Zadar, 17 km (11 miles). ℹ Trg braće Radić 3, (023) 264 280. www.nin.hr

Founded by the Liburnians, the town was important in Roman times, when it was called Aenona. It later became one of the first permanent Croat settlements. The use of Glagolitic script spread from here when it became a Bishop's see in the 9th century. It was the centre of a long controversy between the local Church and the Pope over the use of the Croatian language in liturgy.

Malaria and the difficulty of defending the town caused it to be abandoned once again, and the bishopric was abolished in the 12th century. The few remaining monuments date from this glorious period (9th–12th centuries): the churches of the Holy Cross, St Anselm and St Ambrose.

Inside the town walls is the small 9th-century church of the **Holy Cross** (Sv. Križ), one of the finest examples of pre-Romanesque churches in typical Croatian style *(see p22)*. The name of its founder, the prefect Gladeslaus, is engraved on the lintel. The church's harmony and beauty encapsulate the spirituality of the era.

Nearby is the former cathedral of **St Anselm** (Sv. Anselm), where the kings of Croatia were crowned. It was the first cathedral in Croatia (9th–19th century) and it has a rich treasury with silver reliquaries from the 9th to 15th

The small Romanesque church of St Mary in Ljubač, near Nin

centuries. Near the church stands a large statue by Ivan Meštrović of Bishop Gregory of Nin, promoter of Glagolitic script. Also inside the walls is the church of **St Ambrose** (Sv. Ambroz), built in the 12th century in the Romanesque style with Gothic additions.

In Kraljevac Square is the small but interesting **Museum of Nin Antiquities**.

🔒 **Church of the Holy Cross, of St Anselm and of St Ambrose**
⏱ daily (St Anselm & St Ambrose for mass only).

🏛 **Museum of Nin Antiquities**
Trg Kraljevac 8. **Tel** (023) 264 160. ⏱ May: 9am–2pm daily; Jun & Oct: 9am–8pm daily; Jul–Sep: 9am–10pm daily; Nov–Apr: 9am–2pm daily (by appt). www.amzd.hr

Environs

A short way southwest of Nin stands the church of St Nicholas (Sv. Nikola) in Prahulje. This unusual building, constructed on an Illyrian tumulus, has a dome with an octagonal watch tower from the 12th century on top of it, added during the Turkish invasion. Dating from the 12th century, the church is built on a trefoil plan and once held inscriptions and tombs of members of the court of

Statue of Gregory of Nin, by Ivan Meštrović

Princes Višeslav and Branimir, now in the archaeological museum in Zadar. The church is a fine example of primitive Croatian art.

Ljubač is 13 km (8 miles) northeast of Nin and the site of some ruins: the wall, central buildings and towers of the medieval Castrum Jubae, built by the Templar Knights. It fell into ruin after the order was dissolved. Still standing is the 12th-century Romanesque church of **St Marcela**, noted for its three semicircular apses. Near the village is the small church of St John from the Middle Ages.

🔒 **Church of St Nicholas**
⏱ St Nicholas' Day and St Mark's Day only.

The church of St Nicholas in Prahulje, not far from Nin

A LAND OF SALT WORKS

Salt trading was a very lucrative business in the Middle Ages. Three areas were suitable for its production in the upper Adriatic: the mouth of the River Dragonja, today the border between Slovenia and Croatia, the bay of Pag, and the lowlands around Nin. The salt works of Pag, of Roman origin, which were protected by two ranges of hills, were the largest and most profitable, unlike those of Nin. The possession of these salt flats, still profitable today, has been the cause of various wars ever since.

The salt works on Pag, of Roman origin, still in use today

Paklenica National Park ❺

Nacionalni Park Paklenica

Map C4. 🏠 *Starigrad Paklenica,*
(023) 369 202, 369 155.
🕐 *Apr–Oct: 6am–8:30pm daily;*
Nov–Mar: 7am–3pm daily. 🅿
www.paklenica.hr

Situated in the imposing
Velebit massif, Paklenica
National Park was founded
in 1949. The entrance is in
Starigrad Paklenica – look
out for a road sign on the
Magistrala coastal road (E65).

The park covers an area
of 95 sq km (41 sq miles),
and is formed by two gorges,
Velika Paklenica (Big
Paklenica) and Mala Paklenica
(Small Paklenica), which cut
into the limestone mountains.
The gorges were eroded by
two rivers and parts of the
canyon walls are more than
400 m (1,312 ft) high.

Deep in the cliffs of Velika
Paklenica Canyon there is
an extensive system of underground tunnels built by the
Yugoslav army. The tunnels
are presently being renovated
as the park administration
intend to transform them into
a multi-purpose visitor centre.

The rock faces are pierced
by numerous caves, but
they are not easily accessible.
Only the Manita cave can
be visited, accompanied by
a guide. The bare rock faces
of Velika Paklenica are

Rugged landscape of Paklenica National Park

popular with rock climbers.

High up, majestic birds of
prey make their nests, in an
ideal habitat for breeding.
Golden eagles, hawks, and
especially peregrine falcons
can be seen here. In the
forests there are bears,
wild boar, foxes, roebucks
and hares. A path
in the valley
penetrates far
into the interior
of the park to a
cliff edge where
there is a magnifi-
cent view of the
wooded Vaganski Vrh
mountain, the highest
in the Velebit chain.

The **Velebit**
mountain chain is nearly
150 km (93 miles) long.
The terrain is karst
(limestone) with many sink
holes and plateaux separated
by deep fissures. In 1978
UNESCO listed Velebit as a

**One of many birds of
prey in the park**

biological reserve for
humanity with the aim of
protecting this wild
environment, with its 2,700
plant species and numerous
colonies of large birds of
prey. The *kukovi* – strange,
impressive rock formations
sculpted by wind and water
– are also protected.

Hiking and mountain
biking are other popular
activities in the park and in
summer visitors can stay
overnight in the
Mountain Hut,
located on
the banks
of Velika
Paklenica
creek. A
good camp site is also situated next to a pebble beach.
Along the creek there are
seven disused water mills,
still in good condition,
which can be visited during
the summer.

One of the paths leading into Paklenica National Park

Pag ❻

The island of Pag is 68 km (42 miles) long and has two mountain chains running parallel to the coast: at the southern end cliffs frame a deep bay with numerous inlets. The island was inhabited in the Neolithic Age, and was occupied by the Liburnians in around 1200 BC. When Dalmatia was conquered by Publius Cornelius Scipio in the 1st century AD, the Romans built the town of Cissa and the fortified port of Navalia here. In the Imperial period, villas were built and some mosaic floors and an aqueduct still survive. The Slavs settled in Pag in the 6th century and became sheep farmers. After 1000 AD Zadar and Rab fought over the island to gain control of the salt pans *(see p100)*. When Cissa was destroyed by the inhabitants of Zadar, the islanders chose a new location for a town, Stari Pag, which was fortified by the Venetians in 1192.

Sheep grazing on Pag

in maquis, olive groves and aromatic herbs, particularly sage. As well as the production of olive oil and a distinctive wine called Žutica, sheep farming is one of the main occupations on the island. Pag is famous for its sheep's cheese *(paški sir)*, which has a distinctive taste thanks to the aromatic herbs in the grazing. The cheeses are coated with olive oil, and undergo lengthy maturation.

The dry, barren east-facing coast, swept by the bora wind

Exploring Pag

The island, connected by a bridge to the Magistrala coast road (E65) at its eastern tip, near Miškovići, is dry and barren, with only a few areas cultivated with vines and olive trees. The coastline facing the mainland, rocky and jagged and white in colour, is exposed to the

bora wind and bears little vegetation. The typical dry-stone walls were built to protect the land from the wind and to separate the flocks of sheep belonging to different farmers. The southwest coast is a little flatter with some small beaches. Here the land is covered

Pag Town

The small main island town occupies a sheltered bay facing the mainland. It was granted the status of a free town by King Bela IV in 1244, but rivalry with Zadar brought about its destruction. The walls, the castle, a monastery and the church of St Mary in the old town are in ruins. In 1409, Pag came definitively under the rule of Venice.

KEY

▬ Major road	
▬ Minor road	
▬ Scenic route	
🚢 Ferry	
ℹ Tourist information	
🏖 Beach with facilities	

0 kilometres   5

0 miles   5

For hotels and restaurants in this region see pp226–30 and pp243–6

LACE, SYMBOL OF THE TRADITIONS OF PAG

Pag is renowned for its clean waters and its delicious sheep's cheese, but it is also well-known for its lace. For centuries this lace has been created by the patient hands of the women of the island who, in warm weather, sit by their doorsteps intent on creating this intricate lace. Made using a special stitch, the lace is used to decorate blouses, bedlinen, altar cloths and table centrepieces. Some decades ago a school was established here to train new lacemakers. A collection of antique lace was left to the school by former lacemakers and the examples are used as models. Lace is sold here and some of the rooms are set up as a museum.

Typical Pag lace

VISITORS' CHECKLIST

Map C4. 8,400. Prizna-Žigljen. **Pag** Vela ulica bb, (023) 611 286. Lace exhibition (summer); Carnival of Pag, traditional kolo dance and traditional costumes (Feb & last weekend in Jul). **www.tzgpag.hr Novalja** Trg Briščić 1, (053) 661 404. **www.tz-novalja.hr Karlobag** Trg dr. Tuđmana 2, (053) 694 251. **www.tz-karlobag.hr**

The Skrivanat Tower in the Old Town, Pag

In 1443 the Venetian rulers, with the assistance of local nobles, entrusted the design of a new town to the famous architect Juraj Dalmatinac (Giorgio Orsini). It took several decades to build what is now the present-day Pag.

Venetian rule brought a long period of peace and prosperity, bolstered by the income from the productive salt works. Between the 15th and 18th centuries, important public buildings and a parish church, locally called the cathedral, were built.

The town has preserved its original structure with two main roads intersecting in the main square, and minor roads running parallel.

The high walls with eight towers and four gates were demolished at the end of the 19th century, but some traces (a gate and two bastions) still remain. The 15th-century Duke's Palace (Kneževa Palača), which has been altered, and the unfinished Bishop's Palace by Juraj Dalmatinac face the main square.

A monument to Dalmatinac by Ivan Meštrović and the church of **St Mary of the Assumption** (1443–1448) stand in the same square. The church is a blend of Romanesque and Gothic, with three aisles divided by white stone columns with carved capitals. The façade has a rose window and there is a lunette above the door. Numerous works of art are preserved here, including a wooden 12th-century crucifix, a *Virgin of the Rosary* by Giovanni Battista Pittoni, an organ, and a treasury.

Novalja

Located at the beginning of the narrow peninsula of Lun, Novalja is the second town on the island. It makes its living entirely by tourism, thanks to its level beach. In the centre of the town are the remains of an early Christian basilica and a pre-Romanesque church dating from the 9th–10th centuries.

A ferry service connects the island to the mainland, running from Novalja to Prizna.

Environs

Boat excursions to Pag leave from **Karlobag** on the mainland. Karlobag lies in a pretty bay and takes its name from the fortress that the Archduke of Austria, Charles of Habsburg, built in 1579 on the site of a village destroyed by the Turks.

The fortress lost its importance after the Turkish threat had passed and it was eventually abandoned. Its attractive stones were then salvaged and used to build the houses in the village. Still visible are some of the massive walls and a monastery, which has a famous library and a church.

The harsh but fascinating landscape, characteristic of the island of Pag

Krka National Park ❼

Nacionalni Park Krka

The park covers an area of 109 sq km (42 sq miles) and was established in 1985 to protect the middle and lower stretches of the River Krka, which flows into the bay of Šibenik. The source of the river is near Knin, and the river begins its journey of 75 km (47 miles) inside a canyon on the limestone plateau behind Šibenik. It finally spills over into the spectacular Roški Slap and Skradinski Buk waterfalls, forming a series of lakes and rapids surrounded by vegetation. The bird life in the park is very varied.

Monastery of Visovac
In the middle of the lake is the monastery of Visovac. It was founded by Franciscans in 1445 who were joined by Franciscans from Bosnia in 1576. They brought books, illuminated manuscripts and sacred vestments with them.

Skradin
Once a settlement of Illyrian and Liburnian tribes, then a Roman town, Skradin was a bishop's see from the 6th century. It is one of the main access points to the park; boats go upriver from here to the waterfalls.

Around the lake families of egrets and night herons can be seen perched on the branches of the willows or hidden among the reeds. About 200 species of bird have been counted here.

DEVRSKE

Smrdelje

56

BRIBIRSKE MOSTINE

BRIBIRSKE MOSTINE

Bratiškovci

Entrance 2

Prukljan

Prukljansko Jezero

311 Dubravice

Vis

Skradin ℹ

Raslina

311

Skradinski Buk
From a height of 45 m (147 ft), this impressive waterfall cascades down 17 steps over a distance of 800 m (2,624 ft). Some of the park paths, sprayed by the falls, pass next to what is one of the most spectacular natural displays in Croatia.

8

ŠIBENIK

The lower basin becomes a pool of emerald-green water in the summer and is an attractive place to sunbathe or picnic.

ℹ Lozovac

ŠIBENIK

Entrance 1

Roški Slap

Here the river widens and deepens within the forest before finally cascading from between the trees, producing waterfalls over 25 m (82 ft).

VISITORS' CHECKLIST

Map C–D4. **Park** ⓘ *Trg Ivana Pavla II br 5, Šibenik, (022) 201 777.* **www**.npkrka.hr
🕐 *summer: 8am–7pm; winter: 9am–4pm (Apr, May, Oct, Nov: 8am–6pm). Cars and coaches are not allowed in the park in winter.*
🚤 **Monastery of Visovac:** *can be visited on organized boat trips from Skradinski buk.*

Krka monastery, first mentioned in 1402.

GRAČAC

509

Brljansko Jezero

Kistanje

509

Knin

Vrbnik

33

DRNIŠ ↓

Nečmen

Čitluk

Mratovo

Oklaj

0 kilometres 5

0 miles 5

Lake Visovac is at the heart of the park. After the waterfalls, the river flows through a narrow valley and then widens to form the lake. Some stretches of the banks are steep and others hilly with oak woods.

DRNIŠ ↘

River Čikola

After Lake Visovac, the Krka is joined by the River Čikola and from here the river flows towards the Skradinski Buk and then on to the sea.

56

Siritovci

stery vac

Drinovci

DRNIŠ

Čikola

alik

ŠIBENIK DRNIŠ

VISITING THE PARK

The protected area begins at the Knin valley and continues to the bridge of Skradin. Road signs mark the entrances to the park; each has a parking area, a tourist information centre, and a ticket office. Cars can enter from Lozovac, while the Roški Slap

View of Krka Park

waterfalls can be reached from Miljevci or Skradin. About 15 km (9 miles) from Burnum, other road signs indicate the entrance to the area of the Roški Slap waterfalls. Boats leave from Skradin for trips to the Skradinski Buk waterfalls and from here it is possible to take a short cruise to the Roški Slap falls, crossing the lake of Visovac and visiting the monastery on the island.

KEY

━━ Major road

━━ Minor road

━━ Scenic route

ⓘ Tourist information

★ Waterfall

Šibenik

The town is first documented in 1066 as Castrum Sebenici, when King Petar Krešimir IV described it as a triangular fortified town. In the 12th century it came under Hungarian-Croat rule. Between 1412 and 1797 it was ruled by the Venetians, and the old centre acquired grand buildings and three large forts as well as bastions on the island of St Nicholas. It was a prosperous time and Šibenik became one of the liveliest cultural centres in Renaissance Croatia. Venetian rule gave way to a brief period of French occupation until Austria took over and ruled until 1917. The war during the 1990s brought about the collapse of local industry, and mass unemployment. The situation today is much improved.

Statue of Juraj Dalmatinac

Aerial view of the Cathedral of St James

🏛 Church of St Francis
Sv. Frane

Trg Nikole Tomaszea 1. **Tel** (022) 212 075. ☐ by appt.

Along the busy seafront, on the southern edge of the old town centre, once stood the monastery and church of St Francis, founded in 1229 and destroyed during a raid in 1321. Some capitals, a few statues, and parts of the arches in the cloister remain of the original structure. Towards the middle of the 15th century several new chapels were added on.

The buildings were completely rebuilt in the Baroque style around the middle of the 18th century. The church underwent complete renovation: the wooden ceiling and the sumptuous gilded carved wooden altars were remade, and every wall was decorated with paintings.

Inside, in the first chapel on the left, is a great organ from 1762, made by Petar Nakić.

The large cloister has kept its 14th-century structure and there is a library with manuscripts and liturgical material in the monastery.

🏛 Church of St Barbara
Sv. Barbara

Kralja Tomislava.

The small church of St Barbara, behind the apse of the cathedral of St James, was built around the middle of the 15th century, and conserves parts of an older building. Irregular openings make the façade unusual: the lunette on the main door has a statue of St Nicholas from the workshop of Bonino of Milan (1430). Inside is an altar made by a youthful pupil of Juraj Dalmatinac, Giovanni da Pribislao, who was obliged to match another altar which had been saved from the previous church.

The church also houses a rich and interesting collection of religious art, with paintings, sculptures and illuminated texts dating from the 14th to 16th centuries.

🏛 Count's Palace – Civic Museum
Muzej Grada Šibenika

Gradska Vrata 3. **Tel** (022) 213 880. ☐ call ahead for opening hours. Temporary exhibitions 10am–1pm, 7–9pm daily.

This palace takes its name from the Venetian Count Niccolò Marcello who built it

in the 12th/13th century. It was the Venetian governor's residence and is now a Civic Museum. This late-Renaissance building houses coin collections, archaeological finds from the Neolithic to Roman periods, tomb finds, early Croatian sculptures (7th–9th centuries), and a rich archive of historical documents about the town and its territory, many from the medieval period. There is a statue of the count (1609–11) on the façade next to the entrance.

🏛 Cathedral of St James
Katedrala Sv. Jakova

See pp108–9.

🏛 Old Loggia
Gradska loža

Trg Republike Hrvatske.

In front of the cathedral's Door of Lions stands the Old Loggia, formerly the seat of the town council, built between 1532 and 1543 to a design by Michele Sanmicheli, and restored after it was damaged during World War II.

This is a two-storey structure: the ground floor is an open portico with nine large arches, the upper floor is a loggia, with a balustrade.

The 16th-century Old Loggia, designed by Michele Sanmicheli

🏛 Foscolo Palace
Palača Foscolo

Andrije Kačića.

The Venetian governor, Leonardo Foscolo, built this palace in the Venetian Gothic style in around 1450.

The façade was decorated with Renaissance reliefs by Juraj Dalmatinac's pupils (15th century), and another relief, attributed to the master, has two putti supporting the coats of arms of the noble family, at the side of the entrance door.

View of Šibenik from the medieval Fort of St Anne

⛭ Fort of St Michael
Tvrđava Sv. Mihovila
ℹ️ *(022) 212 075.*
The fort is of medieval origins and the oldest defensive structure in Šibenik. It was destroyed after lightning struck the powder magazine. When it was rebuilt, account was taken of the town's altered defence needs, and the towers were omitted. Its present appearance dates from the 16th–17th centuries. Formerly known as St Anne, it offers magnificent views over the islands.

⛭ Fort of St John
Tvrđava Sv. Ivan
ℹ️ *(022) 212 075.*
Standing on a hill 115 m (410 ft) high, the fort was built in 1646 in a star shape after the town was attacked by the Turks in 1649.

⛭ Šubićevac Fort
Tvrđava Šubićevac.
ℹ️ *(022) 212 075.*
The third large fort called Šubićevac, or Baron's Fort, was constructed rapidly in 1646, in the face of an imminent Turkish attack. The fort, in fact, greatly contributed to the defeat of the Turks in 1647. After a long siege, large parts of it had to be rebuilt. The present structure dates from the middle of the 17th century and a pretty garden is laid out in front of the bastions.

⛭ Fort of St Nicholas
Tvrđava Sv. Nikola
ℹ️ *(022) 212 075.*
The fort was planned by the Italian architect Michele Sanmicheli, and built between 1540 and 1547 on a cliff overlooking the city. It is a fine example of military architecture, both for its strength and for the beauty of the decorations above the entrance gate, in the apertures, in the rooms, and along the corridors. The fort was often used as a prison.

VISITORS' CHECKLIST

Map D5. 🏠 *37,000.*
✈ *Split, 97 km (60 miles).*
🚉 *(022) 333 699.* 🚌 *Draga 44, (060) 368 368, (022) 216 066.*
⛴ *dr. F. Tuđmana 7, (022) 213 468.* ℹ️ **Local:** *Ulica Fausta Vrančića 18, (022) 212 075;*
Regional: *Fra N. Ružića bb, (022) 219 072.*
www.sibenik-tourism.hr

The Fort of St Nicholas, outside the entrance of Šibenik harbour

ŠIBENIK TOWN CENTRE

Cathedral of
  St James pp108–9 ④
Church of St Barbara ②
Church of St Francis ①
Count's Palace –
  Civic Museum ③
Fort of St Anne ⑦
Foscolo Palace ⑥
Old Loggia ⑤

0 metres   200
0 yards   200

Key to Symbols *see back flap*

Šibenik: Cathedral of St James
Katedrala Sv. Jakova

A face on the cornice of the apse

It took Croatian and international experts several years to restore Šibenik's cathedral after its shelling in 1991. Its original construction by renowned Dalmatian and Italian artists began in 1432 and was completed in 1555. The original project was entrusted to the Venetian, Antonio Dalle Masegne, who built the lower Gothic level. His successor, Juraj Dalmatinac (*see p20*), designed the upper Renaissance part of the sculptures by the doors, the 72 faces on the outside of the apse, many of the capitals, the tomb of Juraj Šižgorić and, along with Andrija Aleši, the beautiful baptistry. On Dalmatinac's death in 1475, the work was continued by Nikola Firentinac, who built the splendid presbytery with the choir, the dome, the galleries and vaulted roof. The Adam and Eve by the Door of Lions are by Bonino of Milan.

The Dome, a unique structure built of interlocking slabs of stone, was badly damaged in 1991.

Transept
The transept is supported by a square structure; on three sides is an arch surmounted by a statue. The stones were worked in such a way that they fitted together without the need for mortar.

★ Presbytery
The finely worked stone stalls were made by Juraj Dalmatinac and Nikola Firentinac. Other sculpted reliefs adorn the upper parts.

STAR FEATURES

★ Baptistry

★ Presbytery

The exterior is decorated with 72 sculpted human faces on the cornice, the work of Juraj Dalmatinac and his assistants.

Door of Lions
This door is named after the two stone lions which support statues of Adam and Eve. The doorway is framed by slim, finely carved columns.

★ Baptistry
At the end of the right aisle is an impressive baptistry with many statues and reliefs sculpted by Juraj Dalmatinac, Nikola Firentinac and Andrija Aleši. The fine baptismal font is supported by three putti.

VISITORS' CHECKLIST

Trg Republike Hrvatske 1.
Tel (022) 214 418. ◯ daily.
◙ ঔ ☑ www.sibenik.hr/
vodic-eng/sibenik/kulturno_
povijesna_bastina2.asp

Façade
The symmetrical façade has an arched tympanum in the centre. The taller central section has a rose window in the centre and a smaller one above on the tympanum. The façade is framed by two pilasters and has only one door.

The cathedral was built entirely in local stone and is a tribute to the great technical skill of the stone-cutters.

The Gothic doorway is decorated with groups of sculptures of saints ascending the arch, which is framed by two spires.

Interior
The three-aisle interior is divided by columns with carved capitals supporting pointed arches. The tall central nave has a frieze and women's gallery.

Drniš ❾

Map D4. 🏚 *3,400.*
🚉 *Šibenik, 25 km (15 miles), (022) 333 699.* 🚌 *Šibenik, (022) 216 066.*
ℹ️ *(022) 219 072.*

The town of Drniš first appears in documents towards the end of the 15th century, as the site of a fort built to stop a Turkish invasion, at the point where the River Čikola cuts into the valley and flows down towards Šibenik.

In 1526 the fort was captured and enlarged by the Turks, who made it one of their outposts. A village with a mosque and baths developed around the fort, but during the wars between Venice and the Ottoman empire, from 1640 to 1650, the fort and the village were almost entirely destroyed by the Venetians.

In the reconstruction that followed the mosque was remodelled and became the church of St Anthony. The minaret became the bell tower of the church of St Roch. Serbs populated the town and it became part of the Krajina territory.

Along the road from Drniš to Šibenik, the ruins of defence structures with high walls and a tower can be seen.

Environs
Some 9 km (5 miles) east of Drniš is the village of **Otavice**, the birthplace of Ivan Meštrović's parents. The great sculptor *(see p157)* built the **Church of the Most Holy Redeemer** here for himself and his family. It is simply designed in the form of a stone cube with a shallow dome.

Church of the Most Holy Redeemer in Otavice, near Drniš

Knin ❿

Map D4.🏚 *12,000.* 🚉 *(022) 663 722.* ℹ️ *Dr. Franje Tuđmana 24, (022) 664 822.* **www**.tz-knin.hr

A town on the main road from Zagreb to Split, Knin has long played an important role in Dalmatia's history. It occupies a strategic position on the plateau, and there have been defences of some kind here since prehistoric times. In the 10th century, when the town was known as Ad Tenen, the **Fort of Knin** was built here on Mount Spas. It was used by reigning Croat monarchs, who often stayed in the nearby town of Biskupija and held coronations here.

Early in the 11th century Knin became a bishopric and the residence of several aristocratic Croatian families. Occupied by the Turks in the early 16th century, in 1688 Knin fell to the Venetians.

The Morlachs, in the pay of Venice, distinguished themselves in the battle to retake the fort by scaling the walls. Afterwards they rebuilt the fort and settled in the town.

In 1991, the Serbian army used the fort when most of the inhabitants of Croat origin were forced out. It became a focus for the Serb rebellion and the Republic of the Serb Krajina, of which Knin was the capital, was created. In August 1995 the territory was returned to the Croats.

Environs
About 5 km (3 miles) away is **Biskupija**, once known as the "Field of five churches", for its religious buildings (9th–11th centuries) attended by the Croat kings. King Zvonimir was killed here by Croat nobles who did not accept his allegiance to the pope. By the main building is a church designed by Ivan Meštrović and frescoed by Jozo Kljaković.

The imposing Fort of Knin, on Mount Spas

Sinj ⓫

Map D5. 🏛 *13,000.* 🚉 *Split.* 🚌
Split. 🛈 *Put Petrovca 12, (021) 826
352.* 🎭 *Sinjska Alka, jousting
tournament in costume (1st Sun Aug).*
www.tzsinj.hr

On the Cetina plateau the
Romans founded Aequum,
the present-day Čitluk, on the
road towards Bosnia, but the
unhealthy area and malaria
forced the inhabitants to
abandon the town and move
to a nearby hill called
Castrum Zyn. This was safer
and easier to defend and they
built a fort here.

At the end of the 1400s
some Franciscan monks, who
had fled from a monastery in
Rama, a Bosnian town, came
here, bringing with them an
image of the Virgin believed
to be miraculous and they
built a **Franciscan Monastery**
(Franjevački Samostan)
and a church.

The town,
by now
called Sinj,
was captured by the
Turks in 1513 and
remained in their
possession until
1699 when it was
liberated by the
Venetians. Its
strategic position
urged the Turks to
attempt to recapture
it in 1715, but an
unexpected attack by 600
horsemen, citizens
of the town, against the
Ottoman troops prevented
its capture.

**Sculpture of
the jousting
tournament, Sinj**

This historical event is
commemorated every year on
the first Sunday in August
with a jousting tournament
(Sinjska Alka), when expert
riders take part in a
competition to capture a
shield, the symbol of victory.

The Franciscan church,
which has been rebuilt at
various times, is a popular
pilgrimage site. The monastery has been renovated and
some of the rooms house
archaeological finds from
ancient Aequum.

🏛 **Franciscan Monastery**
A Stepinca 1. **Tel** *(021) 707 010.*
◐ *by appt only.*

Primošten, once an island but now linked to the mainland

Klis ⓬

Map D5. 🏛 *2,300.* 🚉 *Split.* 🚌
Split. 🛈 *Megdan 57, (021) 240 578.*
www.tzo-klis.htnet.hr

The little village of Klis is
dominated by an imposing
Fort which consists of three
concentric walls. It was
founded by the Romans on
a hill above a mountain pass
which led from the plateau
onto the plain. The
Venetians strengthened
the fort and enlisted
the Uskoks to help
fight off the Turks,
who however finally
captured it in 1537.
The Turks enlarged
the fort, building a
mosque and a minaret
and from here they
menaced the city of
Split until 1648
when they were
driven off by
Venetian troops. The
fort was in use until
the Austrians took over. The
mosque was turned into a
church and the minaret
was demolished.

The town's restaurants are
particularly known for their
excellent spit-roasted lamb.

**The Fort of Klis, the scene of
many bloody battles**

Primošten ⓭

Map D5. 🏛 *1,800.*
🚉 *Split.* 🚌 *Split (021) 329 180.*
🚤 *Marina (022) 570 068.* 🛈 *Trg
Biskupa J. Arnerića 2, (022) 571 111.*
🎭 *Gospe od Loreta (May).*
www.tz-primosten.hr

Originally an isolated
island, Primošten is now
connected to the mainland
by a bridge and a causeway.
The name Primošten means
"brought closer by a bridge".
The island was inhabited in
prehistoric times, and was
settled by Bosnian refugees
fleeing from the Turks. Under
Venetian rule, walls were built
around the town.

The top of the town is
dominated by the church of
St George, built in the late
15th century and enlarged
around 1760. Inside is an icon
of the Virgin on a silver
panel, and a Baroque altar.

A popular resort with
pebbly beaches, Primošten is
also famous for its vineyards
(see p129) and a good red
wine called Babić.

Marina ⓮

Map D5. 🏛 *1,000.* 🛈 *Trg Stjepana
Radića 1, (021) 889 015.*

This small holiday resort lies
in a sheltered bay and has a
marina and a pretty beach.
The village has been
inhabited since the 15th
century. In 1495 the Bishop
of Trogir built a massive
tower in the port, now the
Hotel Kaštil.

The two churches in the
village, St Luke and St John,
were built in the 15th century
and restructured at various
times by the Sobota family,
the feudal lords of the village.

Trogir ⑮

Set on a small island just off the mainland, Trogir is one of the jewels of the Dalmatian coast, with many splendid monuments. The Greeks of Issa (now Vis) first settled here in the 3rd century BC, when they founded the fortified town of Tragyrion (island of goats) which became Tragurium under the Romans in 48 BC. In the Middle Ages Trogir was protected by the Byzantine fleet, but in 1123 it was attacked and destroyed by the Saracens, and abandoned by the few surviving inhabitants. It revived again 70 years later and a period of artistic growth ensued, first under the kings of Hungary and, from 1420, under Venetian rule. In 1997 Trogir was listed as a UNESCO World Heritage Site.

The seafront of Trogir, with Kamerlengo castle in the distance

Most of the old historic centre of the town is on an island and is encircled by a wall with two gates. A bridge now joins the island to the mainland and another links it to the island of Čiovo. Tourism is important to the town: ice-cream parlours, restaurants and pizzerias line the small squares. The main public and religious monuments, and other important buildings, have been the subject of restoration work.

🚪 Land Gate
Sjeverna Vrata

Rebuilt in the 17th century, this gate was made from a tall doorway in pale rusticated stone, with grooves which once supported a drawbridge. On the cornice above the arch once stood the lion of St Mark and, above that, on a pedestal, stands a statue of the Blessed John of Trogir (Sv. Ivan Trogirski), one of the town's patron saints.

🏛 Civic Museum
Muzej Grada Trogira

Gradska vrata 4. *Tel (021) 881 406.* ⬜ *Jul–Aug: 9am–1pm, 5–10pm; May, Jun, Sep & Oct: 9am–1pm, 5–10pm; Nov–Apr: 9am–2pm by appt.* 🎨🚫📷🚫

On the other side of the Land Gate is the Baroque Garagnin Fanfogna Palace, now the Civic Museum, with 18th-century furnishings. There are archaeological collections, documents and antique clothes linked to the town's history.

🏛 Stafileo Palace
Palača Stafileo

Matije Gupca 20. ⬛ *to the public.* Stafileo Palace was built in the late 15th century. A series of five windows in Venetian Gothic style punctuates each of the two floors, the openings framed by pillars, capitals and carved arches. Around the arches are reliefs of flowers and leaves. The design is attributed to the school of Juraj Dalmatinac, who worked for many years in Trogir.

⛪ Cathedral of St Lawrence
Sv. Lovre

Trg Ivana Pavla II. *Tel (091) 531 4754.* ⬜ *mid May–Oct: 9am–8pm; Nov–mid May: by appt.*

The cathedral stands on the site of an ancient church, destroyed by the Saracens. Construction started in 1193, but was prolonged for decades and involved dozens of artists. The three-aisle building has three semicircular apses: the central nave is higher than the side aisles from which it is divided by eight columns.

There are two entrances. The side door, known as "the count's", is very simple, and dated 1213. The other entrance is a magnificent Romanesque door under an atrium, to the right of which stands a beautiful Gothic bell tower, built between the late 14th century and the beginning of the 17th century. This door was carved in around 1240 by the Dalmatian sculptor Master Radovan *(see p20)*, and is the finest expression of Romanesque sculpture is found in Dalmatia. Two stone lions support statues of Adam and Eve either side of the door. Next to them are pilasters depicting saints in Byzantine style. Scenes of the different months of the year are carved on the middle pilasters.

Above the door, in the large lunette, is a relief of the Nativity and in the semi-circles are episodes from the life of Jesus. The door is enclosed under a sloping roof with a corbel at the top with a statue of St Lawrence. In the atrium is a baptistry designed by Andrija Aleši in around 1460 with a relief of the Baptism of Christ.

The intricate Romanesque door of the Cathedral of St Lawrence

Aerial view of the square and the cathedral

The church interior contains an octagonal stone pulpit from the 13th century built and sculpted by Mauro, a choir with wooden stalls inlaid by Ivan Budislavić towards the mid-15th century, and a ciborium on the main altar with sculptures depicting the Annunciation. On the altars are paintings by Palma il Giovane and Padovanino.

Along the left aisle is the chapel of the Blessed Orsini, a masterpiece by Nikola Firentinac and Andrija Aleši made in 1468–72, with 12 statues of the apostles in shell-shaped niches and, in the centre, the sarcophagus of the Blessed Orsini, the first bishop of Trogir. The sculptures are by Nikola Firentinac, Andrija Aleši and Ivan Duknović.

In the sacristy are paintings by Salvator Rosa and Gentile Bellini, cabinets carved by Grgur Vidov, and a Treasury with many gold pieces, reliquaries and paintings dating from the 17th-century.

The tall bell tower was built in the 14th century, but was partly destroyed during the wars early in the following century and only the ground floor remains of the original building. When Trogir became part of Venetian territory, the bell tower was rebuilt. The first floor with a balustrade by Matej Gojković (1422), is in the Gothic style, with two narrow mullioned windows

VISITORS' CHECKLIST

Map D5. 🚃 10,500. ✈ Split, 30 km (18 miles). 🚉 Split, 30 km (18 miles). 🚌 (021) 881 405. 🛈 Trg Ivana Pavla II 1, (021) 885 628. 📠 (021) 881 508. **www**.tztrogir.hr

with a trefoil, surmounted by blind arches. The second level has two tall windows on each side: the north and south walls have mullioned windows with four trefoil eyes, those on the east and west walls are surmounted by fretwork grilles, with columns and capitals at the centre and corners, giving a feeling of lightness to the entire floor. Recent studies attribute this work to the Italian sculptor Lorenzo Pincino, who worked in Trogir and Dalmatia for many years, with the assistance of local craftsmen.

The third storey, from the late 16th century, was built by the sculptor Trifun Bokanić and has large arched openings.

TROGIR TOWN CENTRE

Cathedral of St Lawrence ④
Church of St Dominic ⑪
Church of St John the Baptist ⑧
Church of St Nicholas ⑩
Čipiko Palace ⑤
Civic Museum ②
Kamerlengo Castle and St Mark's Tower ⑫
Land Gate ①
Loggia and Clock Tower ⑦
Sea Gate and Fish Market ⑨
Stafileo Palace ③
Town Hall ⑥

Key to Symbols see back flap

0 metres 100
0 yards 100

Exploring Trogir

A good time to visit Trogir is the late spring or early autumn, when the narrow streets, flanked by ancient stone houses, are not so busy with summer visitors, and there is space to stop and admire the ingenious architectural details that make this island so fascinating. A carved doorway, a coat of arms, or a mullioned window may decorate the façade of a building; the entrance to a courtyard may offer glimpses of scented gardens. These are all indications of a once widespread prosperity and also evidence of Trogir's cultural past, when it was an important centre for the arts. After many years of hardship and neglect, the town has been restored to its former glory.

The Clock Tower

supported by six columns with Roman capitals and dates from the 14th century. On the wall are two reliefs, one from 1471 sculpted by Nikola Firentinac *(Justice)*, and one from 1950 by Ivan Meštrović *(Ban Berislavić)*. The Clock Tower stands to the left of the Loggia. It supports a pavilion dome, salvaged in 1447 from the chapel of the oratory of St Sebastian. The saint's statue on the façade was sculpted by Nikola Firentinac.

A Renaissance well in the courtyard of Čipiko Palace

🏛 Čipiko Palace
Palača Čipiko

Gradska ulica. 🚫 *to the public, except courtyard.*

An inscription indicates 1457 as the year of completion of the beautiful Čipiko Palace, built for Trogir's most illustrious family. Over a Renaissance doorway, distinguished by its columns with capitals, is a shell decoration above a finely worked cornice.

The first floor has a mullioned window with a balustrade in light coloured stone. In the centre, two columns with capitals support pointed arches and at the ends of the window are two thin pilasters surmounted by capitals with spiral decorations. Between the arches are four sculptures of angels. Two central ones hold a scroll with the coats of arms

of the Čipiko family. The second floor lacks a balustrade, and is similar in style to the lower floor, although its decorations are less ornate.

A second door, opening on to a side street, has a complex structure. Two fluted door jambs support capitals with carved foliage decoration and a stone cornice with two sculpted lions holding a coat of arms. These are flanked by two sculptures of angels in medallions.

🏛 Town Hall
Gradska vijećnica

Trg Ivana Pavla II.

On the eastern side of the square is the Town Hall. This building originates from the 15th century and has three storeys with open arches and a beautiful mullioned window with a balustrade on the upper floor, which was restored in the 19th century. Numerous coats of arms decorate the façade which has three Renaissance doors framed by projecting stone. The pretty porticoed courtyard is open to the public. However, the interior, which has been altered at various times, has nothing of significant interest.

🏛 Loggia and Clock Tower
Gradska loža

Trg Ivana Pavla II. 🚫 *daily.*

The Loggia and the Clock Tower face John Paul II Square (Trg Ivana Pavla II). The Loggia has a roof

🔒 Church of St John the Baptist
Sv. Ivan Krstitelj

🚫 *ask at tourist office for timings.*

This small Romanesque church, built in the 13th century, is the pantheon of the powerful Čipiko family. The church housed an Art Gallery (Pinacoteca) with collections of medieval illuminated manuscripts, ornaments, paintings and precious gold pieces from various churches, but this is now in the **Museum of Sacred Art** near the cathedral. The collection also includes a sculpture *(Deposition)* by Nikola Firentinac, organ panels by Gentile Bellini *(St Jerome and St John the Baptist)* and two polyptychs by Blaise of Trogir.

The doorway of the Romanesque church of St John the Baptist

The Fish Market, housed in a 16th-century loggia

🏰 Sea Gate and Fish Market
Južna Vrata

Obala Bana Berislavića.
The Sea Gate was built at the end of the 16th century and has two beautiful columns made of blocks of light-coloured stone which frame the opening and support a projecting block on which stands the lion of St Mark.

Nearby is the Fish Market which is held in an open loggia with nine columns supporting the roof. It was built in 1527 and was formerly the customs house.

Ceremonial costumes made by the tailor Boris Burić Gena

BORIS BURIĆ GENA

Trogir can boast a unique present-day success story: Boris Burić Gena, a tailor who specializes in making traditional Croatian suits. His signature jackets are made without lapels and have antique-style brocade buttonholes. They are often worn in ceremonies and parades. The careful choice of fabrics, meticulous design and matching of accessories have made this talented craftsman's name. His workshop, the Burić Palace, now draws wealthy and famous clients from all over Europe.

🔒 Church of St Nicholas
Sv. Nikola

Gradska ulica 2. **Tel** (021) 881 631. .
The church and Benedictine convent date from the 11th century, but were rebuilt in the 16th century. The convent rooms now house the **Zbirka Umjetnina Kairos**, an art collection which includes the *Kairos*, a relief of Greek origins (1st century BC) depicting the god of opportunity, a Gothic Crucifix, and a Romanesque statue *(The Virgin with Child)*.

Relief depicting Kairos, St Nicholas

🔒 Church of St Dominic
Sv. Dominik

Obala Bana Berislavića.
🕐 *summer: 8am–noon, 4–7pm daily.*
The church and monastery of St Dominic are Romanesque-Gothic buildings constructed in the 14th century. They were renovated by Nikola Firentinac in the Renaissance style. The single-nave church contains the tomb of Giovanni Sobota, a lawyer, attributed to Nikola Firentinac (1469), and a splendid painting by Palma il Giovane *(Circumcision of Christ)*.

🏰 Kamerlengo Castle and St Mark's Tower
Kaštel Kamerlengo

In the southwest corner of the island stands Kamerlengo Castle, which was at one time the residence of the Venetian governor. It was built by the Venetians in about 1430, and is a four-sided structure with a hexagonal base. Facing the sea, its high walls connect the three towers and the bastion. This imposing structure was once connected to St Mark's Tower (Kula svetog Marka). The large open space inside the castle is used for outdoor theatre performances and concerts during the summer months.

St Mark's Tower was built by the Venetians after the construction of the castle and has the typical structure of defences built in the Renaissance period. A circular tower stands on a truncated cone base and there is a long series of embrasures on the roof. Artillery was installed on the top level in readiness to defend the strip of water that separates the island from the mainland.

What was once the parade ground, between the castle and St Mark's Tower, is now the town's sports field.

The imposing St Mark's Tower, built for defence in 1470

Salona ⑯

Detail of the Tusculum

The ancient town of Salona, 5 km (3 miles) from Split, is famous for its Roman ruins. The name Salona (or Salonae) derives from the salt *(sal in Latin)* works in the area. Originally an Illyrian settlement, it was then Greek, but did not become an important centre until the Romans built a town next to the Greek city. During the rule of Augustus it became a Roman colony called Martia Julia Salonae and later it was the capital of the province of Dalmatia. In the 1st century AD the Romans built an amphitheatre, theatres, temples, baths, a Forum and town walls reinforced with towers, and Salona became the richest and most populated city in the mid-Adriatic. In 614 the Avars and the Slavs destroyed it and it fell into disuse. The buildings and the churches were stripped and the stone was used for new buildings.

Salona's main road

Ruins of the walls and triangular tower

Exploring Salona

At the end of the 19th century excavations began to bring to light the buried remains of this ancient settlement. The work has clearly shown that the town had two districts dating from different periods: the original, old centre *(Urbs vetus)* and a later part which dates from the Augustan era *(Urbs nova occidentalis* and *Urbs nova orientalis).* The excavations have uncovered only a part of the layout of the **Outer Walls**, which were frequently reinforced over the centuries. However, the foundations and the remains of towers with triangular or rectangular bases are visible.

A good place to begin a tour is the **Necropolis of Manastirine**, the burial area just outside the walls, north of the city (near the parking area). In the 4th century a religious building was constructed here to house the relics of the Salonian saints, victims of Diocletian's persecution of Christians. The ruins of the necropolis and the basilica are well preserved.

From Manastirine, after the entrance, you reach the Tusculum, a villa built in the last century for the distinguished archaeologist Frane Bulić, to enable him to study Salona. A scholar and director of the Archaeological Museum in Split, he devoted much of his life to researching the ancient ruins of this city. The building is now a small museum.

However, the most interesting material is now in the Archaeological Museum in Split *(see p123).*

Further on is the richest area of ruins with the foundations of early Christian basilicas, baths and the Caesarea Gate. The **Baths** were built in the 1st century when the city became the capital of the province of Dalmatia. In the early Christian period the buildings were probably transformed into religious buildings: the **Bishop's Complex** in the northeastern sector of Salona comprised basilicas, a baptistry and the bishop's residence. Before Christianity became widespread, early Christian martyrs were slayed here, including St Domnius (the patron saint of Split), Venantius and Anastasius.

The foundations of two basilicas have been excavated. One is known as the Urban Basilica, the other, called Honorius' Basilica, had a Greek cross

The Necropolis of Manastirine, just outside the walls

Basilica Urbana in the Bishop's Complex

VISITORS' CHECKLIST

Map D5. from Split. (021)
210 048. www.solin-info.com
summer: 7am–7pm; winter:
call to check opening times.

but has now been established as the second half of the 2nd century AD.

From the amphitheatre, another path leads to the Theatre at the edge of the old city. This was built in the first half of the 1st century AD and part of the stage and the foundations of the stalls have been excavated. Next to the theatre is the **Forum**, the political and commercial heart of the city. Unlike the Forum in Zadar (*see pp92–95*), the paving was dismantled and only the foundations remain. In the Roman era some of the most important buildings stood around the Forum, which was begun in the 1st century AD and subsequently modified.

The best-preserved Roman construction in ancient Salona is the **Aqueduct**, built to bring water from the River

plan. This is also the site of what remains of the **Caesarea Gate:** arches flanked by two octagonal towers, showing the building techniques used by the Romans in the Imperial era.

Going west along the walls you reach the **Necropolis of Kapljuč**, another early Christian burial site, and then the imposing ruins of the **Amphitheatre**, in the easternmost part of the city.

The amphitheatre, in brick, was probably covered in stone and stood in the newer part of the city on the northwest edge of *Urbs vetus* (Old Town) close to the walls. According to historians, the amphitheatre could seat 18,000–20,000 people. The foundations and a part of the lower tribune have been excavated and the discovery of a network of underground channels has led to the theory that simulated naval battles were held in the arena.

The amphitheatre's construction date was controversial for a long time,

Jadro to the city and extended in the time of Emperor Diocletian to reach his palace in Split (*see pp120–1*). Repair work was carried out at the end of the 19th century and the southern part of the aqueduct is still in use. Alongside the walls it is possible to see some parts of the aqueduct above the surface – more evidence of the great skills of Roman civil engineers.

From the theatre you return to the Manastirine necropolis. North of this site is the **Necropolis of Marusinac**, built outside the city around the tomb of St Anastasius. In this area a few traces of a basilica dating from the 5th century are still visible.

The Amphitheatre, of which only a part of the lower tribune remains

THE RUINS OF SALONA

Amphitheatre ⑦
Baths ③
Bishop's Complex ④
Caesarea Gate ⑤
Forum ⑨
Necropolis of Kapljuč ⑥
Necropolis of Manastirine ①
Necropolis of Marusinac ⑩
Theatre ⑧
Tusculum ②

0 metres   500
0 yards   500

Key to Symbols see back flap

Split ⑰

Detail of Papalić Palace

Shipyards, factories and a busy port present the modern face of Split, which expanded unchecked after World War II. The old town centre is still full of charm however; it grew up in and around the Emperor Diocletian's vast Roman palace, one of the largest and best-preserved left from the Roman world. In 614, the palace took in refugees from Salona *(see pp116–17)*, which had been razed by the Avars, and these newcomers began to use the Roman structure as housing. Among the refugees were the bishop and other religious dignitaries, who breathed new life into the bishopric of Split. After two centuries of Byzantine rule and the establishment of Croat communities, Split became part of the Venetian territories in 1409. Under the Venetians, new walls and the Gripe Fort were built and the arts flourished.

Baptismal font in the Baptistry of St John, former Temple of Jupiter

View of the port and the seafront of Split

🏛 Golden Gate
Zlatna Vrata
This was the main entrance to Diocletian's Palace *(see p120)* and was the most impressive of the gates, with towers and decorative elements above the arches. In the 11th century, the corridor between the palace and the gate was closed and turned into the church of **St Martin** (Sv. Martin). An inscription commemorates Father Dominic, the founder.

🏛 Split City Museum
Muzej Grada Splita
Papalićeva 1. **Tel** (021) 360 171. ⬤ May–Oct: 9am–9pm Tue–Fri, 9am–4pm Sat–Mon; Nov–Apr: 9am–4pm Tue–Fri, 10am–1pm Sat & Sun. 🕮
The Gothic Papalić Palace, housing the Split City Museum, is one of the most interesting of the 15th–16th-century buildings constructed in the

abandoned parts of the Diocletian complex. It houses an exhibition with various artistic finds, paintings, and books illustrating the city's celebrated history from the 12th to the 18th centuries.

🏛 Peristyle
The interior courtyard of the Roman complex is an impressive part of the complex where the layers of centuries of building can clearly be seen. The slim columns bordering three sides rest on a high plinth and have finely worked capitals. The access to the former private quarters of Diocletian has a tall arched tympanum and relief decorations.

🔒 Baptistry of St John
Sv. Ivan Krstitelj
Tel (021) 345 602. ⬤ 9am–7pm daily.
This small, beautiful building, consecrated in the 6th century, was the Palace's Temple of Jupiter. Inside, the baptismal font incorporates a pre-Romanesque panel of King Zvonimir and other dignitaries. The statue of St John on the end wall is by Ivan Meštrović and was added before World War II. The tomb of Bishop John is from the 8th century and the one in front of it, that of Bishop Lawrence, dates from the 11th century.

🔒 Cathedral of St Domnius
Katedrala Sv. Duje
See p121.

🏛 Silver Gate and Church of St Dominic
Srebrna Vrata i Sv. Dominik
Hrvojeva ulica. **Church of St Dominic** ⬤ am.
Near the Silver Gate there is a market, a wonderful chaos of seasonal fruit and vegetables, homemade cheeses, hams and dried herbs. Because of the open space, this also provides the best view of the Palace of Diocletian. It is still possible to distinguish the different structures of the complex, and part of the guards' corridor, on the walls, can be walked along.
In front of the gate is the Oratory of St Catherine, built in the Middle Ages. It was used by the Dominicans while they built their own monastery (1217). The oratory was almost entirely rebuilt in the 17th century and became the church of St Dominic (Sv. Dominik). Inside the church, which was enlarged in 1930, are a *Miracle in Surian* by Palma il Giovane and an *Apparition in the Temple*, attributed to his school.

🏛 Brass Gate
Mjedena Vrata
Ethnographic Museum
Severova 1. **Tel** (021) 344 164. ⬤ Jun–Sep: 9am–7pm Mon–Fri, 9am–1pm Sat; Oct–May: 9am–4pm Mon–Fri, 9am–1pm Sat. 🕮 ♿
Although the Brass Gate is plain and faces the sea and port, it opens on to the richest

façade of the palace. The upper floor had a portico which was later enclosed to make living quarters. The vast cellars have been excavated to reveal impressive arched vaults and skilful masonry. Shops occupy some of these but other huge cellars house an exhibition about the palace and temporary local displays.

Close to the Brass Gate, on Severova, is the **Ethnographic** **Museum** (Etnografski Muzej), displaying an array of skilled Dalmatian folk crafts.

🏛 Iron Gate
Željezna Vrata
The church of **Our Lady of the Belfry** (Gospa od Zvonika), has an early Romanesque bell tower, the city's oldest (1081), and was constructed in the outer passageway above this entrance to the Palace.

VISITORS' CHECKLIST

Map D5. 🏙 175,000. ✈ Franje Tuđmana 96, Kaštel Štafilić (021) 203 506. 🚋 Obala kneza Domagoja, (060) 333 444. 🚌 Obala Kneza Domagoja, (060) 327 777. ⛴ Jadrolinija: (021) 338 333. 🛈 Peristil bb, (021) 345 606. 🎉 St Domnius Feast (7 May); Split Summer (mid-Jul–mid-Aug). **www**.visitsplit.com

🏛 People's Square
Narodni Trg (Pjaca)
This was the centre of business and administration from the 15th century and the nobility erected prestigious buildings here. Examples are the Venetian-Gothic **Cambi Palace** and the Renaissance **Town Hall** (Vijećnica), built in the first half of the 15th century, with a loggia with three arches on the ground floor and a Gothic window on the upper floor.

The Renaissance Town Hall on People's Square in the centre of Split

SPLIT TOWN CENTRE

Baptistry of St John ④
Braće Radića Square ⑩
Brass Gate ⑦
Cathedral of St Domnius ⑤
Church of St Francis ⑪
Golden Gate ①
Iron Gate ⑧
Museum of Split ②

People's Square ⑨
Peristyle ③
Silver Gate and Church of St Dominic ⑥

Airport 20km (12 miles) ✈

Archaeological Museum POLJUD

KAŠTELA

SINJSKA

ZAGREBAČKA

KRALJA TOMISLAVA

NODILOVA

Strossmayerov Park

KRUŽIĆEVA

NIGEROVA DOMALDOVA

KRALJA

SV. MARIJE

MARMONTOVA

BAN MIKADENOVA

BANA JELAČIĆA

TRG REPUBLIKE

Fish Market

Town Hall

⑨ PEOPLE'S SQUARE

ZADARSKA

Iron Gate ⑧

BRAŠARNA

Golden Gate ①

CARRARINA POLJANA

② Museum of Split

DOMINISOVA DIOKLECIJANOVA

KREŠIMIROVA

③

④ Baptistry of St John

PERISTYLE

KRALJICE JELENE

🛈

HRVOJEVA

⑤ Cathedral of St Domnius

⑥ Silver Gate and Church of St Dominic

⑪ Church of St Francis

Museum of Croatian Archaeological Monuments, Meštrović Gallery

DOBRIĆ

SUBIĆEVA

MAJSTORA

BRAĆE RADIĆA SQUARE ⑩

Cupola

Main Hall

⑦ Brass Gate

Diocletian's Palace

Food Market

RIVA

Harbour

0 metres 100
0 yards 100

Train station 200m (220 yards) 🚉
Ferry port 400m (440 yards) ⛴

Key to Symbols see back flap

Palace of Diocletian

Diocletian, probably a native of Salona, became emperor in 284. He made Maximian joint Augustus, senior co-emperor, in 285, and then in 293 he appointed Galerius and Constantius as Caesars, junior co-emperors (the Tetrarchy). After governing for 20 years, Diocletian retired from public life and in 305 moved to the palace which he had commissioned from the architects Filotas and Zotikos in the bay of Split. After Diocletian's death in 316, the palace was used as administrative offices and the governor's residence. In 615, refugees from Salona found shelter here after the destruction of their city by the Avars. The richest settled in the emperor's apartments, the poorer in the towers and above the gates. The corners of the palace were marked by four square towers, and four towers along the north, east and south sides, while the side facing the sea had a loggia with arches.

Iron Gate and the Clock Tower
This is the best preserved gate: beyond is the church of Our Lady of the Belfry with a 12th-century tower next to it.

Temple of Jupiter
This had an atrium with six columns. The body of the building had a coffered vault and rested on an underground crypt. In the early Middle Ages it was turned into the Baptistry of St John.

The Temples of Venus and Cybele were circular outside and had a hexagonal ground-plan inside. A colonnaded corridor ran around the outside.

The Mausoleum of Diocletian, now the Cathedral of St Domnius

Peristyle
Near the crossroads where the Cardo *and* Decumanus *intersected, the peristyle gave access to the sacred area. On one side were the temples of Venus and Cybele and, further back, that of Jupiter (now the Baptistry of St John); on the other side, the Mausoleum, now the cathedral.*

rait of Diocletian
r reorganizing the empire,
emperor sought the spiritual
fication of its citizens. The state
gion, personified by the emperor,
ned in importance, and temples
e constructed bearing his image.
istians were subject to extremely
ent persecution.

The Golden Gate, facing
Salona, was the main
entrance to the palace. This
was the most imposing of
the gates with two towers
and many decorations.

The Silver Gate, or
eastern gate, was a
simpler copy of the
Golden Gate.

CONSTRUCTION OF
OCLETIAN'S PALACE

e palace, shown here in its
ginal form, was like a typical
nan military camp. It was
5 m (705 ft) long and 180 m
0 ft) wide and was enclosed
very thick walls, at times
m (92 ft) high. The four-sided
onghold was reinforced with
vers on the north, east and
st sides. There is a gate on
h side, connected by two
ds corresponding to the
nan *Cardo* and *Decumanus*.

Cathedral of St Domnius
Katedrala Sv. Duje

Kraj Sv. Duje 5. *Tel (021) 345 602.*
Jun–Aug: 8am–sunset daily; Sep–
May: 9am–noon, 4.30–7.30pm daily.

Originally Diocletian's
mausoleum, the cathedral was
consecrated in the 7th century
when the sarcophagus
containing the body of
Diocletian was removed and
replaced by the remains of St
Domnius. It was the
archbishop of Split at the time
who transformed the
mausoleum into a Christian
church. It has remained
practically unaltered since that
time except for the
construction of a Romanesque
bell tower (12th–16th
centuries) and the addition of
the 13th-century choir inside.

An ancient sphinx in black
granite rests at the foot of the
bell tower. The entrance
doorway has wooden panels
from 1214, with scenes from
the Gospel in floral frames.

The cathedral, built on
an octagonal ground-
plan, has a double
order of Corinthian
columns, most
of them the
Roman originals;
above there is a frieze
decorated with scenes of
Eros hunting, supporting
medallions with portraits
of Diocletian and his wife
Prisca. In the second niche
on the right, with frescoes
dating from
1428, is the

**The 13th-century hexagonal
pulpit, Cathedral of St Domnius**

Altar of St Domnius, the
work of Bonino of Milan
(1427). The wooden choir
stalls in the 17th-century
presbytery are an example
of Romanesque carving
from the beginning of the
13th century.

To the side is a chapel
housing the **Altar of St
Anastasius**, designed in
1448 by Juraj Dalmatinac.
The niche after this was
altered in the 18th century to
create the Baroque chapel of
St Domnius. The 13th-century
hexagonal **pulpit** is supported
by thin columns with carved
capitals. The 14th-century
building behind the
cathedral houses
the sacristy and the
name of one of the
architects, Filotas,
is inscribed by
the entrance. In
the sacristy, now
the Cathedral
Museum, are many
works of art,
including objects
in gold and silver,
ancient manu-
scripts, medieval
icons and vestments.

Of particular
importance are the
Historia Saloniana
written by Arch-
deacon Toma in the
13th century and a
7th-century Gospel.

Detail of the Altar of St Anastasius, Cathedral

Exploring Split

As well as Diocletian's palace, Split has much in the way of historical and artistic interest to offer. In the medieval period, villages were built near the walls and when the city became a free town these settlements were linked in a more orderly fashion. The present-day Brače Radić Square and the People's Square were built, along with the Cambi Palace and the Town Hall. After 1420, construction of the external defences began and town walls were built. Between Split and Trogir, castles built for defence against the Turks still survive.

Distant Accords **by Ivan Meštrović, Meštrović Gallery**

The 15th-century Marina Tower, built by the Venetians

🏛 Brače Radić Square
Trg Brače Radić

This medieval square is at the southwest corner of Diocletian's Palace. The tall **Marina Tower** (Hrvojeva Kula) is the only evidence of the imposing castle built by the Venetians in the second half of the 15th century after the final defeat of Split. Built on an octagonal ground-plan, it stands on the southern side of the square.

On the northern side is the Baroque **Milesi Palace**, which dates from the 17th century. There is also a work by Ivan Meštrović in the centre of the square: the great monument to Marko Marulić, the writer and scholar (1450–1524) who was the founder of literature in the Croatian language. The imposing bronze statue dedicated to the writer has an inscription with some verses by the poet Tin Ujević.

Monument to Marko Marulić

🏛 Church of St Francis
Sv. Frane

Trg Republike. 🛈 *(021) 348 600* *(Tourist office).* ◯ *by appt.*

The church has been rebuilt in recent times but the small Romanesque-Gothic cloister, with thin columns enclosing a flower garden, is original.

The church, with mainly Baroque furnishings, has a 15th-century crucifix by Blaž Juriev Trogiranin. It also houses the tombs of the city's illustrious citizens, including that of Archdeacon Toma (the first Dalmatian historian), writer Marko Marulić and the well-known composer Ivan Lukačić.

🏛 Museum of Croatian Archaeological Monuments
Muzej Hrvatskih Arheoloških Spomenika

Stjepana Gunjace bb. **Tel** *(021) 323 901.* ◯ *Jul–Aug: 9am–1pm, 5–8pm Mon–Fri, 9am–2pm Sat; Sep–Jun: 9am–4pm Mon–Fri, 9am–2pm Sat.* ● *Sun, public hols.* 🔖 ♿ 🚫 www.mhas-split.hr

Set up in 1975, this museum houses finds from the area around Split dating from the early Middle Ages. The collection also includes the works of early Croat sculptors, dating from 800. The stone fragments, salvaged from churches and castles, consist mainly of tombs, capitals, altar fronts, ciboria and windows. Highlights include Prince Višeslav's hexagonal baptismal font in marble, dating from the beginning of the 9th century, and the sarcophagus of Queen Jelena (10th century), discovered in the ancient Roman city of Salona.

🏛 Meštrović Gallery
Galerija Meštrović

Šetalište Ivana Meštrovića 46. **Tel** *(021) 340 800.* ◯ *May–Sep: 9am–7pm Tue–Sun; Oct–Apr: 9am–4pm Tue–Sat, 10am–3pm Sun.* 🔖

The building housing this gallery was the residence of Ivan Meštrović in the early 1930s *(see p157)*. The sculptor himself designed the building to be his family house, studio and gallery. His sculptures, including *Distant Accords* and *Persephone*, decorate the garden and the interior. Among statues in marble, wood and bronze are *The Contemplation*, *The Vow* and *Psyche*. Part of the building still preserves the artist's apartments.

The **Kaštilac**, further down the road at No 39, can be visited with the same ticket. This 16th-century residence belonged to the Capogrosso-Kavanjin family and was bought by Meštrović in 1939 to set up an exhibition hall. The artist also built a small church here to exhibit a series of reliefs called *New Testament*, now replaced by a different work, the *Author of the Apocalypse*.

🏛 National Art Gallery
Galerija Umjetnina

Ulica kralja Tomislava 15. **Tel** *(021) 350 110.* ◯ *May–Sep: 11am–4pm Mon, 11am–7pm Tue–Fri, 11am–3pm Sat; Oct–Apr: 9am–2pm Mon, 9am–5pm Tue–Fri, 9am–1pm Sat.* ● *Sun, public hols.* 🔖 📷 🚫 ♿

The gallery offers a broad overview of art in Split and the rest of Croatia from the 16th to the 20th centuries. As well as the Venetian masters there are also important icons from the so-called school of Bocche di Cattaro (18th–19th centuries) and more contemporary work, including works by Ivan Meštrović and Vlaho Bukovac. Temporary exhibitions are also held here.

Polyptych by Girolamo da Santacroce, Our Lady of Grace

🏛 Archaeological Museum
Arheološki Muzej

Zrinsko Frankopanska 25. *Tel (021) 329 340.* ⏱ Jun–Sep: 9am–2pm, 4–8pm Mon–Sat; Oct–May: 9am–2pm, 4–8pm Mon–Fri, 8am–2pm Sat.

The museum was founded in 1820 and has been on its present site since 1914. It contains a considerable number of finds from the Roman, early Christian and medieval periods

Sarcophagus, Archaeological Museum

which are exhibited in rotation. Of great interest are the finds from Roman Salona, including sculptures, capitals, sarcophagi (those from the 4th–5th century still have pagan reliefs), jewellery, coins, small objects in glazed terracotta and ceramics. There are also finds from the Roman town of Narona *(see p130)*.

🏛 Our Lady of Grace in Poljud
Gospa od Poljuda

Poljudsko Šetalište 17. ℹ *(021) 381 011.* ⏱ by appt.
Towards Zrinsko-Frankopanska in the direction of the suburbs lies an area once

called the marsh *(poljud)*. In the 1400s, the Franciscans built a fortified monastery here with large lateral towers, and a church with a trussed roof. A polyptych by Girolamo da Santacroce from 1549 stands on the main altar, depicting the *Virgin and Saints*: the figure holding a model of the city is St Domnius, patron saint of Split.

Many works of art are on display, including a *Portrait of Bishop Tommaso Nigris* by Lorenzo Lotto (1527) and miniatures by Bone Razmilović.

Not far from the monastery is the stadium of the famous Hajduk Split football team, built in 1979 in the suburb of Poljud and designed by Boris Magaš.

🌿 Marjan Peninsula
This protected nature reserve is on the west side of town, and is reached by a winding flight of steps. On the way is the 13th-century church of St Nicholas (Sv. Nikola). A path leads out to the wooded

peninsula, from where there are fine views out to sea, with the islands of Šolta, Brač and Hvar clearly visible. You can also find the best beaches in Split in this pleasant area.

Environs
Seven Castles (Kaštela) is the name given to a series of fortifications built by the Venetian governor and local nobles to defend the town against the Turks between the end of the 15th century and the 16th century, between Split and Trogir. The village of Kaštela grew up around the complex. Five of the original castles are still preserved, as are the fortified villas which rose from their reconstruction.

St George's Castle (Kaštel Sućurac), the summer residence of the bishop of Split, was built at the end of the 14th century and strengthened the following century by building a wall, of which some traces remain.

Abbess Castle (Kaštel Gomilica) was built on an island which is now linked to the mainland.

Vitturi Castle (Kaštel Lukšić) was transformed into a large villa, keeping only the old external structure. It was built by the Vitturi family, who donated a sculpture by Juraj Dalmatinac to the church of St Raynerius (Sv. Arnir). **Old Castle** (Kaštel Stari) has kept its original aspect; the sea-facing side looks like a palace with Gothic windows.

All that remains of the **New Castle** (Kaštel Novi) are the tower and St Roch church, built by the Čipiko family.

The stadium of the Hajduk football team, built in 1979 in the suburb of Poljud

Šolta ⓲

Map D5. 👥 *1,400.* ⛴ *from Split.*
🛈 *Grohote, (021) 654 657.*
www.visitsolta.com

This long island, indented
with bays and coves, covers
an area of 57 sq km (22 sq
miles). The economy is based
on agriculture thanks to
reasonably fertile soil and,
over recent years, tourism has
also become important. The
Romans called the island
Solenta and it was a holiday
resort for the nobility of
Salona. The ruins of many
villas can be found in lovely
locations on the island.

After the attack on Salona
in 614, some of the refugees
fled here and villages were
built. Some still have small
churches dating from the
early Middle Ages. The island
was later abandoned in favour
of Split, due to constant
Turkish raids – though some
refugees from the mainland
did settle here. Near
Stomorska, Grohote, Donje
Selo and Nečujam, traces of
defence towers can be seen.

Many people from Split
have holiday homes here.

Brač ⓳

Map D5. 👥 *14,000.* ✈ *(021) 559*
711. ⛴ *to Supetar from Split.* 🚌
(060) 393 060. **Supetar** 🛈 *Porat 1,*
(021) 630 551. **www**.supetar.hr
Bol 🛈 *Porat bolskih pomoraca bb,*
(021) 635 638. **www**.bol.hr

The third largest island in the
Adriatic at 40 km (25 miles)
long and 15 km (9 miles)
wide, Brač has an interesting

Bol's famous golden beach, changing with the tides

geological structure. In some
areas the ranges of limestone
hills have sinkholes and are
cut by ravines and gorges. In
other areas a white, hard stone
prevails. The stone has been
quarried since ancient times
(see p134) and is still much
sought after. Extensive woods
cover some parts of the island
and other areas are cultivated.

Although Brač has always
been inhabited, it was first
subject to Salona (the rich
Salonians built villas and
also sought refuge here when
their town was attacked by
the Avars), and then to Split.
Both Split and Brač came
under Byzantine and then
Venetian rule. Under the
Venetians (1420–1797),
villages were built in
the interior but no
defences were built to
prevent the pirates
and Turks landing.

Ferries from Split
on the mainland dock
at the old town of
Supetar, which has
some good beaches.

To the southwest
lies the town of **Milna**,

which was founded at the
beginning of the 18th century
and faces a sheltered bay.
The exterior of the church of
the Annunciation of Mary
(Gospa od Blagovijesti) is
Baroque and the interior is
decorated in the Rococo style.

Nerežišća, in the centre of
the island, was for a long
period the main town. The
Governor's Palace, the Loggia
and a pedestal with the lion
of St Mark are signs of its
former status.

The major attraction at **Bol**,
on the southern coast, is its
famous long beach (Zlatni
Rat, meaning Golden Horn), a
triangular spit of shingle which
reaches out into the sea and

The town of Pučišća on the island of Brač

KEY

▬	Major road
▬	Minor road
⛴	Ferry
✈	Airport
🛈	Tourist information
🏖	Beach with facilities

ŠOLTA
Maslinica — 111 — Grohote — Stomorska
Supetar
Škrip
Milna — 114
Nerežišća — 113
Pučišća — Povlja
Selca
BRAČ — 115
Sumartin — 113
Bol

0 kilometres   10

0 miles   10

changes shape with the seasonal tides. It is a popular spot for windsurfing.

A Dominican monastery, founded in 1475, stands on a headland at the edge of the village. The beautiful church is decorated with paintings, including a *Virgin with Saints* attributed to Tintoretto. A rich treasury includes liturgical objects. From Bol you can climb up **Mount St Vitus** (Vidova Gora), a two-hour walk to one of the highest peaks in the Dalmatian islands (778 m/2,552 ft), near which a fortified monastery (Samostan Blaca) clings to rocks.

In **Pučišća** quarrymen can be seen at work and the Roman quarries where they extracted stone can also be visited. The blocks were loaded onto ships at the port. Pučišća is a charming spot similar to **Sumartin**, further east, which was founded by refugees from the coastal region of Makarska fleeing the Turks in 1645. There is a fine Franciscan monastery, the foundations of which were laid by the poet Andrija Kačić Miošić.

Škrip is probably the site of the first settlement on the island and the presumed birthplace of Helen, mother of Emperor Constantine. The church and a painting by Palma il Giovane on the main altar are dedicated to Helen.

A fortified house houses **Brač Museum** and exhibits archaeological finds, evidence of mankind's ancient presence on the island.

🏛 Brač Museum
Škrip. 📞 *(021) 637 092.*
🕐 *summer: 8am–8pm daily;*
winter: by appt.

KEY

━━ Minor road

🛥 Ferry

ℹ Tourist information

🏖 Beach with facilities

Vis ㉒

Map D6. 🏘 *4,300.* **Vis** 🛥 *(021) 711 032.* ℹ *Šetalište Stare Isse 5, (021) 717 017.* **Komiža** ℹ *(021) 713 455.*

Further out in the Adriatic than the other Dalmatian islands, Vis was until 1989 a military base and closed to tourism. Now gradually being rediscovered by intrepid travellers, it has a jagged coastline with beaches, and an inland mountain chain with Mount Hum reaching a height of 587 m (1,925 ft).

The island was chosen by Dionysios of Syracuse as a base for Greek domination of the Adriatic. The Greeks founded the town of Issa here. Later the island was ruled by the Romans, then Byzantines and, from 1420, the Venetians.

The island played a key role during World War II – in 1944 Marshal Tito used it as a base for co-ordinating partisan

The façade of the church of Our Lady of Spilica in Vis

military operations. The cave is still called "Tito's Cave". Crucial meetings between partisans, the Yugoslav government in exile and the Allies were also held on Vis.

The main town of **Vis** has Venetian Gothic buildings and the Renaissance church of Our Lady of Spilica (Gospa od Spilica), with a painting by Girolamo di Santacroce. In the town of **Komiža**, there is a castle built by the Venetians.

Environs
The **island of Biševo**, to the southwest of Vis, has a Blue Grotto (Modra Spilja), where, at midday, the water takes on beautiful colours. Day trips by boat to the cave depart from Komiža and Vis in the morning (contact the Tourist Office).

A monastery was built here around 1000 AD, which resisted raids by pirates and Saracens for 200 years. The ruins remain, along with a 12th-century church.

Part of the coastline near Komiža, on the island of Vis

Hvar ㉑

Art treasures, a mild climate, good beaches and
fields of scented lavender make this island one of the
treasures of the Adriatic. Limestone hills form the
central ridge. Hvar's story begins in the 4th century BC
when the Greeks from Paros founded Pharos (the
present-day Stari Grad) and Dimos (Hvar). Traces have
been left by the Romans, the Byzantines, the Croatian
sovereigns and the Venetians, who ruled from 1278
until 1797. After 1420, defences were built, and the
capital was moved from Pharos to Hvar. In 1886, under
Austria-Hungary, the "Hvar Hygienic Society" began to
promote the town as a health resort. It is also the
birthplace of a number of famous people: the painter
Juraj Plančić (1899–30), and writer and art critic Tonko
Maroević (b. 1941), a Croat intellectual.

Main square of Hvar, with the
Cathedral of St Stephen

A peaceful bay on the island of Hvar

Hvar Town

This town is one of the most
visited on the Dalmatian
coast, thanks to the treasures
within its walls (1278). During
Venetian rule, governors and
local nobles decided to make
it a safe harbour for the fleets
going to, or returning from,
the Orient. They also
transferred the bishopric
and built monasteries.

Hvar has a long tradition of
art and culture and one of
the first theatres ever built in
Europe is here. It was also
the birthplace of the

Renaissance poet Hanibal
Lucić (c.1485–1553), and the
playwright Martin Benetović
(died 1607).

The town's most important
buildings stand on three sides
of the main square: the fourth
is open to the sea. The
Renaissance **Cathedral of
St Stephen** (Katedrala Sv.
Stjepana) has a trefoil
pediment and a 17th-century
bell tower standing to one
side. The interior houses
many works of art: *Virgin
and Saints* by Palma il

Giovane (1544–1628), *Pietà*
by Juan Boschetus, *Virgin
with Saints* by Domenico
Uberti and a fine 16th-century
wooden choir.

The **Clock Tower**, the **Civic
Loggia** below and **Hektorović
Palace** (Hektorovićeva
Palača), recognizable by the
beautiful Venetian-Gothic
mullioned window, all date
from the 15th century.

On the south side of the
square is the **Arsenal**, which
dates from the late 16th
century. A theatre was built
on the first floor in 1612, the
first "public theatre" in the
Balkans. People of all classes
could come and see drama
here, regardless of their
social standing.

Outside the walls of the
old town is the **Franciscan
Monastery** (Franjevački
Samostan) dating from 1461
and the church of **Our Lady
of Charity** (Gospa od Milosti),
with a relief on the façade by
Nikola Firentinac. Inside are
two paintings by Palma il
Giovane (*St Francis receiving
the Stigmata* and
St Diego), three polyptychs
by Francesco da Santacroce,
a *Christ on the Cross* by
Leandro da Bassano, and
six scenes inspired by the

A field of lavender on the island of Hvar

VISITORS' CHECKLIST

Map D–E5. 🚶 11,500. 🚢 Split, Drvenik. **Hvar** 🚢 (021) 741 007; Jadrolinija: (021) 741 132. 🛈 Trg Svetog Stjepana bb, (021) 741 059. **Stari Grad** 🚢 (021) 765 060; Jadrolinija: (021) 765 048. 🛈 Obala dr. Franje Tudmana 1: (021) 765 763. **Sućuraj** 🚢 (021) 773 228.
🛈 (021) 717 288. **www**.tzhvar.hr

Passion of Christ by Martin Benetović. There are also many works of art in the rooms facing the cloister. The painting of the *Last Supper* in the refectory is of uncertain attribution – possibly Matteo Ingoli, Matteo Ponzone or the school of Palma il Giovane. There are splendid views from the 16th-century Španjola fort and from the Napoleon fort (1811).

The cloister of the Franciscan monastery, outside Hvar

Stari Grad

This town was originally called Pharos and was founded by the Syracusans in the 4th century BC (remains can be seen in Ciklopska ulica). Around Pod Dolom are the ruins of a Roman villa with mosaic floors. Stari Grad lies at the end of a long bay and the main sights are situated around the main square. Facing the square are the 17th-century church of **St Stephen** (Sv. Stjepan) and the

Baroque **Bianchini Palace** (Biankini Palača), the home of a **Nautical Collection**.

The heart of the town is dominated by **Kaštel Tvrdalj**, the fortified residence of Petar Hektorović which has a seawater fishpond. An Ethnographic Collection is now housed in the fort. Hektorović, a humanist poet, built the fort in around 1520. He was the author of the poem *Ribanje i ribarsko prigovaranje (Fishing and Fishermen's Conversation)* in which he vividly describes a fishing trip around the islands of Hvar, Brač and Šolta in which he took part.

The **Dominican Monastery** (Dominikanski Samostan), founded in 1482 and rebuilt and fortified after destruction by the Turks, has a rich library and a collection of paintings. In the town there is also an International School of Painting and Sculpture run by Professor Emil Tanay, for young people and postgraduates.

Kaštel Tvrdalj, Stari Grad

🔒 **Dominican Monastery**
Tel (021) 765 442. ⏰ Jun–Sep: 10am–noon, 4–8pm; Oct–May: by appt.

Vrboska

The road leading to this small village offers a marvellous sight in June: vast fields of scented lavender.

Vrboska is home to the 16th-century church of **St Mary** (Sv. Marija), fortified in 1575 to provide shelter for villagers in the event of a siege. The Baroque church of **St Lawrence** (Sv. Lovro) has a polyptych on the main altar by Paolo Veronese (c.1570) and a *Virgin of the Rosary* by Leandro da Bassano.

Sućuraj

Lying in a sheltered bay is this village with the remains of a castle built by the Venetians in around 1630.

Environs

The **Pakleni Islands**, facing the town of Hvar, are uninhabited and mostly woodland. Their name derives from the resin *(paklina)* at one time extracted from the pines and used to waterproof boats. During the summer boat trips to the islands depart from Hvar. The nearest island, Jerolim, is given over to naturism.

The island of **Šćedro**, south of Hvar, is covered in pines and maquis. Illyrian tombs and parts of a Roman villa have been found here.

KEY

▬	Major road
▬	Minor road
🚢	Ferry
🛈	Tourist information
🏖	Beach with facilities

Boating on the river in the Cetina Valley Nature Park

Omiš ㉒

Map D5. ㈜ *6,100.* ▦ *(021) 864 210.* ▦ *(021) 861 025.* ⓘ *Trg Kneza Miroslava bb, (021) 861 350.* **www**.tz-omis.hr ◈ *Festival Klapa (Jul).*

In the late Middle Ages Omiš was known as the residence of the terrifying corsairs who fought fiercely against Venetian rule from the 12th century until 1444, when the town fell to Venice. Today it is a peaceful holiday resort with some light industry along the coast, and the starting point for visits to the valley of the River Cetina.

In July, the Dalamatinksa Klapa festival attracts many visitors who come to hear Klapa, a kind of plainsong traditional to Dalmatia. It is still very popular, even among the young.

Only a few traces of the Roman *municipium* of Onaeum remain but many of the medieval defences built by the counts of Kačić and Bribir are still visible on a hill, once the site of the Old Town, or Starigrad. These consist of the walls going down to the River Cetina and also the ruins of a large fort (Fortica) with its distinctive high tower. From the fort, built between the 16th and the 17th centuries, there is a splendid view of Omiš and the central Dalmatian islands.

The church of St Peter in Priko, a district of Omiš

There are three interesting religious buildings in the town. One is the Renaissance church of **St Michael** (Sv. Mihovil) with a pointed bell tower, originally a defensive structure. Inside is a 16th-century wooden altar, a large 13th-century wooden cross and two paintings by Matteo Ingoli of Ravenna (1587–1631). At the end of the main road is the 16th-century **Oratory of the Holy Spirit** (Sv. Duh) with *Descent of the Holy Spirit* by Palma il Giovane (1544–1628).

However, the most fascinating monument here is in Priko, on the opposite bank of the River Cetina. This is the 10th-century church of **St Peter** (Sv. Petar), one of the most appealing pre-Romanesque churches in Dalmatia. It has a single nave, a dome and remains from the early Christian period incorporated into the walls.

Environs
The **Cetina Valley Nature Park**, immediately behind Omiš, shelters a river which flows into the artificial lake of Peruča. The river runs out of the lake and parallel to the coast for some distance and then, near Zadvarje, abruptly turns and cascades down before flowing into a narrow gorge. This beautiful natural environment, with its myriad bird species, can be explored on foot or by bicycle, but the most popular way to see it is to take one of the many boats through the park.

Makarska ㉓

Map E5. ㈜ *14,000.* ▦ *Ulica Ante Starčevića, (021) 612 333.* ▦ *(021) 611 977.* ⓘ *Obala Kralja Tomislava bb, (021) 612 002.* **www**.makarska-info.hr

The Makarska coast extends from Brela to Gradac and includes a long stretch of shore with lush vegetation sheltered by the Biokovo massif. Makarska, one of Dalmatia's most popular mainland resorts, lies within a bay sheltered by the peninsula of St Peter's. The town was the site of the Roman Mucurum, which was destroyed by the Goths in

The Makarska coast, with white beaches and a mountainous backdrop

THE VINEYARDS OF DALMATIA

Vines are grown all along the coast of Dalmatia, and on many of the islands. Vineyards first start appearing around Primošten, near Trogir *(see p111)*, where the good quality red wine Babić is made, and become part of the landscape along the Makarska coast. Built on stony hillsides, these vineyards are often "fortified" with low dry-stone walls, painstakingly constructed with geometrical precision by peasant farmers. Low-growing vines cultivated inside the walls are protected from the cold north winds and kept cool in the hot summer months. A monument to human toil, the result of immense patience and effort, without these walls it would not be possible to cultivate this difficult ground.

Vines protected by dry-stone walls

The beach at Gradac, one of the longest in the eastern Adriatic

The Franciscan monastery, Makarska, now a museum

548, and rebuilt at a later date. It belonged to the Kingdom of Croatia until 1499, when it was conquered by the Turks, for whom it was a port and trading centre until 1646, the beginning of Venetian rule.

There are two ancient monasteries in Makarska. St Philip Neri (Sv. Filipa Nerija) was built in 1757, and has medieval and Roman-era fragments in the cloister. The Franciscan monastery (Franjevački Samostan), built in 1614 on the foundations of a 15th-century monastery, houses the **Malacological Museum** (Malakološki Muzej), with a collection of mollusc shells.

The centre of the modern town is the square called Brother Andrija Kačić Miošić

(1704–60), dedicated to the Dalmatian scholar and author of theological and philosophical works. Two seafront promenades extend towards the wide beaches and Kalelarga, where there are 18th-century buildings.

🏛 **Malacological Museum**
Franjevački put 1.
Tel (021) 611 256.

Gradac ㉔

Map E5. 🏠 *1,200.*
🔢 *(021) 697 375 (high season only).*
www.gradac.hr

This town's fame and popularity are due to the fact that it has one of the longest beaches in the eastern Adriatic. Over 6 km (4 miles) long, the beach is lined with hotels and camping sites.

In the town itself there are two large 17th-century towers while nearby, in Crkvine, the remains of a Roman staging post between Mucurum (the present-day Makarska) and Narona *(see p130)* have been found. Gradac gets its name from the fort (grad) built in the 17th century to defend the town against the Turks.

Environs
In **Zaostrog**, 14 km (8 miles) northwest of Gradac, is a Franciscan monastery (Franjevački Samostan) founded in the 16th century and completed a century later. The façade of the church has an inscription written in Cyrillic script. In the rooms around the beautiful cloister there is a fascinating folklore collection, an art gallery, and a library and archive where documents about the period of Turkish occupation are kept. The scholar Andrija Kačić Miošić *(see Makarska, p128–9)* lived and died in the monastery.

Around 20 km (12 miles) from Gradac, towards Makarska, is **Živogošće**, one of the oldest settlements on the Makarska coast. Today it is a busy tourist resort, but it was once famous for a spring which flowed from the rocks.

A Franciscan monastery was founded near this spring in 1616, and its beautiful church boasts an ornate Baroque altar. The monastery is famous for its well-stocked library and archives, which are the main source for the study of the area around the Biokovo massif.

Franciscan monastery, Zaostrog

The delta of the River Neretva in Opuzen, drained and turned into fertile fields

Opuzen ㉕

Map E6. 🏛 *2,800.* 🚌 *Metković, (060) 365 365.* 🛈 *Trg Kralja Tomislava 1, (020) 671 651.* **www**.tz-opuzen.hr

At the edges of the delta of the River Neretva, where the road leaves the Magistrala coast road (E65) and climbs the river valley, stands Opuzen. For centuries it was fortified and has always been considered something of a border town.

Towards the end of the 15th century, the Hungarian-Croat king, Matthias Corvinus, built the fort of Koš here. It was captured by the Turks in 1490 who ruled until 1686, when it came under Venetian rule. There are also traces of a 13th-century castle built by the Republic of Dubrovnik and the remains of a fort (Fort Opus), built by the Venetians to defend the border of their territories. The town takes its name from this fort and the ruins can be seen on the eastern side of town.

In the entrance hall of the former Town Hall are some fragments discovered in the ancient town of Narona.

Narona ㉖

Map E6. 🚌 *Metković, (060) 365 365.* 🛈 *(020) 691 596.* **www**.a-m-narona.hr

The ancient Roman town of Colonia Julia Narona was founded by the Romans in the 2nd century BC. It was an important road junction and a trading centre with the Pannonian hinterland, and had temples, baths, a theatre and other buildings grouped around the Forum. A walled town, it was one of the first dioceses in the Balkans and flourished until the 7th century when it was occupied and destroyed by the Avars. It fell into disuse afterwards.

At the end of the 19th century, after a few chance discoveries, the Austrian archaeologist Karl Patsch began to carry out excavations. Work continued after World War II and uncovered numerous finds from pagan and Christian temples, houses and public works. In 1995, a particularly fine temple was discovered. Large parts of the area still have to be explored, but it is possible to get an idea of the importance of the

Head of Emperor Vespasian, now in Vid's Museum

town by visiting the Archaeological Museum in **Vid**. This village stands on much of the site of ancient Narona, 3 km (2 miles) from Metković. In the museum are statues of gods and emperors, as well as weapons and jewels that were found in Narona. Other finds are in Split's Archaeological Museum *(see p123).*

The 16th-century church of St Vitus (Sv. Vid) stands just outside the town on the site of an old church, of which only parts of the apse remain.

Neum ㉗

Bosnia-Herzegovina. **Map** E6. 🏛 *2,500.* 🚌 *Metković, (060) 365 365.* **www**.neum.ba

All the buses running along the coastal road between Split and Dubrovnik pass through the 9-km (5-mile) stretch of coast that is part of Bosnia-Herzegovina. The main town in this area is Neum, which is a holiday resort and Bosnia's only coastal town. Prices are cheaper here than in Croatia, and as a result it is a popular place for Croatians to stop off and go shopping.

Neum is a border town, and visitors should carry passports. There are several hotels and tourist facilities.

Pelješac Peninsula ㉘

Map E6. ▦ *Metković, (060) 365 365.* **Ston** ▦ *580.* ▦ *(020) 754 026.* ⓘ *Pelješka Cesta 2, (020) 754 452.* **www**.ston.hr **Orebić** ▦ *2,500.* ▦ *(020) 743 542 (Trpanj).* ⓘ *Zrinsko Frankopanska 2, (020) 713 718.* **www**.visitorebic-croatia.hr

The peninsula of Pelješac juts out 65 km (40 miles) from the mainland, but it is only 7 km (4 miles) wide at its broadest point. A mountain chain forms its backbone, which peaks at Mount St Elijah (961 m/3,152 ft). The slopes and plain are covered with vineyards and fruit trees, and the shallow coastal waters are given over to oyster farming.

The peninsula was first colonized by the Greeks, then by the Romans and later by the Byzantines. From 1333 to 1808 it belonged to Dubrovnik.

The Pelješac coast, a centre for oyster farming

Ston

The town closest to the mainland, Ston was formerly called Stagnum because of its shallow waters. There have been salt pans here since the time of the Romans, who built a *castrum* on the site. It was enclosed by walls prior to 1000 AD.

The present defensive walls, still impressive above the town, were begun in the 14th century and completed in the 15th century on Dubrovnik's orders. There are more than 5 km (3 miles) of walls climbing from Veliki Ston, the main heart of the town, to St Michael's Mount and descending the opposite slope until they reach Mali Ston. The 41 towers, seven bastions and two forts make this one of the largest and most interesting defensive structures in the Adriatic and indeed the world. Some of the best military architects such as Michelozzo Michelozzi, Župan Bunić, Bernardino of Parma, Juraj Dalmatinac and Paskoje Miličević contributed to its design and construction. The walls are still in good condition despite being bombed in 1991 and struck by an earthquake in 1996.

The main structures are at **Veliki Ston**, which is built on an irregular pentagonal ground plan. The buildings include the largest fort (Veliki Kaštio), the Neo-Gothic church of St Blaise (Sv. Vlaho), built in 1870 to replace a cathedral from the 14th century which was destroyed by the earthquake of 1850, the Governor's Palace (Knežev Dvor), enlarged in the same century and the Bishop's Palace (1573). The **Church and Franciscan Monastery of St Nicholas** (Sv. Nikola) was built between the end of the 14th century and the 16th century.

Mali Ston, the other focus of the town, is dominated by Fort Koruna, which dates from 1347, with two arsenals and a fortified warehouse for storing salt. There are wonderful views across the peninsula to the north of the town from here.

The Franciscan monastery between Orebić and Lovište

Orebić

Towards the tip of the peninsula, Orebić is the boarding point for ferries to Korčula. It has a **Maritime Museum** (Pomorski Muzej), which illustrates the history of its inhabitants, who were the most sought-after sea captains in the Mediterranean. At the end of their careers these seamen invested in villas along the coast or in the hills.

Just outside the village, towards Lovište, is a massive **Franciscan Monastery** (Franjevački Samostan), founded in the 15th century. In the church alongside are two reliefs: one is a *Virgin with Child* by Nikola Firentinac (1501), who was a pupil of Donatello.

🏛 Maritime Museum
Trg Mimbelli bb. **Tel** *(020) 713 009.* ☐ *Jun–Sep: 9am–noon, 5–8pm daily; Oct–May: 7am–2:30pm Mon– Fri.* 📷

Overlooking the circle of walls connecting the two parts of Ston

Korčula ㉙

Gothic relief in All Saints' Church

Dense forests of aleppo pine, cypress and oak are found all over this island, one of the largest in the Adriatic at 47 km (29 miles) long. Mountains run the length of the island, reaching 560 m (1,837 ft) at their peak. Inhabited since prehistoric times, the Greeks named the island Korkyra Melaina (Black Corfu). After 1000 AD, it was fought over by Venice and the Croat kings and later by the Genoese and the Turks (in the 1298 naval battle between Genoa and Venice, the Genoese captured Marco Polo, said to be a native of the island). Today it is a popular holiday spot for its cliffs and sandy beaches, its villages and Korčula, its main town.

VISITORS' CHECKLIST

Map E6. 🏘 *17,000.* 🚢 *from Orebić, Split and Rijeka.* **Korčula** 🚌 *(020) 711 216.* 🚢 *(020) 715 410.* ℹ *Obala dr. Tuđmana 4, (020) 715 701.* **www**.visit korcula.net 🎭 *Moreška, 9pm Mon & Thu in summer.* **Lumbarda** ℹ *(020) 712 005.* **Blato** ℹ *Trg dr. Franje Tuđmana 4, (020) 851 850.* 🎭 *St Vincenca's Day (28 Apr).* **Vela Luka** 🚌 *(020) 812 023.* ℹ *Obala 3 br 19, (020) 813 619.* **www**.tzvelaluka.hr

The Land Gate, main entrance to the old town of Korčula

Korčula Town

The town is perched on a peninsula, surrounded by strong 13th-century walls, reinforced with towers and bastions by the Venetians after 1420. The whole town is enchanting. The **Land Gate** (Kopnena Vrata) was fortified by a huge tower, the Revelin, which overlooked a canal dug by the Venetians to isolate the town. There are now steps in this area. Narrow streets branching off the main road are designed to lessen the impact of the bora wind.

Facing **Strossmayerov trg**, the central square, is the town's main monument: the 13th-century **Cathedral of St Mark** (Katedrala Sv. Marka), built in pale, honey-coloured stone. Most of it dates from the end of the 15th century. The skill of Korčula's sculptors and stone masons is evident in the door, where two lions guard the entrance, decorated with thin spiral columns and a lunette with the figure of St Mark, attributed to Bonino of Milan. Two further doors open onto the side aisles. On the left stands an imposing bell tower.

Inside are large columns with elaborately decorated capitals and several important sculptural works: a 15th-century holy water stoup, a font from the 17th century, and the tomb of Bishop Toma Malumbra, attributed to the workshop of Marko Andrijić, who also made the ciborium in the presbytery in 1481. There is also a statue of St Blaise by Ivan Meštrović. The paintings include *St Mark with St Jerome and St Bartholomew* by Tintoretto. On a wall are trophies recalling the Battle of Lepanto of 1571.

Next to the cathedral, in the Bishop's Palace, now the Abbot's House, is the **Abbey Treasury** (Opatska Riznica), which is particularly known for its Dalmatian and Venetian art, including a

Impressive entrance to the Gothic Cathedral of St Mark, Korčula

KEY

▬	Major road
▬	Minor road
🚢	Ferry
ℹ	Tourist information
🏖	Beach with facilities

Korčula, the main town on the island, on an isthmus on the northeast coast

polyptych by Blaž of Trogir, two altar paintings by Pellegrino of San Daniele, a *Sacred Conversation* by Titian, a *Portrait of a Man* by Vittore Carpaccio and an *Annunciation* by Titian. A door by Bonino of Milan decorates the Gothic church of **St Peter** (Sv. Petar) to the left of the cathedral. Facing St Peter are the Gothic **Arneri Palace** and the Renaissance Gabriellis Palace (16th century). The latter has been the **Civic Museum** (Gradski Muzej) since 1957 and contains documents on Korčula's seafaring history, an interesting archaeological section covering the period from prehistoric to Roman times and other works of art.

Along the seafront is **All Saints' Church** (Svi Sveti), built in 1301 and remodelled in the Baroque style, which belongs to the oldest brotherhood on the island. Inside is an 18th-century carved wooden *Pietà*, by the Austrian artist George Raphael Donner, and a 15th-century polyptych by Blaž of Trogir.

In the nearby quarters of the brotherhood is the **Icon Gallery** (Galerija Ikona), which is famous for its rich collection of Byzantine icons from the 13th to 15th centuries, many from Crete.

Outside the walls are the **Church and Monastery of St Nicholas** (Sv. Nikola), from the 15th century, with many paintings by Dalmatian and Italian artists.

🏛 **Abbey Treasury**
Trg Sv. Marka.
ℹ *(020) 711 049.* ◯ *call for information.* 📷

🏛 **Civic Museum**
Trg Sv. Marka. **Tel** *(020) 711 420.*
◯ *Apr–Jun: 10am–2pm Mon–Sat; Jul–Sep: 9am–9pm Mon–Sat; Oct–Mar: 10am–1pm; by appt Sun.*

🏛 **Icon Gallery**
Trg Svih Svetih.
ℹ *(020) 711 306 or (091) 593 1281.* ◯ *summer: 10am–2pm, 5–8pm Mon–Sat; Sun & winter: by appt.*

ANCIENT DANCES AND FESTIVALS

The Moreška and the Kumpanjija are Korčula's two most noted folk festivals. Officially, the Moreška sword dance takes place in Korčula on 29 July, the patron saint's day (St Theodore). However, it is repeated on Mondays and Thursdays during the summer for tourists. It commemorates the clash between Christians and Moors in the attempt to free a girl kidnapped by the infidels. In Blato, the Kumpanjija dance is dedicated to the patron saint, St Vincenca, and is celebrated with drum music. At the end of the battle, girls in bright costumes appear, accompanied by pipes and drums. The dance takes place in front of the church on 28 April and is performed once a week for tourists who visit Blato.

Actors performing the ancient Moreška sword dance

Račišće
KORČULA
Pupnat
Korčula
118
Žrnovo
Lumbarda
Pupnatska Luka
118
...ra
...valatica

0 kilometres   5
0 miles   5

The sea and rocky coastline of Korčula

Lumbarda

Lumbarda is a village 6 km (4 miles) southeast of the town of Korčula and is thought to have been founded by Greeks from Vis. It was called Eraclea by the Romans. In the 16th century it became a holiday resort for the nobles of Korčula. Some inscriptions from the Greek period are now in the Archaeological Museum of Zagreb *(see pp162–3).*

Today this village is one of the centres of production for the liqueur-like, white wine called Grk, which is made from grapes of the same name grown in the sand. The nearby small beaches are havens of tranquillity.

Blato

In the central square of Blato, a town where the festival of the Kumpanija *(see p133)* is held every April, are an 18th-century Baroque loggia, the Renaissance **Arneri Castle**, where the Civic Museum documenting local history is being set up, and **All Saints' Church** (Svi Sveti), of medieval origin. This church was enlarged and rebuilt in the 17th century and has an altarpiece of the *Virgin with Child and Saints* on the main altar by Girolamo

di Santacroce (1540) and, in the chapel, the relics of the martyr St Vincenza, the object of veneration in the local community. The cemetery church of the **Holy Cross** and that of **St Jerome** date from the 14th century.

Vela Luka

Situated about 45 km (28 miles) west of Korčula is Vela Luka, called "the oldest and the newest town", because it was built at the beginning of the 19th century on the neolithic site of Vela Spilja. It is one of the largest towns on the island and industries coexist with attractive bays and numerous islands.

The hills surrounding the town shelter this area from the winds from the north and south. Vela Luka is also the main port on the island and there are regular ferry services to Split and Lastovo.

Lumbarda on the island of Korčula, one of the greenest in the Adriatic

The ancient Roman quarries, Brač

THE STONE OF DALMATIA

The excellent quality of the stone in the Dalmatian islands was known to the Romans, who used it to build the monuments of Salona and Diocletian's Palace in Split. On Brač, the old Roman quarries are still visible in Pučišća. Brač stone was used for the cathedral in Šibenik *(see pp108–9),* for which Juraj Dalmatinac devised a method of cutting the stone so that blocks interlocked without mortar. Most of the palaces and churches in Venice are also made of Dalmatian stone. Further afield, part of the White House in Washington and the Royal Palace in Stockholm were faced with stone from Brač. In Korčula, quarrying ceased long ago, and stone cutting skills have largely died out. However, the quarries on the small island of Vrnik, facing Korčula, are still active and stone from here was used in the church of St Sophia in Istanbul, the Duke's Palace in Dubrovnik and the United Nations building in New York.

The Franciscan church and monastery on the island of Badija

Badija ③

Map E6.
🚤 *taxi-boats from Korčula.*
www.badija.com

This is the largest of the small islands, 1 sq km (0.4 sq m), in the archipelago surrounding the island of Korčula, and is covered with pines and cypress trees. It takes its name from the Franciscan monastery built here in 1392 for a community of monks who had fled from Bosnia. The monastery and church were enlarged in the following century and remained the property of the religious community until 1950, when it became a sports resort.

The church, whose furnishings have been transferred to the Civic Museum and the cathedral in Korčula, has a façade in pale-coloured stone and a large central rose window. The cloister is a good example of Gothic architecture at its most charming, with columns and arches.

The Loggia in the main square in Lastovo, venue for festivals

Lastovo ③

Map E6. 🏠 *800.* 🚢 *from Vela Luka (Island of Korčula), Dubrovnik during summer and from Split. Harbour Master: (020) 805 006.* ℹ *Pjevor bb, (020) 801 018.* **www**.lastovo.hr

The island of Lastovo, surrounded by about 40 small islands and rocky outcrops, was a military area and thus closed to tourists. The island is 9 km (5 miles) long and about 6 km (4 miles) wide. Although it is mostly mountainous terrain (Mount Hum reaches a height of 417 m/1,368 ft), vines, olives and fruit are cultivated on the terraced slopes. The coast is rocky apart from the bay close to the town of Lastovo.

Traces of the long period of rule by Dubrovnik (1252–1808) are visible in the upper part of the town and in the fort, built by the French in 1819 on the site of an earlier castle destroyed by Dubrovnik in 1606.

A church from the 14th century and a 16th-century loggia stand in the main square. Religious festivals are celebrated here.

Mention of the small church of **St Blaise** (Sv. Vlaho), situated at the entrance to the village, is found in 12th-century documents. Also of ancient origins, in the cemetery, is the Romanesque **Oratory of Our Lady in the Field** (Gospa od Polja) from the 15th century. Some remnants of buildings and rustic villas testify to the presence of the Romans on the island. The lack of tourism has helped to preserve the old buildings.

Religious holidays are very popular and celebrated with traditional dances with antique musical instruments. The locals wear brightly coloured traditional costumes.

Some of the many uninhabited, unspoilt islands in the sea around the island of Lastovo

Mljet National Park 32
Nacionalni Park Mljet

The island of Mljet, called Melita by the Romans and Meleda by the Venetians, covers an area of 98 sq km (37 sq miles). It is mountainous, with two limestone depressions in which there are two salt-water lakes linked by a channel. In Roman times Mljet was the holiday resort of the wealthy of Salona, who built villas here. Some ruins can still be seen. In 1151, Duke Desa gave the island to the Benedictines of Pulsano in Gargano (Italy), who founded a monastery here. Two centuries later Stjepan, the Ban (governor) of Bosnia, gave it to Dubrovnik, to which it belonged until 1815. In 1960 the western part was declared a national park to save the forest of Aleppo pine and holm oak.

Roman Palatium
In Polače lie the ruins of a Roman settlement named Palatium, including the remains of a large villa and an early Christian basilica and thermae.

Monastery of St Mary
In the centre of Big Lake (Veliko Jezero) is a small island with a 12th-century Benedictine monastery, remodelled in the 1500s. Although currently being restored, it can still be visited.

Big Lake (Veliko Jezero)
The lake covers an area of 1.45 sq km (320 acres) and reaches a depth of 46 m (150 ft). A channel links the lake to the sea, and another channel links it to a smaller lake, Malo Jezero.

National Park
The area of 31 sq km (12 sq miles) is almost entirely forested. The park is home to wild boar, deer, hares, lizards and many bird species.

0 kilometres 3

0 miles 3

VISITORS' CHECKLIST

Map E6. 🏛 *1,300.* 🚢 *from
Dubrovnik.* **Goveđari**
ℹ️ *Polače, (020) 744 086.*
National Park ℹ️ *(020) 744
041.* 🏞 🗓 **www**.mljet.hr
*The park can be visited on foot
or by bicycle following the trails.
Boats must be authorized – call
information office for details.*

Marine Life
*Dozens of species of fish, including grouper,
inhabit the underwater ravines and caves along
the coast. The most valued creature is the
endangered monk seal, protected in these waters.*

The village of Babino Polje
was founded in around the
middle of the 10th century by
a group of refugees from the
mainland. The governor's
residence was built in 1554
when the island became part
of the territory of the Republic
of Ragusa (now Dubrovnik).

Saplunara
*Saplunara lies at the
southernmost point of
the island and boasts the
most beautiful beach in
the area. It has been
declared a nature
reserve for its lush
vegetation.*

Sobra   ℹ️   Prožura
Okuklje
Korita
Maranovići   120
Saplunara

Uninhabited Islands
*Nature is left undisturbed on these islands,
with woods of pine, holm oak and oak going
right down to the rocky shore.*

Fishing Villages
*The island's ancient stone
villages are inhabited
mainly by farmers and
fishermen. These villages
and the delightful bays
and coves around the
island are lovely places in
which to spend time.*

KEY

▬	Minor road
═	Path
—	Park border
ℹ️	Tourist information
🏖	Beach with facilities

A secluded beach on the island of Mljet ▷

Street-by-Street: Dubrovnik ❸

Detail of the door of the Rector's Palace

Set in the limpid waters of the Adriatic, Dubrovnik had been, until war broke out in 1991, one of the top international tourist destinations of Dalmatia, renowned for the beauty of its monuments, its magnificent walls and welcoming atmosphere. According to Emperor Constantine Porphyrogenitus it was founded by fugitives from Roman Epidaurum (now Cavtat) in the 7th century. It came under Byzantine and Venetian (1205–1358) rule, and attained formal independence after 1382, when it became the Republic of Ragusa. In the 15th and 16th centuries its fleet numbered over 500 ships. Artistically it flourished and its wealth was greatly influenced by the discovery of America and new trade routes. Much of the old town centre dates from the rebuilding that took place after the earthquake of 1667.

★ Rector's Palace
The highest level of city government met here. The rector lived here during his period of office, which was limited to one month.

★ Cathedral Treasury
The provenance of the objects here clearly demonstrates how the Dubrovnik merchants developed trading relations with the principal cities of the Mediterranean. The Treasury has works from the Byzantine, Middle Eastern, Apulian and Venetian schools. There are gold and enamel objects and also paintings by great artists.

LUČARICA   GUNDULIĆEVA POLJANA

PRED. DVO

POLJANA MARINA DRŽIĆA

KNEZA DAMJANA JU

KEY

- - - - Suggested route

View of Dubrovnik
Lovely views of Dubrovnik can be seen from the coast about 2 km (1 mile) to the south, where there is an elevated terrace. From here you can look over the entire city and its walls.

Church of St Blaise
This 16th-century church was rebuilt in the following century. At the beginning of the 18th century, it was redesigned by Marino Groppelli.

Sponza Palace
Originating in the 16th century, today the palace houses the State Archives. On the lintel is a Latin inscription: "Falsifying and cheating with the weights is forbidden. While I am weighing the goods, God is measuring me".

VISITORS' CHECKLIST

Map F6. 🚶 43,000. ✈ Čilipi, (020) 773 377. 🚌 Obala pape Ivana Pavla 11, 44A, (060) 305 070. ⛴ Harbour Master: (020) 418 988; Jadrolinja: (020) 418 000. 🛈 **Local:** *Brsalje 5 (020) 323 887;* **Regional:** Vukovarska 17 (020) 324 999. 🎭 Dubrovnik Summer Festival (Jul–Aug).

...ciscan
...astery and
...ig Fountain
...ofrio

PRIJEKO

The outer city walls

...AČA

ZLATARSKA

SVETOG DOMINIKA

★ **Dominican Monastery**
Since its foundation in 1315, the monastery has played a leading role in cultural activities in the city. Important sculptors and architects played a part in its construction.

Ploče Gate
Next to the Dominican monastery is the Ploče Gate, which leads to the port. Goods arrived from, and were sent to, every port in the Mediterranean.

| 0 metres | 50 |
| 0 yards | 50 |

Fort of St John
To make the city impregnable, the governors employed the most important European architects of the time. This fortress was one of many bulwarks.

STAR SIGHTS

★ Cathedral Treasury

★ Dominican Monastery

★ Rector's Palace

Exploring Dubrovnik

From the autumn of 1991 until May 1992, Dubrovnik was the target of relentless, heavy bombing by Yugoslav troops. During this period over 2,000 bombs and guided missiles fell on Dubrovnik, damaging some of the most significant symbols of Dalmatian culture. Over half the houses and all the monuments were shelled. The war also hit the city's productivity, especially tourism, which suffered a dramatic decline for four years. Only after the Erdut Agreement of 1995 did life begin to return to normal. UNESCO and the European Union set up a special commission for the reconstruction of the city, and in a remarkably short space of time much of the damage has been repaired. Dubrovnik has now regained much of its former splendour and tourism is once again flourishing.

The solid Minčeta Tower, part of the wall defences

The splendid view from the impressive city walls

⛨ Walls
Gradske Zidine

ℹ️ *(020) 324 641.* ⏱ *Jun & Jul: 8am–7:30pm; Apr, May, Aug & Sep: 8am–6:30pm; Oct: 8am–5:30pm; Nov–Mar: 10am–3pm. Access to the walls near the Franciscan monastery in Poljana Paška Miličevića, the large square behind Pile Gate near the Dominican monastery.* 🏛

A symbol of Dubrovnik, the walls offer splendid views from the guards' walkway. They were built in the 10th century, with modifications in the 13th century. They were then reinforced at various times by great architects such as Michelozzo Michelozzi and Antonio Ferramolino.

The walls and ramparts are 1,940 m (6,363 ft) long and reach a height of 25 m (82 ft) in some parts. Those facing inland are up to 6 m (20 ft) wide and strengthened by an outer wall with ten semi-circular bastions. Other towers and the Fort of St John defend the part facing the Adriatic and the port. Completing the

defences to the east and west of the city are two fortresses: the Revelin and the fortress of Lovrijenac.

⛨ Pile Gate
Gradska Vrata Pile

This is the main entrance to the old fortified centre. The stone bridge leading to Pile Gate is from 1537. The bridge crosses a moat which is now a garden. The gate is a strong

Pile Gate, leading to the old town

defensive structure built on different levels. In a niche above the ogival arch stands a small statue of St Blaise, the patron saint of Dubrovnik, by Ivan Meštrović. In the ramparts between the inner and outer walls is a Gothic door dating from 1460.

⛨ Minčeta Tower
Tvrđava Minčeta

This is the most visited of the walls' defensive structures. It was designed by Michelozzo Michelozzi in 1461 and completed by Juraj Dalmatinac three years later. The semicircular tower is crowned by a second tower with embrasures at the top.

⛨ Ploče Gate
Vrata od Ploča

The gate faces a small port and is preceded by the polygonal **Asimov Tower**. Dating from the 1300s, the gate is reached by an imposing stone bridge. It is a complex structure with a double defence system.

A moat separates the gate and **Revelin Fort** (Tvrđava Revelin), designed in 1538 by Antonio Ferramolino. It was the last of the defences to be built. It is based on a pentagonal ground-plan and has massive walls enclosing three large rooms and a terrace. The city's art treasures were brought here for safety in times of difficulty because of the fort's strength.

🏰 Fort of St John
Tvrđava Sv. Ivana
Aquarium *Tel* (020) 323 978.
◐ Jun–Sep: 9am–9pm daily;
Oct–May: 9am–1pm Mon–Sat. 🖼
Maritime Museum *Tel* (020) 323
904. ◐ summer: 9am–6pm Tue–
Sun; winter: 9am–2pm Tue–Sun. 🖼
A chain once helped to
defend the harbour, stretching
from this fort to the island in
front and then across to the
Tower of St Luke (Kula Sv.
Luke) along the walls.

The upper areas of the fort
house the **Maritime Museum**
(Pomorski Muzej), where
the seafaring history of
Dubrovnik is told through
model ships, standards, prints,
diaries and portraits.

On the lower level is an
Aquarium (Akvarij) with an
assortment of Mediterranean
marine life, including sea
horses, symbol of the institution. At the top is the circular
Bokar Fort (Tvrđava Bokar),
built by Michelozzo Michelozzi.

⛲ Big Fountain of Onofrio
Velika Onofrijeva Fontana
This is one of the best-known
monuments in the city. It
stands in the square which

The Big Fountain of Onofrio (1438–44)

opens out immediately after
the Pile gate. It was built in
1438–44 by the Neapolitan
architect, Onofrio de la Cava,
who was also responsible for
designing the city's water
supply system. He
decided to draw
the water from the
River Dubrovačka
for this purpose. The
imposing fountain
once had two storeys,
but the upper level
was destroyed in the
earthquake of 1667.

Tucked between
the city walls and the
Franciscan monastery
is the **Church of St
Saviour** (Sv. Spas).
The façade of the
church is an example
of Venetian-Dalmatian
Renaissance
architecture, a style
dating from after
the earthquake
of 1520.

DUBROVNIK TOWN CENTRE

Big Fountain of Onofrio ⑥
Cathedral and Treasury ⑬
Church of St Blaise ⑪
Dominican Monastery ⑭
Dubrovnik Cable Car ⑮
Fort of St John ⑤
Franciscan Monastery ⑦
Minčeta Tower ③
Pile Gate ②
Ploče Gate ④

Rector's Palace ⑫
Sponza Palace ⑩
Stradùn (Placa) ⑧
Square of the Loggia ⑨
Walls ①

0 metres   150
0 yards   150

Key to Symbols *see back flap*

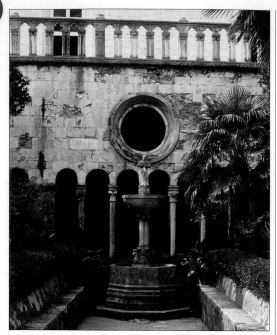

The lovely late Romanesque cloister, Franciscan monastery

⛪ Franciscan Monastery
Franjevački Samostan

Placa 2. **Tel** (020) 321 410. ⏰
summer: 9am–6pm daily; winter:
9am–5pm daily. **Franciscan
Museum** ⏰ Apr–Oct: 9am–6pm
daily; Nov–Mar: 9am–5pm daily. 📷

Construction of the monastery
began in 1317 and was
completed in the following
century. It was almost entirely
rebuilt after the earthquake in
1667, but the south door
(1499), in Venetian Gothic
decorated with a Pietà in the
lunette, and a 15th-century
marble pulpit escaped
damage. The cloister, which
was completely undamaged
by the earthquake, reveals
elements of the Romanesque
and the Gothic style and has
a fountain from the 15th
century in the centre.

One side of the cloister
leads to the **Pharmacy** (Stara
Ljekarna), in use since 1317,
where alembics, mortars,
measuring apparatus and
beautifully decorated jars are
displayed on the old shelves.

The capitular room of the
monastery houses the
Franciscan Museum (Muzej
Franjevačkog Samostana),
which has religious works of
art and objects belonging to
the order. Instruments from
the pharmaceutical laboratory
are kept here.

⛪ Stradun (Placa)

This wide street, which
crosses the city from east to
west between two city gates,
is known as Stradun or Placa.
It was constructed in the 12th
century by draining and filling
in the marshy channel that

Stradun, the main street of Dubrovnik

separated the island of
Ragusa from the mainland.
The street was paved in 1468
and a series of stone houses
was built after the earthquake
of 1667. Today the street is
lined with busy bars and
cafés, and is a popular place
for locals and visitors to
gather in the evening.

⛪ Square of the Loggia
Luža

This square, the political and
economic heart of Dubrovnik,
is situated at the eastern end
of Stradun and surrounded
by important buildings. Today
it is still a popular meeting
place, in particular around
Orlando's Column, which was
built by the sculptor Antonio
Ragusino (1418).

On the eastern side of the
square is a **Clock Tower**
(Gradski Zvonik). Repair
work carried out in 1929
restored a 15th-century look
to the Clock Tower. The
nearby **Loggia of the Bell**,
with four bells, dates from
1463. The bells were rung to
call the citizens to gather
whenever danger threatened.

Next to this stands the
Main Guard House, rebuilt in
1706 after the earthquake of
1667. It has a large Baroque
doorway, similar to a city
gate, and is enlivened on the
first floor by the Gothic
mullioned windows,
reminiscent of the earlier
building which was built in
the late 15th-century.

The **Small
Fountain of Onofrio**
(Mala Onofrijeva
Cesma), dating from
1438, stands alongside
the Guard House.

⛪ Sponza Palace
Palača Sponza

Tel (020) 321 032. ⏰ May–
Oct: 9am–10pm daily; Nov–
Apr: 10am–3pm daily.
To the left of the
square is Sponza
Palace. Remodelled in
1516–22, it has an
elegantly sculpted
Renaissance loggia on
the ground floor and a
beautiful Venetian
Gothic three-mullioned
window on the first
floor, evidence of its

14th-century origins, and a statue of St Blaise on the upper floor. It was the Mint in the 14th century and now houses the State Archives.

🔒 Church of St Blaise
Crkva Sv. Vlaha

Loža. **Tel** *(020) 323 887.*
⬜ *8am–noon, 4.30–7pm daily.*
St Blaise was rebuilt in the early decades of the 18th century according to a 17th-century design and contains many Baroque works of art.

On the main altar stands a statue of the patron saint, Blaise. It was produced in the 15th century in gold-plated silver, and depicts the saint holding a model of the city in the Middle Ages.

Baroque façade of the church of St Blaise

🏛 Rector's Palace
Knežev Dvor

Pred Dvorom 1. **Tel** *(020) 321 422.*
⬜ *Apr–Oct: 9am–6pm daily; Nov–Mar: 9am–4pm daily.*
The Rector's Palace was for centuries the seat of the most important government institutions of the Dubrovnik Republic. It housed the Upper and Lower Council, as well as the rector's quarters and rooms for meetings and audiences. The building was constructed in the early 15th century on the site of a medieval fortress, and designed by the Italian architect Onofrio de la Cava. In 1465 the portico by Petar Martinov from Milan was added. The Gothic works are by Juraj Dalmatinac.

The rooms of the palace house the interesting **Cultural Historical Museum** (Kulturno Povijesni Muzej), which

The Rector's Palace, built in the 15th century as the administrative seat

contains 15 collections of historic items created in art and craft workshops throughout Europe between the 16th and 20th centuries. On the ground floor an authentic jail space, court, notary and archives have been preserved and presented. Coins, medals, stamps and measures, ancient weapons and numerous other works of art as well as an inventory of the state pharmacy "Domus Christi" are on display on the mezzanine floor. On the first floor, rooms contain valuable objects from the 16th–18th centuries.

Also of great interest are the portraits of illustrious personalities who were born or lived in Dubrovnik, whose history is told through their heraldic coats of arms. During the Festival of Dubrovnik concerts are held in the atmospheric internal courtyard.

Next door is the 1863 Neo-Renaissance **Town Hall** (Vijećnica), designed by Emilio Vecchietti. It is also the home of Gradska Kavana, a restaurant, and the Civic Theatre.

🔒 Cathedral and Treasury
Velika Gospa

Kneza Damjana Jude 1.
⬜ *Apr–Oct: 8am–5pm Mon–Sat, 11am–5pm Sun; Nov–Mar: 8am–noon, 3–5pm Mon–Sat, 11am–noon, 3–5pm Sun.* **Cathedral Treasury** *Tel (020) 323 459.* ⬜ *same times as the cathedral.*
The cathedral was built after the earthquake of 1667 by the Roman architects Andrea Buffalini and Paolo Andreotti. Inside are three aisles enclosed by three apses. Paintings by Italian and Dalmatian artists from the 16th–18th centuries decorate

the side altars, while an *Assumption* by Titian (c.1552) dominates the main altar.

Alongside the church is the **Cathedral Treasury** (Riznica Katedrale), famous for its collection of about 200 reliquaries. It includes the arm of St Blaise which dates from the 13th century, and a Holy Cross which contains a fragment of the cross on which Jesus was said to have been crucified. The tondo *Virgin of the Chair* is thought to have been painted by Raphael himself, and is a copy of the masterpiece which is now in Florence.

The treasury also has an extraordinary collection of sacred objects in gold, including a pitcher and basin in gold and silver with decoration that illustrates the flora and fauna of the area around Dubrovnik.

The great dome of Dubrovnik's Baroque cathedral

The church of St Dominic, inside the monastery

🏛 Dominican Monastery
Dominikanski Samostan Bijeli Fratri

Od Sv. Dominika 4. **Tel** *(020) 321 423.* 🕐 *May–Oct: 9am–6pm; Nov–Apr: 9am–5pm.* 📷

Building began in 1315 and it soon became clear that because of the size of the complex, the city walls would have to be enlarged. The monastery was later rebuilt after the earthquake of 1667.

A long flight of steps with a stone balustrade leads up to the church. The door, the work of Bonino of Milan, is decorated with a Romanesque statue of St Dominic. The interior has a wide single nave and, hanging from the central arch, a splendid gilded panel *(Crucifix and Symbols of the Evangelists)* by Paolo Veneziano (14th century).

The various rooms of the monastery, arranged around the Gothic cloister by Maso di Bartolomeo (15th century), house the **Dominican Museum** (Muzej Dominikanskog Samostana). It contains an extraordinary collection of works from the so-called "Dubrovnik school", including a triptych and an *Annunciation* by Niccolò Ragusino, from the 16th century, and works from the Venetian school, including *St Blaise, St Mary Magdalene, the Angel Tobias and the Purchaser* by Titian, as well as precious reliquaries and objects in gold and silver.

Dubrovnik Cable Car
Dubrovačka žičara

Frana Supila 35a. **Tel** *(020) 311 577.* 🕐 *9am–9pm daily.* 📷 **www.** dubrovnikcablecar.com
Destroyed in 1991, the cable car that connects Dubrovnik City Walls and Mount Srđ is in operation again. The route takes three and a half minutes to complete, and offers wonderful views.

Environs
The island of **Lokrum**, 700 m (2,296 ft) across the water from Dubrovnik, is a nature reserve.

The first people to settle on the island were the Benedictines, who founded an abbey here in 1023. This was rebuilt in the 14th century, but later destroyed by the earthquake of 1667. In 1859, Archduke Maximilian of Habsburg built a palace here and renovated the cloister which later became the Natural History Museum.

In **Trsteno**, 20 km (12 miles) northwest of Dubrovnik, is an Arboretum. This was begun in 1502 in the park surrounding a villa built by Ivan Gučetić. The park has the layout of a Renaissance garden with grottoes and ancient ruins.

There are several Renaissance summer houses around Dubrovnik, including the **Villa Stay** in Rijeka Dubrovačka.

A statue in the *Arboretum* in Trsteno

Elaphite Islands ③④

Map F6. 👥 *2,000.* 🚤 *from Dubrovnik.* 🏛 *Dubrovnik regional tourist office (020) 324 999.*

Lying to the north of Dubrovnik, the Elaphite islands (Elafitski otoci) can be reached from Dubrovnik by motorboat. There are several daily crossings. The islands were described by the natural historian Pliny the Elder, who named them after the fallow deer then found here.

Only three of the islands are inhabited: Šipan, Lopud and Koločep, while Jakljan is devoted to farming. Characteristics common to the islands are the woods of maritime pines and cypresses in the uncultivated areas and beautiful beaches and bays frequented by pleasure boats. The islands have long been popular with the aristocracy of Dubrovnik, who built villas here. Some islands had monasteries which were suppressed with the arrival of French troops in 1808. Many of the churches date from the pre-Romanesque period, but few, however, are still intact.

Koločep
This is the nearest island to Dubrovnik and for this reason has been a summer retreat since the 16th century for its

The island of Lokrum in front of Dubrovnik, a protected nature reserve

Sunj beach on the southeast coast of Lopud, one of the Elaphite islands

citizens. Most of the island is covered in maritime pines and subtropical undergrowth.

The churches of St **Anthony** and St **Nicholas** have pre-Romanesque origins, while the **Parish Church** dates from the 15th century.

Lopud

The island, measuring 4.6 sq km (1.7 sq miles), has a fertile valley sheltered from the cold winds by two ranges of hills. Most of the inhabitants live in **Lopud**, a village in a bay. The two forts, now in ruins, date from the 16th century and the Franciscan monastery is from 1483. The monastery church, **St Mary of Spilica** (Sv. Marija od Špilica), contains a polyptych by Pietro di Giovanni (1520), a triptych by Nikola Božidarević, a painting by Leandro da Bassano, a triptych by Gerolamo di Santacroce and a carved choir from the 15th century.

Šunj, in the southeast, draws visitors because of its sandy beach, but the church is also worth visiting for its many works of art, including a painting by Palma il Giovane and a polyptych (1452) by Matej Junčić.

Šipan

This is the largest of the Elaphite Islands (15.5 sq km/ 6 sq miles) and there are two towns. In **Šipanska Luka** stands the pre-Romanesque church of St Michael and the ruins of a Benedictine monastery. In **Suđurađ** there is a castle and the ruins of a bishop's palace.

Cavtat ㉟

Map F6. 🏛 *2,500.* 🚌 *(020) 478 065.* 🚢 *from Dubrovnik.* ℹ *Zidine 6, (020) 478 025.* 🎭 *Summer in Cavtat, Epidaurus Festival.* **www**.*tzcavtat-konavle.hr*

Cavtat is the Croatian name for Civitas Vetus, the site of the Roman town of Epidaurum, destroyed by the Avars in the 7th century (occasional excavations have revealed the remains of a theatre, several tombs and parts of a road). The beauty of the area, the beaches, the luxuriant vegetation and the interesting monuments attract many visitors to the present-day village.

The **Baltazar Bogišić Collection**, assembled and donated by the scholar and jurist of the 19th century, is housed in the 16th-century **Rector's**

Traditional dress of Konavle, still used for festivities

Palace. The works of the painter Vlaho Bukovac are especially fine.

At the end of the seafront is the church of **Our Lady of Snow** (Gospa Snježna) and a Franciscan monastery, both from the end of the 15th century. On the hilltop stands the **Račić Mausoleum** built by Ivan Meštrović (*see p157*) in 1922.

Konavle ㊱

Map F6. ℹ *Zidine 6, Cavtat, (020) 478 025.* **www**.*tzcavtat-konavle.hr*

The area southeast of Cavtat occupies a narrow piece of land between the sea and the mountains of Bosnia-Herzegovina. Its name derives from the channels (*canalis*) which collected the water to supply the aqueduct – of which some traces remain – for the Roman town of Epidaurum.

The hilly areas are covered in vineyards and olive groves. The small villages maintain the old customs and traditional costumes are still worn by the inhabitants. Konavle was heavily damaged by bombing in 1991.

This area is also renowned for its excellent cuisine and there are numerous restaurants. One of the best known is **Konavoski Dvori**, housed in a watermill near the waterfalls of the River Ljuta.

The pretty seafront and port of Cavtat

ZAGREB

The capital of Croatia, Zagreb is also the heart of the political, economic and cultural life of the country. Surrounded by woods and parks, the city lies between the slopes of Mount Medvednica to the north and the River Sava to the south. Located at the centre of continental Croatia, this Central European city constitutes a meeting point between eastern and western Europe.

The political scientist Max Weber once declared that the quality of life in a city could be measured by the number of its cultural institutions. Zagreb has over 20 museums, 10 theatres, 350 libraries, a university, and lively programmes of artistic and cultural events. This is not just because Zagreb is the capital (it has only been the capital since 1991), but is also due to the leading cultural and political role that Zagreb has played over the centuries.

Zagreb was originally two separate medieval towns. Two settlements were built on two adjacent hilltops: Kaptol, the centre of religious power, and a bishopric from 1094, and Gradec (now part of Gornji Grad). In 1242, with the proclamation of a "Golden Bull", Gradec was given the title of royal free city by the Croat-

History of Croatia by Ivan Meštrović, Meštrović Gallery

Hungarian King Bela IV. This granted various economic and administrative privileges to the inhabitants. From the 16th century onwards Gradec was also where the Ban – the governor of Croatia delegated by the Hungarian kingdom – and the Croat parliament carried out their business and where Croat nobles met to govern this turbulent territory. The two towns were both fortified with ramparts, towers, moats and gates, and separated by the Medveščak stream. The stream was often the site of violent clashes between Gradec and Kaptol, and that time is vividly recalled by the street called the Bridge of Blood (Krvavi Most).

In 1880, a terrible earthquake struck the city and many of the major monuments date from after this time.

The colourful Dolac market with fruit and vegetable stalls

◁ View of the centre of Zagreb from Kralja Tomislava square

Exploring Zagreb

The city is divided into two large sectors; the
old town (Gornji Grad or Upper Town), which
includes the two districts of Gradec and Kaptol,
situated in the hills, and the modern area (Donji
Grad or Lower Town) on the plain. The large square
dedicated to the Croat governor Jelačić (Trg bana
Jelačića) is where the upper and lower towns meet.
The old town is home to the main centres of
religious, political and administrative power. The
more modern part developed after 1830 around a
U-shaped series of parks and open spaces (known
as the "green horseshoe"). The major museums,
including the Ethnographic Museum, Mimara Museum, Gallery of Old Masters and Gallery of Modern
Art, are all located here, as well as the National Theatre. To the south of a series of gardens with sculptures lies the Botanical Garden. Around Jelačić Square
there are plenty of cafés with summer terraces.

LOCATOR MAP

0 metres   200
0 yards   200

SIGHTS AT A GLANCE

Museums and Galleries
Archaeological Museum ㉕
City Museum ⑥
Croatian History Museum ⑫
Croatian Museum of Naive Art ⑬
Croatian Natural
  History Museum ⑦
Ethnographic Museum ⑳
Gallery of Modern Art ㉔
*Gallery of Old Masters
  pp164–5* ㉓
Meštrović Atelier ⑧
Mimara Museum ⑲
Museum of Arts and Crafts ⑱
Museum of Contemporary Art ㉖

Churches
Cathedral of the Assumption
  of the Blessed Virgin Mary ①
Church of St Catherine ⑯

Church of SS Cyril
  and Methodius ⑭
Church of St Francis ③
Church of St Mark ⑨
Church of St Mary ④

Palaces and other Buildings
Archbishop's Palace ②
Art Pavilion ㉒
Ban's Palace ⑪
Croatian National Theatre ⑰
Parliament Building ⑩
Stone Gate ⑤
Tower of Lotrščak ⑮

Parks and Gardens
Botanical Garden of the Faculty
  of Science ㉑
Maksimir Park ㉗
Mirogoj Cemetery ㉘

GREATER ZAGREB

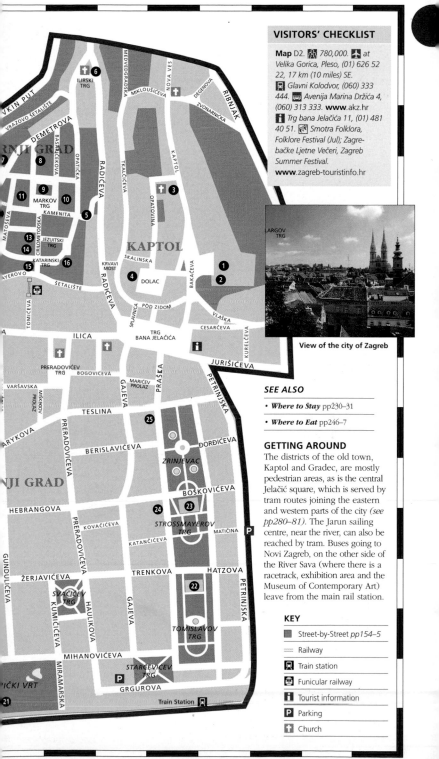

VISITORS' CHECKLIST

Map D2. 🏠 780,000. ✈ at
Velika Gorica, Pleso, (01) 626 52
22, 17 km (10 miles) SE.
🚉 Glavni Kolodvor, (060) 333
444. 🚌 Avenija Marina Držića 4,
(060) 313 333. **www**.akz.hr
🛈 Trg bana Jelačića 11, (01) 481
40 51. 🎭 Smotra Folklora,
Folklore Festival (Jul); Zagre-
bačke Ljetne Večeri, Zagreb
Summer Festival.
www.zagreb-touristinfo.hr

View of the city of Zagreb

SEE ALSO

• **Where to Stay** pp230–31

• **Where to Eat** pp246–7

GETTING AROUND

The districts of the old town,
Kaptol and Gradec, are mostly
pedestrian areas, as is the central
Jelačić square, which is served by
tram routes joining the eastern
and western parts of the city (see
pp280–81). The Jarun sailing
centre, near the river, can also be
reached by tram. Buses going to
Novi Zagreb, on the other side of
the River Sava (where there is a
racetrack, exhibition area and the
Museum of Contemporary Art)
leave from the main rail station.

KEY

▮	Street-by-Street pp154–5
═	Railway
🚉	Train station
🚡	Funicular railway
🛈	Tourist information
🅿	Parking
✝	Church

Cathedral of the Assumption of the Blessed Virgin Mary ❶

Katedrala Marijina Uznesenja

Kaptol. *Tel* (01) 481 47 27. ☐
10am–5pm Mon–Sat, 1–5pm Sun.

Dedicated to the Assumption and St Stephen, this is the most famous monument in the city. Its present appearance dates from renovations carried out by Friedrich von Schmidt and Hermann Bollé after the earthquake of 1880, which destroyed the dome, the bell tower and some of the walls. The rebuilding, which retained the medieval plan of the cathedral, was just the latest in a series of alterations the building had undergone in its long history. The building was already in existence in 1094 when King

Decorative detail of one of the cathedral spires

Ladislaus transferred the bishopric here from Sisak. Destroyed by the Mongols in 1242, the cathedral was rebuilt by Bishop Timotej a few years later. In the centuries that followed, the side aisles were added and the church was decorated with statues and reliefs.

The new Neo-Gothic façade (1880) is flanked by two twin spires. The façade has a large ornate doorway with sculpted decorations, a rose window and three high windows, the whole crowned by a tympanum.

The interior has three aisles and a polygonal apse. During a late 19th-century reorganization, the Baroque and Rococo altars were transferred to other churches in the diocese, and as a result only a few Gothic and Renaissance works remain. These works include a statue of St Paul (13th century), wooden statues of the saints Peter and Paul from the 15th century, a triptych entitled *Golgotha* (1495) by Albrecht Dürer and a 14th-century *Crucifixion* by Giovanni da Udine. The cathedral also contains the tombs and votive chapels of bishops and important personalities in Croatian history, such as Petar Zrinski, Krsto Frankopan and the blessed Cardinal Alojzije Stepinac, whose tomb behind the main altar is by Ivan Meštrović.

Of great interest are the frescoes from the Giotto-esque school in the sacristy: the oldest (12th century) in inland Croatia. In the basement of the bishop's sacristy, the

The central nave in the Neo-Gothic Cathedral of St Stephen

Cathedral Treasury preserves a rich collection of religious objects. These include illuminated manuscripts, finely crafted church ornaments from the 11th to the 20th centuries, and objects of veneration such as the Cloak of King Ladislaus (11th century), a bishop's veil from the 14th century and the so-called Sepulchre of God. This last was made by the embroiderers of the village of Vugrovec, where Bishop Petar Petretić founded an embroidery school in around 1650. Among the oldest works are a 10th-century ivory diptych and a bronze Crucifix from the 11th–12th centuries.

Archbishop's Palace ❷

Nadbiskupska Palača

Kaptol. ⬤ *to the public.*

The enormous Baroque buildings comprising the Archbishop's Palace enclose the other three sides of the cathedral square. The building incorporates three of the five round towers and one square tower, which were part of the fortifications built from 1469 as defence against Turkish attacks. The present palace dates from 1730, when several buildings were linked and united by an imposing Baroque façade.

Inside the complex is the Romanesque chapel of St

The tall spires of the Cathedral

Stephen Protomartyr (13th century). This is the oldest building in Zagreb to have survived in its original form: the frescoes are from the 14th century.

In the square in front of the palace stands a fountain with a column crowned by a statue of Mary with four Angels, the work of the Viennese artist Anton Dominik Fernkorn (1813–78) in around 1850.

The moats that once surrounded the walls have been filled in and turned into the **Ribnjak Public Gardens**, with various statues including one called *Modesty* by Antun Augustinčić (1900–79). The defences were partially demolished in the 19th century, however. At No 18 Ulica Kaptol, opposite the cathedral, is the **Northeast Tower**, which is now a residence. At No 15 stands the **Northwest Tower** (Prišlinova Kula), now part of a 15th-century building.

The Archbishop's Palace by the Cathedral of St Stephen

Church of St Francis ❸

Sv. Franjo

Kaptol 9. **Tel** (01) 481 11 25.
⬜ 7am–noon, 3–7pm daily.

Founded, according to legend, after St Francis' return from the East, this church dates from the 13th century. After the earthquake of 1880, the church was rebuilt in the Neo-Gothic style. It was at this time that

Stained-glass windows by Ivo Dulčić in the church of St Francis

the Baroque altars were removed. Some of the side altars are Neo-Gothic, while on the main altar there is a fine painting of St Francis by Celestin Medović (1857–1920). The brightly coloured stained-glass windows were designed by Ivo Dulčić in the 1960s.

In the adjacent 17th-century **Monastery**, where the saint supposedly stayed, is the much-visited chapel of St Francis (1683), with ornate stucco decorations and Baroque paintings.

Church of St Mary ❹

Sv. Marija

Dolac 2. **Tel** (01) 481 49 59.
⬜ for mass.

Opatovina is a narrow street where some of the houses were built using parts of the late-15th century fortifications. The street leads into the ancient district of Dolac, at the end of which stands the church of St Mary, which dates from the 14th century. It was rearranged in 1740 when several Baroque altars were built by Franjo Rottman, but its present appearance dates

The monument to Petrica Kerempuh, Dolac

back to rebuilding after the earthquake in 1880.

Near the church stands a statue by Vanja Radauš of the legendary wanderer and minstrel Petrica Kerempuh, playing to the figure of a hanged man.

The large, picturesque **Dolac Market**, which was first held in 1930, takes place around the church. This is a characteristic district of the city where Baroque houses face narrow streets and lanes. A historic pharmacy is at No 19 Kaptol and an ancient house at No 7.

Stone Gate ❺

Kamenita Vrata

Kamenita.

In the walls around Gradec, the part of Upper Town built on a neighbouring hill to Kaptol, there were once five gates. Stone Gate is now the only one of these remaining. It was built in the 13th century, and stands beside a square tower from 1266. In 1731 a fire destroyed all the nearby houses, but a painting of Mary with Child on the gate was left undamaged. A chapel was established around this painting and a Baroque wrought-iron grille now protects the work, attributed to a local master from the 16th century.

On the west façade of the church is a statue of a woman, a character from a famous Croation novel and the work of the sculptor Ivo Kerdić in 1929. On the other side of the gate, on the corner of Kamenita and Habdelićeva, stands an 18th-century building. On the ground floor of this building is a **Pharmacy** (Alighieri ljekarna) which has been in existence since 1350 and which, from 1399 onwards, belonged to Nicolò Alighieri, the great-grandson of the great Italian writer Dante.

Street-by-Street: the Upper Town (Gornji Grad)

Pietà by Ivan Meštrović

In the Upper Town there are various institutions which have played a significant part in the history of the city and of Croatia. They now house the political and cultural centres of the country: the presidency of the Republic, Parliament, the State Audit Court and several government ministries. All of these buildings were restored, repaired or rebuilt after the terrible earthquake of 1880. Some of the ancient noble palaces have been converted into museums. There are also three interesting churches: the ancient church of St Mark, the Baroque church of St Catherine built by the Jesuits, and the church of Saints Cyril and Methodius. The daily signal to close the city gates was rung from the medieval tower of Lotrščak (Turris Latruncolorum).

Croatian Natural History Museum
Created from three collections, the museum houses most of the finds from Krapina, which date human presence in Croatia back to the Palaeolithic era ❼

Ban's Palace
The building dates from the 17th century and was built after the city became the seat of the Ban (governor of Croatia) in 1621. It now houses the presidency of the Republic ⓫

Croatian Historical Museum
This museum, housed in the Vojković-Oršić-Rauch palace, has works of art and documents collected since 1959 ⓬

★ Croatian National Museum of Naive Art
Over 1,500 works of Naive art by the founders and followers of the Hlebine school are held here ⓭

Church of SS Cyril and Methodius
Built by Orthodox Christians in the first half of the 19th century, the church, designed by Bartol Felbinger, has a fine iconostasis ⓮

Tower of Lotrščak
At noon every day a cannon is fired from this tower, which dates from the 12th century ⓯

KEY

– – – Suggested route

★ **Meštrović Atelier**
The great Croatian sculptor Ivan Meštrović lived in this 18th-century building from 1922 to 1941. About ten years before his death he donated his home and all the works of art in it to the state ⑧

LOCATOR MAP

Parliament Building
This building dates from 1910, when the provincial administration offices were enlarged. The independence of Croatia was proclaimed from the central window of the building in 1918 ⑩

★ **Church of St Mark**
The coloured tiles on the roof of this fine Gothic church form the coats of arms of Croatia, Dalmatia, Slavonia and Zagreb ⑨

| 0 metres | 50 |
| 0 yards | 50 |

The Stone Gate
is all that remains of the five original gates constructed around the Gradec area in the 13th century ⑤

The Klovićevi Dvori,
an important temporary exhibition site, has been housed since 1982 in a 17th-century Jesuit monastery.

STAR FEATURES

★ Church of St Mark

★ Meštrović Atelier

★ Croatian National Museum of Naive Art

Church of St Catherine
Built on the site of an ancient Dominican church, this is the city's most fascinating Baroque building ⑯

City Museum ⑥
Muzej grada Zagreba

Opatička ulica 20. **Tel** (01) 485 13 61. ☐ 10am–6pm Tue–Fri; 11am–7pm Sat, 10am–2pm Sun. ☑ by appt. ▨ ⬢ ⬿ www.mgz.hr

Three historic buildings (the convent of the nuns of St Clare from around 1650, a 12th-century tower, and a granary from the 17th century, now converted into a school) have been linked to form the City Museum. Its 12 collections, consisting of 4,500 objects on permanent display, illustrate the history and culture of Zagreb from its origins to the present day.

The exhibits include paintings, maps and views of the city, standards, flags, military uniforms, statues and also archaeological finds. Many of the exhibits were donated by the city's famous townsmen and women, including the actress Tilla Durieux, the musician Rudolf Matz, the composer Ivan Zajc, the soprano Milka Trnina and architect Viktor Kovačić.

Along the street is the 19th-century **National Palace**, with the beautiful Illyrian Hall, which houses part of the Croatian Academy of Arts and Sciences, and the **Paravić Palace** (19th century), with fine wrought-iron gates, now the Institute of Historical Studies.

Some of the statues on display in the City Museum

Sculptures in the garden of the Meštrović Atelier

Croatian Natural History Museum ⑦
Hrvatski Prirodoslovni Muzej

Demetrova 1. **Tel** (01) 485 17 00. ☐ 10am–5pm Tue–Fri (to 8pm Thu), 10am–7pm Sat, 10am–1pm Sun. www.hpm.hr

The 18th-century Amadeo Palace, a theatre from 1797 to 1834, has been the Natural History Museum since 1868, when collections from the Department of Natural Science at the National Museum were transferred here. At the end of the 19th century there were three museums of natural history: Mineralogy and Petrography, Geology and Palaeontology, and Zoology. These three merged in 1986 to form the present museum.

A mineral in the Croatian Natural History Museum

There are over 2,500,000 exhibits, including minerals from all over the world and palaeontology collections containing some of the material found in Krapina. The zoological collection documents every species of animal found in Croatia.

Meštrović Atelier ⑧
Atelje Meštrović

Mletačka 8. **Tel** (01) 485 11 23. ☐ 10am–6pm Tue–Fri, 10am–2pm Sat & Sun. ▨ ⬢ ⬿ www.mdc.hr/mestrovic

The atelier building dates from the 17th century; the sculptor Ivan Meštrović himself modernized it to live in from 1922 to 1942. It now houses a collection of his work. It is part of The Museums of Ivan Meštrović, together with the Gallery and the Kaštilac in Split, as well as the burial chapel in Otavice (see p110). There are almost 100 works on display, including exhibits in the courtyard – *History of Croatia, Laookon of our Days* and *Woman in Agony*. The drawings, models and sculptures in wood, stone and bronze testify to the expressive ability and great skills of the sculptor. His personal archives are also here, as well as photographic records and works by other artists associated with the master.

Ivan Meštrović

Regarded as one of the most important sculptors of the 20th century, Ivan Meštrović was born in 1883 in Vrpolje where his parents had gone for the harvest from their native village of Otavice in the Dalmatian hinterland. As a young boy he delighted in making figures out of wood, and his work was noticed by the village mayor and by Lujo Marun, an archaeologist, who sent him to Split when he was 17 to study sculpture. Thanks to donors, he was able to attend the Academy of Fine Arts in Vienna, where he designed works for later production. Here he met and became friends with the great French

Portrait of Ivan Meštrović

sculptor, Auguste Rodin. In 1908 he moved to Paris and his first exhibition established his reputation. He worked in various cities, including Split – creating many of the works now on show in the Meštrović gallery there – and Zagreb. He also took up politics: during World War II he was imprisoned by the Nazi regime and freed on the Vatican's intervention. He then moved to Rome where he sculpted the *Pietà Romana*, now in the Vatican Museum. After the war he taught at universities in the US, where he died in 1962. He was buried in the burial chapel in Otavice *(see p110)* that he designed for himself and his family.

Meštrović, intent on his work

Detail of the Resurrection of Lazarus (1940)

Woman by the Sea *is a splendid female figure in marble (1926) which seems to twist around on itself. The form of the body is vigorous and yet the hands are delicate and slender.*

THE SCULPTOR AT WORK

The speed at which Meštrović executed his works was proverbial, although the preparation time was lengthy. To satisfy demand, he replicated his works in wood, marble and bronze. Three copies, not quite identical, exist of the statue of the Bishop of Nin, in Nin, Split and Varaždin.

Mother and Child *is a wooden sculpture from 1942 which demonstrates the artist's great expressive talent. The figure of the child is almost insignificant, leaving the face of the mother to play the main role.*

History of Croatia *is a work from 1932. There are four originals; one in bronze is in the Meštrović Atelier in Zagreb. The woman's thoughtful gaze looks to the future, symbolizing expectations and hopes.*

The church of St Mark, with its colourful glazed tile roof

Church of St Mark **⑨**
Sv. Marko

Markov trg. **Tel** *(01) 485 16 11.* ◗ *check opening times (01) 481 40 51.*

Today this is the Upper Town's parish church. St Mark's was first mentioned in 1256 when King Bela IV granted the town of Gradec permission to hold a market fair in front of the church. The fair lasted for two weeks and was held to celebrate the saint's day.

The church has undergone various alterations over the centuries. All that is left from the original construction is a Romanesque window and a splendid Gothic doorway, created by the sculptor Ivan Parler between 1364 and 1377. The 15 niches on the door contain statues of Jesus, Mary, St Mark and the 12 apostles. Some of these were replaced by wooden copies in the Baroque era.

On various occasions fires and earthquakes have been responsible for changes in the church's appearance. Its present look dates from 1882, when the coloured glazed tiles on the roof were added. The tiles bear the coats of arms of Croatia, Dalmatia, Slavonia and the city of Zagreb. The church has been refurbished with several statues by the sculptor Ivan Meštrović. On the high altar is a large *Christ on the Cross*, a *Pietà* stands on the altar of the Holy Cross and a bronze statue of *Mary with Child* adorns an altar dedicated to the Virgin Mary. The modern frescoes depicting Croat kings in action were painted by Jozo Kljaković.

Mary with Child by Meštrović, St Mark's

Parliament Building **⑩**
Sabor

Markov trg. ℹ *(01) 456 96 07.* ◗ *groups only by appt.*

Built in Neo-Classical style in 1908 after several 17th- and 18th-century Baroque buildings were razed, this building holds an important place in the story of Croatia. Historic proclamations have been issued from the balcony: the seceding of the nation from the Austro-Hungarian kingdom (29 October 1918) and independence from Yugoslavia after a referendum in 1991. Today the Sabor is still the centre of 21st-century Croat politics.

Viceroy's Palace **⑪**
Banski Dvori

Markov trg. ℹ *(01) 456 92 22.* ◗ *by appt.*

The parliament chamber, the central archives, the law courts, the President of the Republic's residence and government offices are all housed in this building in front of St Mark's, which was badly damaged in an airstrike in 1991. The palace is similar in design to the parliament building and is made up of two long 18th-century structures. In the 19th century two two-storey wings were added.

Croatian History Museum **⑫**
Hrvatski Povijesni Muzej

Matoševa ulica 9. **Tel** *(01) 485 19 00.* ◗ *10am–6pm Mon–Fri,10am–1pm Sat & Sun.* ● *public hols.* 🎫 🚹 🚫 **www.**hismus.hr

The museum, founded in 1846, has been housed here since 1959. It illustrates the history of Croatia from the Middle Ages to the present day by means of all kinds of mementoes. These include documents and paintings of political, military and cultural events, as well as items such as firearms, flags and medals. The exhibitions are not permanent but change frequently due to limited space.

The museum is housed in the Baroque Vojković-Oršić-Kulmer-Rauch Palace, which dates from the second half of the 18th century.

The Parliament Building (Sabor), built in Neo-Classical style in 1908

My Homeland by Ivan Rabuzin (1961), Croatian Museum of Naive Art

Croatian Museum of Naive Art ⑬

Hrvatski Muzej Naivne Umjetnosti

Ćirilometodska ulica 3. *Tel* (01) 485 19 11. ◻ 10am–6pm Tue–Fri, 10am–1pm Sat & Sun. ◉ public hols. 🖼 📷 📷 www.hmnu.org

Since 1967, this 19th-century building with its beautiful Neo-Baroque façade has housed works from an exhibition of Naive painters which opened in Zagreb in 1952. The paintings are characterized by the use of vivid colour and a strong feeling for narrative. There are paintings by the founders of the Naive trend, Ivan Generalić and Mirko Virius, as well as by the Hlebine school (*see p21*), where works by Ivan Večenaj and Mijo Kovačić stand out, and artists from other regions (Ivan Lacković, Ivan Rabuzin, Slavko Stolnik and Matija Skurjeni). Among the sculptures are several by Petar Smajić.

Church of SS Cyril and Methodius ⑭

Sv. Ćiril i Metod

Ćirilometodska ulica. *Tel* (01) 48517 73.

First built in around 1830 in Neo-Classical style by the architect Bartol Felbinger (1785–1871), the church was rebuilt after the earthquake of 1880 in a Neo-Byzantine style designed by Hermann Bollé.

The interior has a large iconostasis painted by the Ukrainian Epaminondas Bučevski, and four large paintings by Ivan Tišov.

The adjacent Greek-Catholic seminary was built in 1774 and enlarged at the beginning of the 20th century.

Tower of Lotrščak ⑮

Kula Lotrščak

Strossmayerovo Šetalište. *Tel* (01) 485 17 68. ◻ Apr–Oct: 11am–7pm Tue–Sun. 🖼

Since the middle of the 19th century, the inhabitants of Zagreb have set their clocks at noon by the cannons fired from this tower. Dating from the 13th century, it is one of the oldest buildings in the city.

At one time this square tower had a bell, which announced the closing of the city gates each evening. Its name comes from the latin *campana latruncolorum* – bell of thieves – anyone left outside at night ran the risk of being robbed.

The tower originally stood alongside the southern side of the walls of Gradec. Even at that time, the walls, nearly 2 m (6 ft) thick, were built with chains inside them as an anti-earthquake measure.

· The tower now houses a gallery. It is worth climbing to the top for spectacular views over the city.

Church of St Catherine ⑯

Sv. Katarina

Katarinin trg. *Tel* (01) 485 19 50. ◻ 8am–8pm daily.

The Jesuits built this church in around 1630 on the site of a Dominican building. The church is considered to be one of the most beautiful religious buildings in Zagreb. The white façade has a doorway and four niches with statues and six prominent pilasters. Above is a niche with a statue of Mary.

The single-nave church is home to numerous Baroque works of art. Of particular interest are the stucco reliefs (1721–3) by Antonio Quadrio, the *Scenes of the Life of St Catherine* by the Slovenian artist Franc Jelovšek (1700–64) in the medallion on the ceiling, a beautiful *Altar of St Ignatius* by the Venetian sculptor Francesco Robba (1698–1757) and, on the main altar (1762), *St Catherine among the Alexandrian Philosophers* by Kristof Andrej Jelovšek (1729–76).

In the nearby square called Jezuitski trg, there is a fountain with a statue of a *Fisherman with a Serpent* by Simeon Roksandić (1908). Facing this is a Jesuit monastery (17th century) and a large building from the same period which was the Jesuit seminary and later, a boarding school for boys of noble parentage.

The rich Baroque interior of the church of St Catherine

The Neo-Baroque building housing the Croatian National Theatre

Croatian National Theatre ⑰
Hrvatsko Narodno Kazalište

Trg Maršala Tita 15. **Tel** (01) 488 84 18. ⬚ for performances only. ⬤ public hols. **www**.hnk.hr

The Croatian National Theatre stands in the square marking the beginning of a U-shaped series of parks and squares forming a "green horseshoe", the design of the engineer Milan Lenuci (1849–1924). The theatre, one of a number of imposing buildings in the square, was completed in 1895 and is a blend of Neo-Baroque and Rococo. It was designed by the Viennese architects Hermann Helmer and Ferdinand Fellner. The roof has two small domes at the front and a higher dome further back. The exterior is ornamented with two orders of columns running along its entire length.

The interior is richly decorated with works by Croatian and Viennese artists. Five stage backcloths include one called *The Croatian Renewal,* a splendid work by Vlaho Bukovac.

In the area in front of the theatre stands a masterpiece by Ivan Meštrović, *The Well of Life,* which consists of a group of bronze figures huddled around a well.

Museum of Arts and Crafts ⑱
Muzej Za Umjetnost i Obrt

Trg Maršala Tita 10. **Tel** (01) 488 21 11. ⬚ 11am–7pm Tue–Fri, 11am–2pm Sat & Sun. 📷 🎫 by appt. 🏠 🍴 🚫 **www**.muo.hr

This museum was first established in 1880 to house collections of artworks by craftsmen and artists. The building was designed by Hermann Bollé and was built between 1887 and 1892. More than 3,000 objects of applied arts from the Gothic period to the present provide an overview of Croatia's cultural history and its close ties to the rest of Europe.

A 19th-century clock, Museum of Arts and Crafts

The collections offer an insight into the Croatian and European production of arts and crafts, spanning from late Medieval times to Art Deco and right up to the more contemporary era. The collections housed at the museum include religious art, Judaica, and items including clocks and watches, ivories, metalworks, glass, ceramics, textiles and fashion. As the museum is supported by international backing, impressive temporary exhibitions from abroad occasionally take place here. The adjacent library has a total of 65,000 books on arts and crafts.

Mimara Museum ⑲
Muzej Mimara

Rooseveltov trg 5. **Tel** (01) 482 81 00. ⬚ Oct–Jun: 10am–5pm Tue, Wed, Fri & Sat, 10am–7pm Thu, 10am–2pm Sun; Jul–Sep: 10am–7pm Tue–Fri, 10am–5pm Sat, 10am–2pm Sun. ⬤ Mon. 📷 🎫 🏠

In 1972, Ante Topić Mimara, a businessman who was also a collector, painter and restorer, donated his extensive collections to the city of Zagreb, and the Mimara Museum was set up for their display. The museum is housed in an enormous Neo-Renaissance building built in 1895 by the German architects Ludwig and Hülsner.

The works are displayed chronologically from the prehistoric era to the present day. The archaeological section is particularly fascinating, with important finds from ancient Egypt, Mesopotamia, Persia, Pre-Columbian America, as well as the Middle and Far East (Japan, Cambodia, Indonesia and India are represented).

The icon collection not only contains Russian pieces, but also has icons from Palestine, Antioch and Asia Minor dating from the 6th to the 13th centuries. There are ancient Persian, Turkish and Moroccan carpets, and about 300 exhibits cover over 3,500 years of the development of Chinese art, from the Shang to the Qing dynasties.

The 550 glassware exhibits come from Europe, as well as Persia, Turkey and Morocco. About 1,000 objects and

The Bather by Renoir (1868) in the Mimara Museum

pieces of furniture give a good overall picture of European craftsmanship from the Middle Ages to the 19th century.

There is also a wide-ranging collection of 200 sculptures, which date from ancient Greece to the time of the Impressionists. They include works by the Italian sculptors Giambologna, the Della Robbias and Verrocchio, and the Frenchmen Jean-Antoine Houdon and Auguste Rodin. Italian painting is represented by, among others, Veronese, Paolo Veneziano, Pietro Lorenzetti, Raphael, Canaletto, Giorgione and Caravaggio.

Dutch Baroque painting is represented by Rembrandt, Jacob Van Ruisdael and Jan Van Goyen. Flemish masters here include Rogier van der Weyden, Hieronymus Bosch, Van Dyck and Rubens. Diego Velázquez, Bartolomé Esteban Murillo and Francisco Goya represent the Spanish painters.

The museum also has paintings by the English artists John Constable and JMW Turner and the French painters Edouard Manet, Pierre-Auguste Renoir and Camille Pissarro.

Putto by Verrocchio, Mimara Museum

Ethnographic Museum ⑳
Etnografski Muzej

Mažuranićev trg 14.
Tel (01) 482 62 20. ☐ 10am–8pm Tue–Sun. ● Mon, public hols. 📷 ♿ 🎥 📷 (without flash) www.emz.hr

This is the most important museum of its kind in Croatia. It was founded in 1919 and set up in this harmonious domed building, constructed in 1902 in the Art Nouveau style by the architect Vjekoslav Bastl, for exhibitions held by the Chamber of Commerce. The statues decorating the central part of the façade are by the sculptor Rudolf Valdec and the frescoes on the dome inside were painted by Oton

Traditional Croatian costumes on display, Ethnographic Museum

Iveković. Only a small proportion (2,800 pieces) of the 80,000 exhibits which the museum possesses are on display. Croatian culture is illustrated through exhibits of gold and silver jewellery, musical instruments, splendid embroidery, furnishings, kitchen utensils, tools, beautiful traditional women's costumes embroidered in gold and men's ceremonial dress. A reconstruction of a farmhouse room illustrates the customs and way of life of Croat farmers and fishermen.

There is also a fascinating collection of dolls dressed in traditional costumes, called the Ljeposav Perinić collection.

The valuable collection of pieces from non-European civilizations, including Latin

America, Africa, the Far East, Melanesia and Australia, was assembled from donations made by scholars and explorers, among them Dragutin Lerman and brothers Mirko and Stevo Seljan.

Botanical Garden of the Faculty of Science ㉑
Botanički Vrt Prirodoslovno-matematičkog fakulteta

Marulićev trg 9a. ℹ (01) 489 80 60. ☐ Apr–Oct: 9am–2:30pm Mon & Tue; 9am–7pm Wed–Sun. 🎫 http://hirc.botanic.hr/vrt

Part of the "green horseshoe" designed by Milan Lenuci is a large, English-style garden created in 1890 by Antun Heinz, a professor of botany, and entrusted to the faculty of Mathematics and Natural Sciences at Zagreb University.

The garden, covering an area of 50,000 sq m (540,000 sq ft), is an oasis of tranquillity and for this reason it is a popular place in which to stroll. There are about 10,000 plant species here, including around 1,800 tropical plants from all over the world, with Asia particularly well represented.

Paths link the conifer woods, artificial ponds, the exhibition pavilions, rock gardens and glasshouses. A wonderful display is provided by the different varieties of trees, shrubs and flowers which are grown here. Aquatic plants are cultivated in special ponds.

A pond in the Botanical Gardens

The Art Pavilion, venue for major exhibitions

Art Pavilion ㉒
Umjetnički Paviljon

Trg Kralja Tomislava 22. *Tel (01) 484 10 70.* ☐ *11am–7pm Tue–Sat; 10am–1pm Sun.* ☒ www.umjetnicki-paviljon.hr

In 1896 the Art Pavilion represented Croatia at the international exhibition in Budapest. It was set up on this site in 1898 by Ferdinand Fellner and Hermann Helmer. Since then it has been used for large-scale, diverse art exhibitions. A work by Ivan Meštrović, a monument to the Renaissance painter Andrija Medulić, stands in front of the pavilion.

The pavilion faces onto a square, Trg Kralja Tomislava, dedicated to the first Croatian king, Tomislav. An equestrian statue by the sculptor Robert Frangeš-Mihanović stands here in commemoration.

Gallery of Old Masters ㉓
Galerija Starih Majstora

See pp164–5.

Gallery of Modern Art ㉔
Moderna Galerija

Andrije Hebranga 1. *Tel (01) 604 10 55.* ☐ *11am–7pm Tue–Fri; 11am–2pm Sat & Sun.* ☒ *public hols.* ☒ ☒ ☒ ☒ ☒ www.moderna-galerija.hr

Since 1973, Vranyczany Palace (1882) has housed works by the most eminent Croat painters and sculptors of the 19th and 20th centuries. The institution itself dates from 1905 when the first works of Ivan Meštrović, Mirko Rački and F Bilak were acquired. Later purchases and donations added to the gallery's extensive collections which now boast 9,500 paintings, sculptures, watercolours, drawings and prints.

At the entrance, the large painting, *Gundulić Imagining Osman*, 1894 by Vlaho Bukovac, immediately establishes the standard of the collection. The gallery also has works by Ljubo Babić, Miljenko Stančić, V Karas, M Mašić, Emanuel Vidović, C Medović, MC Crnčić, B Csikos-Sessia, Ivan Meštrović, Robert Frangeš-Mihanović, Josip Račić, Miroslav Kraljević, V Becić, O Hermann and Edo Murtić.

Archaeological Museum ㉕
Arheološki Muzej

Trg Nikole Šubića Zrinskog 19. *Tel (01) 487 30 00.* ☐ *10am–6pm Tue–Sat (to 8pm Thu), 10am–1pm Sun.* ☒ ☒ *by appt.* ☐ www.amz.hr

A large 19th-century building, the Vranyczany-Hafner Palace, has housed the Archaeological Museum since 1945. The institution itself, however, was founded in 1846.

Around 400,000 pieces from all over Croatia, and particularly the area around Zagreb, are on display here. The museum has five main sections: pre-historic, Egyptian, ancient and medieval, and a part devoted to coins and medals.

The first section covers the period from the Neolithic to the late Iron Age and includes the famous *Vučedol Dove*, a pouring vessel shaped like a bird. Despite the rustic materials used, it nonetheless reveals the technical skills that the pre-Illyrian civilizations had acquired.

Another important exhibit is the bandage used to bind the Mummy of Zagreb. This bandage has mysterious origins and

Gundulić Imagining Osman by Vlaho Bukovac, founder of modern Croat painting, Gallery of Modern Art

An avenue in Maksimir Park, home of the Zoo

bears text in the Etruscan language, which has not yet been completely deciphered.

The museum's ancient collection is the most important of all and includes the Lapidarium which can be found in the courtyard. It is a collection of stone monuments dating from the Roman period (it is open every day except for Monday). The valuable exhibit of the *Head of Plautilla*, from the Roman town Salana (*see pp116-7*), is not currently on display but is the emblem of the museum.

An archaeological conservation laboratory dedicated to preserving the exhibits is also part of the museum. In addition the museum has developed several educational projects aimed at school children. The archaeological library next door houses over 45,000 volumes, some of which are very rare.

Head of Plautilla, Archaeological Museum

Museum of Contemporary Art ㉖

Muzej suvremene umjetnosti

Avenija Dubrovnik 17. *Tel (01) 605 27 00.* ◯ *11am–6pm Tue–Sun, 11am–8pm Sat.* **www**.msu.hr

The museum holds a collection of 12,000 works of art by Croatian and foreign artists. Drawings, posters, films, photography, sculptures and paintings cover the period from the 20th century onwards, although most pieces are from the second half of the 20th century. The museum moved into a new building, designed by the architect Igor Franić, in 2010.

Maksimir Park ㉗

Maksimirski Perivoj

Maksimirski perivoj bb. ◯ *daily.* **www**.park-maksimir.hr

The largest park in the city (covering over 3 sq km/ 1 sq mile), is considered one of Croatia's living monuments. It is named after Bishop Maksimilijan Vrhovac, who initiated the project in 1794. The park was finally completed in 1843.

The park is landscaped in the English style with wide lawns and flower beds, small woods and lakes. A **Zoo** (Zoološki vrt), has hundreds of different animal species. Among the follies scattered around the park is one called **Vidikovac** (Belvedere).

Mirogoj Cemetery ㉘

Groblje Mirogoj

Mirogoj. ◯ *winter: 7.30am–6pm daily, summer: 6am–8pm daily.*

At the foot of Mount Medvednica, 4 km (2 miles) from the centre of the city, is the Mirogoj Cemetery, built in 1876 by Hermann Bollé. This great architect had already demonstrated his ability and talent with the building of the new city district. The cemetery covers an area of 28,000 sq m (6.91 acres) and the tombs of the most illustrious figures in the political, cultural and artistic life of Croatia lie here.

An imposing façade covered in ivy forms the entrance to the Catholic and Orthodox chapels. From here branch two long Neo-Renaissance arcades which house the burial rooms of the most important families.

A long tree-lined avenue divides the area into two sections which in turn are divided into squares of trees and bushes. Among the areas of greenery stand funeral monuments by leading Croatian sculptors and engravers. There are works by Ivan Meštrović, Jozo Kljaković, Ivan Rendić, Antun Filipović, Antun Augustinčić, Edo Murtić, Ivan Kerdić and Robert Frangeš-Mihanović.

As well as the tombs of notable personalities there is also a monument dedicated to the memory of the soldiers who died during World War I, by Juri Turkalj and V Radauš, and a monument dedicated to the Jews who died in World War II, by Antun Augustinčić. On one of the cemetery lawns there is a monument dedicated to the German soldiers killed in the war.

The well-preserved cemetery is a real open-air museum and is often visited by the local inhabitants, who regularly put fresh flowers and candles on the tombs of great Croats of the past.

Arcade in the Mirogoj Cemetery, one of the most beautiful in Europe

Gallery of Old Masters ㉓
Galerija Starih Majstora

In 1880 Josip Juraj Strossmayer, the rich
and powerful Bishop of Đakovo and one
of the leading proponents of a pan-Slav
movement, had this gallery built to house
the Academy of Arts and Sciences and
the Gallery of Old Masters, to which he
donated his own impressive collection of
about 250 works of art.

The Neo-Renaissance building has a
large internal porticoed courtyard. Nine
rooms on the upper floor house around
200 works from the major European
schools from the 14th to the 19th century. Behind
the building is a large statue of Bishop Strossmayer
sculpted by Ivan Meštrović in 1926.

**Virgin with Child
and St Francis
and St Bernardine
of Siena**
*This painting is one
of the few works by
Bartolomeo Caporali
(c.1420–1505) to be
found outside
Perugia in Italy.*

Susanna and the Elders
*The three figures depicted in the
painting stand out against the
landscape in the background. The
faces of the two old men are very
expressive; it is as though they
are revived by gazing at the
beautiful Susanna. The artist,
Master of the Prodigal Son,
demonstrates great technical
skill and vivid use of colour.*

**Second
floor**

GALLERY GUIDE
*The gallery is on the second
floor of the building. Exhibits
include works by important
Italian, German, Flemish and
French masters, representing
schools and artistic trends
from the 14th to the 19th
century. Before visiting the
gallery, note, in the entrance
hall, the Baška Tablet, one of
the oldest documents of Croat
culture (11th century),
written in Glagolitic script.*

Madame Recamier
*This portrait by Antoine Jean Gros
(1771–1835) was probably painted
around 1825. It is of a Madame
Recamier who was a leading figure
of some notoriety in Parisian high
society of that time.*

Virgin Mary with Jesus, John and an Angel
This tondo by Jacopo del Sellaio uses exuberant colour. The Tuscan artist belonged to the circle of Filippo Lippi and Sandro Botticelli.

VISITORS' CHECKLIST

Trg Nikole Šubića Zrinskog 11.
Tel *(01) 489 5117.* ◯
*10am–7pm Tue, 10am–4pm
Wed–Fri, 10am–1pm Sat & Sun.*
📷 🎥 📷 *(without flash)*

Adam and Eve
This lively oil on panel painting is by Mariotto Albertinelli (1474–1515), a Florentine painter. It shows Adam and Eve being expelled from Earthly Paradise.

KEY

▢	Italian School 14th–16th century
▢	Italian School 16th–18th century
▢	Flemish and Dutch Masters and European School 15th–17th century
▢	French Masters 18th–19th century
▢	Non-exhibition space

★ St Augustine and St Benedict
The work reveals the expressive skill of the great Venetian master, Giovanni Bellini (1430–1516). The figures of the saints occupy simple niches.

★ St Sebastian
This delicate image of the saint by Vittore Carpaccio (1465–1525) was part of a polyptych. In this painting with its vivid colouring, the Venetian master expresses the drama of the martyrdom through the smile of the young man at the moment of his death.

Main entrance

STAR PAINTINGS

★ St Augustine and St Benedict

★ St Sebastian

CENTRAL CROATIA

*C*entral Croatia is bordered to the west by the vine-covered hills of Samobor, which continue on towards Karlovac and Ogulin, and to the south by the Bosnia-Herzegovina border as far as Jasenovac. To the northeast is a stretch of fertile valley formed by the Sava river, which goes from Zagreb to the Lonjsko Polje Nature Park. These wetlands, south of Sisak, are home to all kinds of birds.

This region of Croatia has long been a meeting point for different civilizations. Until the 12th century BC, this area was inhabited by the Illyrians, who were joined by Celts in the 4th century BC. The first Illyrian cities became Roman towns after the 1st century AD. The most important was Siscia (now called Sisak), which was sacked by the Huns in 441 and raided by the Avars in the 6th century.

Head of Mitra, 2nd century AD, Sisak

The southern border with Bosnia, which dates back to 271 AD, was confirmed at the time of the division between the Western and Eastern Churches in 1054, and later re-confirmed when the Turks occupied the Balkans. To stop the continuous Turkish raids, in 1578 the Austrian Emperor established a *Vojna Krajina* (Military Frontier) in areas which had mostly been abandoned by the Croats, who had fled to the coastal cities for refuge. To help guard the borders, Serbian refugees were brought in, along with minorities of Vlachs, Albanians, Montenegrin and German-speaking groups. Villages sprang up which were inhabited by Catholics, Muslims and people of the Orthodox faith. These diverse communities lived together without any serious tension until the mid-19th century, when feelings of nationalism swept across Europe. The most recent war, fought in the name of nationalism, not only created widespread destruction but also "ethnic cleansing", resulting in the exodus of thousands of Serbs.

This part of Croatia is the area least visited by tourists, although it offers magnificent scenery with rivers and wood-covered hills and good Croatian cuisine. There is plenty to see, with ancient castles, churches, museums and nature reserves.

Horses grazing in the Lonjsko Polje Nature Park

◁ *The Assumption*, a fresco by Franc Jelovšek in the Franciscan church of St Anastasia, Samobor

Exploring Central Croatia

Three distinct areas make up this part of the country:
the lowlands around the capital, Zagreb, with numerous
18th-century buildings constructed on the sites of
ancient castles; the hilly area between Samobor and
Karlovac, renowned for its wine production; and the
strip of border with Bosnia-Herzegovina, south of Sisak.
The landscape of Central Croatia is varied, with areas of
rolling plains alternating with vine-covered hills. Higher
areas are covered in thick woods and there is also an
area of wetlands that comprise Lonjsko Polje Nature
Park. In the cities and larger towns there are Baroque
churches, monasteries, castles, fortresses and
museums. Most suffered damage in the 1991–95
war, but some have been repaired since.

**Roman piece,
Civic Museum, Sisak**

**Interior of the church of
St Mary in Jastrebarsko**

SAMOBOR ①

OKIĆ ③

JASTREBARSKO ④

OZALJ ⑤

KARLOVAC ⑥

OGULIN ⑦

TOPUSKO TOPLICE ⑧

Ljubljana   Laduč   Zabok

Zaprešić ②

Žumberačko Gorje

Kerestinec

Brezovica

Velika Gorica

Kupa

GRAD ZAGREB

OZALJ

Duga Resa

Rijeka

Tušilović

KARLOVAČKA

Vojnić

Glina

Josipdol

Korana

Drežnica

Slunj

Plaški

Zadar

Mala Kapela

Broćanac

Rakovica

Velika Kapela

Poku

GETTING AROUND

The road network which crosses
central Croatia is good. Recently roads
have been improved and the motorways
extended. From Zagreb the A3 motorway goes
to Samobor and the Lonjsko Polje Nature Park.
State road number 30 serves Sisak, while a secondary road network connects the other towns. All the
main towns and cities are served by the Croatian railway
system, except for the city of Samobor. Buses go to all
villages, however small.

0 kilometres   20

0 miles   20

SIGHTS AT A GLANCE

Garić **15**
Jasenovac **11**
Jastrebarsko **4**
Karlovac **6**
Hrvatska Kostajnica **10**
Kutina **14**
Lonjsko Polje Nature Park **13**
Novska **12**
Ogulin **7**
Okić **3**

Ozalj **5**
Samobor **1**
Sisak **9**
Topusko Toplice **8**

Tour
*Tour of Country Houses
pp172–3* **2**

LOCATOR MAP

SEE ALSO

• *Where to Stay* p231–2

• *Where to Eat* p247–8

The River Sava near Sisak

The vine-covered hills around Okić

KEY

━━ Motorway
━━ Major road
━━ Minor road
━━ Main railway
━━ County border
━━ International border

The main altar in the church of St Mary, Samobor

Samobor **❶**

Map C2. 🧍 *15,200.* 🚌 *(01) 336 72 76.* 🚉 *Trg kralja Tomislava 5, (01) 336 00 44.* 🎭 *Carnival (Feb); Day of the city (3rd Sat in Oct).* **www**.tz–samobor.hr

Samobor is built below the ruins of what was once a large fort (Stari Grad). In 1242 it was granted the status of a royal free town, and became an important trading centre. Today it is one of the capitals of Croatian gastronomy, priding itself on its traditional local dishes.

In the oldest area (Taborec) is the Gothic church of **St Michael** (Sv. Mihalj), which was remodelled in the Baroque period. Dating from the same time is the church of **St Anastasia** (Sv. Anastazija) and a Franciscan monastery with the church of St Mary (Sv. Marija): the *Assumption* behind the main altar was frescoed by Franc Jelovšek in 1752, while the altar on

the left was decorated by Valentin Metzinger (1734). The adjacent monastery is laid out around a beautiful quadrangular cloister and has Baroque frescoes in the refectory and library.

The history of the city and local area is well documented in the **Civic Museum** (Muzej Grada Samobora), housed in the 18th-century Livadić Palace. The section dedicated to the history of Croatian mountaineering is especially interesting.

🏠 St Anastasia
Ulica Sv. Ane 2. **Tel** *(01) 336 00 82.* ◐ *by appt.*

🏛 Civic Museum
Livadićeva 7. **Tel** *(01) 336 10 14.* ◐ *9am–3pm Tue–Fri, 9am–1pm Sat, 10am–5pm Sun.* 📷 📹 ✗ 🏠

Tour of Country Houses **❷**

See pp172–3.

Okić **❸**

Map C2.
🚉 **County:** *Preradovićeva 42, Zagreb, (01) 4873 665.*

On the isolated hilltop above Okić stand the ruins of a fortified town. These consist of the remains of a wall with round towers, an entrance gate and a Gothic chapel. The town, mentioned in documents from 1183, belonged to the counts of Okić, Zrinski,

Frankopan and Erdödy. It was destroyed by the Turks and the town was eventually abandoned in 1616.

In the village around the foot of the hill is the church of **St Mary** (Sv. Marija). It was rebuilt in 1893 incorporating a decorated doorway from 1691. Inside are some Baroque altars, a splendid pulpit and a font. In front of the church is an octagonal bell tower with a vestibule.

A painting by Metzinger in the church of St Mary in Jastrebarsko

Jastrebarsko **❹**

Map C2. 🧍 *5,500.* 🚉 *from Zagreb.* 🚌 *from Zagreb.* 🚉 *Strossmayerov trg 4, (01) 627 2940;* **www**.tzgj.hr

At the foot of the Plešivica mountain chain, between Samobor and Karlovac, stands Jastrebarsko. The town appears in documents of 1249. It assumed greater importance in 1257 when it was declared a royal free town by Bela IV and became a trading centre for timber, livestock and the wine which is still produced locally.

In the 15th century the town was a feudal holding of the Erdödy family, who built an imposing **castle** on a square ground-plan with round towers at the corners and an internal porticoed courtyard. Two centuries later it was altered and turned into a residential building which is now closed to the public.

The Baroque church of **St Nicholas** (Sv. Nikola; 1772–75) contains a fresco by

The ruins of the fortified town of Okić, perched on a hilltop

Rašica and the tomb of Petar Erdödy (1567). In the church of **St Mary** (Sv. Marija; 1740), originally Dominican and later Franciscan, the altars are all Baroque. The painting on the altar dedicated to Mary is by Valentin Metzinger and dates from 1735.

Ozalj ❺

Map C2. 🏛 1,200. 🚉 (047) 731 158. 🚌 Karlovac, (060) 338 833, Ozalj, (047) 731107. 🚶 Kurilovac 1, (047) 731 196. 🎭 Day of the city (30 Apr); Summer evenings in Ozalj (15–20 Aug). **www**.ozalj-tz.hr

A castle (Stari Grad) which belonged to royalty once stood on this rocky spur. It was built in the 13th century to monitor the roads and the traffic on the river Kupa which flows below it. The castle was strengthened by the Babonić counts and was also the property of the Frankopan family and, in the late 16th century, of Juraj Zrinski. After the Ottoman threat had passed, a village grew up around the castle which had become a residential manor.

Parts of the fortress remain visible: two encircling walls with five semicircular towers. Next to these are some more recent buildings: the granary *(palas)* (16th century) and a Gothic family chapel.

Coat of arms, Civic Museum, Karlovac

Ozalj castle, once owned by the Frankopans and Juraj Zrinski

The main building, on several levels, was renovated in 1928 by the Thurn und Taxis family who had inherited it. For a time the building was abandoned but in 1971 it became a **Museum**. Exhibits explain the history of the fort and local area and there are some Glagolitic inscriptions.

🏰 **Castle and Museum**
Ulica Zrinskih i Frankopana. 🚶 (047) 731 170. 📷 for restoration. The outer parts can be visited; guided tours for groups to some parts of the castle: 8am–3pm Mon–Fri. 🎭

Karlovac ❻

Map C2.
🏛 60,000. 🚉 (060) 333 444. 🚌 (060) 338 833. 🚶 **Local:** Ulica Petra Zrinskog 3, (047) 615 115; **Regional:** A Vraniczanya 6, (047) 615 320. **www**.karlovac-touristinfo.hr 🎭 Spring Promenades (May); St John's Bonfires (Jun); International folk festival (Aug).

Today Karlovac is an industrial city and an important junction for roads to Slovenia. It originated as a bulwark against Turkish raids, but was actually founded in 1579 by the Archduke of Austria, Charles of Habsburg, from whom the town gets its name.

The town was planned by the Italian N Angelini as a city-fort at the confluence of the rivers Korana and Kupa. The layout was based on a six-pointed star with bastions and moats which have now been transformed into public gardens. The interior contained 24 buildings, all similar, all of which are still preserved today – although they are used for different purposes.

The heart of the city is Strossmayer Square with the Baroque Frankopan Palace which houses the **Civic Museum** (Gradski Muzej). The archaeological and ethnographic collections document the city's history.

Clock tower of the church of the Holy Trinity in Karlovac

In the square Trg Bana Jelačića is a Franciscan monastery, with a **Museum of Sacred Art** in the cloisters.

The town is also the site of the Catholic church of the **Holy Trinity** (Presvetoga Trojstvo), mainly from 1683–92 with an 18th-century clock tower (1795). The church has an elaborate black marble altar made by Michele Cussa in 1698. The Orthodox church of St Nicholas (Sv. Nikola) dates from 1786.

To the east the city now extends as far as **Dubovac Castle**, a medieval construction. The castle was used as a hotel, but is being restored to its original design.

🏛 **Civic Museum**
Strossmayerov trg 7. **Tel** (047) 615 980. 🕐 8am–4pm Mon–Fri, 10am–noon Sat–Sun. 🎭 🏛 by appt. **www**.gmk.hr

🏛 **Museum of Sacred Art**
Trg bana Jelačića 7. **Tel** (047) 615 950/1. 🕐 by appointment.

🏰 **Holy Trinity**
Trg bana Jelačića 7. **Tel** (047) 615 950/1. 🕐 before mass. Other times by appt.

Tour of Country Houses ❷

To the south and west of Zagreb are several small towns which are easily reached from the A1 motorway, where there are numerous buildings of great architectural interest. Several of them are found along the road which goes from Zaprešić to the Zagorje hills. They were built by members of the Croatian aristocracy after the threat of Turkish invasion had passed and are mainly 18th- and 19th-century reconstructions of older houses. Almost all of the buildings were expropriated after World War II when the Croatian state was set up, and put to different uses. Most of the interiors are not open to the public.

Lužnica ④
Built in the 18th century, this large building has two storeys and a U-shaped ground plan. The central part is flanked by four round towers with conical roofs. The centre of the long façade culminates in a high tympanum and there are three arched windows on the upper floor above a splendid doorway.

Januševec ⑤
This building, 6 km (4 miles) from Zaprešić, is one of the most beautiful examples of Neo-Classical architecture in Croatia. It was built around 1830 and has three storeys and a rectangular ground plan centred around a central hall lit by a lantern in the roof. In the centre of the Palladian façade is a three-arched portico with four columns above, crowned by a large tympanum.

| 0 kilometres | 3 |
| 0 miles | 3 |

Laduč ⑥
This castle, 7 km (4 miles) west of Zaprešić, was constructed by the architect K Waidman in 1882 for Baron Vladimir Vraniczany. The pastel colour of the large two-storey building blends harmoniously with the deep green lawns in front. In the centre of the façade is a three-arched portico with an arched loggia above. Today the building is home to an institution providing social services.

Novi Dvori ③

This Neo-Romanesque building near Zaprešić stands on the site of an older structure which was once the country residence of the Ban, Josip Jelačić (1801–59). The house, surrounded by a large park, was partly restored in 1991. The façade has a high stepped tympanum and in front of the entrance is an arched portico with a terrace above. The family tomb stands in the grounds.

TIPS FOR DRIVERS

Departure point: Brezovica.
Length of tour: 40 km (25 miles) one way.
Information: All the houses included in this tour can be seen from the outside. Some may be partially open for visitors.
🛈 Zagreb Tourist Office: Trg bana Jelačića 11, (01) 481 40 51, 481 40 52. **Stopping-off points:** Samoborska Klet, Trg kralja Tomislava 7. **Tel** (01) 332 65 36, is a traditional restaurant in Samobor. Cheaper restaurants include the Samoborska Pivnica beerhall.

KRAPINA

aprešić

E59

Kerestinec ②

This villa, southwest of Zagreb, was built in 1575 over older buildings by the Erdödy family. It is famous as a place where many intellectuals were imprisoned in World War II. The square building stands in a lovely park and has four round corner towers, a fine doorway and an internal arcaded courtyard.

Bestovje

v. Nedjelja

KEY

▬▬ Tour route

▬▬ Motorway

═══ Other roads

ZAGREB

E65

VARAŽDIN

E71

②

①

KARLOVAC

Brezovica ①

The Drašković family built a house here in the 16th century. It was converted into a Baroque palace two centuries later and for some time has been a luxury hotel. The two-storey building has a U-shaped ground plan and the façade has two round corner towers and a raised central section.

The 15th-century castle of the Frankopan counts in Ogulin

Ogulin ❼

Map C2. 🏘 8,800. 🚉 (047) 525 001. 🛈 Kardinala A. Stepinca 1, (047) 532 278. **www**.tz-grada-ogulina.hr

When Marshal Tito was imprisoned here in 1927 and 1933 *(see p42)* this town became well-known throughout Croatia. The prison was part of a castle built by the Frankopan counts in the 15th century. The castle walls enclosed a large building with two tall towers at the ends, a Gothic chapel and several houses which were built when Ogulin became a staging post on the *Vojna Krajina* (Military Frontier, *see p39*) in 1627. Part of the structure is given over to the **Regional Museum** which has sections on archaeology, folklore and mountaineering.

A short distance from the fortified town is the Old Castle (Zulumgrad) situated near the Đula abyss: a chasm formed by the Dobra river.

Topusko Toplice ❽

Map D2. 🏘 800. 🚌 from Zagreb, Sisak, Karlovac. 🛈 Trg bana Jelačića 4, (044) 885 203. 🎭 Days of Honey (Feb); Folklore Day (Jun); Half Marathon (Aug). **www**.turizam-topusko.com

The presence of a Cistercian abbey made this a centre for spreading Christianity in the Banovina area (a region of green valleys south of Sisak, between the Sava and Glina rivers). The abbey was founded in 1204 by King Andrew II and a village grew up around it in the Middle Ages. The remains can be found in Opatovina Park.

The nearby hot water springs (up to 78°C/ 172°F) were used in Roman times and in the first half of the 19th century a thermal spa was established which was frequented by the Emperor Franz Joseph and other court dignitaries. Today the spa treats rheumatic and neurological problems, and the after-effects of incapacitating injuries. The spa has three main thermal sources and the water comes from a depth of 1,500 m (4,920 ft). The quality of the water has not changed in the last 200 years. There are two hotels in Topusko and a number of private accommodations.

Sisak ❾

Map D2. 🏘 36,800. 🚉 (044) 524 724. 🚌 (060) 330 060. 🛈 Rimska ulica bb, (044) 522 655. **www**.sisakturist.com

The city of Sisak, at the point where the rivers Kupa and Odra flow into the Sava, has always played an important role in Croatian history. Its name has changed a number of times over the course of its 2,000 years of existence. It originated as the Illyrian-Celtic Segestica, becoming Siscia with the Romans, and later Colonia Flavia Siscia. Rome conquered the town after a bloody battle

Hercules (1st century AD), Sisak museum

in which Emperor Augustus was wounded. After the conquest of the Balkans, the emperor made it the capital of the Pannonia Savia province and it became a trading centre.

It was destroyed by Attila in 441, and in the 6th century it was raided by the Avars and Slavs. The town was finally rebuilt by the Croats and became Sisak. It was from here that Prince Ljudevit began the conquest of Croatia in the 8th century. Sisak was destroyed again by the Hungarians in the 10th century, and was also abandoned by the bishop, who transferred the see to Zagreb, but built a fort here. In 1593 this fort was the site of a battle which resulted in the first Turkish defeat in the Balkans.

The town rose again nearby and began to enjoy a long period of prosperity, thanks to the tolls on river traffic. It still has some Baroque buildings, including the old and new town halls.

A park surrounds the **fortress** (Stari Grad) on the River Kupa, south of the city. The fortress was built in the middle of the 16th century at the time of the Turkish invasions. It has a triangular ground plan, with three large round brick towers (1544–55), connected by a high wall with openings for firearms. In the park is a beautiful traditional farmhouse. The **Civic Museum** (Gradski Muzej) has material from the Roman settlement.

🏰 **Fortress**
Tome Bakača Erdödyja. 📞 (044) 811 811. ⏰ contact for info.

🏛 **Civic Museum**
Kralja Tomislava 10. **Tel** (044) 811 811. ⏰ Apr–Sep: 10am–6pm Tue–Fri, 9am–noon Sat–Sun; Oct–Mar: 7:30am–3:30pm Mon–Fri, by appt. Sat & Sun. 📷 📵 **www**.muzej-sisak.hr

---

Environs
About 20 km (12 miles) south-west is **Gora** which, in the Middle Ages, was the centre of a Županija (county) of the same name. The county seat

Fortress of Sisak next to the Kupa river, built in the 13th century was a castle which appears in documents in 1242, but which was destroyed by the Turks in 1578. The Gothic church of the **Assumption of the Blessed Virgin Mary** (Uznesenja Blažene Djevice Marije) was also badly damaged and was restored in the 18th century in the Baroque style. The church has chapels on all corners and resembles a castle, with a marble altar and pulpit inside.

Hrvatska Kostajnica ⓾

Map D2. 🏘 *2,000.* 🚆 *from Zagreb, Sisak.* 🚌 *from Zagreb, Sisak.* 🛈 *Vladimira Nazora 17, (044) 851 800.*

Standing on the left bank of the River Una which, for much of its length, marks the border between Croatia and Bosnia-Herzegovina, this town still bears the signs of damage from the war in the 1990s. By the river, near a bridge, is a renovated castle built in the Middle Ages but frequently razed. Only three towers connected by a high wall remain in the wake of the last war. The church and monastery of **St Anthony of Padua**, built after the Turks left at the end of the 17th century, have been restored and are discreetly furnished (some of the Baroque altars were famous for their beauty).

Environs
Around 14 km (9 miles) to the southwest is **Zrin**, where the ruins of a castle built in the 14th century by the Babonić family stand on a hill. In 1347 it passed to the Bribir princes

The tulip-shaped monument by Bogdanović in Jasenovac cemetery

of Šubić. A branch of the family took the name of Zrinski after the village around the castle. It was occupied by the Turks from 1577 until the end of the 17th century when they destroyed it.

The Zrinskis played an important role in Croatia's history: as fierce defenders against the Turks; then as the authors of the failed attempt to free the territory from Habsburg rule *(see p177)*.

Jasenovac ⓫

Map E2. 🏘 *780.* 🚆 *from Sisak.* 🚌 *from Sisak.* 🛈 *Trg kralja Petra Svačića 3, (044) 672 490.*

This town is notorious as the place where, during World War II, tens of thousands of prisoners of war, Jews, Gysies, Serbs and Croats, perished in the concentration camp which was located here. In memory of this terrible genocide, a

large tulip-shaped monument, designed by the artist Bogdan Bogdanović, has been erected in the centre of what used to be a concentration camp.

The church of St Luke in Novska

Novska ⓬

Map E2. 🏘 *7,300.* 🚆 *from Zagreb, Sisak, (044) 892 421.* 🚌 *from Zagreb, Sisak.* 🛈 *Potočna ulica 1a, (044) 601 305.*

The town of Novska is the starting point for visiting the Lonjsko Polje Nature Park *(see p176)* and for excursions to the Psunj mountains. A number of recreational sports can be enjoyed here too.

The church of **St Luke** (Sv. Luka) is a Baroque church dating from 1775. It has a fine altar and a painting by the modern painter Z Šulentić.

In the **Bauer Gallery** there are many works by Naive and contemporary artists.

Novska's economy is based on industry and trade and rail and road links are good.

The castle of medieval origins in Kostajnica, on the banks of the Una

Nesting storks in the Lonjsko Polje Nature Park

Lonjsko Polje Nature Park ⓭

Map D2. **Park office (Krapje)**
🛈 (044) 672 080. Entrance at Čigoč
🛈 (044) 715 115 (Čigoč). ◯ Apr–Oct: 8am–4pm daily; Nov–Mar: by appt. 🖳 **www**.pp-lonjsko-polje.hr

The wide bend in the River-Sava between Sisak and Stara Gradiška has been a special ornithological reserve since 1963. It became a nature reserve in 1990 to protect an area of 506 sq km (195 sq miles). This vast area was regularly flooded by the river and its tributaries (Lonja, Ilova, Pakra and Čazma) during the thaw, and in the summer and early autumn the waters would recede. Since the 1960s parts of the wetlands have been drained, but they still remain some of Europe's most important marshland.

Woods of oak, poplar, ash and willow trees grow along the banks of the river and on the higher ground, while the dry fields are used as grazing for sheep in the summer months. Wild boar live here, as well as deer, and there are also Turopolje pigs and Posavina horses, both of which are protected species.

The park is an important stopping place for black storks, which arrive in spring and leave in autumn after nesting, for numerous species of heron, for egrets and a variety of birds of prey, including the rare harrier and white-tailed eagles.

Kutina ⓮

Map D2. 🏠 15,000. 🚉 (060) 333 444. 🚌 (060) 355 060. 🚺 Crkvena 42, (044) 681 004. **www**.turizam-kutina.hr

Kutina, in the Moslavina region, was built over the ruins of a Roman *castrum* (a Roman military camp or fort) and numerous archaeological finds have been discovered. The town is linked to two castles; Kutinjac Grad, documented in 1256, and the fortress of Plovdin, however only ruins and parts of the walls remain.

Kutina flourished again in the 17th century, developing on the plain south of the fortress. It is here that the church of **Our Lady of the Snow** (Marija Snježna) was built by Count Karl Erdödy in around 1770. The church is surrounded by a covered portico and is decorated inside with stucco and *trompe-l'oeil* paintings by Josip Görner. The sculpture and the inlaid wooden furnishings which enclose the altar of the Holy Sepulchre are a unique example of Baroque composition.

Erdödy Castle, which was rebuilt in 1895, houses the **Museum of Moslavina** (Muzej Moslavine) which tells the history and folklore of Moslavina through an extensive collection of documents, objects and traditional costumes.

🏛 Museum of Moslavina
Trg kralja Tomislava 13. **Tel** (044) 683 548. ◯ 8am–1pm Tue–Fri.

Interior of the church of Our Lady of the Snow in Kutina

Environs
Around 50 km (31 miles) northwest of Kutina is **Ivanić-Grad** and the nearby towns of **Kloštar Ivanić** and **Križ**. In Ivanić-Grad there are workshops making pretty flax and linen products, keeping local traditions alive.

In Kloštar Ivanić there is a Franciscan monastery founded in 1508 and the church of St Mary (Sv. Marija), with collections of silver, paintings and richly illustrated music codices.

In Križ, the parish church of the Cross was founded by the Knights Templar in the 11th century. The church has a decorative Baroque interior and a magnificent 1787 organ.

Some remains of the old fortifications around Garić

Garić ⓯

Map D2. 🏠 76 (Podgarić). 🚺 **Regional**: Trg Eugena Kvaternika 4, Bjelovar, (043) 243 944.

On a hill in the Moslavačka chain (Moslavačka Gora) near Podgarić stand the ruins of the fortified town of Garić, noted as a *castrum* in 1256. In 1277, it was granted by the king to Timotej, Bishop of Zagreb, who entrusted its defence to the counts of Gardun, and later to the counts of Celje. Nearby, below Garić, the Pauline order founded the monastery of St Mary in 1295. In 1544 the town and the monastery were destroyed by the Turks.

The fortified town was protected by high walls and was an irregular shape. There was a moat with towers, and further towers inside the walls.

The Zrinski and Frankopan Dynasties

Dujam, count of Krk, died in 1163 and his descendants took the name of Frankopan *(Frangere Panem)* after Venice confirmed the family's rule over Krk. They were allied with Venice until 1480 when they were forced to surrender the island. However, they still had vast estates given to them by the Hungarian kings. The Šubić family became counts of Bribir, when they were granted the town by King Andrew II in 1290, and counts of Zrinski in 1347 when they were obliged to move to Zrin *(see p175)*. The execution of the Ban of Croatia, Petar Zrinski, and his brother-in-law Fran Krsto Frankopan in 1671 ended the two most powerful Croatian dynasties. The Habsburgs confiscated their property and the Zrinski line died out. A branch of the Frankopan family still survives in Friuli, Italy.

Fran Krsto Frankopan *(1643–1671), great grandson of Krsto Frankopan and Mario Frangipane's heir (the Roman branch of the family), was publicly executed in Wiener Neustadt in 1671, for his part in a plot against the Empire.*

Krsto Frankopan, *(1480?–1527), son of Bernard, Ban of Croatia, and Louise of Aragon, was Emperor Maximilian's general in the war against Venice in the early 16th century. He was imprisoned in Milan and died fighting for the independence of Hungary, of which Croatia was part.*

Fran Krsto Frankopan awaiting execution

Petar Zrinski

EXECUTION OF THE REBELS

On 30 April 1671, in the town square in Wiener Neustadt, the Ban of Croatia, Petar Zrinski, and his brother-in-law, Krsto Frankopan, were beheaded on charges of high treason on the orders of Emperor Leopold I. The two brothers-in-law had attempted to form a coalition of the Croatian feudal lords in order to limit Austro-Hungarian influence.

Nikola Zrinski *fought against the Turks and was a defender of Christianity. He died in the Battle of Siget in 1566, after he refused the sultan's offer to make him Governor of Croatia if he abandoned the Emperor.*

Petar Zrinski *was the Ban (governor) from 1664, and the leader of the movement which sought to limit Habsburg activity in Croatia. The attempted revolt was foiled by betrayals and the promise of a possible agreement. The two leaders went to Vienna to negotiate with the Emperor. When they reached the capital they were imprisoned, and a few months later were beheaded.*

Waterlilies in the Lonjsko Polje Nature Park, a paradise for many species of birds and animals ▷

SLAVONIA AND BARANJA

The easternmost part of northern Croatia, between Hungary, Serbia and Bosnia-Herzegovina, is one of the most fertile areas of Europe, known as "the granary" of Croatia. The landscape of Slavonia and Baranja is characterized by expanses of wheat and maize fields and hills covered with vineyards or ancient woods. The main city, Osijek, is famous for its fortified centre.

First inhabited by the Illyrians, present-day Slavonia and Baranja came into contact with the Roman world in the 2nd century BC. It took the Romans more than 200 years to subdue the inhabitants of this region, which they referred to as Pannonia. From 402 Pannonia was invaded, first by the Goths, then the Huns, Visigoths, Burgundians, Gepids, Longobards, Sarmatians and finally the Avars. When the Slavs arrived, very little remained of Roman rule, and the land, ever since then called Slavonia, was practically uninhabited.

Fresco in the church of St Francis, Požega

In 925 the Kingdom of the Croat Sovereigns was set up and this lasted until 1097, when King Koloman came to rule Slavonia and created the Hungarian-Croat kingdom. Following the Battle of Mohács in 1526, Slavonia became part of the Ottoman Empire, and remained so until 1689.

To confront the constant disputes between the Turks and the Holy Roman Empire, the Habsburgs set up a Military Frontier (*Vojna Krajina*), which lasted until 1881, when Austria-Hungary took Bosnia-Herzegovina from the Turks. The frontier was abolished and absorbed into Croatia.

When war broke out in 1991, the presence of Serb villages was a pretext for the Serbian occupation of Slavonia. In 1995, under the auspices of the United Nations, control of Slavonia reverted back to the Croatians. Although war damage is still visible along the border, particularly in Vukovar, great efforts are being made with rebuilding and Slavonia is once again well worth visiting for its historical treasures. It is also an area of great natural beauty and includes the nature reserve of Kopački Rit, a wetlands sanctuary for wildfowl.

Local people in the typical traditional costumes of the region

◁ The tall spires of the Neo-Gothic cathedral in Osijek *(see p188)*, with the River Drava in the background

Exploring Slavonia and Baranja

Slavonia, the region between the rivers Sava, Drava and Danube, is made up of a vast rolling alluvial plain with chains of hills at its edges which are covered in woods and vineyards. At one time the rivers turned the area into an enormous swamp for many months of the year. Baranja is a triangular are a of land in the far northeast, bordered at the extreme tip by the rivers Drava and Danube and the Hungarian border.

The plains are covered in fields of maize and the hills are given over to viticulture. In the southern corner, the Drava river regularly overflows from spring to autumn to create a broad area of marshland, now the Kopački Rit Nature Park. The park is an important wildlife sanctuary, a refuge for hundreds of different species of bird, including the rare black stork.

On the right bank of the Drava river is Slavonia's main city, Osijek. It has wide avenues, parks, and 19th-century, Viennese-style buildings, as well as a Neo-Gothic cathedral.

The Baroque belfry of St Roch in Virovitica

SIGHTS AT A GLANCE

The countryside around Slavonski Brod

GETTING AROUND

For many years Osijek was a rail, road and river junction of some importance. Since the war in the 1990s, rail and river traffic has become less significant. However, Osijek is still the centre of the road system in the area and, thanks to a good network, the city can easily be reached from Slavonia and Baranja using state road number 2 heading south from Varaždin, or the same number 2 road north from Vukovar and the E73 from Hungary. There is also an efficient public bus service. About 7 km (4 miles) from Osijek there is a domestic airport with daily connections to Zagreb. Osijek itself has an excellent tram service which makes it easy to get around the city.

LOCATOR MAP

SEE ALSO

- *Where to Stay* pp232–3
- *Where to Eat* pp248–9

The traditional costumes of Bizovac

KEY

▬	Motorway
▬ ▬	Motorway under construction
▬	Major road
═	Minor road
▬	Main railway
▬	County border
▬	International border

The ruins of Grad Ružica, near Orahovica

0 kilometres 15

0 miles 15

Daruvar **❶**

Map E2. 🏛 *10,000.* ✈ *Osijek, 130 km (81 miles); Zagreb, 150 km (93 miles).* 🚌 ➡ 🛈 *Trg kralja Tomislava 12, (043) 331 382.* 🍷 *Wine exhibition (May/June).* **www**.tz-daruvar.hr

This spa town was known as Aquae Balissae in the time of the Roman Empire for the quality of its hot water spring, the source of which is at the foot of the Papuk mountains.

The town developed from three medieval settlements. In 1760 the area was bought by a Hungarian count, Antun Janković, who built a Baroque castle he named Daruvar, and the first **spa**. Today, Daruvar (meaning "city of the crane") has hotels, a **Medical Centre** (Daruvarske Toplice) offering the spa waters, the Daruvar wine road and a thermal water park, Aquae Balissae.

There are two 18th-century churches in the town, one Catholic and one Orthodox. Daruvar is also a centre for the Czech people in Croatia, who maintain the Czech language and customs.

💧 Spa
Julijev Park. ***Tel*** *(043) 623 620.*

Lipik **❷**

Map E2. 🏛 *2,300.* ✈ *Osijek, 93 km (58 miles); Zagreb, 155 km (96 miles).* 🚌 ➡ *from Pakrac.* 🛈 *Trg kralja Tomislava 3, (034) 421 600.* 🍷 *Day of the city (4 Nov).* **www**. tz-lipik.com

The area (Aquae Balissae) was known in Roman times for its waters. In the early 19th century a hot water spring, rich in minerals, was rediscovered and Lipik became one of the most famous spas in Croatia. It was especially popular between the two World Wars. Lipik was damaged in the 1991 war, but a new **spa** has been built and the hotels and medical centres restored. Lipik is also known for breeding the famous Lipizzaner horses, which originated in the 16th century in Lipizza, Slovenia.

💧 Spa (Toplice)
Marije Terezije 13. ***Tel*** *(034) 440 700.*

Baroque building in Požega's main square

Nova Gradiška **❸**

Map E2. 🏛 *13,300.* ✈ *Osijek, 93 km (58 miles); Zagreb, 155 km (96 miles).* 🚌 *(035) 361 610.* ➡ *(035) 361 219.* 🛈 *Matije Antuna Reljkovića 9, (035) 361 494.* **www**.tzgng.hr

In 1748 this town was founded as Fredrichsdorf by the Viennese, who planned to build a fortress here. The town, situated at the foot of Mount Psunj, is built on a fertile plain. An agricultural market is regularly held in the main square, which is lined with Baroque buildings.

The Neo-Classical church of St Stephen of Hungary (Sv. Stjepan Kralj) is now the **Immaculate Conception**. The Baroque **Sanctuary of St Theresa** (Sv. Terezija) dates from 1756.

⛪ Immaculate Conception
Aloizija Stepinca 1. ***Tel*** *(035) 362 203.* ⏲ *8am–6pm daily.*

The Baroque Sanctuary of St Theresa in Nova Gradiška

Požega **❹**

Map E2. 🏛 *21,000.* ✈ *Osijek, 67 km (42 miles); Zagreb, 175 km (109 miles).* 🚌 *(034) 273 911.* ➡ *(034) 273 133.* 🛈 *Antuna Kanižlića 3, (034) 274 900.* 🍷 *Feast of St Gregory (12 Mar), Music Festival Zlatne žice Slavonije (3rd weekend in Sep).* **www**.pozega-tz.hr

The Romans first founded this town, a halfway settlement between the towns now called Sisak and Osijek, with the name of Incerum. In the 11th century it was one of the centres from which the heretical movement of the Bogomili spread; after their repression in the 12th century the city was granted to the Templars by King Bela IV.

In 1285 the Franciscans founded a monastery, the church of which was used as a mosque during the Turkish occupation. In the 18th and 19th centuries the town was called the "Athens of Slavonia" for the cultural events held to commemorate the expulsion of the Turks in 1691. The city took on a new look during this period: in the main square, Trg Sv. Trojstva, buildings with stucco and Baroque porticoes were built.

In the square stands a column, a memorial to plague victims made in 1749 by Gabrijel Granicije. To one side of the square is the renovated 18th-century church of **St Francis** (Sv. Franjo). The monastery alongside still houses a community of Franciscan monks.

Interesting examples of Baroque architecture in the town include the Jesuit College (1711) and Gymnasium (1726), opened by the Jesuits who, in 1763, also founded the Požega Academy. Dating from 1763, the church of **St Theresa** (Sv. Terezija Avilska) became a cathedral in 1997. The frescoed walls are by Celestin Medović and Oton Iveković.

The church of **St Lawrence** (Sv. Lovro, 14th century) was renovated in Baroque style in the early 18th century. It still has some 14th-century frescoes. There are also tombstones testifying to the city's glory; one is for the poet Antun Kanižlić (1699–1777). In the square between the church of St Francis and the Jesuit College is a statue of Luka Ibrišimović, a Franciscan who distinguished himself in the battles against the Turks.

14th-century fresco in the church of St Lawrence, Požega

The **Civic Museum** (Gradski Muzej) contains an assortment of archaeological finds, Romanesque reliefs and Baroque paintings.

Every year on 12 March Požega holds an event called Grgurevo, to commemorate a local victory over the Turks won in 1688.

🏛 **Civic Museum**
Matice Hrvatske 1. **Tel** (034) 272 130. ⬭ 9am–2pm Mon–Fri, by appt. Sat & Sun.

🏛 **St Theresa**
Trg Sv. Terezije 13. **Tel** (034) 274 321. ⬭ 8am–noon, 3–6pm daily.

Kutjevo ❺

Map F2. 🏘 2,800. 🚉 Osijek 62 km (38 miles). 🚍 Našice, 27 km (17 miles). 🛈 Republike Hrvatske 77, (034) 315 008. 🎪 Feast of St Gregory (12 Mar).

An important wine-producing centre, the town is famous for a winery founded by the Cistercians. In 1232, the order built a monastery here and encouraged the cultivation of vines. After Turkish rule, at the end of the 17th century, Jesuits took over the monastery and wine-making resumed. The Cistercian cellars are still intact and wine is still an important industry.

The Jesuits also built the church of **St Mary** (Sv. Marija) in 1732, which houses a painting of the Madonna with Child by A Cebej (1759).

Slavonski Brod ❻

Map F3. 🏘 59,510. 🚉 Osijek, 100 km (62 miles); Zagreb, 197 km (122 miles). 🚍 (060) 333 444. 🚆 Trg Hrvatskog proljeća, (060) 310 310. 🛈 **Local:** Trg Pobjede 30, (035) 448 594. **Regional:** Petra Krešimira IV 2, (035) 408 393. 🎪 Brodsko kolo: folk festival (mid-Jun). **www**.tzgsb.hr

Built on the site of the Roman town Marsonia, this town was placed so as to monitor the traffic on the river Sava, the border with Bosnia-Herzegovina. The town

Baroque altar in Holy Trinity church in Slavonski Brod

belonged to the counts Berislavić-Grabarski from the Middle Ages to 1526 when it was conquered by the Turks, who occupied it until 1691.

To defend the border, in 1741 the Viennese government built a fort with barracks, residences for governors and religious buildings. Damaged during World War II and again in the war in 1991, the buildings are under repair: some are used as schools and others house museums and galleries.

The town has grown beyond the original ramparts. Along the banks of the Sava is a **Franciscan Monastery**, dating from 1725, which has been renovated, and the Baroque church of the **Holy Trinity** (Sv. Trojstvo) with many statues, paintings and altars.

The **Regional Civic Museum** (Muzej Brodskog Posavlja) contains historic documents and archaeological, geological and ethnological finds from the region.

The well-known Croatian writer, Ivana Brlić-Mažuranić (1874–1938), spent much of her life in this town. She wrote fairytales for children: among her most famous works are *Fisherman Palunco*, *Jagor* and *The Forest of Stribor*. The town is also known for its folklore festival (Brodsko kolo) held in June.

🏛 **Regional Civic Museum**
Ulica Ante Starčevića 40. **Tel** (035) 447 415. ⬭ 10am–1pm, 5–8pm Mon–Fri, 10am–1pm Sun. 🔒 25 Dec, 1 Jan. 📷 (by appt) 📷 (without flash). **www**.muzejbp.hr

The cloisters in the Franciscan monastery, Slavonski Brod

View of the 19th-century red-brick Cathedral of St Peter in Đakovo

Vrpolje ⑦

Map F3. 🏠 *2,200.*
🚉 *Osijek, 39 km (24 miles).* 🚌 *from Osijek.* 🛈 **Regional:** *Petra Krešimira IV, 2, Slavonski Brod (035) 408 393.*

A small country town, Vrpolje is known as the birthplace of the sculptor Ivan Meštrović (1883–1962) *(see p157).* Many of the artist's works, donated to the town he held in great affection, can be seen here. In the small parish church of **St John the Baptist** (Sveti Ivan Krstitelj, 1774) is his statue of St John the Baptist, a relief and a crucifix, while outside is a striking *Bust of a Woman.* The **Ivan Meštrović Gallery** (Spomen Galerija) has 30 of his works on display: casts, bronzes and wooden sculptures.

Bust of a Woman by Meštrović, Vrpolje

Đakovo ⑧

Map F2. 🏠 *21,000.* 🚉 *Osijek, 48 km (22 miles).* 🚌 *(031) 811 360.* 🚌 *(060) 302 030.* 🛈 *Kralja Tomislava 3, (031) 812 319.* 🎭 *Đakovo embroidery, Đakovački Vezovi (first week in Jul).* **www**.tz-djakovo.hr

In medieval times this town was known by the name of Civitas Dyaco, and later as Castrum Dyaco. Late in the 13th century it became a bishopric, and its influence extended over most of Slavonia and Bosnia.

Conquered and destroyed by the Turks in 1536, it became a Muslim centre and a mosque was built. After Turkish rule, the city was renovated. Only the mosque, at the end of the central avenue, was retained. It was converted into the parish church of All Saints (Svi Sveti) in the 18th century.

The central square is dominated by the **Cathedral of St Peter** (Sv. Petar), built between 1866 and 1882 by Bishop Josip Juraj Strossmayer; the project was the work of the Viennese architects Karl Rösner and Friedrich von Schmidt. The imposing façade is flanked by two 84-m (275-ft) belfries. The interior has frescoes by Maksimilijan and Ljudevit Seitz, sculptures by Ignazio Donegani and Tomas Vodcka and decorations by Giuseppe Voltolini from the 19th century. The crypt houses the tombs of the bishops Strossmayer and Ivan de Zela. Next to the church is the 18th-century Bishop's Palace, which has an ornate Baroque doorway.

The Festival of Embroidery of Đakovo (Đakovački Vezovi) is held at the beginning of July with displays of traditional local costumes, folk dancing and wine tasting.

🛈 **Cathedral of St Peter**
Strossmayerov trg.
Tel (031) 802 200. ⏰ 6:30am–noon, 3–7pm daily.

Novi Mikanovci ⑨

Map F2. 🏠 *700.* 🚉 *Osijek, 50 km (31 miles).* 🚉 *Stari Mikanovci, 3 km (2 miles).* 🛈 *(032) 344 034.*

The village is famous for the small Romanesque church of **St Bartholomew** (Sveti Bartol), from the first half of the 13th century, a rare example of architecture from before Turkish rule. The church stands in a cemetery and is called the "Tower of Pisa of Slavonia" because of its leaning bell tower, which appears to be held up by the façade. At the cemetery entrance is a colourful statue of St Bartholomew.

Županja ⑩

Map F3. 🏠 *13,800.* 🚉 *Osijek, 67 km (41 miles).* 🚉 *(032) 831 183.* 🛈 *Veliki kraj 66, (032) 832 711.* 🎭 *Folklore Festival, Šokačko Sijelo (Feb).* **www**.tz-zupanja.hr

On the border with Bosnia-Herzegovina, Županja lies along a wide bend in the Sava River. The area has been inhabited since ancient times; Bronze Age finds have been discovered in a necropolis. One of the first Croat settlements was set up here. After Turkish rule it became one of the military staging posts on the *Vojna Krajina* (Military Frontier) *(see p39)* and a trading centre.

The **Frontier House** is a wooden building originally from the early 19th century, used by tax collectors.

Embroidered head-dress in the Ethnographic Museum, Županja

Damaged during the bombings in the 1990s and now restored, it houses the **Ethnographic Museum** (Zavičajni Muzej "Stjepan Gruber").

🏛 **Ethnographic Museum**
Savska 3. *Tel (032) 837 101.*
⬜ 7am–7pm Mon–Fri, 5–7pm
Sat–Sun. 🈂 📷 (by appt).

Vinkovci ⓫

Map F2. 🏠 33,300. 🛬 Osijek, 43
km (27 miles). 🚆 (032) 308 215. 🚌
(060) 332 233. 🛈 **Local:** Trg bana
Josipa Šokčevića 3, (032) 334 653;
Regional: Glagoljaška 27, (032) 344
034. 🎭 Autumn in Vinkovci,
Vinkovačke Jeseni (Sep).
www.tz-vinkovci.hr

A settlement existed here as far back as 6000 BC; the Romans named it Aurelia Cibalae. It was the birthplace of the Emperors Valens and Valentinian, and a bishop's see from the 4th century. In the Middle Ages it was called Zenthelye, because of the presence of the (now abandoned) church of **St Elias** (Sv. Ilija). The church dates from the 12th century, and is one of the oldest monuments in Slavonia.

The **Civic Museum** (Gradski Muzej), situated in the former 18th-century Austrian barracks in the main square, holds finds from the Roman necropolis and has a folklore collection. Large Roman sarcophagi are displayed in the museum's lapidarium.

Exhibit in the Civic Museum, Vinkovci

Facing the garden is the church of SS Eusebius and Pollio (Sv. Euzebije i Polion) from 1775, and the Town Hall.

Each September a festival of music and popular traditions is held in the town and groups from all over the country take part. The streets are decorated, stallholders sell local produce, and artists perform.

🏛 **Civic Museum**
Trg bana Šokčevića 16. *Tel (032)
332 504.* ⬜ 10am–1pm, 5–7pm
Tue–Fri; 10am–1pm Sat–Sun (Aug:
10am–1pm Tue–Sun). 📷 📸

The church of St Ivan, next to the
fortified walls in Ilok

Ilok ⓬

Map G2. 🏠 5,900. 🛬 Osijek,
62 km (38 miles). 🚆 Vukovar, 39 km
(24 miles). 🛈 **Local:** Trg Nikole
Iločkog 2, (032) 590 020. 🎭 Grape
harvest festival (first week in Sep).
www.turizamilok.hr

Overlooking a wide loop in the River Danube, Ilok is the easternmost city in Croatia and the centre of the region of Srijem, famous since Roman times for its wine.

In the late Roman era the city grew in importance and took the name of Cuccium.

In the Middle Ages it was a *castrum* with high walls, towers and fortified buildings. The defences were reinforced in 1365, and the town was given to Nikola Kont, whose family later acquired the title of Counts of Ilok.

Around the middle of the 15th century, the church and monastery of **St Ivan Kapistran** (Sv. Ivan Kapistran) were built inside the fort. St Ivan Kapistran was a Franciscan who was famous for uniting Christian forces against the Turks and who died here in 1456. When Ilok became a major Turkish administrative and military centre in the 16th century, mosques and baths were added to the fortress.

Both the church and the monastery have been renovated and between them, long stretches of the ancient walls can still be seen. Parts of one of the Turkish baths are still visible.

In 1683, after his role in winning the battle of Vienna, Commander Livio Odescalchi was given the town of Ilok by the Austrian Emperor. In this idyllic setting he built a U-shaped mansion, **Odescalchi Manor**. Today, the mansion houses a restaurant, public offices and the **Civic Museum** (Gradski Muzej) with archaeological and ethnographic collections. The wines of Ilok are still produced here in the cellars, among them a dry white wine called Traminac.

🛐 **Church and Monastery of St Ivan Kapistran**
O.M. Barbarića 4.
Tel (032) 590 073.
⬜ by appt or before mass.

🏛 **Odescalchi Manor and Civic Museum**
Šetalište oca Mladena Barbarića 5.
Tel (032) 827 410. ⬜ 8am–6pm
daily wine tastings only.
Civic Museum ⬜ 9am–6pm Fri;
9am–3pm Tue–Thu; 11am–6pm Sat.
🈂 📷 🈁 🏠 🚫

The mansion built by Commander Livio Odescalchi in Ilok

Tabernacle in the Franciscan monastery in Šarengrad

Šarengrad ⑬

Map G2. 🏠 100. 🛫 Osijek, 53 km (33 miles). 🚍 Vukovar, 30 km (19 miles). 🅸 **Regional:** Vinkovci, (032)344 034.

A medieval fort once controlled the heavy traffic along the river Danube at this spot. In the 15th century, Count Ivan Morović added a **Franciscan Monastery**. The fort, however, was destroyed during the war with the Turks and the area remained uninhabited until their departure late in the 17th century.

With the return of the inhabitants, the monks set up a school and collected archaeological items for a museum.

During the break-up of former Yugoslavia between 1991 and 1995, the area was heavily bombed. The church and monastery have since been restored and the statue of St Anthony of Padua has been put back in position. From the hill there are good views of the Danube.

Vukovar ⑭

Map G2. 🏠 31,700. 🛫 Osijek, 23 km (14 miles). 🚍 Priljevo 2. 🚍 from Vinkovci. 🅸 **Local:** J.J. Strossmayera 15, (032) 442 889.
www.turizamvukovar.hr

This Baroque city was once known for its churches, elegant 18th-century buildings, numerous museums and art galleries. However, Vukovar has come to symbolize the war which raged in Slavonia in 1991, when it was bombed by the Serbs and the JNA (Yugoslav People's Army). The historic Baroque nucleus was almost totally destroyed. Plans for repair in collaboration with UNESCO are under way but hampered by the lack of international funds.

Vukovar has a very long history, as evidenced by the famous "Dove of Vučedol" from 2000 BC. This vessel was found 5 km (3 miles) from Vukovar and is now in the Archaeological Museum in Zagreb (see pp162–3).

The city, at the confluence of the Danube and the river Vuka, was known by the name of Vakovo in the Middle Ages. Later it was given to various families: the Horvat, the Gorjanski and the Talovci. Conquered by the Turks, Vukovar became a military garrison and a key trading centre. After liberation from the Turks in 1687, it resumed its role as an advance post of the Christian Catholic world against the Muslim and Orthodox religions.

The Dove of Vučedol, symbol of Vukovar

In 1736, it was given to the Eltz counts, who called the town Vukovar. As the inhabitants were Catholics or of the Orthodox faith, churches were built for both religions, including a Franciscan monastery (1727).

In 1751, the Eltz family built a huge Baroque mansion. It was nationalized after World War II and then housed the **Civic Museum** (Gradski Muzej). The palace was badly damaged in 1991 and the contents of the museum, along with the Bauer Collection and the Franciscan monastery treasury, were seized and taken to museums in Belgrade and Novi Sad. In 2001 the collections were returned, and gradually restored. The Catholic church of SS Philip and James (Sv. Filip i Jakov) and the Orthodox church of St Nicholas (Sv.

Nikolaj) were also badly damaged in 1991.

🏛 **Civic Museum**
Županijska 2. **Tel** (032) 441 270.
🕐 7am–3pm Mon–Fri, Sat & Sun by appt only.

Erdut ⑮

Map G2. 🏠 1,500. 🛫 Osijek, 37 km (23 miles). 🚍 from Osijek. 🅸 **Regional:** Kapucinska 40, Osijek, (031) 214 852.

The town of Erdut gained a place in history when, on 13 November 1995, an agreement between Croatia and Yugoslavia was drawn up here, setting out the return of Slavonia and Baranja to Croatia after almost four years of Serb occupation.

The town occupies an important strategic position overlooking the Danube, and a fortification was erected in Roman times. In the medieval period a **Castle** was built. It was damaged by the Turks, but then rebuilt by them. The castle was also used by the Habsburgs. Two towers, one circular and one square, survive from the old castle.

The large **Cseh Mansion**, where the 1995 agreement was drawn up, is now under repair. It was built in the 19th century by the Cseh family, the lords of the manor.

The circular tower of the medieval castle, Erdut

Osijek ⑯

See pp190–93.

A naive outdoor sculpture, Ernestinovo

Ernestinovo ⑰

Map F2. 🏘 *1,200.* ✈ *Osijek, 20 km (12 miles).* 🚌 *from Osijek.* 🛈 **Regional:** *Kapucinska 40, Osijek, (031) 214 852.* 🎨 *Open-air exhibition of sculpture (Aug).*

For many years, well-known sculptors have been meeting in Ernestinovo to present their work in a summer show. This small village is now famous for its open-air exhibitions. The first exhibition was organized in 1976 by the sculptor Petar Smajić. It took place in exile from 1991 to 1996 and returned to Ernestinovo the following year. Many works of art are displayed and offered for sale in the village galleries. Ernestinovo was badly damaged during the war in the 1990s.

Kopački Rit Nature Park ⑱

See pp194–5.

Topolje ⑲

Map F2. 🏘 *200.* ✈ *Osijek, 46 km (28 miles).* 🚊 *Beli Manastir, 16 km (10 miles).* 🚌 *from Osijek.* 🛈 **Regional:** *Kapucinska 40, Osijek, (031) 214 852.*

In 1687, after the victory in Vienna over the Turks, Prince Eugene of Savoy, commander of the Imperial forces,

decided to build a church to commemorate the victory in the countryside surrounding Topolje. The location has particular charm as the church is set among trees standing alone among a patchwork of fields of maize and tobacco. The church was sacked, however, and nearly completely destroyed in the conflicts following the break-up of former Yugoslavia. The building is now undergoing extensive restoration although the splendid furnishings have sadly been lost.

Here, as in Darda, there are several Hungarian communities, who, together with the Croats, are gradually returning after their exile during the Yugoslav occupation. The Hungarian-style houses with their overhanging roofs add a distinctive character to the area. In the autumn, long strings of chilli peppers can be seen hanging out to dry in the sun.

Environs
Around 10 km (6 miles) east of Topolje is the town of **Batina**. In Roman times this was the site of a fortress on the banks of the River Danube and was known by the name of Ad Militarae. Until the war of 1991, which depopulated this small town set among hills and vineyards, there was a bridge connecting Baranja with Hungary and Vojvodina, but since its destruction, both river and road traffic have stopped.

On one of the small hills near Topolje, a tall monument

Hungarian-style houses with chilli peppers hanging to dry, Topolje

in white stone with a female figure in bronze representing Victory commemorates the fallen of World War II. It is the work of one of the great Croatian artists of the 20th century, Antun Augustinčić *(see p20).*

Mansion of the Esterházy barons, now the Town Hall of Darda

Darda ⑳

Map F2. 🏘 *5,400.* ✈ *Osijek, 15km (9 miles).* 🚌 *from Osijek.* 🛈 **Regional:** *Kapucinska 40, Osijek, (031) 214 852.*

An elegant mansion built by the Esterházy barons in the second half of the 18th century, now renovated and used as the Town Hall, is the only evidence of Darda's history. Darda was once a fortified city, represented on 17th-century maps as a large fortress, connected to Osijek by the 8-km (5-mile) bridge of Solimano. Built in 1566 to cross marshland, the bridge was destroyed in 1664 by Nikola Zrinski *(see p177)* to block the Turkish army. On that occasion the city was subsequently devastated.

In the recent war in the 1990s, two 18th-century churches were destroyed: the Catholic church of St John the Baptist (Sv. Ivan Krstitelj) and the Orthodox church of St Michael (Sv. Mihajlo).

Environs
Bilje, 4 km (2 miles) south of Darda, is the site of the information office for the Kopački Rit Nature Park *(see pp194–5).* It is housed in a palace built by Prince Eugene of Savoy, who was granted the small town of Bilje after the victory in Vienna over the Turks (1687).

Osijek ⑯

The capital of Slavonia sits in the middle of a fertile plain. It is a centre of industry, a university town, and a lively Central European city with wide roads linking three districts: the Fort (Tvrđa), Lower Town (Donji grad) and Upper Town (Gornji grad). The city developed in 1786 when the three areas merged. Due to its position on the River Drava, Osijek has always played a strategic role. In 1809 Emperor Francis I declared it a Royal Free Town (this document is now in the Museum of Slavonia). In 1991, after the declaration of independence by Croatia, the city was bombed for over a year by Yugoslav forces and much of the old centre (Upper Town) was damaged. Liberated in 1995, in 1998 Osijek became part of the Croat state again.

View of the main square in the heart of Tvrđa

Exploring Osijek

The fort (Tvrđa) is the fortified centre of Osijek. It was constructed in the early 18th century after liberation from the Turks. Fortunately, Tvrđa did not suffer serious damage during the war in the 1990s. As a result it has preserved its Baroque architecture, which is characterized by simple, austere lines, unusual at this time. This lack of ornamentation was due to the fact that the buildings were intended for use by soldiers and office workers.

Facing Trg Sv. Trojstva, the central square of Tvrđa, named after the Holy Trinity, are various Baroque buildings, including the Building of the Guard, with an 18th-century clock tower, and the General Headquarters of Slavonia, which is now part of the university, and recognizable by its monumental Baroque entrance.

The heart of city life is the main square in the Upper Town, Trg Ante Starčevića.

With its shops, bars and restaurants, this is Osijek's modern face, dating back to the second half of the 19th century and the early 20th century. Facing the square is the County building, built in the early 20th century in the Renaissance style.

🏛 Museum of Slavonia
Muzej Slavonije

Trg Sv. Trojstva 6, Tvrđa. **Tel** (031) 250 730. ◻ 9am–7pm Tue–Fri (to 10pm Thu), 5–9pm Sat, 10am–2pm Sun. 🗓 🛇 🗖 🗭 🖥 www.mso.hr
On the eastern side is the old Town Hall which has housed the Museum of Slavonia since 1946. Geological, prehistoric, Greek, Illyrian and Roman objects are on display here. One section is dedicated to ancient Roman Mursa with statues, tombstones, architectural pieces and a coin collection.

Other sections are dedicated to folklore with exhibits of richly decorated costumes. Today these clothes provide models for a flourishing handicrafts industry making golden silk fabrics.

🄰 Church of the Holy Cross
Sv. Križ

Franjevačka ulica, Tvrđa. **Tel** (031) 208 177. ◻ 8am–noon, 3–8pm.
Northeast of the main square, on the site of a sacred medieval building, stands the church of the Holy Cross, built by the Franciscans between 1709 and 1720. Next to this is the monastery (1699–1767) which housed the first printing press in Slavonia (1735), and from the mid-18th century also housed schools of philosophy and theology. In the church is a statue of the Virgin from the 15th century and some liturgical furnishings.

🄰 Church of St Michael
Sv. Mihovil

Trg Jurja Križanića, Tvrđa. **Tel** (031) 208 990. ◻ before mass.
Standing a little way back from the square is the church of St Michael, which was built by the Jesuits. The façade is flanked by two bell towers, and the monastery has a splendid doorway (1719). Below street level the foundations of the 16th-century Kasim-paša mosque are still visible.

War memorial in Kralja Držislava park

🏭 Europe Avenue
Europska Avenija

This is the main road of Osijek, linking the Fort (Tvrđa) to the Upper Town (Gornji grad). It crosses some of the city's parks, one of which is Kralja Držislava park, site of a striking bronze memorial to the fallen of the 78th Infantry Regiment *(Soldier in the Throes of Death)*, by Robert

Interior of the Neo-Gothic church of SS Peter and Paul

Frangeš-Mihanović (1894), which is regarded as the first modern sculpture in Croatia.

🏛 Gallery of Fine Arts
Galerija Likovnih Umjetnosti

Europska Avenija 9. *Tel (031) 251 280.* ◯ *Jul & Aug: 10am–8pm Mon–Fri; rest of year: 10am–6pm Tue–Fri (to 8pm Thu); 10am–1pm Sat & Sun.* 🈲 📷 *by appt.* 🚫 🔗 www.gluo.hr
The Gallery of Fine Arts, founded in 1954, is housed in an elegant 19th-century house. There are collections of paintings from the 18th and 19th centuries, as well as works by contemporary Croatian artists. There is also a section dedicated to the "Osijek School".

🔒 Church and Monastery of St James
Sv. Jakov

Kapucinska ulica 41, Gornji grad. *Tel (031) 201 182.* ◯ *6.30am–noon, 4–8pm & by appt.*
The oldest building in Upper Town is the church of St James (1702–27), with a Capuchin monastery. In the sacristy are mid-18th-century paintings about the life of St Francis.

🔒 Church of SS Peter and Paul
Sv. Petar i Pavao

Trg Marina Držica, Gornji grad. *Tel (031) 310 020.* ◯ *2–6.30pm Mon, 9am–6.30pm Tue–Fri.*
This imposing Neo-Gothic church is dedicated to St Peter and St Paul. The church is known as "Katedrala" (cathedral) by the locals because of its size: the façade has towers 90 m (295 ft) high. It was designed by Franz Langenberg and built in the late 19th century. The 40 stained-glass windows and some of the sculptures are by the Viennese artist Eduard Hauser. Most of the windows were bomb-damaged but have been restored.

VISITORS' CHECKLIST

Map F2. 🏘 *90,500.* ✈ *20 km (12 miles) Vukovarska 67, (060) 339 339.* 🚌 *Bartola Kašića, (060) 334 466.* 🚃 *Trg Ružičke, (031) 205 155.* ℹ **Local:** *Županijska 2, (031) 203 755;* **Regional:** *Kapucinska 40 (031) 214 852.* 🎉 *City day (2 Dec), Summer Nights of Osijek (Jun–Aug).* **www**.tzosijek.hr

🎭 Croatian National Theatre
Hrvatsko Narodno Kazalište

Županijska ulica 9, Gornji grad. *Tel (031) 220 700.*
The Croatian National Theatre was built in the Moorish style in the 19th century. Opera and drama productions are put on from September to June.

Interior of the Croatian National Theatre

OSIJEK CITY CENTRE

Church of the Holy Cross ②
Church of St James ⑥
Church of St Michael ③
Church of SS Peter and Paul ⑦
Croatian National Theatre ⑧
Europe Avenue ④
Gallery of Fine Arts ⑤
Museum of Slavonia ①

0 metres   500
0 yards   500

Key to Symbols *see back flap*

Street-by-Street: the Fort (Tvrđa)

The fortified centre of Osijek (Tvrđa) was built on the site of the Roman settlement of Mursa, which, in 131 AD, became the capital of Lower Pannonia with the name of Colonia Aelia Mursa. Destroyed by the Avars and rebuilt by the Croats, it

Parchment with the title of "Royal Free Town"

remained a military and administrative centre until it was attacked and burnt by the Turks in 1526. Making the most of the strategic position, the Turks rebuilt the Fort and, under Suleyman II, also constructed a bridge across the Drava. After the expulsion of the Turks in 1687, the Austrian Emperor destroyed the mosques and other reminders of Turkish rule. He then built a fortified series of buildings more like a city than a fort. Tvrđa now houses the Town Hall, the university faculties, and the Museum of Slavonia. The only remaining part of the ramparts is towards the river Drava and includes the "Water Gate" (Vodena Vrata).

★ **Church of St Michael**
Constructed by Jesuits in the first half of the 18th century, the church has a Baroque façade flanked by two towers.

TRG J. KRIŽANIĆA

FRANJE KUHAČA

KAMILA FIRINGERA

PINTEROVIĆ

MARKOVIĆA

KAMILA FIRINGERA

BOŠKO

Building of the Guard
On the western side of the square stands the Building of the Guard, with a clock tower from the 18th century. It now houses the Archaeological Museum.

Croatian Academy of Science and Arts

KEY

– – – Suggested route

STAR SIGHTS

★ Church of St Michael

★ Museum of Slavonia

Plague Column
The centre of the square is dominated by the "column of the plague", erected in 1729 in thanks for the ending of an outbreak of the disease.

Church and Monastery of the Holy Cross
The church, erected by Franciscans between 1709 and 1720, is next to the monastery which housed the first printing press in Slavonia.

View of Osijek and the River Drava
Splendid views of the city can be enjoyed from the banks of the Drava. It was once important for river trading, but trade is now practically non-existent.

TRG VATROSLAVA LISINSKOG

BOSENDORFERA

FRANJEVAČKA

FAKULTETSKA

FRANJE

KUHAČA

...VAČKA

JAGIĆA

0 metres 100
0 yards 100

Darda
(See p189)

KNEZA TRPIMIRA

Đakovo
(see p184)

★ Museum of Slavonia
This museum contains interesting collections of geological, prehistoric, Greek, Illyrian and Roman material.

Headquarters of Slavonia
On the northern side of the main square of Tvrđa is the former Headquarters of Slavonia, now the University Rectorate, easily recognized by the imposing façade.

Kopački Rit Nature Park ⑱
Park Prirode Kopački Rit

This triangular piece of land is bordered by the final stretch of the river Drava before it meets the Danube. The landscape changes with the seasons and becomes flooded when the Danube overflows. The area covers 177 sq km (68 sq miles) and can turn into an immense wetland marsh. At other times it is a vast grassland plain with pools and ponds. There are also dry areas which support enormous willows and tall oak trees. A nature reserve since 1967, it has a rich and varied fauna and for many months of the year provides a sanctuary for hundreds of different species of bird, both migratory and domestic. A high embankment on the western side stops the further spread of the flood waters. On top is a road which allows cars to cross this part of the park.

White Storks
One of the park's symbols, the white stork is especially visible in the breeding season.

Park Entrance
The main entrance to the Kopački Rit Park is in the village of Bilje (see p189).

OSIJEK

0 kilometres 2

0 miles 2

Black Storks are rare; only a few dozen pairs of the bird inhabit the park.

Sakadaš Canal

Sarvaš Pond

Drava

Lakes
Forty different species of fish live in the lakes and ponds which form in the park.

White-Tailed Eagle
The many birds of prey maintain a balance among the bird population. The white-tailed eagle is the rarest eagle in Europe.

Drava

Waterfowl
Ponds and lakes provide an ideal habitat for the wading birds and swans which are present all year round.

VISITORS' CHECKLIST

Map F–G2. ⓘ *Titov Dvorac 1, Lug, (031) 285 370.* ◯ *9am–5pm daily.* 🅿 🚲 *Information on boat rides and bike hire is available at the entrance.* **www**.kopacki-rit.com

Deer and Roe deer in their hundreds congregate in the flooded areas of the park, for brief periods of the year.

Great Crested Grebe
The mating display of these birds is one of the more spectacular sights in the park.

Ducks and Geese
The mallard duck is a much photographed bird for its bright plumage. There are also pochards, shovelers and tufted ducks.

Wild Boar
During the spring it is sometimes possible to see whole families of this shy animal in the oak woods.

Cormorant
Usually found in colonies, cormorants build their nests in trees. Here, thousands of their nests can be seen in the tall willow and poplar trees.

KEY

━━ Major road

━━ Scenic road

ⓘ Tourist information

Danube

Bijelo Lake

Hulbajski Canal

Danube

Drava

The thermal spa in the village of Bizovac

Bizovac ㉑

Map F2. 🏠 2,300. ✈ Osijek, 20 km (12 miles). 🚉 from Osijek. 🚌 from Osijek. 🚶 Kralja Tomislava 136, (031) 675 112.

During the search for petroleum in the middle of the 20th century, a hot water spring was discovered here. The water of the spring reaches a temperature of 90°C (194°F) and is rich in minerals. A few years later, the thermal spa of **Bizovačke Toplice** was built. The spa proved to be extremely successful and it is now an enormous complex including a hotel, two large swimming pools, and cabins for thermal baths. Every day hundreds of guests come here to undergo thermal treatments which are helpful in treating rheumatic and respiratory illnesses, and in healing injuries.

The small centre of Bizovac is also well known in Slavonia for its exquisite gold and silver embroidery. The work is carried out by the young women of the area, usually to a commission.

🛁 **Bizovačke Toplice**
Sunčana 39. **Tel** (031) 685 100. www.bizovacke-toplice.hr

Environs
Around 9 km (5 miles) south of Bizovac is the village of **Brođanci**, famous for the Olympics of Ancient Sports, held here in August every year. During the competition, athletes take part in some of the sports once practised by the peasants of Slavonia, such

as tug-of-war, boulder-throwing, bare-back riding and other strenuous challenges and competitions.

A lively popular festival has developed around the event; musicians perform in the streets and there are displays of old crafts. Local handicrafts can be bought and regional food can be sampled.

Valpovo ㉒

Map F2. 🏠 8,000. ✈ Osijek, 30 km (18 miles). 🚌 (060) 390 060. 🚶 Ulica Matije Gupca 32, (031) 656 200. 🎭 Summer in Valpovo: dancing, folk music and theatrical shows (summer). www.tz-valpovo.com

The centre of Valpovo stands on the remains of the fort of Lovallia, one of many fortified settlements which the Romans established on the Pannonian plain. In the Middle Ages, a castle was erected to keep a look-out over the nearby Drava river. The castle was later granted to the Morović, Gorjanski and Norman families. After the Turkish conquest in 1526, the castle was used as a garrison.

In 1687, after the expulsion of the Turks, the area was handed over to the Hilleprand Prandau family. At the beginning of the 19th century the castle was destroyed by fire and was then extensively rebuilt into a larger building, which today houses the **Valpovo Museum** (Muzej Valpovštine). The museum contains period furniture and interesting archaeological finds. The complex stands in

The imposing castle at Valpovo, now a museum

a large park and a moat surrounds the medieval walls, the tower, the new building and the church. A town developed around the fort, and with it the splendid Baroque church of the **Immaculate Conception** (Začeće Marijino) of 1722.

🏛 **Valpovo Museum**
Dvorac Prandau Norman. **Tel** (031) 650 639. ☐ 4–7pm (8pm in summer) Mon, Thu; 10am–noon Tue, Wed, Fri.

Majláth, a mock-medieval manor in the town of Donji Miholjac

Donji Miholjac ㉓

Map F2. 🏠 6,700. ✈ Osijek, 45 km (28 miles). 🚉 Valpovo, 20 km (12 miles); Našice, 30 km (18 miles). 🚌 (060) 357 060. 🚶 Trg Ante Starčevića 2, (031) 633 103. 🎭 Miholjačko Sijelo: festival in costume (summer). www.tz-donjimiholjac.hr

On the banks of the Drava river, this small town lies on the Hungarian border. All traces of the past have been erased, except for the church of **St Michael** (Sv. Mihovil). The mock-medieval **Majláth Manor** was built at the beginning of the 20th century by the Majláth family. It has pinnacles and a tall tower on the façade. The manor is now the town hall.

🏛 **Majláth Manor**
Vukovarska 1. **Tel** Tourist Office (031) 633 103. ☐ by appt. 🌐

Environs
About 25 km (15 miles) west is the village of **Čađavica**. Traces from ancient Croatian settlements have been discovered near here. The Romanesque church of St Peter was used by the Turks as a mosque and was renovated in the 18th century.

Našice ②④

Map F2. 🏠 *8,300*. ✈ *Osijek, 42 km (26 miles)*. 🚃 *(060) 333 444*. 🚌 *(060) 334 030*. ℹ️ *Pejačevićev trg 4, (031) 614 951*. **www**.*tznasice.hr*

A small plateau is the setting for the town of Našice, which is surrounded by vineyards and woods. Built on the site of an ancient settlement, it was referred to in the first half of the 13th century under the name of Nekche, as property of the Templar Knights. After the dissolution of this order in 1312, it passed to the Gorjanski nobles and, later, through marriage, to the counts of Ilok, before falling into the hands of the Turkish forces in 1532.

After the expulsion of the Turks, Našice's fortunes changed. The Franciscans returned and restored the church of **St Anthony of Padua** (Sv. Antun Padovanski). They also rebuilt their monastery, which had been founded here at the start of the 14th century. Both needed repairing after war damage suffered in 1991.

A short distance away is a large manor house, built at the beginning of the 19th century in Neo-Classical style by the Pejačević family, where the musician Dora Pejačević (1885–1923) lived. Situated in a large park, the two-storey building has been restored.

The church of St Anthony of Padua in Našice

This building is now the **Civic Museum**.

🏛 **Civic Museum**
Pejačevićev trg 5. **Tel** *(031) 613 414*. ◻ *8am–3pm Mon–Fri; 9am–noon Sat.* 📷 🎥 *(by appt)*. 📷 **www**.*zmn.hr*

Orahovica ②⑤

Map F2. 🏠 *4,300*. ✈ *Osijek, 62 km (38 miles)*. 🚃 *(033) 646 079*. 🚌 *(033) 673 231*. ℹ️ *Trg sv. Florijana bb, (099) 2620 336.* 🎭 *Spring in Orahovica: folklore event (Jun).* **www**.*tzgorahovica.hr*

The town of Orahovica is well known in Croatia for its wines. It was a feudal estate in 1228, and later a Turkish garrison, acquiring its present-day look in the 18th century.

On one of the hills around the town stand the ruins of **Rosetta** (Ružica Grad), one of the largest of Croatia's medieval forts. The walls were 9m (29 ft) thick and enclosed military buildings, a church, and the governor's residence. The complex was so large it was often referred to as a city.

The Turks burnt down the fort, then partially restored it and used it as a military garrison. Liberated in 1690, the fort was once again used for defence, and a village, inhabited by Serbs, developed around its base.

Environs
Along the road to Kutjevo, 5 km (3 miles) south of Orahovica, near the village of Duzluk, is the Orthodox **Monastery of St Nicholas** (Manastir Sv. Nikola), which has ancient frescoes and illuminated manuscripts. Some 30 km (18 miles) from Orahovica, following the road to Virovitica, then turning left for Čeralije, is **Voćin**, a small village where the destruction caused by the war in 1991 is still evident. The village lies at the foot of a large castle

built in the second half of the 13th century by the Aba counts. Today, the houses in Voćin are in ruins. All that remains of the church of **St Mary** (Sv. Marija), which was built by King John Corvinus in the first half of the 15th century, is part of the apse wall.

The ornate altar in the Baroque church of St Roch, Virovitica

Virovitica ②⑥

Map E2. 🏠 *15,600*. ✈ *Osijek, 89 km (55 miles)*. 🚃 *Ulica Stjepana Radića, (033) 730 121.* 🚌 *Trg Fra. B. Gerbera 1, (033) 721 113.* ℹ️ *Trg Kralja Tomislava 1, (033) 721 241.* 🎭 *Day of the City (16 Aug).*

Documents from the end of the first millennium give the town its Hungarian name of Wereuche. It was declared a free town by King Bela IV in 1234 and it developed into an agricultural and trading centre. Later occupied by the Turks, it remained under their rule until 1684. When it later flourished, all Ottoman traces were destroyed.

The Baroque church of **St Roch** (Sv. Rok), decorated by the sculptor Holzinger and the painter Göbler, dates from the 18th century. On the site of the ancient Wasserburg Castle stands the imposing **Pejačević Manor** (1800–4), now the **Civic Museum** (Gradski Muzej) with archaeological and folklore collections and an art gallery.

🏛 **Civic Museum**
Dvorac Pejačević, Trg Bana Jelačića 23. **Tel** *(033) 722 127.* ◻ *8am–3pm Mon, Fri; 8am–7pm Tue–Thu; 10am–1pm Sat.* 📷 🎥 *(by appt).* 📷 **www**.*muzejvirovitica.hr*

THE NORTHERN COUNTIES

*T*he landscape in this part of Croatia is made up of a variety of elements: the rolling hills of Zagorje with their therapeutic spring waters and thermal spas; the county of Međimurje, which is famous for its wines; the cities of Varaždin and Čakovec, which developed around ancient castles; Koprivnica, surrounded by lush countryside and vineyards, and Bjelovar and Križevci with their palaces.

The principal towns in the area have ancient origins and two, Varaždin and Križevci, were also at various times the seat of the Sabor, the Croatian Parliament. Bjelovar is the most recent and largest city-fortress in the country. Even before the 1991 war which affected the south of this area, the wars of the second half of the 18th century had already destroyed all evidence of the Middle Ages and Turkish occupation.

However, there are many religious buildings in the area, including a number of Catholic Franciscan and Pauline monasteries in places once inhabited by Orthodox communities. Religious life is still very active here and church buildings are cherished.

Porcelain plate in the Naive Museum in Hlebine

The high hills of Zagorje are covered in forests, broken up only by the clearings created for imposing medieval castles, many of which have since been transformed into sumptuous Baroque residences. In Podravina, drained by the River Drava, which in some parts flows along the Hungarian border, the hills are lower and are characterized by vineyards and sparse woodland.

This part of Croatia has preserved all kinds of ancient customs and traditions, a source of inspiration for the Naive art movement. The home of Naive art is Hlebine, where artists such as Ivan Generalić encouraged and fostered the talent of local amateur painters.

Typical countryside between Belec and Marija Bistrica

◁ Café life in the pretty Baroque town of Varaždin

Exploring the Northern Counties

This is an area of good, fertile agricultural land and the lush countryside produces an abundance of maize, tobacco and sunflowers. The hillsides are covered in vineyards as far as the eye can see and yield wines, good whites in particular, which can be bought along the Wine Road, from wineries or in the village shops. Despite these attractions, the region does not see a great deal of international tourism. This is particularly true of Međimurje, the valley crossed by the River Mura, granted to Croatia after World War I. Part of the population here is of Hungarian origin and the people have preserved their Hungarian customs and traditions.

A side chapel of St Mary of the Snows, Marija Bistrica

View of the castle in Veliki Tabor

0 kilometres   15

0 miles   15

SEE ALSO

- *Where to Stay* p233
- *Where to Eat* p249

SIGHTS AT A GLANCE

Map labels: Maribor, ŠTRIGO, VINICA **4**, VARAŽDINS, Maribor, TRAKOŠĆAN **6**, VARAŽDI, Ivanec, Kn, LEPOGLAVA **5**, PREGRADA **8**, KRAPINA **7**, Ivanščica, Po, VELIKI TABOR **9**, KRAPINSKO ZAGORSKA, Mihovljan, BELEC **15**, Miljana, Zlatar, Krapinske Toplice, **14**, THERMAL SPAS, KUMROVEC **10**, TOUR OF THE, KLANJEC **11**, BEDEKOVČINA **12**, Krapina, Zabok, Konjčina, Oroslavje, MARIJA BISTR **13**, Sveti Ivan Zelina, Stubičke Toplice, Jakovlje, Medvednica, Kašina, Zaprešić, Zagreb, Zagreb

GETTING AROUND

Motorways connect Zagreb to Maribor in Slovenia, and pass through Krapina and Hungary (and serve Varaždin). Cars still use state roads which run more or less parallel to the two motorways. State road 2 goes from the Slovenian border, northwest of Varaždin, and continues on towards Osijek. A railway line runs alongside state road 3 and at Varaždin interconnects with railway lines from Zagreb, Slovenia and Hungary. There are also train connections to Slovenia and Hungary from Čakovec and Koprivnica stations.

LOCATOR MAP

A Naive painting from the Hlebine Gallery

Varaždin Castle in winter

KEY

▬▬	Two lane motorway, toll-free
▬	Major road
▬▬	Minor road
▬	Main railway
▬	County border
▬▬	International border

Varaždin ●

Door detail, church of the Assumption

Traces of occupation from the Neolithic age, the La Tene civilization and the Roman period have been found around Varaždin castle. Despite this, the first mention of the town is found in a document from 1181, when King Bela III confirmed the rights of the Zagreb Curia to the thermal spas in the area. In 1209, it was declared a free town by King Andrew II and it began to develop as a trading centre. In the late 14th century it passed into the hands of the counts of Celjski, followed by the counts of Frankopan, Brandenburg and Erdödy. In 1446, it was destroyed in a fire and in 1527 the Turks attacked. In 1776 another fire destroyed the houses, but the Baroque buildings, for which the town is famous, were fortunately spared.

Aerial view of the Castle, today home to the Civic Museum

Castle and Civic Museum
Stari Grad & Gradski Muzej
Strossmayerovo šetalište 7. *Tel (042) 658 754.* ◯ *9am–5pm Tue–Fri, 9am–1pm Sat & Sun.* 🈳 🎫 🚫
It is unknown when exactly this castle was built, though some documents suggest it dates back to the 12th century. It was built over the ruins of an observation tower and, in the 15th century, two round towers were added. The castle was rebuilt in 1560 by the Italian architect Domenico dell'Allio, who created a Renaissance structure on two floors with arcades and corridors facing courtyards.
The castle's present look dates from the time of the Erdödy counts, who added the bastions and a moat. It is now the Civic Museum which has collections of weapons, porcelain, furniture, handicrafts, and a pharmacy from the 18th century. Remains of the wall and the Lisak tower, to the east of the castle, are the only evidence remaining of the ancient walls that existed at this site.

Gallery of Old and Modern Masters
Galerija Starih i Novih Majstora
Stančićev trg 3. *Tel (042) 214 172.* ◯ *9am–5pm Tue–Fri, 9am–1pm Sat & Sun.* 🈳 🎫 🚫
The gallery has a large collection of works by artists from all over Europe, particularly landscapes by Flemish and Italian artists, and portraits by German and Dutch painters.

Tomislav Square
Trg Kralja Tomislava
Town Hall (Gradska Vijećnica): Trg kralja Tomislava 1. *Tel (042) 402 508.* ◯ *by appt.* **Drašković Palace** (Palača Drašković): Trg kralja Tomislava 3. ● *to the public.*
This square is the heart of the town. Facing the square is the **Town Hall** (Gradska Vijećnica), one of the oldest buildings in Varaždin. Built in the Gothic style in the 15th century, it has since been altered and a clock tower added. It has been the Town Hall since 1523, when Prince George of Brandenburg gave

it to the city. It is guarded in summer by the Purgers, who wear richly decorated blue uniforms and bearskin hats.
To the east of the square stands **Drašković Palace** (Palača Drašković), built in the late 17th century with a Rococo façade. The Croat Parliament met here in 1756–76. Opposite stands the Renaissance Ritz House, one of the oldest in the town, as evidenced by the date (1540) engraved on the doorway.

✚ Cathedral of the Assumption
Uznesenja Marijina
Pavlinska ulica 4. *Tel (042) 210 688.* ◯ *9.30am–12.30pm, 4–7pm daily.*
The church of the Assumption became a cathedral in 1997. Both the church and the annexed monastery were built in the first half of the 17th century by the Jesuits. Later, the Pauline order moved in.
The cathedral's tall façade is enlivened by pillars. The interior is a triumph of the Baroque. The main altar occupies the width of the central nave and has gilded columns, stuccoes and engravings. At the centre of the altar is an *Assumption of the Virgin,* reminiscent of Titian's work in Venice. Evenings of Baroque music concerts are held here.

The rich Baroque altar in the Cathedral of the Assumption

Church of St John the Baptist
Sv. Ivan Krstitelj
Franjevački trg 8. *Tel (042) 213 166.* ◯ *8.30am–noon, 5.30–7pm daily.*
The church was built in 1650 in the Baroque style on the site of a 13th-century church. The façade has a Renaissance

The bell tower of St John the Baptist in Tomislav Square

doorway with a tympanum and two statues of St Francis of Assisi and St Anthony of Padua. The interior has eight side chapels and an ornate gilded pulpit from the late 17th century. The bell tower is 54 m (177 ft) high.

In front of the church is one of the copies of the *Monument of Bishop Gregory of Nin* by Ivan Meštrović. The adjacent pharmacy has many works of art, among them some allegorical frescoes by Ivan Ranger *(see p206)*.

🏛 Hercer Palace
Palača Hercer

Franjevački trg 6. ◯ *9am–5pm Tue–Fri, 9am–1pm Sat & Sun.* **Entomological Museum: *Tel** (042) 658 760. ◯ *same opening times as the palace.* 🦋 🅿

Built at the end of the 18th century (the founders' coat of arms is on the door), the palace has housed the well-organized **Entomological Section of the Civic Museum** (Entomološki Odjel Gradskog muzeja) since 1954. The museum was founded thanks to the entomologist Franjo Košćec (1882–1968), who, in 1959, donated his natural history collection to the city. From 1962 to 1980, his work was carried on by his daughter Ružica, a biologist. As well as thousands of insects, the museum also has a herbarium. From time to time, temporary exhibitions on a variety of themes are organized.

🛐 Church of the Holy Trinity
Sv. Trojstvo

Kapucinski trg 7. *Tel* (042) 213 550. ◯ *9am–noon, 6–7pm Mon–Sat, Sun before and after mass.*

The church dates from the early 18th century and houses

numerous Baroque paintings, furnishings by local masters, and an organ with figures of angels playing instruments.

The neighbouring monastery, which dates from the same period, is famous for its library which contains many parchments, incunabula and manuscripts, and some of the oldest documents written in ancient Croatian *(kajkavski)*.

🏛 National Theatre
Narodno Kazalište

Ulica Augusta Cesarca 1. *Tel* (042) 214 688. ◯ *for performances only.*

Built by Hermann Helmer in 1873, this is one of the main cultural centres in the city. During the summer and autumn, theatre-goers from all over Europe come to attend the performances.

VARAŽDIN TOWN CENTRE

Castle and Civic Museum ①
Cathedral of the Assumption ④
Church of St John the Baptist ⑤
Church of the Holy Trinity ⑦
Gallery of Old and Modern Masters ②
Hercer Palace ⑥
National Theatre ⑧
Tomislav Square ③

0 metres   200
0 yards   200
Key to Symbols *see back flap*

Vineyards in the countryside around Čakovec

Čakovec ②

Map D1. 🏠 *15,800.* 🚆 *(040) 384 333.* 🚌 *Masarykova ulica, (040) 313 947.* ℹ️ **Local:** *Kralja Tomislava 1, (040) 313 319.* **Regional:** *J.B. Jelačića 22, (040) 390 191.* 🎭 *Carnival in Međimurje (Feb); The Town of Čakovec Day.* **www**.tourism-cakovec.hr

In the second half of the 13th century, on a site once inhabited by Romans, Count Demetrius Chaky, a magistrate at the court of King Bela IV, built a tower here which was called Chaktornya. In the following century, the main defensive structure in Međimurje was built around the tower. In 1547 Emperor Ferdinand gave it to the Ban (governor) of Croatia, Nikola Zrinski (*see p177*), together with a large estate, as a reward for the victory against the Turks and to settle a debt.

Nikola Zrinski died heroically while fighting against the Ottomans in defending Siget, and became a national hero. On 29 May 1579, one of his successors, a member of the Zrinski family of Siget, guaranteed tax privileges to whoever went to live in the city that was developing around the fort. This date is considered the founding of the city and is celebrated with a festival. Bastions and a moat were added in this period as defence against cannon fire. Inside the walls, a four-storey palace was built around a square courtyard.

In 1671 Petar Zrinski led a plot to separate Croatia from the Kingdom of Hungary. The plot was discovered and Zrinski and his co-conspirator Fran Krsto Frankopan were beheaded on 30 April 1671. Čakovec then came under the direct rule of the Emperor.

The Renaissance "**Old Castle**", of which only the first floor remains, and the Baroque "**New Castle**" with a rectangular plan, face each other inside the medieval walls. For a long time the Old Castle was used as a prison. It is now being restored and is to be used in future for cultural activities. The church has been reopened for worship.

The **Međimurje Civic Museum** of Čakovec has on display exhibits of prehistoric material, many Roman finds, and ethnographic collections. There is also an exhibition dedicated to the local composer, J Slavenski (1896–1955), who was known for his love of the traditional music of the region.

Čakovec is the main administrative centre of the Međimurje, a frontier region which borders Slovenia and Hungary. The land in the western part of the region is hilly with broad valleys, and is renowned for its wines, while the fertile plains of the eastern part produce cereal crops.

🏛 **Međimurje Civic Museum**
Trg Republike 5. **Tel** *(040) 313 285.* ⏰ *8am–3pm Mon–Fri; 10am–1pm Sat–Sun.* 🎫 ⬚ ⊘ 📷

Environs
In the village of Šenkovec, 2 km (1 mile) from Čakovec, stands the church of **St Helen** (Sv. Jelena). What little remains of its original Gothic

The Old and New castles of Čakovec

form has been integrated into an overall Baroque appearance. The church is all that survives of the monastery founded by the Paulines in 1376. It has been rebuilt at various times, firstly after a Protestant revolt, then because of a fire and finally after an earthquake.

Inside the church are the tombstones of the powerful Zrinski family, the lords of Čakovec: that of Nikola Zrinski and his wife Catherine Frankopan, and also that of Petar Zrinski.

The church also contains several tombs of members of the Knežević family, who became the successors to the Zrinskis.

Fresco on the door of the church of St Jerome, Štrigova

into a palace in the 17th century. At one time the palace was famous for its rich furnishings, its art collections, and for the fact that the Hungarian king, Matthias Corvinus, was often a guest here.

The church of **St Jerome** (Sv. Jerolim) stands on a hill at the edge of the village. Restoration has uncovered the frescoes above the doorway and in the niches on the façade, which is flanked by two harmonious bell towers and culminates in a curvilinear tympanum.

In the church are numerous *trompe-l'œil* paintings by the Tyrolean artist Ivan Ranger (*see p206*), depicting *Angels*, the *Evangelists* and the *Life of St Jerome*. There are also statues representing the fathers of the Church.

Vinica ❹

Map D1. 🏛 *1,200.* 🚌 *from Varaždin.* 🛈 **Regional:** *Uska 4, Varaždin, (042) 210 096.*

This small town lies at the foot of vine-covered hills. It was first mentioned in documents in 1353 as the site of a medieval fortress. At one time it was known for the large palace built by the Patačić counts on the site of their old castle. The palace

The frescoed façade of the church of St Jerome, Štrigova

is now in ruins, as is that of the Drašković counts, which was situated in the centre of a large park.

In the late 19th century, Count Marko Bombelles created **Opeka Park**, 2 km (1 mile) south of Vinica. This large arboretum was at that time the only one of its kind in Croatia. Here Bombelles planted exotic trees and plants from around the world, including the Americas, Japan, Tibet and the Caucasus, over an area of flat and hilly ground.

Next to this wonderful park, declared a protected nature reserve in 1961, a School of Horticulture has been set up. This school has several glasshouses and a large garden of flowering plants.

🌺 **Opeka Park**
🚪 *at all times.*

One of the frescoes decorating the church of St Helen, Čakovec

Štrigova ❸

Map D1.
🏛 *450.* 🚉 *from Čakovec.* 🚌 *from Čakovec.* 🛈 **Regional:** *J.B. Jelačića 22, Čakovec, (040) 390 191.*

Numerous finds of Roman origin have been discovered here, leading historians to believe that this village was built on the site of the Roman city of Stridon, the birthplace of St Jerome.

The counts of Štrigovčak lived here, but their castle was destroyed during a raid by the Turks. Nearby, the Bannfy counts also built a castle, which was transformed

Colourful floral display in Opeka Park, near Vinica

Choir stalls in the church of St Mary, frescoed by the artist Ivan Ranger

here. Also of interest is the pulpit and the altar of St Anne by the Pauline monk and sculptor Aleksije Königer.

> 🔒 **Church of St Mary**
> Trg 1. hrvatskog sveučilišta 3.
> **Tel** (042) 792 566.
> ☐ by appt.

Lepoglava ❺

Map D1. 🏛 8,700. 🚇 (042) 791 193. 🚌 for Ivanec. 🚶 **Local:** Hrvatskih pavlina 7, (042) 494 317; **Regional:** Ivanec, (042) 784 284. 🎭 International Lace Festival (Sep). www.lepoglava-info.hr

This town is famous for the intricate lace which is made here, thanks to its Lace School, which was founded some centuries ago.

The town is also notorious in Croatia as being the site of a historic prison. At various times, Marshal Tito and Archbishop Stepinac, head of the church in Croatia in World War II, among others, were imprisoned here.

The prison building was formerly a Pauline monastery, built on the orders of the Count of Celje at the end of the 14th century. It was embellished and enlarged in the second half of the following century by King Matthias Corvinus. It was used as a school of theology, grammar and philosophy, as well as a secondary school open to lay pupils.

In 1854, after the dissolution of the Pauline order, the monks' cells became prison cells. Behind the large, ancient cloisters a more modern prison was built. Nowadays, this prison is Croatia's largest.

Restoration has been completed on the beautiful Gothic church of **St Mary** (Sv. Marija), which was rebuilt in

the Baroque style in the late 17th century. The church has a single nave and polygonal choir. The façade has prominent pilasters enclosing niches, and two tympana. Inside is 18th-century stucco-work by Antonio Giulio Quaglio alongside magnificent works by the fresco painter Ivan Ranger (of note is his *Apocalypse* in the choir stalls). Ranger's largest cycle of frescoes can be found

Typical lace from Lepoglava

Trakošćan ❻

Map D1. 🚌 for Trakošćan. 🚶 Trakošćan, (042) 796 281. www.trakoscan.hr

The pretty surroundings of the **Castle of Trakošćan**, and its excellent state of conservation, make this one of the most visited tourist sights in Zagorje. The castle was built to guard the road which descends from Ptuj towards the valley of the River Sava. The castle was listed in 1434 as one of the properties granted by Sigismund of Austria to the Count of Celje. It was used for defence purposes until the end of Turkish rule.

IVAN RANGER (JOHANNES BAPTISTE RANGER)

Born in Götzens, near Innsbruck in Austria, in 1700, Ivan Ranger joined the Pauline order at a very early age. Not much is known of his years as an apprentice, but it is certain that he lived for a time in Italy, where he encountered the Baroque style in Venice, Rome, Bologna and Mantua. At the age of 30 he was invited to Lepoglava, then the headquarters of the order, to which he remained loyal until his death in 1753. He also worked in nearby towns and in Slovenia (at the monastery of Olimje and the castle-monastery of Sveti Jernej in Rogatec). In line with Pauline principles, he created a school of fresco painters. With these artists he produced colourful fresco cycles which were full of expression (the *trompe-l'œil* paintings also reveal great technical skill). His themes were always religious, and he was much imitated.

Fresco painted by the Pauline monk Ivan Ranger

The Castle of Trakošćan, now a museum

In 1568 it became the property of the Drašković counts.

During the second half of the 19th century, it was transformed into a splendid Neo-Gothic residence by Juraj Drašković. He also added an artificial lake, a park and gardens, while at the same time preserving some of the military aspects of the castle. It stands on a wooded hilltop and is surrounded by a high wall with a tower, which encircles the imposing palace.

All 32 of the rooms of the castle are now a **Museum** where furniture, armoury, vestments and paintings, as well as a rare series of portraits of the Drašković family, are on display.

🏰 Castle and Museum
Tel (042) 796 422. ◯ Apr–Oct: 9am–6pm daily; Nov–Mar: 9am–4pm daily. 📷 🎫 📷 📷

Krapina ❼

Map D1. 🏛 4,500. 🚉 Frana Galovića bb, (049) 328 028. 🚌 A. Starčevića, (049) 315 018. 🗓 Magistratska 11, (049) 371 330. 🎭 Week of music and Kajkaviana culture (Sep). **www**.tzg-krapina.hr

The town is well-known in the scientific field because the remains of Krapina man, *Homo krapinensis*, who lived in the Palaeolithic age, were found nearby. The Neanderthal skeleton, discovered in 1899 in a hillside cave, is now in the Archaeological Museum in Zagreb. The **Museum of**

Krapina Neanderthal Men is one of the most modern museums in Croatia. Multimedia presentations and exhibits explore the life and culture of Neanderthal man.

Krapina is first documented in 1193 as the site of a castle, now destroyed, built to guard the river of the same name. After the danger of Turkish attack had passed, it was conceded to the Keglević counts and became an important administrative town.

It also became a religious centre. In the mid-17th century, a Franciscan monastery and the Baroque church of **St Catherine** were built. The sacristy and some of the monastery rooms are decorated with vivid frescoes by Ivan Ranger.

In one of the town squares is a monument to Ljudevit

Gaj, born in Krapina in 1809. During the first half of the 19th century he was a prominent figure in the movement which promoted the revival of Croatian politics and culture.

🏛 Museum of Krapina Neanderthal Men
Šetalište V Sluge bb. *Tel* (049) 371 491. ◯ Apr–Sep: 9am–7pm Tue–Sun; Nov–Feb: 9am–4pm Tue–Sun; Mar & Oct: 9am–4pm Mon–Fri, 7am–6pm Sat & Sun. 📷 📷 by appt. 📷

Environs
A short way northeast of Krapina is the sanctuary of the **Madonna of Jerusalem** in Trški Vrh, regarded as one of the most magnificent examples of Baroque art in Croatia. Built in 1750–61, on a square plan, the façade has a bell tower with an onion dome. Inside is an arched portico with rounded corners and four chapels similar to the tower. The walls, vaults, ceilings and dome of the church are covered with a cycle of frescoes of biblical subjects and scenes from Mary's life by the Styrian artist, Anton Lerchinger. The ornate main altar (with a statue of the Virgin brought from Jerusalem in 1669) is by sculptor Filip Jacob Straub of Graz, while the pulpit and the other three altars are the work of Anton Mersi, a gilder and sculptor.

Bust of Ljudevit Gaj, Krapina

Fresco in the Baroque church of the Madonna of Jerusalem in Trški Vrh

Pregrada ⑧

Map C1. 🏠 *1,700.* 🛈 *Local: Trg Gospe Kunagorske 2, (049) 377 050;* 🎭 *Carnival (Feb), Branje grožđa, grape harvest (Sep).* **www**.pregrada.hr

The village church has ancient origins but now presents a 19th-century appearance, made distinctive by the façade flanked by two pointed bell towers. Inside, as well as the tombs of members of the Keglević and Gorup families, there is also a very large organ, which was at one time in Zagreb Cathedral.

On the site of a medieval castle, in the Hrvatsko Zagorje woods, along the Wine Road, stands **Gorica Castle**, once owned by the Keglević family and the feudal manor of the area. Two round towers frame the structure of the elaborate façade. Other buildings behind the towers are now used as a winery.

Environs

On a vineyard-covered hill, 7 km (4 miles) west of Pregrada, in **Vinagora,** stands an unusual sanctuary of ancient origins. This place of worship became the parish church in 1780. The church of St Mary of the Visitation (Sv. Marija od Pohoda) contains some Gothic statues and rich furnishings. The church is surrounded by walls which encircle the hill.

Two round towers guard the sanctuary entrance, which also once had a drawbridge. These towers are now used as chapels.

Inside the church of St Mary of the Visitation, Vinagora

Veliki Tabor ⑨

Map C1. 🚌 *from Krapina or Zagreb for Desinić.* 🛈 **Regional:** *Košnički Hum 1, (049) 374 970.* 🎭 *Knights tournament (Sep).* **www**.velikitabor.com

One of the most famous and best preserved castles in Croatia, Veliki Tabor stands on a bare hilltop, making it visible from a great distance. It was royal property in the 14th century at the time of King Matthias Corvinus I (the

fact that it was royal property justified its imposing appearance). It was granted to the family of the Ratkaj counts, who in the 16th century transformed it into a sumptuous residential palace.

Walls with four semicircular towers encircle the main body of the castle, which is built on a pentagonal ground plan. Two floors with porticoes face the central courtyard. The bastions (no longer extant), made Veliki Tabor a fortress to be feared. The castle is now a museum.

> 🏛 **Castle**
> Košnički Hum 1, Desinić. **Tel** *(049) 343 963.* **Fax** *(049) 301 533.*
> ⏰ *Apr–Sep: 9am–5pm Tue–Fri, 9am–7pm Sat & Sun; Mar & Oct: 9am–4pm Tue–Fri, 9am–5pm Sat & Sun; Nov–Feb: 9am–4pm Tue–Sun.*

Environs

Miljana, just to the southwest of Veliki Tabor, is home to one of the most picturesque Baroque castles in Croatia. Construction began in the 17th century but was not completed until the mid-19th century. This time span resulted in a variety of styles; there are striking 18th-century Rococo frescoes in some rooms, and some delightful artworks.

Kumrovec ⑩

Map C1. 🏠 *300.* 🚉 *(049) 553 129..* 🚌 *from Zagreb.* 🛈 *Cesta Lijepe naše 6a, (049) 502 044.* 🎭 *Marriage of Zagorje (Sep).* **www**.kumrovec.hr

This was the birthplace of Marshal Tito, born Josip Broz in 1892. His house, which dates from 1860, was turned into a museum in 1953. On display are the furniture and household goods which belonged to his family.

In the square in front of the house is a monument to Tito, the work of Antun Augustinčić in 1948. Along with other village houses, Tito's birthplace is now part of a folk museum, the **Ethnological Museum – Staro Selo**, which means "old village". The preserved thatched houses are furnished with utensils and household

The Castle of Veliki Tabor, one of the best-preserved castles in Croatia

◁ Vineyards around Kumrovec, in the hilly region of Zagorje

Birthplace of Marshal Tito, part of the Staro Selo museum in Kumrovec

goods of the time.
Reconstructed workshops
have been set up to
demonstrate crafts such as
hemp- and flax-weaving.

🏛 **Ethnological Museum –
Staro Selo**
Josipa Broza 19A.
Tel (049) 225 830.
☐ May–Oct: 9am–7pm daily; Nov–
Apr: 9am–5pm daily. 🖼 🔲

Klanjec ⓫

Map C1. 🏔 600. 🚇 (049) 550404.
🚌 from Zagreb, Krapina, Zabok.
🛈 Trg A. Mihanovića 2, (049) 550
235. 🎭 Carnival (Feb). 🖼 🔲
www.klanjec.hr

Antun Augustinčić
(1900–79) is one of
the most important
Croatian sculptors
of the 20th century,
and his works can
be seen around the
world. He was born
here, and the
**Antun Augustinčić
Gallery** has displays
of his work.

Statue of Antun
Mihanović, Klanjec

Also of interest are the
Franciscan monastery and the
annexed church of St Mary,
both built in the 17th century
by the powerful Erdödy
family, whose tombs lie here.
In the main square is a
monument by Robert
Frangeš-Mihanović, dedicated
to the poet Antun Mihanović,
who wrote the Croatian
national anthem.
Another memorial dedicated
to Antun Mihanović is the 9-m
(29-ft) memorial stone which
stands in Zelenjak, 3 km (2
miles) north of Klanjec, in the
direction of Tuheljske Toplice.

🏛 **Antun Augustinčić Gallery**
Trg A. Mihanovića 10.
Tel (049) 550 343.
☐ Apr–Sep: 9am–5pm daily; Oct–
Mar: 9am–3pm Tue–Sun.

Bedekovčina ⓬

Map D1. 🏔 3,500. 🚇 Trg A
Starčevića 12, (049) 213 106.
🚌 from Zagreb. 🛈 **Regional:** D.G.
Krambergera 1, Krapina, (049) 233
653. 🎭 Wine fair (Jun).

This town is home to a
particularly attractive castle
and palace, one of many
buildings erected over the
ruins of ancient castles in
the Zagorje hills. The
majority of these were
destroyed during the
wars against the Turks.
This particular castle
was built in the
early 18th century,
and now houses
public offices.
The castle is built
on a quadrangular
plan, on two levels
and with a sloping
roof. Coats of arms are
emblazoned above the two
entrance doors.

Marija Bistrica ⓭

Map D1. 🏔 1,000. 🚇 Zlatar
Bistrica, 5 km (3 miles). 🚌 from
Zagreb. 🛈 Zagrebačka bb, (049)
468 380. 🎭 Bistrica week (Jul).
www.info-marija-bistrica.hr

This small village on the
northern side of the
Medvednica mountain is
home to the **Sanctuary of
St Mary of Bistrica** (Majke
Božje Bistričke), one of the
best-known pilgrimage sites
in Croatia. There has been a
church on this site since 1334.
In the mid-16th century,
when a Turkish invasion
seemed imminent, a wooden
statue of the *Black Madonna
with Child* was hidden in
the church. Some decades
later, it was miraculously
rediscovered, to great joy
and emotion. It still inspires
tremendous devotion today.
The church has been
enlarged several times and
was the first to be declared
a sanctuary of Croatia by
Parliament (1715). It was
rebuilt in 1883 by the
architect Hermann Bollé. He
adopted an eclectic approach,
combining Romanesque,
Gothic and Baroque styles.
The church also has a large
frescoed portico.
The sanctuary possesses a
rich store of beautiful
religious objects: gold and
silver pieces, furnishings and
sacred vestments adorned with
gold embroidery. Some objects
are now on exhibit in the
Diocesan Museum in Zagreb.

🛕 **Sanctuary of St Mary of
the Snows**
Trg pape Ivana Pavla II 32.
Tel (049) 469 156. ☐ by appt.

Sanctuary of St Mary of the Snows in Marija Bistrica, a place of pilgrimage

Tour of the Thermal Spas ⑭

Between Varaždin and Zagreb are six thermal spas (*toplice*), dating from different eras. Set in a pleasant hilly landscape of vineyards and woods, the spas are popular with Croatians and visitors from nearby European countries. As well as being attracted by the well-equipped thermal spas, visitors are also drawn by the cities and towns nearby. In addition there are numerous castles, sanctuaries, churches and museums, making this a very pleasant area to stay in.

0 kilometres   10

0 miles

Decorative detail from the Roman baths, Varaždinske Toplice

Krapinske Toplice ④

This thermal spa was built in the second half of the 19th century near a hot water spring rich in calcium, magnesium and carbonate. The hospital treats rheumatic, cardiovascular and neurological illnesses with bathing in its three indoor pools (the hotel also has outdoor pools and a whirlpool) and mud treatments.

Sutinske Toplice ⑤

Located 8 km (5 miles) northwest of Zlatar, at an altitude of 170 m (557 ft) this site has been famous since the 13th century for its curative waters, which are slightly radioactive and rich in minerals, particularly calcium and magnesium. Mud baths are particularly effective for the treatment of a variety of ailments. Outdoor pools only.

Terme Jezerčica ①

This thermal spa is located in Danja Stubica. There is a hotel (with thermal water conducted to every bathroom), a wellness spa and beauty centre, a sauna, fitness programmes, massage, face and body treatments and several pools.

Terme Tuhelj ③

This spa town is 40 km (25 miles) from Zagreb. At the hotel with its eight pools, rheumatic, respiratory, urological and gynaecological illnesses are treated.

Stubičke Toplice ②

This spa is at the foot of Mount Medvednica, 3 km (2 miles) from Donja Stubica. The spa dates from 1776. There is a hotel with a pool, and a hospital specializing in the treatment of degenerative diseases of the joints and spine. The hot spa waters emerge at 69°C (156°F).

For hotels and restaurants in this region see p233 and p249

TIPS FOR DRIVERS

Length of tour: 100 km (62 miles). **Stops:** Toplice Hotel, A. Mihanovića 2 (049) 202 202; Hotel Matija Gubec, V. Šipeka 31, Stubičke T., (049) 282 501/630; Hotel Minerva, Trg slobode 1, Varaždinske T., (042) 630 534.
🛈 Stubičke T., V. Šipeka 24, (049) 282 727; Krapinske T., Zagrebačka 4, (049) 232 106; Terme Tuhelj, Gajeva 4, (049) 203 000; Sutinske T., (049) 466 627; Varaždinske T., (042) 633 133.

Varaždinske Toplice ⑥

The spa resort in Varaždinske Toplice is one of the oldest in Croatia. The first baths were set up at the end of the 18th century and the first public spa was opened to the public in 1829. The thermal waters are used to treat rheumatic and orthopaedic conditions.

KEY

■ Tour route

■ Motorway

⎓ Other roads

🛈 Tourist information

The decorated interior of the church of St Mary of the Snows, Belec

Belec ⑮

Map D1.
🏠 500. 🚌 from Zabok.
🛈 D.G. Krambergera 1, Krapina, (049) 233 653.

Among the hills of Zagorje is the village of Belec, much loved by art historians, because on its outskirts is the small church of **St George** (Sv. Jurja), one of the few Romanesque buildings preserved in inland Croatia. The bell tower takes up nearly all of the façade (it resembles a defensive tower rather than a campanile). On the right is a small portico with two thin columns. This leads to the interior, where there is an ornate Gothic altar and interesting frescoes dating from the year of its construction.

Lower down the hillside is the church of **St Mary of the Snows** (Sv. Marija Snježna), constructed by the Keglević family in 1674. This church is considered a masterpiece of Croatian Baroque, because of its sumptuously decorated and ornamented interior. The monk and artist Ivan Ranger (see p206) painted some of his trompe-l'œil masterpieces here, including Scenes from the Old Testament and Episodes of the Virgin Mary's Life. The church also has a magnificent main altar, surrounded by cherubs and saints.

🏛 **Church of St Mary of the Snows**
Tel (049) 460 040. 🔘 by appt.

Varaždinske Toplice ⑯

Map D1. 🏠 2,000. 🚊 from Zagreb and Novi Marof. 🚌 from Zagreb.
🛈 Trg Slobode 16, (042) 630 000.
www.varazdinsketoplice.com

The waters that gush from a sulphurous spring at the foot of the hill south of Varaždin were known to the Jasi, an Illyrian tribe, in the 3rd century BC. The town was known as Aquae Jasae by the Romans, and the spa rapidly developed, as shown by the numerous archaeological finds discovered here. The baths were used until the area was invaded by the Goths. Later, a landslide buried the baths in mud and for centuries they were forgotten.

In the 12th century, under the rule of the bishop of Zagreb, a village was founded with the name of Toplissa and the inhabitants began to use the hot water from the spring once more. During the construction of the present-day resort, the Roman town was rediscovered.

Varaždinske Toplice also boasts a medieval district which includes a castle, part of which houses a **History Museum**. Inside a small fortress is the parish church with an organ from 1766 and two carved altars made by Francesco Robba.

In a nearby park is Seoska Kuća, an 18th-century rural house with furniture and objects from the same era.

The sanctuary dedicated to the Trinity, Ludbreg

Ludbreg ⓱

Map D1. 🏘 *3,800.*
🚉 *from Zagreb via Koprivnica or
Varaždin.* 🚌 *from Zagreb.* 🛈 *Trg Sv.
Trojstva 14, (042) 810 690.* 🎭
*Celebration of Miraculous Blood (1st
Sun in Sep).* **www**.*tz-ludbreg.hr*

Many traces from the
Roman era, such as
walls and baths, have been
found in this area. In
researching these finds, some
historians have identified
Ludbreg as being the Roman
site of Jovia.

The town later became one
of the first bishop's sees in
inland Croatia. In 1411,
during a mass, a priest saw
the wine in the chalice turn to
blood and the town chapel
where this miracle took place
became a destination for
pilgrims. In 1513 Pope Leo X
declared Ludbreg the only
Sanctuary of the Trinity (Sv.
Trojstvo) in Croatia.

The church, originally
Gothic, was altered in 1829,
and now features a Baroque
altar and frescoes by M Rački
(1937). The portico is typical
of churches of pilgrimage
and dates from 1779.

In 1739, Parliament voted to
build a large chapel dedicated
to the Precious Blood of
Christ here, in order to
preserve the miraculous
chalice in an appropriate
place. The chapel was not
finally consecrated until 1994.

A manor house in Baroque
and Classical style, built by
the Battahyany family in 1745,
today houses workshops
belonging to the Croatian
Restoration Institute.

Koprivnica ⓲

Map D1. 🏘 *24,800.*
🚉 *Kolodvorska 31, (060) 305 040.*
🚌 *Zagrebačka ulica, (048) 621 282.*
🛈 *Local: Trg Bana Jelačića 7, (048)
621 433; Regional: Nemčićeva 5,
(048) 624 408.* 🎭 *Podravski Motivi,
Naive art exhibition (first week of Jul).*
www.*koprivnicatourism.com*

Koprivnica (originally
Kukaproncza), was founded
by the powerful Ernust family,
and was a key trading centre
for the Podravina area as well
as a royal city from 1356. It
was burnt down by the Turks
in the 16th century, destroying
one of Croatia's first free towns.

Slowly rebuilt in the 17th
century, the town took on a
Baroque appearance with a
wide avenue flanked by the
main buildings. At one end
stands the 19th-century County Hall of Koprivnica and
Križevci. There are many Serbian immigrants here, hence
the Orthodox Church of the
Holy Spirit (Sveti Duh), dating
from the late 18th century.

A significant event for the city
was the establishment in 1685
of a **Franciscan Monastery**
and the church of St Anthony
of Padua. The monastery
was a source of culture and
learning for the whole region
and it has resumed this role
in recent times.

Nearby is the **Civic
Museum** (Gradski Muzej) with
archaeological, historical and
cultural collections, and the
Koprivnica Gallery with a
collection of Naive works
linked to the Hlebine school
(*see p21*). Next door, in a
former old brewery, is the
beer hall Kraluš (*see p247*),
much loved by the locals.

🏛 **Civic Museum**
Trg Leandera Brozovića 1.
Tel (048) 642 538. ⏲ *8am–2pm
Mon–Fri; 10am–1pm Sat.*

🏛 **Koprivnica Gallery**
Zrinski trg 9/1. **Tel** (048) 622 564.
⏲ *8.30am–3.30pm Mon–Fri,
9.30am–1pm Sat.* 🖼

Environs
Hlebine, 13 km (8 miles) east
of Koprivnica, owes its fame
to the peasant painters fostered
by the artist Krsto Hegedušić.
In the 1930s this group
founded the so-called "Hlebine
school" (*see p21*) of Naive art:
the core of a trend in painting
which represented the
landscape and people of this
region in a simple and original
way. Their work is exhibited
in both the **Hlebine Gallery**
and the Koprivnica Gallery.

🏛 **Hlebine Gallery**
Trg Ivana Generalića 15. **Tel** (048)
836 075. ⏲ *10am–4pm Mon–Fri,
10am–2pm Sat.* 🖼

A work of Naive art of the Hlebine school in the Koprivnica Gallery

The medieval castle in Đurđevac, today housing a gallery

Đurđevac 🔟

Map E1. 🏘 *6,700.*
🚉 *Kolodvorska 21, (048) 813089.*
🚌 *(048) 812 002.* 🛈 *Vladimira Nazora 2, (048) 812 046.*
🎉 *Đurđevo, City Day (23 Apr); Legend of the Picoki, culture and folklore show (last week of Jun).*

Although the town's name derives from an ancient religious building dedicated to St George (Sv. Jurai), the town is now known for the **Castle** (Stari grad), whose ancient name is mentioned as Wasserburg, meaning castle on the water. In the Middle Ages the structure was much larger (excavations reveal a rectangular plan with a drawbridge and tower). All that remains now is a roughly octagonal building with an internal courtyard. A gallery occupies the upper floor.

Bjelovar 🔟

Map D1. 🏘 *27,800.*
🚉 *Masarykova ulica, (043) 241 263.*
🚌 *Masarykova ulica, (043) 241 269.*
🛈 **Local:** *Trg Eugena Kvaternika 2, (043) 243 944;* **Regional:** *Trg Eugena Kvaternika 4, (043) 243 944.*
🎉 *Terezijana, cultural display (Jun).*
www.turizam-bilogorabjelovar. com.hr

In the Middle Ages this town was called Wellewar. It acquired greater status in 1756, when Maria Theresa of Austria built a fort here. It became a military town, and was built on an octagonal layout, centred around two intersecting roads. These are now home to the cathedral of

St Theresa, schools, the Orthodox church of the Holy Spirit and the barracks. The **Civic Museum** (Gradski Muzej) has an extensive and varied collection.

🏛 Civic Museum
Trg Eugena Kvaternika 1. **Tel** *(043) 244 207.* ⬜ *10am–7pm Tue–Fri, 10am–2pm Sat–Sun.*

The iconostasis in the Church of the Holy Trinity, Križevci

Križevci 🔟

Map D1.
🏘 *11,600.* 🚉 *(048) 716 193.*
🛈 *Nemčićev trg 6, (048) 681 199.*
www.tz-krizevci.hr 🎉 *Križevačko Veliko Spravišče, cultural and gastronomic event (mid-Jun).*

References to this town are found in acts from the early 12th century. In 1252 it was declared a royal free town, and at various times it was chosen as the meeting place for the Croatian parliament. During a meeting in 1397 certain nobles considered traitors to King Sigismund were massacred.

Of these, one was the Prince palatine, Stjepan Lacković. The town was later fortified but after Turkish rule, only the towers' foundations and pieces of the wall remained. The town prospered with the arrival of the railway in 1871.

The oldest building is the medieval **Church of the Holy Cross** (Sv. Križ), but only the side doorway dates from this period. The church was restructured in the Baroque style in the second half of the 18th century. The altar of the Holy Cross was sculpted by Francesco Robba in 1756 for the cathedral in Zagreb.

The Greek Catholic **Church of the Holy Trinity** (Sv. Trojstvo) has an iconostasis, frescoes by Celestin Medović and Ivan Tišov from the early 19th century, and a magnificent main altar, the work of 18th-century artist Sante Pardoni.

The attached monastery became the **Bishop's Palace** (Biskupski Dvor). It houses paintings, icons, manuscripts and holy objects. The **Civic Museum** (Gradski Muzej) has interesting archaeological and art collections.

🏛 Church of the Holy Cross
Ivana Dijankovečkog 1. **Tel** *(048) 711 711.* ⬜ *by appt.*
🏰 Bishop's Palace
Tel *(048) 712 171.* ⬜ *by appt.*
🏛 Civic Museum
Sermageova 2. **Tel** *(048) 711 210.* ⬜ *8am–3pm Mon, Wed & Fri, 8am–7pm Tue & Thu, 10am–noon Sat.* 📷 📹

Altar by Francesco Robba in the church of the Holy Cross, Križevci

TRAVELLERS' NEEDS

WHERE TO STAY

Croatia has for some time been quite a popular holiday destination and with Germans, Austrians and Italians in particular.

Hotel sign at Bežanec, near Pregrada

villages, especially along the coast. Simpler but perfectly acceptable facilities can be found on camping sites or when renting private rooms.

Over the years facilities have improved and there are now more accommodation options available to visitors. Although the tourist industry suffered badly during the war of the 1990s, the damage has largely been repaired and resorts are able to offer a wide range of places to stay. There are plenty of modern hotels, apartments and holiday

Numerous tour operators and travel agencies offer package holidays to different resorts in Croatia, but it is not difficult to make your own travel arrangements. Accommodation is best booked in advance, and planning ahead is a good idea in the peak summer months of June, July and August, as hotels and camping sites get very busy.

The Hotel Palace-Bellevue in Opatija (see p223), on the Istrian coast

HOTELS

Tourism boomed in Croatia in the 1970s and 1980s and most of the hotels, particularly those in the resorts along the coast, date from this period. Facilities are generally of a modern type although decor and furnishings can seem rather monotonous. This type of accommodation may not offer the charm of old-fashioned hotels elsewhere in Europe but service is usually good, rooms are clean and spacious and all the basic facilities (most rooms will have an en-suite bathroom) are provided.

Grander, turn-of-the-century hotels, built during the 19th and 20th centuries, are really only found in Zagreb, the capital, and in Opatija, in the Kvarner gulf. Opatija became a popular seaside resort at the time of the Austro-Hungarian

Empire, when the Habsburgs were regular visitors, and it still has several hotels dating from this time. They offer a style and somewhat faded elegance not found in the more modern multistorey buildings along the coast.

Zagreb is also home to larger luxury hotels including several belonging to well-known international hotel chains, such as Sheraton. The facilities and services offered by these hotels are of a very high standard which is reflected in the prices.

PRIVATE ROOMS

A good value alternative to staying in a hotel is to look for accommodation in private lodgings (*privatne sobe*). This is not only cheaper, but it also gives you a chance to get to know the local people and understand their culture and way of life. Rooms offered in private accommodation are gradually being classified into three standards (the category of the room will also be reflected in the price).

The first and best category is three-star and this includes all rooms with a private bathroom. The two-star

Typical large resort-style hotel on the Croatian coast

◁ **A harvest of figs drying in the sun**

Hotel Regent Esplanade in Zagreb *(see p231)*

category indicates rooms where the bathroom is shared with one other room. Lastly, the one-star category indicates the most basic level.

Private lodgings can be booked through the various agencies which can be found in all the tourist resorts. A tourist tax and commission are charged and in summer landlords may require stays of a minimum of four nights.

A cheaper way of finding rooms is by contacting local families directly. A good place to start is at your point of arrival or meeting places such as bus stations, ferry landing stages and at main cafés. These places are often frequented by landladies with rooms for rent. It is always a good idea to check the location and price before committing yourself.

Another way of finding accommodation without official help is by looking for the signs offering rooms – *sobe* in Croatian, *Zimmer* in German or *camere* in Italian – hanging outside the door. It is a good idea to begin looking fairly early in the day. If you find somewhere you like, you can ask to be shown the room and, if you are happy with what you see, you can arrange the terms and the price of your stay. It may even be possible to negotiate the price, especially out of season.

In general this kind of accommodation is offered on a room-only basis, though many rooms have a kitchen corner. Some families offer half-board or even full-board.

SELF-CATERING

Some of the larger hotel complexes on the coast offer self-catering apartments as well as hotel rooms. These can be an excellent solution for families or groups of friends travelling together, as prices are reasonable and you still have access to hotel facilities such as pools and restaurants.

GRADING

Croatia has adopted the standard star system for cate-gorizing hotels common in other European countries, which ranges from one star for simple accommodation to five stars for a luxury hotel. The old Croatian classification system was by letter. According to this system, hotels were divided into five categories. The highest category was "L", which are now five-star

Sign indicating rooms for rent

hotels. This indicates hotels offering a high standard and a wide range of services and facilities. This type of hotel will usually have one or more restaurants, a night club, sports facilities, a swimming pool, and on the coast, perhaps a private beach. There are not very many five-star hotels in Croatia – most of them are in Dubrovnik with a few in Zagreb.

Four-star hotels (formerly category "A") offer facilities and services similar to the five-star category, but the furnishings are less luxurious and more standardized and there are fewer facilities.

Most of the hotels in Croatia fall within the three-star category (formerly B), which indicates hotels offering a good standard of comfort. Hotels in the old "C" and "D" categories are now two-star hotels. These are cheaper and are generally more spartan in their furnishings and offer fewer services.

It is common practice in Croatia for hotels to offer half-board *(polupansion)*, with the price including bed and breakfast, as well as another meal (usu-ally an evening meal). Prices for half-board are very rea-sonable; often not much more than you would pay for just the room. However, hotel res-taurant food is often based on rather standardized "interna-tional" cooking, and may lack local character.

The swish reception at the Westin Zagreb hotel *(see p231)*

Sign indicating a camping site, or *Autocamp* nearby

CAMPING SITES

There are plenty of camping sites in Croatia. These range from small, often privately run camping sites to the large *Autocamps*, which offer services and facilities such as restaurants and shops. Almost all Croatian camp sites are located in woods by the sea, so you can keep cool under shady trees on hot summer days. The majority of camping sites are located in Istria and the Kvarner area, and in Dalmatia.

All camping sites are open in the summer months of June, July, August and until the middle of September. However, it is best to check with the camping site itself if you are planning to stay in camping sites during May and late September, as the opening periods can vary from year to year.

Some of the loveliest camping sites, situated as they are in hidden-away spots, are those marked "FKK" (*see p266*), which are for naturists only.

Camping outside designated areas is prohibited in Croatia

so do not be tempted to stop overnight in the woods or forests, on the beaches or in any areas not specifically reserved for campers.

YOUTH HOSTELS

An economical alternative for young people is to stay in one of the hostels run by the **HFHS** (the **Croatian Youth Hostel Association**).

There are ten youth hostels in Croatia. Rates vary according to the season and a Youth Hostelling Card (available from the YHA in your home country) will entitle you to a discount.

PRICES

The hotels and camping sites in the main tourist resorts, such as the coastal areas, the Plitvice lakes and the capital Zagreb, usually charge higher prices compared with similar hotels in other places in Croatia. Prices rise in the high season, particularly in the month of August, at least in the seaside resorts, regardless of a hotel's star rating. However, even these higher prices are still reasonable and visitors to Croatia will find that prices are about 10 per cent to 20 per cent lower compared with other parts of Europe for accommodation of a similar standard.

Prices in Zagreb stay the same all year round.

BOOKINGS

Tourism in Croatia is very much a "do-it-yourself" affair. If you prefer not to opt for an all-in package holiday (*see p275*), you can plan your excursions as you go along. Excluding the peak of the high season (August), rooms can usually be found without booking in advance.

The Croatian National Tourist Board (*see p267*) can supply information ahead of your trip. Local tourist offices (there is one in every town) will help you find a room or you can apply to a hotel directly to find out if there are rooms available.

The foyer of the Hotel Dubrovnik in Zagreb

DISABLED TRAVELLERS

Care for the disabled in Croatia is good, for the grim reason that the numbers of disabled people have risen as a result of the 1991–95 war. However, despite renewed sympathy and consideration, it is taking time to improve disabled access to buildings such as hotels and restaurants. Many hotels can be unsuitable for persons with restricted mobility. This can often be the case with hotels built on steep slopes which are well provided with steps but not ramps or lifts. For further information, contact Hrvatski Savez Udruga Tjelesnik Invalida, the Association of Disabled Organizations of Croatia or RADAR in the UK (*see p267*).

Outdoor pool – a common facility despite the proximity of the sea

Aerial view of the Sveti Andrija lighthouse near Dubrovnik

LIGHTHOUSES

A delightful and unusual accommodation option in Croatia is the chance to stay in one of the lighthouses which stand on strategic points on the islands and the promontories along the coast. Availability changes from season to season.

Savudrija is 9 km (5 miles) from Umag, and is the oldest lighthouse in the Adriatic and is built in an ideal spot for windsurfers.

Rt Zub is on the Lanterna peninsula, 13 km (8 miles) from Poreč and Novigrad. Even though it is in a relatively isolated position, it is within reach of a number of tourist resorts.

Sveti Ivan na pučini is situated on an island which is part of the archipelago off Rovinj, which is 3.5 km (2 miles) away, ideal for those who love fishing or diving.

The **Porer** lighthouse, on the island of the same name, is 20 km (12 miles) from Pula. It offers truly spectacular views and is in a particularly isolated position. **Veli Rat** stands among pine trees on the northwestern promontory on the island of Dugi Otok, 35 km (22 miles) from Zadar, while at the entrance to the port of Makarska, near one of the most beautiful beaches in

the Adriatic, stands the **Sveti Petar** lighthouse.

Pločica is situated on the island of the same name between the islands of Hvar and Korčula and the Pelješac peninsula.

The lighthouse of **Sušac** was built in 1878 on the island of the same name, 40 km (25 miles) from Hvar. It stands 100 m (328 ft) above sea level and offers a wonderful view of the open sea. It is possible to scuba dive near the rocks at the southern end of the island.

The lighthouse of **Palagruža** is situated 68 km (42 miles) from Split, between the Italian and Croatian coasts, while on the island of Lastovo, 80 km (50 miles) from Split, is the **Struga** lighthouse, dating from 1839. This is a great location for those who love fishing.

The **Sveti Andrija** lighthouse stands on the island of the same name and is 10 km (6 miles) from Dubrovnik. Finally, there is **Prišnjak** lighthouse on the island of Murter, surrounded by a thick pine wood.

The lighthouses contain one or two apartments, able to accommodate four or more people. For more information and bookings, contact **Plovput**, or agencies such as **Adriatica.net** and **Kompas.hr**.

DIRECTORY

ASSOCIATIONS OF TRAVEL AGENCIES

UHPA Association of Croatian Travel Agencies
I. Kršnjavoga 1, Zagreb.
Tel (01) 230 49 93,
230 49 92.
Fax (01) 236 06 55.
www.putovanja.hr

HUPA Croatian Association of Travel Agencies
Rooseveltov trg 2, Zagreb.
Tel (01) 4561 570.
Fax (01) 4828 499.

Studentska Turistička Agencija Zagreb (Students' Tourist Agency)
Krvavi most 3, Zagreb.
Tel (01) 4886 340.

CAMPING SITES

Kamping Udruženje Hrvatske (Croatian Camping Union)
Bože Milanovića 20, Poreč.
Tel (052) 451 324, 451 292.
www.camping.hr

YOUTH HOSTELS

Youth Hostel Association England & Wales
Trevelyan House, Dimple Road, Matlock, Derbyshire DE4 3YH.
Tel 01629 592 600.
www.yha.org.uk

HFHS Croatian Youth Hostel Association
Savska 5, Zagreb.
Tel (01) 482 92 96.
Fax (01) 487 04 77.
www.hfhs.hr

LIGHTHOUSES

www.lighthouses-croatia.com

Plovput
Obala Lazareta 1, Split.
Tel (021) 390 600.
Fax (01) 390 630.
www.plovput.hr
Bookings can be made online.

Choosing a Hotel

Hotels have been selected across a wide price range for facilities, good value and location. Most hotels consider July–August to be the high season. Prices will often be much lower outside this period – sometimes reduced by as much as a third. The hotels are listed by area and map references refer to the inside back cover.

PRICE CATEGORIES
The following price ranges are for a standard double room and taxes per night during the high season. Most prices include breakfast.
(ⓚ) Under 500 KUNA
(ⓚ)(ⓚ) 500–750 KUNA
(ⓚ)(ⓚ)(ⓚ) 750–1000 KUNA
(ⓚ)(ⓚ)(ⓚ)(ⓚ) 1000–1200 KUNA
(ⓚ)(ⓚ)(ⓚ)(ⓚ)(ⓚ) Over 1200 KUNA

ISTRIA AND THE KVARNER AREA

BRIJUNI ISLANDS Karmen
Veliki Brijun. **Tel** *(052) 525 807* **Fax** *(052) 521 367* **Rooms** *54*   **Map** *A3*

The Brijuni islands are beautiful, not too developed and very quiet. This hotel has a pretty waterside location and is surrounded with the fragrant pines that cover the island. Sea view rooms are obviously desirable but there's a supplement to pay. One of three similar hotels on the island. **www.brijuni.hr/en**

CRES Kimen
Melin 1/16, Cres. **Tel** *(051) 573 305* **Fax** *(051) 573 002* **Rooms** *223*   **Map** *B3*

A large resort-style hotel, Kimen is good for families as it has its own good beach and plenty of other sports activities and facilities available. The rooms are on the small side and basic but you'll probably spend most of your time outside them – good value overall. It is a 15-minute walk to town. **www.hotel-kimen.com**

CRIKVENICA Hotel Esplanade
Strossmayerovo šetalište 52. **Tel** *(051) 785 006* **Fax** *(051) 785 090* **Rooms** *62*   **Map** *B2*

Despite having a pretty old-fashioned building at the front, most of the hotel is modern and low-slung, and more functional than charismatic. Still, it has a forest setting and is almost on the beach, making it a good choice for families. Try to get a room with a balcony and a sea view. **www.jadran-crikvenica.hr**

CRIKVENICA Kaštel
Frankopanska 22. **Tel** *(051) 241 044* **Fax** *(051) 241 490* **Rooms** *74*   **Map** *B2*

Located in a 14th-century building that was once a monastery and then a castle, this hotel therefore has an imposing exterior. Right by the river and close to the beach the hotel is conveniently situated. Unfortunately the interior leaves a little to be desired, unless 70s decor is your thing. **www.jadran-crikvenica.hr**

KRK Marina
Obala hrvatske mornarice 17, Krk. **Tel** *(051) 221 128* **Fax** *(051) 221 357* **Rooms** *10*   **Map** *B3*

A small charming hotel in the old centre of town right on the pretty harbourfront. The staff try hard to please and there's an agreeable restaurant terrace in front of the hotel perfect for people-watching. The rooms are pretty good value for money given the location. **www.hotelikrk.com**

KRK Koralj
Vlade Tomačića, Krk. **Tel** *(051) 655 400* **Fax** *(051) 221 063* **Rooms** *193*   **Map** *B3*

This is a large hotel located close to a beautiful bay. There's plenty of facilities on hand making it a good hotel for families: pools, gym and sauna etc. The rooms are modern and comfortable, with special romantic suites for couples. Other attractions include the restaurant with a terrace, tavern, cocktail lounge and beach bar. **www.valamar.com**

LOŠINJ Alhambra
Čikat Mali Lošinj. **Tel** *(051) 232 022* **Fax** *(051) 232 042* **Rooms** *40*   **Map** *B3*

Hotel Alhambra is a substantial and attractive country villa in pretty Čikat Bay. Surrounded by cypresses and pines, the hotel stands just feet away from the water. Rooms are a decent size and attractively furnished, if a little plain. A sea-view room costs marginally more but is still good value. **www.losinj-hotels.com**

LOŠINJ Bellevue
Čikat, Mali Lošinj. **Tel** *(051) 231 222* **Fax** *(051) 231 268* **Rooms** *245*   **Map** *B3*

A large and modern hotel thankfully cloaked by the beautiful pine woods of Čikat, close to the sea and 1.5 km (1 mile) from town. Comfortable and well-equipped, it has a better than usual range of entertainments, sports facilities and activities. The rooms are OK too. **www.losinj-hotels.com**

LOŠINJ Punta
Sestavine bb, Veli Lošinj. **Tel** *(051) 662 000* **Fax** *(051) 236 301* **Rooms** *235*   **Map** *B3*

Large resort hotel in Veli Lošinj, the smaller sister town to Mali Lošinj. Sitting just around the bay from town and built on the rocks leading to the sea, this establishment has a beautiful location. Usual range of sports facilities and activities including diving and spa and beauty treatments. **www.losinj-hotels.com**

Key to Symbols *see back cover flap*

LOŠINJ Apoksiomen

Riva Lošinjskih kapetana 1, Mali Lošinj. **Tel** *(051) 520 820* **Fax** *(051) 520 830* **Rooms** *25*　　　　**Map** *B3*

This is a lovely boutique hotel set on the harbourfront. It doesn't have every facility going (but it does have Wi-Fi) and the rooms are good but nothing special. However, it has an understated sense of style, attention to detail and some great views over the water. There's even a non-smoking floor. **www.apoksiomen.com**

LOŠINJ Villa Favorita

Sunčana Uvala bb. **Tel** *(051) 520 640* **Fax** *(051) 232 853* **Rooms** *8*　　　　**Map** *B3*

Small, four-star boutique hotel in a delightful setting surrounded by fragrant pines and a mere stone's throw from beautiful clear water. This elegant 19th-century mansion has well-appointed sea-view rooms, a nice garden, a basic sauna and a small swimming pool. **www.villafavorita.hr**

LOVRAN Bristol

Šetalište Maršala Tita 27. **Tel** *(051) 710 444* **Fax** *(051) 710 399* **Rooms** *100*　　　　**Map** *B2*

Attractive late 19th-century wedding cake of a building on the promenade, this hotel has excellent sea views. The best rooms have large windows, high ceilings and a balcony. Despite no air conditioning this is still good value for money. The hotel beach is a little disappointing – stone platforms – but not unusual for Croatia. **www.liburnia.hr**

MOTOVUN Hotel Kaštel

Trg Andrea Antico 7. **Tel** *(052) 681 607* **Fax** *(052) 681 652* **Rooms** *33*　　　　**Map** *A2*

Restored 17th-century town house at the top of a spectacular hill with great views over Istria's interior. The "olde-worlde" steep and winding cobbled streets will do wonders for your fitness. There's a wellness and spa centre, and a fine restaurant serving local specialities – truffles and wines – with spectacular views. **www.hotel-kastel-motovun.hr**

OPATIJA Galeb

Maršala Tita 160. **Tel** *(051) 271 177* **Fax** *(051) 711 935* **Rooms** *20*　　　　**Map** *B2*

A lovely little hotel in the centre of town and on the waterfront offering good value for money. There are nice, clean and good-sized rooms with balconies and sea views (those without come a little cheaper). The staff are very friendly and the restaurant and bar come in handy if you want to take it easy locally. Recommended. **www.hotel-galeb.hr**

OPATIJA Istra

Maršala Tita 143. **Tel** *(051) 710 444* **Fax** *(051) 710 399* **Rooms** *130*　　　　**Map** *B2*

Fairly modern medium-sized hotel standing right on the *lungomare* – the promenade that follows the shoreline. The interior is a little drab and dated, but it has a good range of facilities for its price. Centrally located in Opatija and therefore good for wining and dining; only 5 minutes from the main town beach. **www.liburnia.hr**

OPATIJA Palace-Bellevue

Maršala Tita 144–6. **Tel** *(051) 710 444* **Fax** *(051) 710 399* **Rooms** *210*　　　　**Map** *B2*

Actually a combination of two impressive late 19th-century piles next to the town beach, this hotel harks back to the days of the Austro-Hungarian imperial resort. The grand rooms are a little tired around the edges but the basic architecture – marble columns and chandeliers – is wonderful. Good for nostalgia buffs. **www.liburnia.hr**

OPATIJA Villa Ariston

Maršala Tita 179. **Tel** *(051) 271 379* **Fax** *(051) 271 494* **Rooms** *10*　　　　**Map** *B2*

Managing to be both grand in architecture yet small in the number of rooms, this exclusive boutique hotel is set in a beautiful 1924 villa. Standing just a stone's throw from the rocky coastline there's a splendid view. Statuary dots the grounds and adds to the romantic mood. There's also an excellent restaurant. **www.villa-ariston.com**

OPATIJA Hotel Milenij

Maršala Tita 109. **Tel** *(051) 278 007* **Fax** *(051) 278 021* **Rooms** *99*　　　　**Map** *B2*

Luxury hotel (almost boutique) set in impressive seafront villa-style buildings with classic interiors and nice furniture. A full complement of pools, sauna and beauty therapies add to your relaxation. Good quality catering too. Some rooms have much better views than others though, so be sure to have a look first. **www.milenijhoteli.hr**

OPATIJA Admiral

Maršala Tita 139. **Tel** *(051) 710 444* **Fax** *(051) 710 399* **Rooms** *180*　　　　**Map** *B2*

A great ziggurat built on the seafront with fitness studio, beauty parlour, massage, all sorts of saunas, disco and marina. Unlike a lot of the large hotels these facilities are well-maintained. Some may be put off by the modernity and size, but the Admiral Hotel keeps everything nicely shipshape – and so it should at the price. **www.liburnia.hr**

OPATIJA Hotel Mozart

Maršala Tita 138. **Tel** *(051) 718 260* **Fax** *(051) 271 739* **Rooms** *29*　　　　**Map** *B2*

Five-star hotel located in the centre of town on the main drag close to the waterfront. A substantial five-storey building, its pastel-shading and elegant architecture render it a 19th-century classical idiom. The rooms are nice – with dark wooden floors, good furniture and fresh flowers. Private beach. **www.hotel-mozart.hr**

PLITVICE Grabovac

Grabovac bb, Rakovica. **Tel** *(053) 751 999* **Fax** *(053) 751 892* **Rooms** *31*　　　　**Map** *C3*

A modern, plain looking building that actually shapes up more as a motel than a hotel. There's a self-service restaurant (and an à la carte one). The rooms are simple and basic. This is away from the main resort complex and 12 km (7 miles) north of the park. Cheap and reasonably cheerful. **www.np-plitvicka-jezera.hr**

PLITVICE Plitvice

Plitvička Jezera. **Tel** *(053) 751 100* **Fax** *(053) 751 165* **Rooms** *51*   **Map** *C3*

Set in the delightful Plitvice Lakes Park, this is probably the best of the four park-run hotels. While the communal areas lack character, the rooms are clean and simple. You can always use the facilities at the main complex if you feel the need for a sauna, sports centre, disco or swim. **www.np-plitvicka-jezera.hr**

POREČ Hotel Hostin

Rade Koncara 4. **Tel** *(052) 408 800* **Fax** *(052) 408 857* **Rooms** *41*   **Map** *A2*

Not the prettiest of hotels this is typical Croatian hotel complex architecture – a modern construction, glaringly white-washed. Short on character but near a safe beach and stacked with facilities such as Internet and satellite TV, gym, swimming pool and sauna. Good for families and very close to town. **www.hostin.hr**

POREČ Parentium

Zelena Laguna. **Tel** *(052) 411 500* **Fax** *(052) 451 536* **Rooms** *368*   **Map** *A2*

Large resort-hotel set on its own peninsula amid shady pines. There's a marina round one side of the promontory and some good beaches round the other. The hotel provides the usual array of facilities and there's plenty for children to do. The rooms are clean but be aware that the pine trees hide some sea views. **www.plavalaguna.hr**

POREČ Valamar Club Tamaris

Lanterna 6. **Tel** *(052) 401 000* **Fax** *(052) 443 500* **Rooms** *390*   **Map** *A2*

A large resort-hotel complex set about 10 km (6 miles) from Poreč. It has a secluded setting (well, as quiet as a possible 700 people can be) and there's oodles of activities for those who want them. The pebble beach is nearby with pine trees providing the shade. Good for families. **www.valamar.com**

POREČ Valamar Riviera

Obala Maršala Tita 15. **Tel** *(052) 400 800* **Fax** *(052) 431 351* **Rooms** *105*   **Map** *A2*

Its location at the heart of this ancient town, on the promontory looking out to sea over the harbour, will delight some but this hotel is susceptible to a little noise. It's the best bet in town though, so go for front rooms with harbour views. There's a free boat service to the island of St Nicholas, where there is a private beach for hotel guests. **www.valamar.com**

PULA Hotel Omir

Sergia Dobrića 6. **Tel** *(052) 218 186* **Fax** *(052) 213 944* **Rooms** *19*   **Map** *A3*

This is a tidy two-star hotel in the heart of the city. A friendly family-run establishment, it has a certain individual air – it has its own pizza restaurant and a petshop – with good deals for pampering guests' pets. The rooms are functional but fairly inexpensive; and at least they are air-conditioned. **www.hotel-omir.com**

PULA Hotel Riviera

Splitska 1. **Tel** *(052) 211 166* **Fax** *(052) 219 117* **Rooms** *65*   **Map** *A3*

With an imposing, classically-columned façade in the Austro-Hungarian style, this city guesthouse looks grander than its price would suggest. It has plain but clean rooms and, although it's no longer a first-division hotel, it's still a good bet for the centre of town. **www.arenaturist.hr**

PULA Hotel Scaletta

Flavijevska 26. **Tel** *(052) 541 599* **Fax** *(052) 540 285* **Rooms** *12*   **Map** *A3*

Plain but tastefully decorated family-run boutique hotel. Located near to the main sights in the centre of town, this hotel offers excellent value for money. Well-known restaurant offers the traditional food of the area and has a terrace for fine dining indoors or out (try the yummy scampi ravioli with truffles). **www.hotel-scaletta.com**

PULA Hotel Park Plaza Histria

Verudela 17. **Tel** *(052) 590 000* **Fax** *(052) 214 175* **Rooms** *241*   **Map** *A3*

This is a large and well-equipped resort hotel located 4 km (2 miles) outside the city, opposite Marina Veruda. The rooms are large and there are some excellent sea views, so make sure you get one. Half-board in big resort hotels like this may be economical but is only recommended if you enjoy mass catering. **www.parkplaza.com/histria**

PULA Hotel Valsabbion

Pješčana Uvala 1X/26. **Tel** *(052) 218 033* **Fax** *(052) 383 333* **Rooms** *10*   **Map** *A3*

A very good establishment that does things right. Past guests include John Malkovich, Placido Domingo and Naomi Campbell. This is a smart, intimate, family-run boutique hotel in a seaside villa, 6 kms (4 miles) south of Pula. The hotel is closed in January. **www.valsabbion.hr**

RAB Imperial

Palit bb. **Tel** *(051) 724 522* **Fax** *(051) 724 126* **Rooms** *134*   **Map** *B3*

This large hotel is located close to the heart of Rab town in a quiet leafy park with some tennis courts nearby. It has large, simple but nicely furnished rooms, some with balconies and there's a choice of park or sea views – the latter, as usual, cost a few kuna more. **www.imperial.hr**

RAB Padova

Banjol bb. **Tel** *(051) 724 544* **Fax** *(051) 724 418* **Rooms** *175*   **Map** *B3*

A large and modern hotel located across the bay from Rab's Old Town, this has good sports facilities including 19 tennis courts, indoor and outdoor pools, and sauna and beauty treatments. Excellent views across the bay to Rab. Note that not all rooms have air conditioning. For business travellers, there is a conference hall. **www.imperial.hr**

Key to Price Guide *see p222* **Key to Symbols** *see back cover flap*

RABAC Hotel Mimosa

52221 Rabac. **Tel** *(052) 872 024* **Fax** *(052) 872 097* **Rooms** *217*   **Map** *B3*

Large, low-slung block of a hotel, one of three that dominate the seafront. For people who like resort hotels, it's full of facilities and activities, the restaurants are easily accessible and everything you need is on your doorstep. Those who don't should look elsewhere. Miniclubs for kids, watersports, tennis etc. **www.maslinica-rabac.com**

RABAC Villa Annette

Raška 24. **Tel** *(052) 884 222* **Fax** *(052) 884 225* **Rooms** *12*   **Map** *B3*

In a wonderful position on a hill overlooking the bay of Rabac, this hotel is about a 15-minute's walk from the sea. A modern building, it is nevertheless the opposite of the huge resort hotels. The rooms are tastefully decorated, bright and comfortable, and there's a stylish swimming pool on the terrace. Good restaurant too. **www.villa-annette.com**

RIJEKA Best Western Jadran

Šetalište XIII divizije 46. **Tel** *(051) 216 600* **Fax** *(051) 216 458* **Rooms** *69*   **Map** *B3*

Situated on the Rijeka-Split coastal road, this monolithic building has the sea lapping at its foundations. The refurbished rooms are large, well-furnished and most have big windows and expansive views out over the sea (rooms overlooking the road are cheaper). Wi-Fi available. **www.jadran-hoteli.hr**

RIJEKA Grand Hotel Bonavia

Dolac 4. **Tel** *(051) 357 100* **Fax** *(051) 335 969* **Rooms** *121*   **Map** *B3*

Despite the building dating back to the 19th century, this looks like a modern hotel. Set in the centre of town, it is upmarket and business oriented. The rooms are nice and some have sea views. Service is top notch and the hotel can arrange all sorts of tours and excursions. Internet in every room and good restaurants and bars. **www.bonavia.hr**

ROVINJ Valdaliso

Monsena bb. **Tel** *(052) 805 500* **Fax** *(052) 811 541* **Rooms** *121*   **Map** *A3*

A short distance around the bay from Rovinj, this hotel provides great access to good pebble beaches and bathing rocks. The rooms are decent if uninspiring. Wide range of activities – sports, diving and even a painting class. Good for families. There's also two annexes to the hotel and a large campsite, so it can get busy. **www.maistra.hr**

ROVINJ Hotel Adriatic

Obala P. Budicin bb. **Tel** *(052) 803 510* **Fax** *(052) 803 520* **Rooms** *27*   **Map** *A3*

Located at the very heart of Rovinj, it has a superb position on the one of the prettiest waterfronts in Croatia. Large, sea-view rooms (most of them – do check first). This is the oldest hotel in town (1912), but still the best choice in Rovinj if you like being near the hustle and bustle of the harbour. **www.maistra.hr**

ROVINJ Katarina

Otok Sv. Katarina bb. **Tel** *(052) 804 100* **Fax** *(052) 804 111* **Rooms** *120*   **Map** *A3*

This hotel is situated on an island overlooking the historic centre of Rovinj. The main reception is located in a former castle. It has a beautiful pebble and rocky beach and also a special beach for children. There is a regular boat service to Rovinj. **www.maistra.com**

ROVINJ Hotel Heritage Angelo D'Oro

V Švalba 38–42. **Tel** *(052) 840 502* **Fax** *(052) 840 111* **Rooms** *23*   **Map**

Boutique hotel created in a lovingly restored 17th-century palace – the period detailing really adds atmosphere. There's a pleasant suntrap of a patio and a shady loggia or balcony to look out over the red-tiled roofs to sea. Enjoy the gourmet restaurant and good service – and it should be good at this price. **www.rovinj.at**

ROVINJ Park

I. M. Ronjgova bb. **Tel** *(052) 808 000* **Fax** *(052) 808 550* **Rooms** *202*   **Map** *A3*

This is a very popular hotel just across the bay from the old town of Rovinj (about a 20-minute walk). The rooms are fair to good and those with sea views get a beautiful vista. Plenty of facilities on offer, good for families. Those on a budget may have to look for less facilities or further away from town. **www.maistra.hr**

UMAG Komfor Adriatic

Jadranska bb. **Tel** *(052) 741 644* **Fax** *(052) 741 470* **Rooms** *93*   **Map** *A2*

An unprepossessing looking building, it is at least situated right on the coast with some excellent sea views. The rooms are looking a little tired and there is no air conditioning. Having said that it is only ten minutes walk to town and it does have plenty of sports facilities. Good for those on a budget. **www.istraturist.com**

UMAG Sol Aurora

Katoro. **Tel** *(052) 717 000* **Fax** *(052) 717 999* **Rooms** *306*   **Map** *A2*

This large resort-style hotel has been refurbished and is now one of the best of the large hotel complexes around Umag. Set 2.5 km (1.5 miles) from the town centre, and right on the coast – views may be obscured by pine trees so be warned. Rooms are plain but clean. Plenty of activities for everyone. **www.istraturist.com**

VRSAR Belvedere

Petalon 1, Vrsar. **Tel** *(052) 689 100* **Fax** *(052) 689 555* **Rooms** *134*   **Map** *A3*

This is a large holiday resort that has all the usual facilities and is good for families. The rooms are functional, clean and modern. In a beautiful location looking out to the islands, this complex offers value for money if you enjoy such large holiday resorts. Note – there's also 176 apartments that offer far better value. **www.maistra.hr**

VRSAR Petalon

Petalon, Vrsar. **Tel** *(052) 426 100* **Fax** *(052) 426 280* **Rooms** *176*   **Map** *A3*

This hotel resort is situated on a peninsula next to a pebble beach. It has an impressive range of sport and recreation facilites, as well as a daily entertainment programme, including activities for children. All its modern, light guestrooms have balconies. **www.maistra.hr**

VRSAR Pineta

Vrsar. **Tel** *(052) 637 500* **Fax** *(052) 637 550* **Rooms** *95*   **Map** *A3*

A luxurious hotel with delightful sea views, this gets the best of both worlds as it is both close to town and on the sea. There's an indoor pool and guests can use the next door Belvedere's outdoor pool. If activities are your thing, there's plenty to keep you busy, if not just lounge by the pool or on the fine gravel beach. **www.maistra.hr**

DALMATIA

BRAČ Hotel Kaštil

F. Radića 1, Bol. **Tel** *(021) 635 995* **Fax** *(021) 635 997* **Rooms** *32*   **Map** *D5*

Excellent choice for a medium-sized two-star hotel with personality. Built in traditional white stone (it was once a Baroque fortress) and set peacefully by the town harbour, all rooms and the terrace restaurant look out across the sea. It's away from the package tours, too, although the restaurant does get busy in the evening. **www.kastil.hr**

BRAČ Hotel Kaktus

Put Vele Luke 4, Supetar. **Tel** *(021) 631 133* **Fax** *(021) 631 344* **Rooms** *120*   **Map** *D5*

Part of a huge modern super-complex this is bright, modern and the best-equipped four-star hotel in town. It has sea-view rooms and is in Supetar which, with its harbour and riva, has slightly more authentic charm and fewer daytripping tourists than Bol. Offers plenty of activities. **www.watermanresorts.com**

BRAČ Bluesun Hotel Borak

Put Zlatnog rata bb, Bol. **Tel** *(021)306 202* **Fax** *(021)306 215* **Rooms** *136*   **Map** *D5*

Best large four-star resort hotel in Bol set amid the cypresses and pines with a few other large hotels. This has been renovated and has all the usual facilities. The best thing about it is that it is right beside Croatia's most famous beach, Zlatni Rat (hence the high price). Crowded in high season. **www.bluesunhotels.com**

BRAČ Bluesun Hotel Elaphusa

Bračka Cesta 13, Bol. **Tel** *(021) 306 200* **Fax** *(021) 635 447* **Rooms** *300*   **Map** *D5*

Situated in a typical island pine wood, not far from the famous Bol beach and ten minutes from town, this hotel has been renovated. Half the rooms have air conditioning and most have balconies (sea views cost extra but beware of the pine trees). Facilities galore including sports activities and beauty treatments. **www.bluesunhotels.com**

CAVTAT Hotel Iberostar Cavtat

Tiha bb. **Tel** *(020) 478 246* **Fax** *(020) 478 651* **Rooms** *94*   **Map** *F6*

Modern, low-rise hotel secluded by trees, not far from the town centre and overlooking the beach. This hotel provides solid, if rather functional, three-star value in the lovely town of Cavtat (consider staying here rather than Dubrovnik as you can still get a boat over to the big city and Cavtat is so much more genteel). **www.iberostar.com**

CAVTAT Hotel Supetar

Obala Dr A. Starčevića 27. **Tel** *(020) 479 833* **Fax** *(020) 479 858* **Rooms** *28*   **Map** *F6*

In an old stone house on the waterfront with sea views and a "beach" nearby (a concrete platform with sun loungers), the Supetar is hard to beat for charm, setting and value for money, although the interior is a little drab. Don't worry about the beach, the nearby pine-covered peninsula has beautiful swimming places. **www.hotelsupetar.com**

CAVTAT Croatia

Frankopanska 10. **Tel** *(020) 475 555* **Fax** *(020) 478 213* **Rooms** *487*   **Map** *F6*

Like a Bond-villain's hideout, this supersized hotel clings to the side of a wooded hill, all but hidden from sight until you're right on top of it. The rooms are well-furnished and it has its own private bathing ledges off the rocks into the open sea. There are recreational facilities including restaurants and bars, but it feels quite exclusive. **www.hotelcroatia.hr**

DUBROVNIK Adriatic

Masarykov put 9. **Tel** *(020) 433 520* **Fax** *(020) 433 530* **Rooms** *158*   **Map** *F6*

Set in a modern yet dated building, this hotel has fewer facilities than some places but with an appropriately lower price. Please note, it's not for those with walking difficulties as there's quite a few steps around. The rooms are a little tired but the hotel remains popular for its location, sea views and price. **www.dubrovnikhotels.travel**

DUBROVNIK Hotel Sumratin

Šetalište Kralja Zvonimira 9. **Tel** *(020) 436 333* **Fax** *(020) 436 006* **Rooms** *41*   **Map** *F6*

Out of town on the Lapad Peninsular, this three-storey 1922 villa has a pleasant garden, is located near the beach and is handily placed for restaurants and bars. It has been renovated, though its dated interior and basic facilities are still not quite enough to transcend its two-star status. **www.hotels-sumratin.com**

Key to Price Guide *see p222* **Key to Symbols** *see back cover flap*

DUBROVNIK Zagreb

Šetalište Kralja Zvonimira 27. **Tel** *(020) 438 930* **Fax** *(020) 436 006* **Rooms** *23*

Map F6

A small but comfortable hotel set in a pretty late 19th-century villa, surrounded by a pleasant palm tree-filled garden 4 km (2 miles) from Dubrovnik Old Town, in Lapad. The staff are helpful and friendly. The bathrooms can be a little small. There's a regular bus that runs into town. **www.hotels-sumratin.com**

DUBROVNIK Excelsior

Frana Supila 12. **Tel** *(020) 430 830* **Fax** *(020) 430 835* **Rooms** *158*

Map F6

Top of the market luxury hotel situated to the east of the city, up the hill. Built into the cliffs it reaches right down to the water. The rooms are nice and the views are fantastic; there's good restaurants and a lovely terrace. Facilities and service are sometimes not quite what you'd expect given the price – it is *very* expensive. **www.alh.hr**

DUBROVNIK Hotel Pucić Palace

Od Puća 1. **Tel** *(020) 326 222* **Fax** *(020) 326 223* **Rooms** *19*

Map F6

This five-star boutique hotel is set in a 17th-century palace overlooking the old town's market square (Gundulić). Fashionable, luxurious rooms with antique furniture and dark wooden beams are the norm, and very expensive; this is where high society stays – good restaurants and a winebar too. **www.thepucicpalace.com**

DUBROVNIK Hotel Stari Grad

Od Sigurate 4. **Tel** *(020) 322 244* **Fax** *(020) 321 256* **Rooms** *8*

Map F6

A tiny boutique hotel, rare for its location in the Old Town and furnished like an aristocrat's mansion – chandeliers, rugs, mirrors and paintings etc. The hotel's star feature is the panoramic view from the roof terrace where you can have your breakfast. Light sleepers note, the Old Town is not the quietest of places. **www.hotelstarigrad.com**

DUBROVNIK Hotel Vis

Masarykov put 4. **Tel** *(020) 433 555* **Fax** *(020) 433 550* **Rooms** *151*

Map F6

Overlooking Lapad Bay, this wide, white modern complex has all the comforts and regular hotel facilities, with views out to the open sea (make sure you have one). Clean, modern enough and the service is good too. It might be a bit short of character but it works well on its own level. **www.dubrovnikhotels.travel**

DUBROVNIK Villa Dubrovnik

Vlaha Bukovca 6. **Tel** *(020) 500 300* **Fax** *(020) 500 310* **Rooms** *56*

Map F6

Across the bay facing the Old Town and nestled in the cliffs, this hotel has a superb location – rooms have balconies and sea views. The restaurant is on a terrace over the sea for romantic sunset meals. The hotel staff are helpful and there's a boat service to Dubrovnik. Best not to take the half-board option if you can. **www.villa-dubrovnik.hr**

DUGI OTOK Hotel Lavanda

Božava, Dugi Otok. **Tel** *(023) 291 291* **Fax** *(023) 377 682* **Rooms** *80*

Map C4

Small hotel complex in a good location in Božava, only a few steps from the waters of a tranquil cove. All rooms have been refurbished and have balconies with sea views. The hotel has a lot of the usual facilities – pool, sauna, massage; access to tennis, bowling, table tennis and diving etc. **www.hoteli-bozava.hr**

DUGI OTOK Hotel Sali

Sali bb. 23281, Sali. **Tel** *(023) 377 049* **Fax** *(023) 377 078* **Rooms** *48*

Map C4

Top value for money here. This hotel provides basic no-frills accommodation (although there is air conditioning) but in a really beautiful location. The food's good in the restaurant attached and being in a lovely cool forest by the sea is the icing on the cake. **www.hotel-Sali.hr**

HVAR Amfora

Ulica biskupa Jurja Dubokovića 5, Hvar. **Tel** *(021) 750 300* **Fax** *(021) 750 301* **Rooms** *324*

Map D5

Large hotel (it includes 100 apartments) on the beachfront not far from Hvar town. It is modern and stylish inside and has made a real effort to furnish the rooms nicely. There are four pleasant restaurants with sea views (one with live music in the evenings). There's good tennis facilities and a diving school too. **www.suncanihvar.com**

HVAR Hotel Podstine

Put Podstina 11, Hvar. **Tel** *(021) 740 400* **Fax** *(021) 740 499* **Rooms** *40*

Map D5

Just under 2 km (1 mile) south-west of Hvar town centre, this four-star hotel is set apart in a quiet cove, surrounded by shade-giving trees and with its own private beach (with a sun lounger for each guest) and soothing outdoor seaside terraces. The rooms are modern – most of which have views out over the sea and balconies. **www.podstine.com**

HVAR Hotel Riva

Riva bb, Hvar. **Tel** *(021) 750 100* **Fax** *(021) 750 101* **Rooms** *46*

Map D5

Once the modest Slavija Hotel, a major renovation has seen it emerge as an upmarket luxury boutique establishment. The rooms have been completely revamped – flat-screen TVs and designer furniture. It has a superb location in the centre of town and near to the lively Carpe Diem bar/club – so don't expect complete quiet. **www.suncanihvar.com**

HVAR Palace

Trg sv. Stjepana 5, Hvar. **Tel** *(021) 741 966* **Fax** *(021) 742 420* **Rooms** *62*

Map D5

The oldest hotel in Hvar at the heart of the Old Town and overlooking Hvar bay. There's an elegant rooftop terrace over an archaic and pretty loggia. The Palm restaurant and Arsenal bar are pleasant and occasionally host live bands. The rest is more modern, with satellite LCD TVs in every room, but the decor is getting a bit tired. **www.suncanihvar.com**

KORČULA Bon Repos

Korčula. **Tel** *(020) 726 800* **Fax** *(020) 726 699* **Rooms** *278*　　　　　　　　　　　　　**Map** *E6*

Large hotel built in classic 70s architecture and close to the sea. Surrounded by pines and cypresses, the hotel has a water taxi to town in the high season or it's a pleasant 15 minute walk around the bay. The rooms are clean and simple but meal times can be a bit of a scrum when busy. Plenty of facilities. **www.korcula-hotels.com**

KORČULA Korčula

Korčula. **Tel** *(020) 711 078* **Fax** *(020) 711 746* **Rooms** *24*　　　　　　　　　　　　　**Map** *E6*

A small and traditional looking hotel in the centre of town with a great waterfront terrace. Built in light-coloured Korčula stone, this has an old-fashioned feel about it, but some rooms are a bit tired. The hotel's not perfect by any means but the location is unbeatable. **www.korcula-hotels.com**

KORČULA Liburna

Put od luke 17, Korčula. **Tel** *(020) 726 006* **Fax** *(020) 726 272* **Rooms** *83*　　　　　　**Map** *E6*

In a quiet and secluded position about a five-minute walk around the bay from Korčula town, the hotel has a great location looking out to sea. Built in the 80s, it has a 70s look about it but is fine. The rooms are good-sized, though basic and not the best hotel for small children. It has a small hotel beach. **www.korcula-hotels.com**

MAKARSKA Hotel Meteor

Kralja Petra Krešimirna IV 21300, Makarska. **Tel** *(021) 564 200* **Fax** *(021) 611 419* **Rooms** *270*　　**Map** *E5*

One of the most comfortable hotels in the area with the facilities to match. Set in shady woodlands on a beachfront west of the town centre, all rooms have sea-view balconies (although you have to crane your neck for those on the side). The food lets it down a bit, so plan to eat out. Seawater pool. **www.hoteli-makarska.hr**

MAKARSKA Biokovo

Obala Kralja Tomislava bb. **Tel** *(021) 615 244* **Fax** *(021) 615 081* **Rooms** *55*　　　　　　**Map** *E5*

Centrally located hotel that stands on the seafront with a palm-lined road separating the building from the delightful bay. Well equipped rooms, plenty of beauty treatments and a nearby sports centre. Scores highly for its location in town – those seeking solitude may wish to look elsewhere (outside Makarska even). **www.hotelbiokovo.com**

METKOVIĆ Villa Neretva

Krvavac 2. **Tel** *(020) 672 200* **Fax** *(020) 671 199* **Rooms** *8*　　　　　　　　　　　**Map** *E6*

This hotel is situated in the valley of the River Neretva on the road from Opuzen to Metković. The rooms are simple but comfortable and the hotel boasts an excellent restaurant *(see p244)*. The surrounding region offers plenty of opportunities for excursions and activities. **www.hotel-villa-neretva.com**

OREBIĆ Hotel Bellevue

Obala pomoraca 36. **Tel** *(020) 713 148* **Fax** *(020) 714 310* **Rooms** *54*　　　　　　　　**Map** *E6*

Close to the older part of town and situated a stone's throw from a pleasant pebble beach, the amount of facilities on offer belies its two-star status. Most rooms have sea views and some have balconies. Good value and not too far from one of Dalmatia's best beaches – Trstenica – which is almost sandy. **www.orebic-htp.hr**

OREBIĆ Grand Hotel Orebić

Petra Krešimira IV 107. **Tel** *(020) 798 000* **Fax** *(020) 713 880* **Rooms** *184*　　　　　　**Map** *E6*

Outside of town on a woodland beach, the main advantage of this fairly large hotel is its secluded location. The usual raft of facilities and activities is provided – otherwise everything is acceptable rather than memorable. It is like a lot of these hotels that came out of state ownership (service can be inconsistent). **www.grandhotelorebic.com**

PAG Pagus

Ante Starčevića 1, Pag. **Tel** *(023) 611 310* **Fax** *(023) 611 101* **Rooms** *116*　　　　　　**Map** *C4*

A modern low hotel stretching along a pebble beach close to the town of Pag. The rooms are large and those on the front have lovely sea views. There's the opportunity for plenty of watersports (in Pag, however, not on the beach in front of the hotel). All in all, one of the better hotels in the area. **www.coning-turizam.hr**

POMENA Hotel Odisej

Pomena bb, Mljet. **Tel** *(020) 430 830* **Fax** *(020) 430 835* **Rooms** *157*　　　　　　　　**Map** *E6*

The picturesque harbour of Pomena is in the heart of the Mljet National Park, meaning that this place is located miles off the beaten track on a remote lip of land surrounded by water and unspoilt forest. You can really get away from it all and relax or enjoy the cycling and watersports galore. Worth a detour to stay there. **www.alh.hr**

PRIMOŠTEN Zora

Raduča 11. **Tel** *(022) 570 048* **Fax** *(022) 571 120* **Rooms** *324*　　　　　　　　　　**Map** *D5*

Nestled in a thick blanket of pines and cypresses, this large resort-style complex has an excellent location on a narrow isthmus facing Primošten. Nice rooms with balconies, and equipped with plenty of amenities including Internet and satellite TVs. It's a pleasant walk into town and the hotel is good for families. **www.hotelzora-adriatiq.com**

ŠIBENIK Hotel Jadran

Obala Dr Franje Tudmana 52. **Tel** *(022) 242 009* **Fax** *(022) 212 480* **Rooms** *57*　　　　　**Map** *D5*

If you prefer to stay in town, this is the only place. It's a modern building which looks a little out of place among the old stone buildings of Šibenik, but it's relatively sympathetically styled. The hotel is very good value for money and has an attractive harbourside location. **www.rivijera.hr**

Key to Price Guide *see p222* **Key to Symbols** *see back cover flap*

ŠIBENIK Solaris Hotel Jakov

Hotelsko naselje Solaris bb. **Tel** *(022) 365 951* **Fax** *(022) 364 945* **Rooms** *236*   **Map** *D5*

Large, modern complex 6 km (4 miles) outside of town but right on a beautiful beach. There's also bucketloads of facilities: seawater swimming pool; volleyball, mini-football, basketball and tennis courts; mini golf and children's playground. Expect full occupancy in high season. **www.solaris.hr**

ŠIBENIK Solaris Hotel Jure

Hotelsko naselje Solaris bb. **Tel** *(022) 362 951* **Fax** *(022) 362 945* **Rooms** *256*   **Map** *D5*

One of several hotels all owned by the same company and in the same area, about 6 km (4 miles) from Šibenik Old Town. Close to the pebble beach and surrounded by pine trees, the location is pleasant enough. The decor of the hotel complex is a little industrial and functional but the rooms are OK. There's a bus to town. **www.solaris.hr**

SPLIT Consul

Tršćanska 34. **Tel** *(021) 340 130* **Fax** *(021) 340 133* **Rooms** *19*   **Map** *D5*

Located in a peaceful residential area, a 15-minute walk away from the town centre, the Consul doesn't look very grand but all its rooms are comfortable and include Wi-Fi and bathrooms with Jacuzzi tubs. The hotel restaurant offers traditional Dalmatian as well as international dishes. **www.hotel-consul.net**

SPLIT Hotel Globo

Lovretska 18. **Tel** *(021) 481 111* **Fax** *(021) 481 118* **Rooms** *33*   **Map** *D5*

Spacious, refined bedrooms and four-star comforts throughout supplemented by a similarly high quality of service offset the bland exterior and rather ordinary urban setting of the hotel. It's a 15-minute walk into town and further for the beaches, but beaches are not really Split's forte (Marjan peninsula excepted). **www.hotelglobo.com**

SPLIT Hotel Peristil

Polijana kraljice Jelene 5. **Tel** *(021) 329 070* **Fax** *(021) 329 088* **Rooms** *12*   **Map** *D5*

A wonderful location right in the heart of Split's historical centre and within the walls of Diocletian's palace. The hotel's rooms look out onto Peristil and St Dominus Cathedral, and some of the rooms even have parts of the original palace walls. Its restaurant Tifani offers local and international cuisine. **www.hotelperistil.com**

SPLIT Hotel President

Starčevićeva 1. **Tel** *(021) 305 222* **Fax** *(021) 305 225* **Rooms** *73*   **Map** *D5*

This is an upmarket hotel with nicely furnished and well-appointed rooms. There's an element of the corporate hotel atmosphere that comes from having business customers, but that's not always a bad thing. It delivers sophisticated service right in the centre of Split, and the prices aren't too high either. **www.hotelpresident.hr**

SPLIT Radisson Blu Resort Split

Put Trstenika 19. **Tel** *(021) 303 030* **Fax** *(021) 303 031* **Rooms** *246*   **Map** *D5*

Located along the stunning, crystal-blue Adriatic Sea, the Radisson Blu Resort Split is an oasis offering a beautiful pebble beach, two pools, three restaurants and several chic bars. Rooms, including 25 suites and two exclusive presidential suites, are modern and stylish. **www.radissonblu.com/resort-split**

STON Hotel Ostrea

Ante Starčevića 9, Mali Ston, Ston. **Tel** *(020) 754 555* **Fax** *(020) 754 575* **Rooms** *13*   **Map** *E6*

Surprisingly large rooms in this lovely tiny boutique hotel delightfully located in the harbour. Family-run, the standard of service is friendly and professional. Added bonus: two excellent restaurants on your doorstep serving platefuls of the famous oysters and shellfish of the area, with good local wines. **www.ostrea.hr**

TROGIR Hotel Concordia

Obala bana Berislavića 22. **Tel** *(021) 885 400* **Fax** *(021) 885 401* **Rooms** *11*   **Map** *D5*

Impressive 18th-century stone townhouse converted into an attentive boutique hotel in the centre of Trogir's Old Town. Most of the rooms have sea views but do check beforehand. Some of the accommodation is a little snug but, in general, it offers value and services beyond its modest two-star rating. **www.concordia-hotel.net**

TROGIR Trogirski Dvori

Kneza Trpimira 245. **Tel** *(021) 885 444* **Fax** *(021) 881 318* **Rooms** *15*   **Map** *D5*

Small family-run hotel about a ten-minute walk from the centre of town, and two minutes to the nearest beach. There's a tennis court belonging to the hotel but more importantly the restaurant is actually quite good. It serves the usual Dalmatian cuisine and Croatian wines on a pleasant vine-shaded terrace. **www.hotel-trogirskidvori.com**

TROGIR Villa Sikaa

Obala Kralja Zvonimira 13. **Tel** *(021) 798 240* **Fax** *(021) 885 149* **Rooms** *10*   **Map** *D5*

Small, boutique hotel in a 300-year old building set on the waterfront looking across at the old island town of Trogir. It only has ten rooms, but most of them are large. The hotel has been sympathetically updated inside with decent furniture and fittings and the staff are most helpful. Outstanding value. **www.vila-sikaa-r.com**

TROGIR Vila Tina

Cesta domovinske zahvalnosti 63, Trogir. **Tel** *(021) 888 001* **Fax** *(021) 888 336* **Rooms** *20*   **Map** *D5*

Charming, good value place to stay, 5 km (3 miles) east of Trogir. It offers large functional rooms with balconies. Set right on the coast, with easy-access swimming close to hand, the family-run Vila Tina also has a lovely terrace for sipping cool drinks while watching the sun go down. Good restaurant for grilled fish too. **www.vila-tina.com**

VIS Hotel Tamaris

Obala sv. Jurja 20. **Tel** *(021) 711 350* **Fax** *(021) 711 349* **Rooms** *27*   **Map** *D6*

Stately Austro-Hungarian 19th-century villa, with characteristically high ceilings and wooden floors, right in the centre of Vis. Provides a surprising number of activities given its location. The rooms are simply furnished but inexpensive. Getting a room with a harbour view is a must. **www.vis-hoteli.hr**

VIS Issa

Šetalište Apolonija Zanelle 5, Vis. **Tel** *(021) 711 124* **Fax** *(021) 711 740* **Rooms** *125*   **Map** *D6*

Sitting on the edge of Vis bay about 800 m (900 yards) from the centre of Vis, this is a modern hotel with plenty of sports facilities. These include tennis, mini-soccer, volleyball, basketball etc. It's a modern building set close to the water. All the rooms have balconies but check for a sea or park view. **www.vis-hoteli.hr**

VIS Hotel San Giorgio

Petra Hektorovića 2, Vis. **Tel** *(021) 711 362* **Fax** *(021) 717 501* **Rooms** *10*   **Map** *D6*

This hotel is located in the oldest part of the city of Vis. There is a garden with palm, lemon and orange trees, and the bedrooms are elegant and modernly furnished. Free Wi-Fi is available and rooms have air conditioning, satellite TV and a mini-bar. A restaurant serves Mediterranean cuisine. **www.hotelsangiorgiovis.com**

ZADAR Hotel Donat

Majstora Radovana 7. **Tel** *(023) 555 600* **Fax** *(023) 555 680* **Rooms** *240*   **Map** *C4*

Large and functional modern complex with better than standard three-star facilities. Renovations have seen the addition of a swimming pool and better sports facilities. However, its selling point remains its economy and position right on the beach on a lovely stretch of coast. **www.falkensteiner.com**

ZADAR Hotel Adriana

Majstora Radovana 7. **Tel** *(023) 555 600* **Fax** *(023) 555 680* **Rooms** *48*   **Map** *C4*

Part of the same group as the Hotel Donat but a totally different concept. Set in an attractive 19th-century villa, near the beach and upgradingly restored into what they call a lifestyle hotel – they don't have rooms, they have "junior suites". A bit pretentious, but there's a good swimming pool and an excellent restaurant. **www.falkensteiner.com**

ZADAR Hotel President

Vladana Desnice 16. **Tel** *(023) 333 696* **Fax** *(023) 333 595* **Rooms** *27*   **Map** *C4*

Smart hotel, verging on plush. The interior is slightly over-the-top – covered in dark cherrywood and thickly draped curtains with plenty of swashes. Nevertheless it exudes calm and quality. As you'd expect there's good service, and a restaurant well worth eating in. The hotel is also close to the beach. **www.hotel-president.hr**

ZAGREB

ZAGREB Hotel Ilica

Ilica 102. **Tel** *(01) 37 77 522* **Fax** *(01) 37 77 722* **Rooms** *25*   **Map** *D2*

Near the main square, this small family hotel is top value for money. It has been decorated in an eclectic and individual style. If you want corporate uniformity, don't come here but if you enjoy a bit of character then do consider it. This place gets booked up early and doesn't take credit cards. **www.hotel-ilica.hr**

ZAGREB Hotel Jadran

Vlaška 50. **Tel** *(01) 45 53 777* **Fax** *(01) 46 12 151* **Rooms** *48*   **Map** *D2*

This is a conveniently located hotel only minutes from the central square. However, the façade looks a little austere and some of the the rooms are a bit dowdy – others though are fine so ask to see the room first. Take rooms at the back to avoid any street noise. **www.hotel-jadran.com.hr**

ZAGREB Hotel Sliško

Supilova 13. **Tel** *(01) 61 84 777* **Fax** *(01) 61 94 223* **Rooms** *18*   **Map** *D2*

Modest hotel in mid-town location near the bus station. The rooms are simply furnished in a modern fashion and the hotel offers offers air conditioning and satellite television. The level of facilities is very good for the low prices. Overall it's remarkable value for money. **www.slisko.hr**

ZAGREB Laguna

Kranjčevićeva 29. **Tel** *(01) 3047 000* **Fax** *(01) 382 00 35* **Rooms** *160*   **Map** *D2*

A pleasant and modern hotel located a few minutes taxi drive out of the centre of the city. This means that the hotel offers better facilities at a better price than city-centre hotels. The rooms and common areas are well-furnished and of good quality, but the gym is for women only. Another good value Zagreb hotel. **www.hotel-laguna.hr**

ZAGREB Central

Branimirova 3. **Tel** *(01) 484 11 22* **Fax** *(01) 484 13 04* **Rooms** *76*   **Map** *D2*

A modern hotel close to the train and bus station, this is convenient for those on the move and for those doing some sightseeing. The rooms are a bit small but also fairly well furnished. There's an uninspiring bar, but the Wi-Fi connection is free of charge for guests. **www.hotel-central.hr**

Key to Price Guide *see p222* **Key to Symbols** *see back cover flap*

ZAGREB Hotel Vila Tina

Bukovačka cesta 213. **Tel** *(01) 24 45 138* **Fax** *(01) 24 45 204* **Rooms** *25*   **Map** *D2*

Relatively modern, upmarket hotel in a quiet residential area near to the centre of town. Well-equipped with air conditioning, good indoor swimming pool and beauty centre. It's near the beautiful green open spaces of Maksimir Park. Pretty good value. **www.hotelvilatina.hr**

ZAGREB International

Miramarska 24. **Tel** *(01) 610 88 00* **Fax** *(01) 610 87 00* **Rooms** *207*   **Map** *D2*

Part of an ultramodern looking complex in the business area of town (but still walking distance to the sights). It is geared mainly towards business travellers, although it does have family rooms. Good room facilities and service. There's a large but ultimately disappointing casino in the complex. **www.hotel-international.hr**

ZAGREB Hotel Palace

Trg J.J. Strossmayera 10. **Tel** *(01) 489 96 00* **Fax** *(01) 481 13 57* **Rooms** *123*   **Map** *D2*

This hotel is located in a palace, which was built in the early 20th-century Modernist style, in the centre of the city. There are 118 luxury rooms, three hotel suites and two mini-suites, all of which have been decorated in a retro-chic style. Free Wi-Fi and car-parking facilities are available to guests. **www.palace.hr**

ZAGREB The Westin Zagreb

Kršnjavoga 1. **Tel** *(01) 489 20 00* **Fax** *(01) 489 20 01* **Rooms** *349*   **Map** *D2*

Top-notch luxury hotel within a modern building, this was once known as the Opera Hotel. Now rebranded and refurbished, it provides international levels of service and facilities at a good price. The hotel is located in the very heart of the city near the major cultural and historical attractions. **www.hotelwestinzagreb.com**

ZAGREB Regent Esplanade

Mihanovićeva 1. **Tel** *(01) 456 66 66* **Fax** *(01) 456 60 50* **Rooms** *209*   **Map** *D2*

Set in a wonderfully regal building (circa 1925), the Esplanade is a refined establishment with excellent service – probably the best hotel in Zagreb. The rooms are tastefully decorated with luxurious bathrooms and the communal areas are swathed in marble and dripping with chandeliers. Good restaurants and bars too. **www.regenthotels.com**

CENTRAL CROATIA

ČAKOVEC Hotel Aurora

Franje Punčeca 2. **Tel** *(040) 310 700* **Fax** *(040) 310 700* **Rooms** *10*   **Map** *D1*

This grandiose building for a hotel, harbouring only ten bedrooms, has most essential and luxury facilities – fitness centre, solarium, spa, sauna, hairdresser and sporting opportunities. The rooms are pleasantly spacious and therefore this hotel is probably the best bet for accommodation in Cakovec. **www.hotelaurora-ck.com**

ČAKOVEC Park

Zrinsko Frankopanska bb. **Tel** *(040) 311 255* **Fax** *(040) 311 244* **Rooms** *106*   **Map** *D1*

The largest hotel in the city, about five-minutes walk from the centre of town, this is handily located for sightseeing. The rooms are small, cosy and inexpensive, so it is a good choice if you are on a budget or Hotel Aurora is fully booked. **www.hotel-park.info**

KARLOVAC Hotel Carlstadt

Vraniczanyeva 1. **Tel** *(047) 611 111* **Fax** *(047) 611 111* **Rooms** *40*   **Map** *C2*

Excellent central location. The rooms are simple if uninspiring but offer all necessary facilities. There's a decent restaurant on the ground floor (although the terms "casino" and "cocktail bar" are really triumphs of optimism over truthful description). Popular with travelling businessmen, especially at this price. **www.carlstadt.hr**

KARLOVAC Hotel Korana Srakovčić

Perivoj Josipa Vrbanića 8. **Tel** *(047) 609 090* **Fax** *(047) 609 091* **Rooms** *16*   **Map** *C2*

This is, by far, the best hotel in the area – it has a delightful location right on the River Korana. The hotel is in a grand, sophisticated and exclusive villa set apart from the town and there's everything you could want – at a price. Plenty of sports facilities for those who want to tire themselves out. **www.hotelkorana.hr**

SAMOBOR Hotel Livadić

Trg kralja Tomislava 1. **Tel** *(01) 336 58 50* **Fax** *(01) 3365 588* **Rooms** *21*   **Map** *C2*

Close to the historic picture-postcard centre of Samobor, this little hotel fits in perfectly. Pastel exterior, antique furniture, plush bedding and friendly service all create a wonderful atmosphere. There's also a nice café with a terrace where you can enjoy the treat of the region – a custard slice called a *Samoborske kremsnite*. **www.hotel-livadic.hr**

SAMOBOR Lavica

Ferde Livadića 5. **Tel** *(01) 336 80 00* **Fax** *(01) 336 80 00* **Rooms** *33*   **Map** *C2*

Housed in a historical building that once belonged to a local court councillor, this hotel offers comfortable accommodation in the very centre of Samobor. Rooms are simple but neat and have attached bathrooms. Guests can park their cars free of charge in the private car park. **www.lavica-hotel.hr**

SAMOBOR Garni Hotel Samobor
Josipa Jelačića 30. **Tel** *(01) 336 69 71* **Fax** *(01) 336 69 71* **Rooms** *15* **Map** *C2*

A pretty alpine-style building housing this friendly hotel nestles into the wooded hills just outside the town of Samobor. The rooms are fairly plain and simple but the communal areas are quirkily decorated. There's a nice terrace bar/restaurant overlooking the hotel tennis courts. Some limited business facilities. **www.garnihotel-samobor.hr**

SISAK Toplica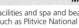
Trg bana J. Jelačića 16, Topusko. **Tel** *(044) 886 001* **Fax** *(044) 886 417* **Rooms** *146* **Map** *D2*

This is not a very attractive establishment, but it makes up for that by offering sports facilities and spa and beauty treatments to guests, as well as two restaurants and a bar. Trips to nearby attractions such as Plitvice National Park and Moslavačke wine cellars can be organized by the hotel. **www.topterme.hr**

SISAK Panonija
Ivana Kukuljevića Sakcinskog 21. **Tel** *(044) 515 600* **Fax** *(044) 515 601* **Rooms** *42* **Map** *D2*

Possibly one of the least attractive hotel exteriors there can be, this hotel thankfully is much nicer on the inside. The refurbished rooms are actually quite tastefully furnished. There's a good restaurant in the same building as the hotel. Not great but there's not a lot of choice in Sisak. **www.hotel-panonija.hr**

SLAVONIA AND BARANJA

ĐAKOVO Blaža
A Starčevića 158. **Tel** *(031) 816 760* **Fax** *(031) 816 764* **Rooms** *18* **Map** *F2*

Strange-looking hotel 1.5 km (1 mile) from the centre of Dakovo with a surprising number of facilities – a large outdoor swimming pool, access to tennis courts and gym. These have elevated its star rating undeservedly. Rooms are very plain, there is a restaurant but the communal areas are not great. **www.hotel-blaza.hr**

DARUVAR Hotel Balise
Trg Kralja Tomislava 22. **Tel** *(043) 440 220* **Fax** *(043) 440 230* **Rooms** *17* **Map** *E2*

Small, centrally located budget hotel set within a once-grand building but now looking slightly down-at-heel – although a renovation of the façade is being planned. The rooms are fairly basic and without pretentions but the hotel offers good value for money. **www.hotel-balise.hr**

DARUVAR Termal
Julijev Park 1. **Tel** *(043) 623 623* **Fax** *(043) 331 455* **Rooms** *150* **Map** *E2*

Large modern hotel (built 1980) located in a leafy park in Daruvar near the thermal springs. Provides the usual Croatian spa experience – a cross between a hospital and a sports club – health treatments and gyms, swimming pools, saunas etc. More intimate accommodation is available next door at Vila Arcadia. **www.daruvarske-toplice.hr**

ILOK Dunav
Julija Benešića 62. **Tel** *(032) 596 500* **Fax** *(032) 590 134* **Rooms** *16* **Map** *G2*

Located on the bank of the Danube, this hotel is surrounded by greenery. It has a few summer terraces, which are perfect for relaxing and admiring the area's natural beauty. All rooms have attached bathrooms and Internet access. The hotel restaurant offers local Continental cuisine and a good selection of Ilok wines. **www.hoteldunavilok.com**

OSIJEK Hotel Central
Trg A Starčevića 6. **Tel** *(031) 283 399* **Fax** *(031) 283 891* **Rooms** *32* **Map** *F2*

Medium-sized traditional hotel set in the heart of town and catering to a discerning clientele. Rooms are good with modern but classic-styled furniture. The common areas are cosy, characterful and dated, but in the best way – it was originally built in 1889. **www.hotel-central-os.hr**

OSIJEK Hotel Osijek
Šamačka 4. **Tel** *(031) 230 333* **Fax** *(031) 230 444* **Rooms** *147* **Map** *F2*

Large modern building that has been completely renovated and updated. Now aimed at the business market there's wireless Internet in the rooms, a wide range of catering outlets and other business facilities. The rooms are smart and modern and you can always relax in the wellness centre once the work is done. **www.hotelosijek.hr**

OSIJEK Hotel Waldinger
Županijska ulica 8. **Tel** *(031) 250 450* **Fax** *(031) 250 453* **Rooms** *16* **Map** *F2*

A lovely old-fashioned hotel, near the centre and only 100 metres/yards from the Drava Promenade. It has only 16 elegant rooms (some with a Jacuzzi) but offers an intimate four-star experience. All rooms have Wi-Fi. There's a coffee shop in the hotel for some rich pastry consumption. **www.waldinger.hr**

ŠPIŠIĆ BUKOVICA Hotel Mozart
Kinkovo bb. **Tel** *(033) 801 000* **Fax** *(033) 801 016* **Rooms** *14* **Map** *E2*

This hotel, with only 14 rooms, has all the comforts of town but is right out in the middle of the countryside. The interior decor has an over-the-top period charm, but that seems appropriate in a country house hotel. Idyllic peace and quiet in pretty rural grounds – you can go horse riding or even hunting. **www.hotelmozart.hr**

Key to Price Guide *see p222* **Key to Symbols** *see back cover flap*

VINKOVCI Slavonija

Duga ulica 1. **Tel** *(032) 342 555* **Fax** *(032) 342 550* **Rooms** *89*　　　　**Map** *F2*

A tall modern-looking building in the centre of town, overlooking the turgid Bosut river (famed for its slow flow!), this hotel offers the best facilities in town. Not a great boast perhaps but its restaurant and café will keep you well fed. **www.hotel-slavonija.eu**

VINKOVCI Cibalia

A Starčevića 51. **Tel** *(032) 339 222* **Fax** *(032) 339 220* **Rooms** *23*　　　　**Map** *F2*

Situated a short distance north of the centre of town, this hotel provides large clean rooms with a decent level of facilities. There is a small restaurant inside. The atmosphere lacks a little in character but the rooms represent good value for the price. Handy for train and bus connections. **www.hotel-cibalia.com**

VUKOVAR Hotel Lav

J J Strossmayera 18. **Tel** *(032) 445 100* **Fax** *(032) 445 110* **Rooms** *44*　　　　**Map** *G2*

By far and away the smartest hotel in Vukovar. This is a modern and impressive building. Four-star facilities and clean and functional rooms (although lacking a little in character) with pretty river views. Good levels of service and Wi-Fi access. **www.hotel-lav.hr**

THE NORTHERN COUNTIES

KRAPINSKE TOPLICE Villa Magdalena

Mirna ulica 1. **Tel** *(049) 233 333* **Rooms** *9*　　　　**Map** *D1*

Situated on a small hill in the centre of this peaceful thermal spa town, Villa Magdalena has luxurious rooms that have Jacuzzis with spring thermal water in the living room of each suite. Internet access is also available in every room. The restaurant offers traditional yet creative Zagorje cuisine. **www.villa-magdalena.net**

STUBIČKE TOPLICE Hotel Matija Gubec

Ulica Viktora Šipeka 31. **Tel** *(049) 282 501* **Fax** *(049) 282 403* **Rooms** *97*　　　　**Map** *D1*

It's here or nowhere in Stubičke Toplice. Another medium-to-large fairly uninspiring spa hotel. The rooms are plain but you can have plenty of fun in the wealth of pools, waterfalls, whirlpool baths available and the natural water baths are steamy hot. There's also a gym and sauna. **www.hotel-mgubec.com**

TRAKOŠĆAN Trakošćan

Trakošćan bb. **Tel** *(042) 440 800* **Fax** *(042) 440 977* **Rooms** *126*　　　　**Map** *D1*

With a wonderful location next to a lake and the beautiful Castle of Trakošćan, this modern and comfortable hotel offers rooms equipped with Wi-Fi, mini bars and fabulous views. There are plenty of sport facilities and recreational activities available for guests. **www.hotel-trakoscan.hr**

VARAŽDIN La'Gus

Varaždinbreg. **Tel** *(042) 652 940* **Fax** *(042) 652 944* **Rooms** *26*　　　　**Map** *D1*

Because this small hotel is a fifteen-minute drive from Varaždin, it is probably only an option if the hotels in town are booked up or you really like the countryside – a nice vineyard setting. The rooms are pleasant enough and there's a large terrace out the back, but it's not terribly appealing from the road. **www.hotel-lagus.hr**

VARAŽDIN Hotel Turist

Aleja kralja Zvonimira 1. **Tel** *(042) 395 395* **Fax** *(042) 215 028* **Rooms** *104*　　　　**Map** *D1*

This is a large modern hotel in the centre of town, aiming at the business market. It has basic business facilities, a bar, a very good restaurant serving local Croatian dishes and a café. The rooms are nice but the rest of the hotel lacks character. As often is the case, the casino is not worth it. **www.hotel-turist.hr**

VARAŽDIN Pansion Garestin

Zagrebačka 34. **Tel** *(042) 214 314* **Fax** *(042) 214 314* **Rooms** *13*　　　　**Map** *D1*

This combination of a hotel and restaurant is only a few minutes' walk from the Baroque centre of town. An attractive building with a faux-Baroque exterior on one side and a modern rustic-style on the other. Rooms are plain but there is a restaurant and a large terrace serving excellent food. **www.gastrocom-ugostiteljstvo.com**

VARAŽDINSKE TOPLICE Minerva

Trg slobode 1. **Tel** *(042) 630 534* **Fax** *(042) 630 826* **Rooms** *269*　　　　**Map** *D1*

This large hotel was built in 1981 near the site of the original Roman baths (hence the name Minerva). The hotel is modern and equipped with sports facilities good enough for most Olympians. The rooms are not bad but meal times are always going to be a bit characterless. **www.minerva.hr**

ZABOK Hotel Dvorac Gjalski

Gredice Zabočke 7, Zabok (near Bedekovčina). **Tel** *(049) 201 100* **Fax** *(049) 201 135* **Rooms** *19*

Set in a splendid castle surrounded by the gentle hills of Hrvatsko zagorje. Guests at this hotel are welcomed by knights resplendent in suits of armour. The rooms are elegant and the whole hotel has an attractive atmosphere of yesteryear. **www.dvorac-gjalski.hr**

WHERE TO EAT

**Veljko Barbieri,
cook and writer**

The food in Croatia is very varied, from the fresh fish and seafood found in towns along the coast to the Central European dishes, such as goulash, offered in inland Croatia. Croatia has its own gastronomic traditions, but the coastal areas have been greatly influenced by the long years of Venetian rule and inland areas reflect the cuisines of Central Europe, in particular those of Vienna and Hungary. Pasta dishes and pizza (with a thin base, in the Italian style) can be found virtually everywhere. Croatian kitchens commonly make the most of a wide range of fresh produce including meat, fish and vegetables. The specialities include the famous sheep's milk cheese *(paški sir)* of Pag and air-dried hams called *pršut*. Prices are generally lower than in other western European countries, making eating out in Croatia a value-for-money experience.

Valsabbion Restaurant, Pula *(see p242)*

RESTAURANTS

The Croatian word *restoran* is used almost in exactly the same, broad way as we use restaurant. It is used to refer to any place where you can eat, which offers a somewhat upmarket, more formal dining experience compared to a straightforward eatery or café. This can range from expensive, fine dining at a hotel *restoran* to low-key, family-run establishments offering simple menus. Equally, prices, too, can range from the very expensive to reasonable cheaper options.

Less formal places to try out are the numerous *gostionica* or *konoba* (both are similar to a trattoria or taverna). These are often family-run businesses and they are good places to try good, traditional, local dishes. Another establishment that serves food is the *pivnica* or beer hall, where you can have a traditional hearty meal along with a glass of beer.

One of the drawbacks of these establishments, from a tourist's point of view, is that some do not display a menu outside indicating the kind of dishes on offer. If you are unsure about a place, it is best to go in and ask to see the menu (or get the owner or waiter to tell you the dishes of the day) and then decide whether to stay or not. Remember you are under no obligation and can feel completely free to leave if the food, the service or the prices on offer are not to your liking.

Most of the *gostionica* and *konoba* fall within the mid-price range and some offer very good value for money. The average cost of a meal is from around 120 to 200 kuna (from about £10–17). This sum would include a starter, a main course (always served with a vegetable) and a dessert. Prices vary according to the standard of the place and its location. A *gostionica* or *konoba* along the coast will almost certainly be more expensive than those inland. Sometimes there is an extra charge for bread, but the service charge is usually included in the price of each single dish.

Along the coast, fresh fish is plentiful though not inexpensive. On menus, prices of fish and seafood are generally given by the kilo. A useful rule of thumb is that a good-sized portion of fish or seafood will usually weigh about 250 grams (10 ounces) and so you should be able to predict roughly how much you will be spending. The choice of fish and seafood on offer will vary daily depending on the catch.

Wine is often drunk with restaurant meals in Croatia (for an overview of Croatia's wines *see pp238–9*), but it is very common for restaurants to serve a drink consisting of a mixture of wine and water *(bevanda)*, or *gemišt*, which is mineral water and local

Sign of one of many *gostionica* offering traditional cooking

Tables outside a pizzeria on the seafront in Umag

wine, brought to the table separately for you to mix.

Ice-cream and pastry shops are called *slastičarnica* and are a great place to enjoy something sweet.

PIZZERIAS AND BISTROS

Pizzas are always a good choice for the visitor travelling on a budget in Croatia. Croatian pizzas are very good and can compete with the best Italian tradition. The prices are always reasonable and are on average 30–40 per cent lower than similar meals in many other parts of Europe.

Another type of restaurant is the bistro, offering a range of straightforward dishes: from *rižot* (risotto) and spaghetti, to simple basic dishes such as *ražnjići* (pork kebabs), *čevapčići* (meatballs) and seafood dishes such as fried octopus or squid rings *(lignje)*.

Beer, called *pivo*, is normally drunk with meals in pizzerias and bistros, but soft drinks, mineral water and wine are also available.

PICNICS AND SELF-CATERING

There are many temptingly beautiful places to visit in Croatia. If you are planning an excursion to one of the unspoilt but isolated spots where refreshment facilities will not be available, you can always take a picnic. Food can easily be bought from food shops, supermarkets or from one of the typical open-

air markets where you can find a great variety of salami, cheeses, bread and olives, as well as fresh fruit and drinks.

Food prices are very reasonable and shopkeepers usually try to be helpful. You may ask for staff to prepare rolls or sandwiches at the counter at no extra cost. Sometimes it is also possible to find some simple ready-made dishes such as *burek*. This is a type of savoury pastry, filled with meat *(meso)* or cheese *(sir)*, and baked in the oven. Buy *burek* in bakeries or small "fast food" shops.

Families or groups staying in self-catering apartments should also have no problem stocking up. Many hotel complexes with apartments also have mini-supermarkets.

VEGETARIAN FOOD

More and more restaurants now offer vegetarian dishes and there are a few that specialize in vegetarian food. Be

aware that some dishes that look vegetarian, like *manistra* (vegetable soup), may contain meat stock. However, restaurants, pizzerias and cafés serving Italian-style food will provide various options from pizzas with vegetable toppings to pasta dishes. Otherwise several side orders of vegetables are usually an option and omelettes *(omlet)* may be available in some places. The choice increases in autumn with the fresh mushroom season, especially in the Istria region.

PAYING

Increasingly, you will find that most Croatian restaurants, whether small or large, now accept credit cards, although it is still possible to come across a few where the bill has to be paid in kuna.

However, credit cards are often not accepted in the *gostionica* and *konoba* or in smaller bars or cafés, so make sure that you carry enough cash with you.

OPENING HOURS

Places serving food and drinks have very flexible opening hours, and it is possible to eat at more or less any time of the day, especially in the tourist resorts. However the meal times of the local people do not vary much from other Mediterranean countries. Lunch is generally served from about noon to 2pm and dinner is served from around 8 to 10pm.

Elegant Zinfadels Restaurant *(see p247)* in Zagreb

The Flavours of Croatia

Croatia can be broadly divided into four main culinary regions: Istrian cuisine is proud of its Italian heritage and features elegant pasta, gnocchi and truffle dishes; Dalmatian cuisine is seafood based and has Venetian echoes; the fertile farmlands of Slavonia have a more Hungarian influence of peppers and spice; while central Croatia retains Austrian predilections – schnitzel, desserts and cakes. However, there are some consistent characteristics – bread is key and is always freshly made either at home or in the local bakery *(pekara)*; fish is important all over the country given the length of the coastline and the many lakes and rivers; and grilling is the preferred cooking method.

Wild aparagus

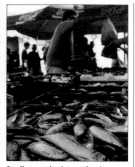

Sardines and other seafood on sale at Split's busy fish market

ISTRIA

With a noticeably Italianate cuisine, food is taken more seriously in Istria than anywhere else outside of Zagreb. Here the truffle, *tartufi*, is venerated. Although freshest in autumn, truffles are used dried all-year-round in risottos and pasta dishes such as *mare monti* (a "surf and turf" combination of mushrooms and shellfish). Many restaurant kitchens roast food in a *peka* – a lidded pot buried in hot ashes – to retain all the flavour and juices. Look out for *srnetina*, venison stew with gnocchi, or roasted, meadow-fed lamb. Other delights are the soft, Istrian smoked ham *(pršut)* and don't miss the best oysters and mussels in Croatia, farmed in the clean waters of the Limski Channel.

DALMATIA

The Adriatic supplies Croatia with much of its fish. Gilthead bream, red mullet, sole and John Dory are common, as are clams, mussels, oysters, octopus, squid, shrimp and even crab and lobster. The channels created by hundreds of islands are perfect for cultivating excellent quality shellfish. Produce is prepared with olive oil, garlic and herbs, cooked quickly – fried, grilled or boiled – and served

Mussels **Octopus** **Sardines** **Sea bass** **Scampi**
Prawns   **Red mullet**
                                                Clams

Selection of typical seafood popular throughout Croatia

CROATIAN DISHES AND SPECIALITIES

Pršut – smoked ham

Many of Croatia's religious and folk holiday festivals are traditionally associated with a particular dish. *Bakalar* (salt cod), for example, is eaten on Christmas Eve and Good Friday, *kulen* (spiced salami) is a Harvest Thanksgiving dish and *guska* (goose) served with chestnuts is a St Martin's Day treat. The Turkish occupation, over 200 years ago, has left behind a legacy of grilled meats and kebabs, *sarma* (cabbage leaf stuffed with rice and mince), *burek* (filo pastry tube filled with meat or curd cheese), and *baklava* (pastries filled with nuts and drenched in sweet syrup). Coastal specialities include *brudet* (fish stew with polenta), *crni rižot* (cuttlefish ink risotto) and *lignje* (squid), served lightly fried in breadcrumbs or *na žaru* (grilled whole).

Manestra *A filling soup made of smoked meat, beans, pasta and vegetables – an Istrian version of minestrone.*

Fresh-baked bread and pastries for sale at a Croatian bakery (pekara)

simply. Easy Italian cooking reigns here – risottos, pizza and pasta feature on menus as a result of history, proximity and the sheer number of Italian visitors. Try Dalmatian *pršut*, firmer than the Istrian version, or *janjetina* – lamb fed on lush island grass and herbs; it's great spit-roasted.

CENTRAL & NORTHERN CROATIA

Inland the food is much richer – olive oil is replaced by butter, lard or dripping. Menus are meat-driven with hearty, filling side dishes such as dumplings and noodles – legacies from Austrian rule. Zagreb has a sophisticated gastronomy but outside of the capital, rustic flavours and styles abound and there is a greater use of veal and game. As well as being grilled, meat

is often cooked in a rich stew or spit-roasted *(pečenje)* – goose, duck, lamb, wild boar and venison are favourites. But perhaps the most obvious Viennese influence are the rich desserts – pancakes, strudels and ribsticking *štrukli*.

Croatian cheese shop, with a variety of hard, soft and goat's cheeses

SLAVONIA & BARANJA

The Austro-Hungarian Empire has also affected Slavonian cooking but with a Hungarian flavour. Large portions of warming dishes insulate the mainly rural population from a cold, wet and often snowy climate. Expect meat or fish in rich sauces, spiced with paprika. The Drava river provides a good supply of freshwater fish like pike and carp. Do try a few slices of Slavonia's famous appetizer, *kulen*. This smoke-cured salami, flavoured with chilli and paprika, is often served with peppers, tomatoes, *turšija* (pickled vegetables) and sometimes curd cheese.

ON THE MENU

Fiš paprikaš: Fiery fish stew from Slavonia often made with carp and spiced with paprika.

Zagrebački odrezak: Veal, ham and cheese fried in breadcrumbs – a super-schnitzel.

Ajvar: A savoury red pepper sauce/relish – everyone has their own secret recipe.

Čevapčići: A Turkish legacy – spicy meat rissoles served with raw onion, flatbread and ajvar.

Blitva s krumpirom: Popular side dish of chard boiled with potatoes, olive oil and garlic.

Palačinke: One of Croatia's top desserts: jam-filled pancakes, with chocolate and walnuts.

Škampi na buzaru *Scampi is gently simmered in wine, tomatoes, garlic and herbs; finished with breadcrumbs.*

Pašticada *A beef joint and seasonal vegetables are slowly pot-roasted in wine – prunes are also sometimes used.*

Štrukli *This Northern Croatia dish of parcels of curd cheese, boiled and then baked, can be either sweet or savoury.*

What to Drink in Croatia

A wide variety of locally made drinks is available throughout Croatia, from beers to wines to fiery fruit brandies. Croatian beer is usually of the lager type but dark beers can also be found. Foreign brands such as Stella Artois, Tuborg and Kaltenberg are brewed in Croatia under licence, and there are Irish pubs selling Guinness and other Irish beers. Croatia's vineyards yield all kinds of red and white wines, most of which are rarely seen outside the country. Spirits based on grapes are popular as aperitifs rather than after-dinner drinks, as are other fruit brandies made from plums or pears. Brandies flavoured with herbs, walnuts or even honey are also popular. Tap water is safe to drink but if the taste does not appeal there is a wide range of bottled mineral waters, both sparkling and still.

Typical sign for a pub, *pivnica* in Croatian

Traditional utensils for the preparation of strong Turkish coffee

COFFEE AND TEA

Coffee *(kava)* is drunk throughout Croatia. All over the country it is served very strong and black, in little cups, like an *espresso* coffee. If it is too strong you can add a little milk or order a *cappuccino* (freshly ground coffee with frothy hot milk). Strong Turkish coffee is also available in some places. Herbal teas *(čaj)* are sold everywhere. Indian teas can also be found, usually served with lemon, but you can ask for milk.

BEER

Karlovačko beer

Another very popular drink sold in cafés and pubs is beer *(pivo)*, which is always served very cold. Most bottled beers are of the lager-type, but some darker beers can be found. The most well-known brands of lager beer are Ožujsko, made in Zagreb and Karlovačko (Karlovac). Another common brand is Pan. Well-known international beers such as Stella Artois are also widely available (some brewed under licence in Croatia), but tend to be more expensive.

Ožujsko beer

SPIRITS

A wide variety of spirits is available in Croatia, demonstrating the nation's fondness for strong alcoholic drinks, in particular fruit-based eau-de-vie. One of the most popular spirits is a plum brandy originating in Slavonia called *Šljivovica*. It is found all over the country. *Loza* is a grape-based eau-de-vie with a high alcohol content, and *Travarica* is a herb-based spirit. *Vinjak* is a brandy, *Pelinkovac* is a herb liqueur, and *Maraskino*, a liqueur from Zadar, is flavoured with maraschino cherries.

Pelinkovac liqueur   Zrinski brandy

Šljivovica eau-de-vie

Many spirits are drunk as aperitifs. A spirit called *Bermet* is produced in Samobor, near Zagreb, and is made according to an ancient, well-guarded recipe. It is drunk as an aperitif, served with ice and a slice of lemon.

Some bottles of eau-de-vie with fruit, made at home all over the country

MINERAL WATER, SOFT DRINKS AND FRUIT JUICES

All bars and cafés offer a wide range of fruit juices, as well as internationally known brands of soft drinks and fizzy drinks like cola. Tap water is safe to drink everywhere in Croatia and bottled mineral waters *(mineralna voda)* are also widely available. The most common brands of mineral water in Croatia are Studena, Jamnica and Jana, but there are also many imported brands available as well.

Mineral water

Orange juice

Pubs and bars with live music: a popular way to socialize

DRINKING CUSTOMS IN CROATIA

Pubs, bars and cafés are not only places to stop at various times of the day for refreshment, but also places to meet friends and socialize. For visitors this can also be a good way of meeting and getting to know local people.

One tradition found in Croatia is that of mixing wine with other drinks such as mineral water or even cola. A *bevanda* is red or white wine with plain water, while *gemišt* is white wine mixed with sparkling mineral water. One of the most popular summer drinks is red wine and fizzy cola, a drink called *bambus*.

Croatians like a drink or two, as is demonstrated by the custom in the Slavonian region of wine drinking with friends. This traditional ritual should only be undertaken by people with a very strong head for alcohol. It begins with the first phase, which is before any wine is consumed, known as the *Dočekuša*. This is then followed by the *Razgovoruša*, during which you chat while sipping at least seven glasses of wine. The final phase is called the *Putnička*, reserved for the leave-taking, when yet more glasses are emptied before people say their final farewells.

WINES

Croatia is also a land of vineyards, with vines grown on rolling hills inland and in pockets of stony soil on the coast and islands. Production varies in quantity and quality but standards are improving and there are some very decent wines around. From the Kvarner area come the white wine Žlahtina (from Vrbnik on Krk), red Cabernet (from Poreč) and Teran (from Buzet), a light red.

Žlahtina

Dalmatia is known for Pošip and Grk from Korčula (both white wines), Dingač (one of the best Croatian reds) and Postup from the Pelješac peninsula. Plavac (red) comes from Brač and Malmsey from Dubrovnik. Finally, from Slavonia come Kutjevačka Graševina, Kutjevo Chardonnay and Riesling, and Krauthaker Graševina.

Dingač **Postup**

WHERE TO DRINK

There are various types of establishments which serve drinks and it is useful to know a few of the basic categories. A *kavana* is equivalent to a café, and serves both alcoholic and non-alcoholic drinks, while a *pivnica* serves mainly beer. Irish pubs can also be found, selling Guinness and other Irish beers. Wine is generally drunk in a *konoba* in coastal towns. In the larger towns you can have a snack with your drink in one of the *bife*, the Croatian equivalent of a snack bar. However, there are not really rigid distinctions between the types of drinks served in one or other of these places. Cafés open early and close late – usually around 11pm or later in the summer.

Drinks of various kinds (though rarely alcoholic) are also served in pastry shops – *slastičarna*. The close links that Croatia's gastronomic tradition has with Austria, and in particular with Vienna, has influenced the production of delicious cakes and pastries as well as excellent *sladoled* (ice cream). Pastry shops close earlier than cafés in general.

A snack bar with outdoor tables in Fažana, a coastal resort

Choosing a Restaurant

The restaurants here have been selected across a wide price range for facilities, good value and location. They are listed by region, starting with Istria and the Kvarner area. Most restaurants in Croatia do not have separate non-smoking areas. For road map references, see the inside back cover.

PRICE CATEGORIES
For a complete meal with drinks (except wine), including service (a tip is recommended):
Ⓚ Under 100 KUNA
ⓀⓀ 100–200 KUNA
ⓀⓀⓀ 200–300 KUNA
ⓀⓀⓀⓀ 300–400 KUNA
ⓀⓀⓀⓀⓀ Over 400 KUNA

ISTRIA AND THE KVARNER AREA

BUZET Toklarija ⓀⓀⓀⓀⓀ
Sovinjsko Polje 11, Buzet. **Tel** *(091) 926 67 69*   **Map** *A2*

In a cottage on a hilltop outside of town, reservations are essential at this fine restaurant. Long menus of food that is "slow cooked" mean a meal that's going to be an event. Attention to detail in the cooking from wood-fired stoves to genuinely local produce make it one of the best restaurants in Croatia.

CRES Gostionica Belona ⓀⓀ
Šetalište 20 travnja 24, Cres. **Tel** *(051) 571 203*   **Map** *B3*

This restaurant is popular with the locals and particularly lively in the evening. The decor is rustic and so is some of the cooking but it's none the worse for that. On offer is seafood and fish, the *lignje na žaru* (grilled squid) is particularly good, as well as meat and pasta dishes.

CRES Riva ⓀⓀ
Obala Creskih Kapetana 13, Cres. **Tel** *(051) 571 107*   **Map** *B3*

Located at the heart of Cres town, this restaurant is doubly blessed. On the one side it faces onto the renovated square, while on the other it has a large terrace that overlooks the harbour. As you'd expect the fish is good and fresh – try sea bass, scampi or seafood risotto. Closed in winter.

KASTAV Kukuriku ⓀⓀⓀⓀⓀ
Trg Lokvina 3, Kastav. **Tel** *(051) 691 519*   **Map** *B2*

Providing a gastronomic highlight of the area, Kukuriku prides itself on its creative cooking. Ingredients such as honey, cheese and mushrooms are locally sourced along with the famous lamb. The menu is also seasonal – asparagus in spring and truffles in autumn. Go along with the chef's recommendations.

KRK Konoba Šime Ⓚ
Ulica Antuna Mahnića 1, Krk. **Tel** *(051) 220 042*   **Map** *B3*

This restaurant sits right on the main harbour promenade. It is a little dark and medieval inside but has a covered seating area right on the promenade overlooking the sea. They serve simple dishes such as large meaty grilled squid and *blitva* – a garlicky green chard and potato mixture.

KRK Konoba Nono ⓀⓀ
Krckih Iseljenika 8, Krk. **Tel** *(051) 222 221*   **Map** *B3*

Set in the centre of town, this traditional restaurant specializes in local dishes and as well as serving the usual array of seafood – fish, prawns and pasta – has a few more authentic meat dishes. Try the home-made *šurlice*, pasta tubes, usually served with a thick goulash sauce enriched with wine. Closed in winter.

KRK Marina ⓀⓀ
Puntica 7, Punat. **Tel** *(051) 654 380*   **Map** *B3*

Used as a harbour since Roman times, Punat bay is a delightful setting for a restaurant. The simple interior is decorated with paintings by a local Naif painter, while outside there is a simple if not terribly aesthetic terrace. The food is good – fish, of course, and the usual Mediterranean fare and locally-made olive oil.

LIMSKI CHANNEL Viking ⓀⓀ
Lim, Sveti Lovreč. **Tel** *(052) 448 119*   **Map** *A3*

The Limski Channel is famous for its shellfish and that's what you should eat here – oysters, the locally-farmed mussels, or scampi served with noodles and porcini mushrooms. The restaurant is traditionally furnished (1970s style) but the location in the winding narrow channel is breathtaking.

LOŠINJ Lanterna Ⓚ
Sv Marije 12, Mali Lošinj. **Tel** *(051) 233 625*   **Map** *B3*

Far from the crowds which fill the town, particularly in summer, this small establishment is off the beaten track but it's well worth the effort – head east up the hill from the harbour towards the church. The food is the usual Mediterranean fare of seafood, grilled meats and pasta, but rather well-executed.

Key to Symbols *see back cover flap*

LOŠINJ Villa Diana

Čikat bb, Mali Lošinj. **Tel** *(051) 232 055*

Map *B3*

Part of a small hotel set in secluded Čikat Bay, Villa Diana has a beautiful location with a large waterfront terrace pleasantly shaded by cypress trees. The restaurant offers a wide range of typical Croatian and international dishes. A restaurant genuinely worth seeking out. Closed in winter.

MOTOVUN Mondo

Ulica Barbacan 1, Motovun. **Tel** *(052) 681 791*

Map *A2*

Excellent value restaurant with a romantic candlelit interior, and an outside terrace. The kitchen makes a point of putting truffles in everything – from home-made paté to beef. However, if you want to try something without them, there is a selection of truffle-free dishes every week.

MOTOVUN Restoran Zigante

Livade 7, Motovun. **Tel** *(052) 664 302*

Map *A2*

Restaurants that are inland differ from those on the coast in that they are not fed by a regular stream of tourists regardless of quality – and they are all the better for it. Istria's most famous temple to the truffle (look out for pictures of a record specimen) offers tasting menus and pictures of the international clientele who've dined there. Enjoy!

OPATIJA Istranka

Bože Milanovića 2, Opatija. **Tel** *(051) 271 835*

Map *B2*

This restaurant is situated in the centre of Opatija. Its speciality is local Istrian cuisine, including dishes such as truffles, home-made *fuži* (a type of pasta typical of Istria) and *maneštra* (Istrian vegetable soup). Fresh fish, meat and pasta dishes are also available. The interior is very pleasant.

OPATIJA Amfora

Črnikovica 4, Volosko. **Tel** *(051) 701 222*

Map *B2*

This is a grand and pleasant restaurant that is definitely better than your average seaside *konoba*. A short distance from the centre on the edge of Volosko bay, it has a large terrace overlooking the sea. Fish and shellfish is a speciality fresh from their own aquarium. The owner is a well-known Croatian gastro guru.

OPATIJA Bevanda

Zert 8, Lido, Opatija. **Tel** *(051) 493 888*

Map *B2*

Another good Opatija seafood restaurant, this has a choice seaside location on a small peninsula with its own little lido. The terrace is really beautiful and the music is (usually) not too loud. Choose from over 20 starters and all that the sea can offer – known for its excellent lobsters.

OPATIJA Plavi Podrum

Ulica Frana Supila 12, Opatija. **Tel** *(051) 701 223*

Map *B2*

There's been a restaurant here for over 100 years and this one is very good. Try the fresh Mediterranean soup. It specializes in fish, of course, but also takes pride in its meat dishes. The excellent cellar contains local and international wines by the bottle or glass, and there's a first class sommelier.

POREČ Nono

Zagrebačka 4, Poreč. **Tel** *(052) 453 088*

Map *A2*

Serves probably the best pizza in Croatia, and if not, then certainly the largest. Also does other meat and fish dishes (good steaks and grilled squid) but the crowds gather here mainly for the pizzas. The small size of the restaurant means it's usually full but it is worth the wait.

POREČ Konoba Ulixes

Dekumanus 2, Porec. **Tel** *(052) 451 132*

Map *A2*

Situated in the Old Town of Poreč this small and intimate restaurant is a bit of a gem. Here you can try Istrian truffle dishes without breaking the bank. Good fish and seafood as well. It's rustic and cosy inside but there's also a small sun-trap of a terrace with an olive tree or two.

POREČ Sv. Nikola

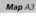

Obala maršala Tita 23, Poreč. **Tel** *(052) 423 018*

Map *A2*

An impressive, award-winning restaurant situated on Poreč's seafront overlooking the island of Sv. Nikola. The superb menu offers sophisticated fish and meat dishes, with specialities such as carpaccio made of scampi frogfish and octopus fish fillet with asparagus and truffles. It is luxuriously decorated.

PULA Vodnjanka

D. Vitezića 4. **Tel** *(052) 210 655*

Map *A3*

An excellent find, this little restaurant with a few tables outside offers very good value Istrian home cooking (Istrian cooking has a more obvious Italian influence). Not the most sophisticated establishment, this is an informal place where the locals come to relax, drink good, cheap wine and eat honest food.

PULA Stari Grad 2

Sisplac 3, Pula. **Tel** *(052) 386 808*

Map *A3*

Head to this restaurant just outside the town centre to sample some typical Istrian dishes, especially the home-made pasta. Try the traditional *fuži* (a type of Istrian pasta) and *pljukanci* (spindle shaped pasta) accompanied by one of 40 wines on offer. Vegetarian dishes are also available. Reservation recommended.

PULA Milan

Stoja 4, Pula. **Tel** *(052) 300 200*

Map *A3*

This is a good hotel restaurant that has been going since 1967. In that time it has built up a repertoire of 350 wines. It serves some marvellous fish – monkfish, sardines, cuttlefish, red mullet. Try the creamy lobster lasagne (*lazanje sa jastogom*). The decor is restrained, fairly modern, and simple.

PULA Vela Nera

Franja Mošnje 3b, Sišan. **Tel** *(052) 300 621*

Map *A3*

Situated in Sišan, a little place 7 km (4 miles) from Pula, this is a modern restaurant with a terrace by the pool and olive trees. The menu features Mediterranean and international cuisine, with a splash of local Istrian flavour. There's also a wide range of wines from Croatia, Europe and the rest of the world.

RAB Konoba Riva

Biskupa Draga 3, Rab. **Tel** *(051) 725 887*

Map *B3*

Good mid-range restaurant with typical *konoba* decor – fishing paraphernalia, wooden beams and a stone-walled interior. There's a nice sea-view terrace, and occasionally live music. They will also deliver to yachts in the marina, which is handy if you want to enjoy fine dining on your own boat.

RAB Marco Polo

Banjol, Rab. **Tel** *(051) 725 846*

Map *B3*

Located in Banjol, not far from the town of Rab, is this delightful restaurant. The dishes are created with ingredients from the sea or from the restaurant's garden. There's also a good choice of Croatian and foreign wines, and a sommelier on hand to make recommendations.

RAB Astoria

Trg Municipium Arba 7, Rab. **Tel** *(051)774 844*

Map *B3*

Ancient Venetian palace with old beams and great stone walls. Situated above the main square, this restaurant has a fine kitchen and terrace with fantastic harbour views. They make a point of growing their own herbs and only using the best local produce. Rab's best dining establishment.

RIJEKA Arca Fiumana

Adamićev gat, Rijeka. **Tel** *(051) 319 084*

Map *B2*

Situated on the upper deck of a ship in Rijeka harbour, so you can be certain that the fish is always as fresh as possible. They also serve excellent home-made pasta from the island of Krk, dishes with truffles and also a variety of meat dishes. There is a good selection of Croatian wines.

RIJEKA Konoba Tarsa

Josipa Kalfaneka 10, Rijeka. **Tel** *(051) 452 089*

Map *B2*

Located in the historic part of Rijeka known as Trsat, this restaurant has a rustic wooden interior. Classic Mediterranean dishes are prepared imaginatively; specialities include home-made gnocchi with venison and boiled lamb. Horse meat is also featured on the menu as well as a selection of over a hundred wines. Live music on weekends.

RIJEKA Kamov

Dolac 4, Rijeka. **Tel** *(051) 357 100*

Map *B2*

Set inside the aspirational Grand Hotel Bonavia – motto "five-star service in a four-star hotel" – this fine dining restaurant offers good quality food and service. The restaurant combines a gastronomic tradition of over 130 years with a modern and almost avant-garde style of cooking.

ROVINJ Amfora

Obala Aldo Rismondo 23, Rovinj. **Tel** *(052) 816 663*

Map *A3*

A firm favourite with the regulars, this restaurant consistently supplies good food in delightful surroundings and an ideal harbourside location. Standard grilled seafood, pasta and meat dishes skillfully executed. Try the local variation of "surf and turf" – *mare monti* – seafood and mushrooms with pasta.

ROVINJ Veli Jože

Svetoga Križa 1, Rovinj. **Tel** *(052) 816 337*

Map *A3*

This attractive restaurant serves traditional Istrian dishes such as *bakalar* (salt cod) in a white sauce or lamb stew cooked with potatoes; pasta and grilled fish – all washed down with the extremely drinkable, local Malvasia white wine. There's also a good-sized terrace.

ROVINJ Puntulina

Ulica Svetog Kriza 38, Rovinj. **Tel** *(052) 813 186*

Map *A3*

Set romantically on a balcony over the sea at the edge of the old town, this is Rovinj's best. It delivers an Italian/Istrian mix and tasting menus too. Stop off at the bar on the ground floor for a sundowner before heading upstairs with your beloved to the delightful restaurant.

UMAG Badi

Lovrečica. **Tel** *(052) 756 293*

Map *A2*

This is a fine restaurant in a small village, Lovrečica, 10 minutes' drive along the coast from Umag. It has a pleasant terrace and a leafy green setting. No surprises in the menu offerings, but good seafood, pasta, and risottos, with definite Italian characteristics. Try the house specials – baked fish dishes.

Key to Price Guide *see p240* **Key to Symbols** *see back cover flap*

DALMATIA

BRAĆ Konoba Mlin

Ante Starčevića 11, Bol. **Tel** *(021) 635 376* **Map** *D5*

Situated in an old mill in a beautiful part of Bol, this restaurant serves traditional dishes of the area using fish, shellfish, grilled meat, Dalmatian *pršut* (a kind of smoked ham) and cheese. Local wines are also available. There are lovely views of the coast from the outside terrace.

BRAĆ Ribarska Kućica

Ante Starčevića, Bol. **Tel** *(021) 635 033* **Map** *D5*

From the terrace there are beautiful views out over the sea with its own secluded beach. There is a wide choice of fish dishes and a fixed price menu after 8pm every evening. Also does pizza, but try rather the gnocchi with *pršut* in a cheese sauce – it's a bit of a rib-sticking dish but perfect if you've tired yourself out swimming.

BRAĆ Taverna Riva

Frane Radića 5, Bol. **Tel** *(021) 635 236* **Map** *D5*

Bol is such a popular place that some restaurants don't bother trying very hard as they'll still be full. Thankfully, this is not one of those – it has a large stone terrace, and serves excellent versions of the usual fish dishes – try *salata od hobotnice* (octopus salad), *pršut* (dalmatian ham), or *rižot od liganja* (squid risotto).

CAVTAT Galija

Vuličevićeva 1. **Tel** *(020) 478 566* **Map** *F6*

Cavtat's top restaurant – close to the main promenade on the way to the peninsula near the Franciscan monastery. Old-fashioned tavern with lovely terrace under pine trees and by the sea – all tables still have linen and candles. The menu is a little more adventurous than most. Worth booking ahead, especially at weekends.

CAVTAT Kolona

Put Tiha 2, Cavtat. **Tel** *(020) 478 787* **Map** *F6*

This is a nice restaurant with a cosy and traditional interior. It also has a terrace, surrounded by aromatic greenery with views out over the sea. The food is good – typical seafood specialities – but what really marks this place out is the genuinely friendly service – they've even been known to drive the last diners home.

DUBROVNIK Lokanda Peskarija

Na Ponti. **Tel** *(020) 324 750* **Map** *F6*

Where the locals go for fried sardines and seafood. Traditional wood-heavy interior, quite cosy and small with a buzzing bar – food is served in "traditional" black pots. Next to the harbour fish market (so be sensible and order the delicious fish). Always busy – so booking ahead is advised. They can put tables outside in summer.

DUBROVNIK Tabasco

Cvatatska 11. **Tel** *(020) 429 595* **Map** *F6*

This pizzeria is situated just outside the old fortified part of town to the north of the Ploče Gate. It serves decent-sized pizzas and large portions of *panzerotti* (large pasta parcels stuffed with cheese and ham topped with tomato sauce). Also has some pasta dishes and fresh salads. The vibe here is filling and cheap.

DUBROVNIK Mimoza

Branitelja Dubrovnika 9. **Tel** *(020) 411 157* **Map** *F6*

This restaurant is located just outside the city walls, near the Pile Gate. You can opt to dine outside on the large terrace, or eat inside in the elegant dining room. The menu is varied and includes traditional *ispod saća* dishes, which means the food has been cooked "under an iron bell", and fish, meat and vegetarian plates.

DUBROVNIK Taverna Arsenal

Pved Dvorum 1. **Tel** *(020) 321 065* **Map** *F6*

Apart from its rich gastronomic offerings and a choice of about 40 mainly local wines, what makes this restaurant special is its interior. Oak wood panelling is rich in details and there is a wonderful terrace with stunning views over the port, where there are two replicas of old sailing ships in the harbour.

DUBROVNIK Levanat

Šetalište Nika i Meda Pucica 15, Lapad. **Tel** *(020) 435 352* **Map** *F6*

Top place in Lapad with rather formal interior. This small restaurant is set right by the sea in Lapad Bay and has an outdoor terrace with panoramic views – ideal for the regular rosy-red sunsets. The food is simple but very good – the usual seafood, grilled meats and traditional pancakes (*palačinke*) filled with chocolate and walnuts.

DUBROVNIK Orhan

Od Tabakarije 1. **Tel** *(020) 414 183* **Map** *F6*

Unpretentious fish restaurant with other options, hidden away down some steps in a secluded cove just by the Old Town. Not being within the walls of the city is an actual advantage as the day-trippers rarely make it here from the cruise boats. Fine terrace with views of Dubrovnik's mighty sea walls.

DUBROVNIK Nautika

Brsalje 3. **Tel** *(020) 442 526* **Map** *F6*

This is probably the most elegant restaurant in the city, and offers a lovely view of the walls and sea just by the Pile Gate. The food is of a similarly high standard and although fairly expensive, the fish dishes are definitely worth trying. The grilled lobsters are excellent as is the fish stew (*brodet*) with polenta. Reserve ahead at weekends.

DUBROVNIK Proto

Široka 1. **Tel** *(020) 323 234* **Map** *F6*

Situated in the heart of the old town, this restaurant has been around since 1886 and is well-known for its fish specialities, as well as meat dishes. Beef consommé with home-made noodles, grilled fish fillet, shrimps in saffron sauce and hazelnut parfait are just some of the choices available to diners. Reserve a table in advance.

DUGI OTOK Tamaris

Sali II 18, Sali. **Tel** *(023) 377 377* **Map** *C4*

Sali is the main village on the island of Dugi Otok and this restaurant, although it doesn't look anything special from the outside (and not much better from the inside) serves decent food and is popular with the locals (especially the bar and nearby pool room). Usual fish dishes such as grilled scampi and spaghetti with shellfish.

HVAR Jurin Podrum

Donja kola 11, Stari Grad. **Tel** *(021) 765 448* **Map** *D5*

The restaurant is in a small street off the beaten track. It has a spartan air – simple stone decor that matches the simple but good food. Try the octopus stew with grilled polenta or shellfish in tomato sauce (*buzara*) – great washed down with the cold white local wines. Also serves good local cheeses.

HVAR Eremitaž

Priko, Stari Grad. **Tel** *(021) 765 056* **Map** *D5*

Located in what was once a hospital for sailors in quarantine, this family-run restaurant serves up a wide range of excellent fish specialities. Situated on the quieter side of the bay, the restaurant has a fine shady terrace facing the old part of town over the sea. It's a romantic spot at night looking across the water at the town lights twinkling.

HVAR L'Antica

Stari Grad. **Map** *D5*

Well-known small restaurant in the pretty cobble-stone centre of old Hvar – supposedly the favoured haunt of artists and intellectuals. As much a bar as a restaurant it serves decent cocktails. The food is good too – tuna steaks in caper sauce, monkfish with dill sauce and seafood risottos. Open-air roof terrace.

HVAR Hanibal

Trg sv. Stjepana, Hvar. **Tel** *(021) 742 760* **Map** *D5*

Named after the 16th-century Hvar poet Hanibal Lucic, and situated by the Church of St Stephen, this restaurant has a very nice designer interior – old stone and wooden beams. Serves excellent fish cuisine – scampi, lobster, prawns, oven-cooked octopus but also grilled lamb and steaks. Best to book in advance, as it can get quite busy.

HVAR Macondo

Groda, Hvar. **Tel** *(021) 742 850* **Map** *D5*

Fine restaurant set up the hill from the main square (look for the signs) – serves good fish cuisine. Try the sublime spaghetti with lobster; finish off with the home-made *prosec* (fortified wine). From the terrace you get a good view of the passers-by. Can get busy at weekends with the glitterati of Hvar.

HVAR Panorama

Smokovnik, Hvar. **Tel** *(021) 742 515* **Map** *D5*

Set in a small Austrian fort with a terrace and a wonderful view of the bay, 2 km (1 mile) from Hvar Town. One of its specialities is lamb roasted in a covered metal pot (*peka*) with other vegetables – the outside of the food caramelizes and the juices combine for a delicious sauce (must be ordered 24 hours in advance). Closed in winter.

KORČULA Morski Konjić

Šetalište Petra Kanavelića, Korčula. **Tel** *(020) 711 878* **Map** *E6*

An intimate *konoba* (sort of fishing-themed restaurant) right on the end of the fortified peninsula. It can get busy so be prepared to queue for the fresh cooked fish dishes and excellent shellfish. It's plain inside – chequered tablecloths and a few nautical items but there's tables outside too. Stocks a wide range of good Croatian wines.

MAKARSKA Jež

Petra Krešmira IV 90. **Tel** *(021) 611 741* **Map** *E5*

Traditional Dalmatian cuisine served in a modern, light and airy environment. The olive oil they use comes from the nearby olive grove. Excellent fish dishes and Croatian wines. Handily located near the Split-Dubrovnik motorway for a proper lunch if you're on the road (although absolutely no drinking if driving – it's the law).

METKOVIĆ Villa Neretva

Kravac 2. **Tel** *(020) 672 200* **Map** *E5*

Located in the heart of the fertile valley of the River Neretva, on the road from Opuzen to Metković, this is one of the best restaurants in Croatia. Traditional but smart inside, with a curved wooden roof, the restaurant serves good fish dishes (both freshwater and sea). The special local cuisine features fish, eels and frogs legs.

OREBIĆ Amfora

Kneza Domagoja 6. **Tel** *(020) 713 779* **Map** *E6*

Handily located right on the waterfront, this is a popular family restaurant. You can tell the food is good as the restaurant is full of locals attacking large portions of splendid seafood. Meat's on the menu, too. You can get a good value feed up here before getting the local ferry to Korčula just round the corner.

PAG Konoba Bodulo

Vangrada 19. **Tel** *(023) 611 989* **Map** *C4*

Fresh and simple food is served in the welcoming shade of a grapevine in this inexpensive family-run restaurant. Typical country dishes of the ubiquitous Dalmatian ham (*pršut*), local cheeses, delicious soupy fish stew (*brodet*), all sorts of grilled meats and pasta dishes.

ŠIBENIK Tinel

Trg Pučkih Kapetana 1. **Tel** *(022) 331 815* **Map** *D5*

One of the finest restaurants in town and definitely the best wine list. Situated in a small square just near the Church of St Chrysogonus, this restaurant covers two floors and serves up all the usual Dalmatian classics – seafood, grilled meat, stews, sausages and steaks.

ŠIBENIK Uzorita

Bana Josipa Jelačića 58. **Tel** *(022) 213 660* **Map** *D5*

A bit of a hidden gem – it's a little off the beaten track but it combines a stylish modern interior within a characterful stone vine-clad building. It specialises mainly in seafood (it produces a lot of its own ingredients such as shellfish, olive oil and wines). Be adventurous and try one of the delicious house specialities such as octopus and mussels in aspic.

SPLIT Galija

Tončićeva 12. **Tel** *(021) 347 932* **Map** *D5*

Central Split is not known for its good restaurants – pizzas are the budget order of the day. Try this place for the best, large brick-oven baked pizzas. It's not enormous, so it can get busy. Good *pršut* and prawn, and tuna and olive pizzas with thin and crispy bases. It's located near the fish market, north of the main square (Trg Republike).

SPLIT Stellon

Preradovićevo Šetalište. **Tel** *(021) 489 200* **Map** *D5*

Set in a concrete and glass pavilion of dubious architectural taste, located above the town beach and resort of Bačvice, this restaurant offers good value pizza, pastas and fried fish dishes. It looks out over the bay. It's not terribly stylish but it's very popular in the evening and a good spot for people watching.

SPLIT Boban

Hektorovićeva 49. **Tel** *(021) 543 300* **Map** *D5*

Well-respected restaurant whose style of decor is modern but a bit cheap and dated (lots of chrome and smoked glass). Nevertheless the food (eg veal steaks with mushrooms) is extremely good and the fish fresh so everyone has a good time. Ask what the catch of the day is. One of the top destinations of the great and glorious Split.

SPLIT Kadena

Ivana pl. Zajca 4. **Tel** *(021) 389 400* **Map** *D5*

Enjoy Mediterranean-Dalmatian cuisine from a terrace with fine sea views. Kadena has a modern interior and a creative menu along with a selection of over 400 wines. Specialities include John Dory fillet in a caper sauce and wheat with smoked seafood or frogs. Worth the walk from the Old Town. Open till midnight; reserve in advance.

SPLIT Kod Joze

Ulica Sredmanuška 4. **Tel** *(021) 347 397* **Map** *D5*

Tucked away in an old stone house, this traditional tavern can be a little tricky to find, but it's worth doing as it serves fine fish (depending on what has come in that day) and well-cooked traditional meat dishes in generous portions. Cool and shady terrace as well. North of the Golden Gate and popular with the locals.

SPLIT Noštromo

Kraj sv. Marije 10. **Tel** *(091) 405 66 66* **Map** *D5*

An elegant and richly decorated establishment, which is located next to the fish market so the fish is always fresh. The menu has a wide variety to choose from – Dalmatian octopus salad, black risotto, roasted squids and T-bone steak are just some of the dishes on offer. Reservation recommended.

STON Kapetanova Kuća

Mali Ston. **Tel** *(020) 754 264* **Map** *E6*

This "Captain's Cabin" serves excellent oysters, shellfish and black cuttlefish ink risotto, as well as all the other usual seafood food dishes. Also has a good selection of the excellent wines of the area. Save a big space for their legendary Macaroni Cake made with pasta, nuts and chocolate – it is filling. Idyllic location on the harbour front.

TROGIR Kamerlengo

Vukovarska 2, Trogir. **Tel** *(021) 884 772* **Map** *D5*

In the heart of the old town this restaurant has a lovely walled patio garden which also houses its wood-burning oven and char-grill. Its speciality is seafood but it also serves anything else that can be roasted, grilled or barbecued. The restaurant is a little hidden down a cobbled side street but you should see the sign.

TROGIR Fontana

Obrov 1. **Tel** *(021) 884 811*   **Map** *D5*

Although the interior is a trifle drab, the terrace of this hotel restaurant is an excellent choice for dining on this beautiful island-town with a spectacular waterfront vista. Everything from pizzas to local fish specialities and classic Dalmatian beef stew (*pašticada*).

VIS Villa Kaliopa

V Nazora 32, Vis. **Tel** *(021) 711 755*   **Map** *D6*

A restaurant set in the middle of the walled garden of a 16th-century Garibaldi palace, dotted with statues and unusual plants. Very atmospheric this establishment attracts the well-heeled yachting crowd and romantic couples. The food and wines are excellent, if a little on the expensive side.

ZADAR Foša

Kralja Dimitra Zvonimira 2. **Tel** *(023) 314 421*   **Map** *C4*

Situated inside the city's 16th-century walls, this restaurant's interior successfully combines stone with modern furnishings. The best tables are outside on the terrace overlooking the harbour. The menu includes fish and meat dishes with a twist, a long wine list and an impressive selection of olive oils.

ZADAR Pet Bunara

Trg Pet bunara bb. **Tel** *(023) 224 010*   **Map** *C4*

This restaurant, nicely decorated in natural stone and wood, is situated in Zadar's Old Town. The menu features a good selection of cold and warm starters, meat specialities (some of them served with delicious fig jam), seafood and some interesting desserts.

ZAGREB

ZAGREB Mimice

Jurišićeva ulica 21. **Tel** *(01) 481 45 24*   **Map** *D2*

A bit of an institution and deservedly popular with the locals, offering a limited range of simple hot or cold fish dishes. More of a food bar than a restaurant, this can be crowded at any time of the day. Fried fish is served informally – the local style is to eat it standing and then get back to work. Try the sardines or anchovies.

ZAGREB Boban

Gajeva ulica 9. **Tel** *(01) 481 15 49*   **Map** *D2*

A restaurant in a basement with sweeping brick arches, it serves an Italian inspired menu – pasta is a speciality. Try Rustica – pieces of steak, baked potatoes, arugula, cherry tomatoes and radicchio – and home-made pasta. There's a popular bar upstairs although it can get smoky – but at least this has a terrace if you need some fresh air.

ZAGREB Ćiho

Pavla Hatza 15. **Tel** *(01) 48 17 060*   **Map** *D2*

Basement restaurant with walls of bric-a-brac giving the place a somewhat wacky ambience. Predominantly a fish restaurant serving specialities from the island of Korčula, the food is very good – especially if you consider the price. The service can seem slow, so just relax end enjoy a bit more of the good house wine.

ZAGREB Kaptolska Klet

Kaptol 5. **Tel** *(01) 481 48 38*   **Map** *D2*

This restaurant is in obvious tourist territory situated just in front of the cathedral; but it is nonetheless a beautiful location. It is a large barn of a building with a cosy, old-fashioned interior despite its size. It also has large covered terraces. The food is traditional and good value, if not particularly inspiring. There is live music on weekend nights.

ZAGREB Nokturno

Skalinska 4. **Tel** *(01) 481 33 94*   **Map** *D2*

Situated in a picturesque street with lovely views of the cathedral from its terrace, Nokturno is very popular with locals and tourists alike. The menu has a lot of variety and features breakfast options, lasagne, pizza, pasta, meat and fish dishes and desserts at very affordable prices. Ideal for a quick and tasty meal.

ZAGREB Vallis Aurea

Tomićeva 4. **Tel** *(01) 48 31 305*   **Map** *D2*

Located near the funicular, this place has a pleasantly old-fashioned interior – whitewashed walls and dark wood. Often busy, it serves mainly Slavonian food – try the beef stew with prunes (*pašticada*) and the stuffed pastries (*štrukli*). Other specialities are trout dishes. Wines are okay too and the staff are helpful.

ZAGREB Baltazar

Nova Ves 4. **Tel** *(01) 466 69 99*   **Map** *D2*

An old favourite on the Zagreb scene, just north of the cathedral – and justifiably acclaimed. All the classic dishes, good service plus a wonderful atmosphere created within a traditional arched basement. On sunny days reserve ahead for one of the desirable summer courtyard tables.

Key to Price Guide *see p240* **Key to Symbols** *see back cover flap*

ZAGREB Bistro Apetit

Jurjevska 65. **Tel** *(01) 467 73 35* **Map** *D2*

An interesting combination of French, Croatian and Italian cuisine can be found at this elegantly furnished restaurant. The menu features interesting dishes such as young boar with a quiche of kale, tuna tartare and pear, cranberry and potato ravioli. A selection of over 250 wines is also available. Closed Monday.

ZAGREB Dubravkin Put

Dubravkin Put 2. **Tel** *(01) 483 49 75* **Map** *D2*

A good restaurant based just outside the centre in a leafy setting beside a park. The owner gets daily deliveries from Dalmatia, thus guaranteeing the freshness of the produce. As a result, the seafood is definitely worth trying at this restaurant. There's a pleasant terrace in summer.

ZAGREB Gračanka Kamanjo

Gračanka cesta 48. **Tel** *(01) 461 75 55* **Map** *D2*

A little out of the centre of the city, on the way towards Mount Medvednica, this restaurant is popular with the locals and, it claims, actors, sportsmen and politicians. That aside, the food on the Mediterranean menu is good, especially the meat and excellent mushroom dishes – in season, of course.

ZAGREB Ivica i Marica

Tkalčićeva 70. **Tel** *(01) 482 89 99* **Map** *D2*

The English translation of this restaurant's name is Hansel and Gretel, and it offers traditional Croatian dishes prepared from organic ingredients. The interior is rustic and cosy. Next door is a pastry shop of the same name, where you can sample healthy cakes made with wholegrain flour and brown sugar.

ZAGREB Okrugljak

Mlinovi 28. **Tel** *(01) 467 4112* **Map** *D2*

This large country-style restaurant on the road between Zagreb and Mount Medvednica has a garden for children and large shady terraces. At simple wooden tables you can try the specialities of the house: roasted lamb, duck, or turkey, served with *mlinci* – a traditional Croatian dish of pasta strips that are boiled and then baked.

ZAGREB Pod Gričkim Topom

Zakmardijeve stube 5. **Tel** *(01) 48 33 607* **Map** *D2*

Take the funicular to the top and then, in an almost rural setting, you will find this delightful and characterful restaurant. There's a nice terrace and plenty of meat dishes Croatian style, but also tasty grilled fish served with a loose mix of *blitva* – green chard – garlic and potatoes.

ZAGREB Zinfadels

Hotel Esplanade, Mihanoviceva 1. **Tel** *(01) 456 6666* **Map** *D2*

Set within an architecturally stunning building, this the place for gourmet haute cuisine in Zagreb. It may be an uber-posh hotel dining room but there's no dress code and a pleasantly relaxed ambience. The interiors are elegantly designed, and the only let down is the occasional intrusion of piano music – although some like that sort of thing.

CENTRAL CROATIA

JASTREBARSKO K Lojzeku

Strossmayerov trg 12. **Tel** *(01) 628 11 29* **Map** *C2*

A well-respected restaurant with a large and shady terrace. The kitchen tries to give traditional Croatian home-cooking a creative twist – turkey breast with gorgonzola sauce and olives; but it's not always successful. However, it does the standard grills, pastas and fish well. Large choice of wines.

KARLOVAC Žganjer

Turanj-Jelaši 41. **Tel** *(047) 641 304* **Map** *C2*

This restaurant is also a motel on the road to Plitvice. Most of the dining is enjoyed outdoors on a covered terrace. The kitchen prides itself on serving Croatian specialities like lamb from the islands and roast suckling pig (but also has ostrich on the menu). If you eat or drink too much you can always sleep it off in one of the rooms.

SAMOBOR Pri Staroj Vuri

Giznik 2. **Tel** *(01) 336 05 48* **Map** *C2*

In a cottage in a charming village you can enjoy proper country cooking – try their *Hrvatska pisanica* (steak with mushrooms, onions, tomatoes and red wine sauce), or rib-sticking dumplings with beef or, for dessert, *štrukli*. The decor includes gingham curtains and clocks all over the walls (the name means Ancient Clocks).

SAMOBOR Samoborska Klet

Trg kralja Tomislava 7. **Tel** *(01) 332 65 36* **Map** *C2*

This is a family-run restaurant situated in the heart of the picturesque town of Samobor. Its gastronomic offerings are varied and include traditional methods of food preparation such as *na ražnju* (on a spit), *ispod peke* (under an iron bell) and *u krušnoj peć* (in a traditional oven).

SISAK Cocktail

A Starčevića 27. **Tel** *(044) 549 137* **Map** *D2*

A restaurant in the centre of Sisak near the town museum, serving traditional and more up-to-date Croatian and Italian cuisine. The establishment is in a modern building with refreshing clean lines (no gingham in sight). The food is pretty good value and there's a good selection of wines.

SLAVONIA AND BARANJA

ĐAKOVO Trnavački Vinodom

A Starčevića 52. **Tel** *(031) 814 810* **Map** *F2*

A small simple Slavonian restaurant serving simple Slavonian food at very good prices. Try the fried carp or the *ražnjići* (pork kebab) with a glass or two of local Graševina or Traminac wine. The interior is a bit drab but the restaurant is conveniently located by near the road for those driving around the country (but no drinking and driving).

ĐAKOVO Croatia Turist

Preradovića 25. **Tel** *(031) 813 391* **Map** *F2*

This restaurant serves typical Slavonia food – they have their own smoke-house so be sure to try something home-smoked – smoke-cured spicy sausage (*kulen*), locally caught venison and freshwater fish. Try the *čobanac* a typical Hungarian-influenced goulash dish. Wash it all down with the excellent regional white wines.

DARUVAR Terasa

Julijev Park 1. **Tel** *(043) 331 705* **Map** *E2*

Located near the thermal spas of Croatia, this restaurant has mock-Baroque furnishings, as though it expects the Austro-Hungarian aristocracy come back and take the waters. Its menu is suitably historical too – it serves Croatian, Hungarian, Czech and Italian cuisine. A large terrace unsurprisingly (the name is a clue).

KUTJEVO Schön Blick

Zagrebačka 11, Vetovo. **Tel** *(034) 267 108* **Map** *F2*

In a rural location and scenically situated next to a lake, 8 km (5 miles) from Kutjevo, this place offers typical country cuisine. You can find the this popular restaurant on the Kutjevo to Velika road. Be sure to try the famous wine – *Kutjevački Risling* – as the local wine industry was started by Cistercian monks.

LIPIK Lipa

Marije Terezije 5. **Tel** *(034) 421 244* **Map** *E2*

This eaterie forms part of a small, candy pink hotel, whose main clientele consists of people travelling to enjoy the medicinal thermal waters of Lipik. The restaurant is a bit bland but it serves good examples of the local hearty, Slavonian cuisine – which is actually not everyone's idea of a healthy diet.

NAŠICE Ribnjak

Stjepana Radića 1, Ribnjak, Našice. **Tel** *(031) 607 006* **Map** *F2*

This rustic restaurant has a very scenic location, 10 km (6 miles) from Našice, on the road from Osijek. This watery region is known for its freshwater fish and, as such, is a good place to try Slavonian fish dishes and specialities including *fiš paprikaš* – with obvious Hungarian influences.

NOVA GRADIŠKA Slavonski Biser

Nikole Tesle 2–4, Nova Gradiška. **Tel** *(035) 363 259* **Map** *E2*

Conveniently located for travellers near the train and bus station, this restaurant offers Croatian cooking and the standard range of international dishes. The terrace is unfortunately next to the road but it's not too busy a thoroughfare. It's a large establishment that also operates as a motel.

OSIJEK Kod Ruže

Kuhačeva 25a, Osijek. **Tel** *(031) 206 066* **Map** *F2*

Located in the historic centre of Osijek, Kod Ruže is a delightfully old-fashioned inn. The menu features plenty of tasty and hearty Slavonian specialities featuring local meat, freshwater fish and frogs, but there are some salads for health-conscious diners too. There is also a good selection of spirits and local wines.

OSIJEK Slavonska Kuća

K. Firingera 26, Osijek. **Tel** *(031) 369 955* **Map** *F2*

Traditional Slavonian food is served at this popular, rustic restaurant. Freshwater fish features heavily on the menu, and the *fiš paprikaš*, a typical Slavonian soup made of different kinds of fish, and prepared in a cauldron above a fire, is definitely worth a try. Other specialities include a sausage made of smoked fish.

SLAVONSKI BROD Onyx

Zrinska 50, Slavonski Brod. **Tel** *(035) 445 555* **Map** *F2*

This modern restaurant is situated within walking distance of the centre of Slavonski Brod. The menu is a pleasant mix of Croatian, Italian and international dishes. If you're in doubt, try the fresh fish from Dalmatia, which is delivered on a daily basis.

Key to Price Guide *see p240* **Key to Symbols** *see back cover flap*

VUKOVAR Vrške

Parobrodarska 3. **Tel** *(032) 441 788* — **Map** *G2*

Riverside restaurant with laidback charm, specialising in regional freshwater fish dishes – choose from spicy fish stew (*fiš paprikaš*), sturgeon (*kečiga*), fried carp (*šaran*) or catfish with mushrooms (*som u šampinjonima*). Also on offer are Slavonian specialities and home-made desserts. One of the few restaurants to have survived the war and still going strong.

THE NORTHERN COUNTIES

KOPRIVNICA Kraluš

Zrinski trg, 10. **Tel** *(048) 622 302* — **Map** *D1*

Traditional 250 year-old beer hall on a square at the centre of town. Although the region is proud of its wines, there's also a strong beer culture. This establishment brews its own beers and has special tasting menus designed for specific beers. Try the beer sausage (*pivska kobasica*) with beans (*podravski grah*).

KOPRIVNICA Podravska Klet

Prvomajska 46, Starigrad. **Tel** *(048) 634 069* — **Map** *D1*

Rustic restaurant with a thatched roof, stained-glass windows and solid wooden tables. There's a lot of good local produce on offer – home-made sausage, creamy cows' cheese, home-prepared cows' tongue and a house special rustic stew (*Gorički gulaš*). Local wines too. Sometimes features traditional live music.

KRAPINSKE TOPLICE Zlatna Lisica

Martinišče 38a. **Tel** *(049) 236 627* — **Map** *D1*

With a great view overlooking the rolling hills of the surrounding region, this is a simple restaurant serving good, honest country food. Try the sausages "by the metre" (*kobasice na metre*), game stews (*gulaš od divljači*) and especially the locally caught roasted boar (*pečena veprovina iz banjica*).

STUBIČKE TOPLICE Academia

Zagrebačka bb, hotel Kaj, Marija Bistrica. **Tel** *(049) 326 600* — **Map** *D1*

Located in the Kaj hotel, this restaurant offers an intimate dining experience. Traditional Zagorje cuisine with a twist is prepared using fresh ingredients from local farms, which ensures quality meals. Try any of the meat dishes on the menu or the home-made *štrukli* – cooked or baked pastry filled with cream cheese. Reserve a table in advance.

TRAKOŠĆAN Trakošćan

Trakošćan bb. **Tel** *(042) 440 800* — **Map** *D1*

Set by a lake and near to the medieval castle of Trakošćan, this large hotel complex restaurant serves Croatian specialities from the Zagorje hills. The hotel is set in the beautiful countryside below the imposing castle. There's a nice large terrace. Try the pork cutlets in grape juice (*svinjski kotlet u moštu*).

VARAŽDIN Grenadir

Kranjčevićeva 12. **Tel** *(042) 211 131* — **Map** *D1*

Conveniently located in the town centre, this restaurant offers tasty food at very reasonable prices. There is plenty to choose from on the menu. For those who don't want to try the local cuisine, there are also pasta dishes, such as *gnocchi* served with mozzarella, and pasta with salmon. Or have a light salad to freshen up a hot summer's day.

VARAŽDIN Restoran Raj

Gundulićeva 11. **Tel** *(042) 213 146* — **Map** *D1*

Although the restaurant has stone arches, and medieval chandeliers, it is pleasantly minimalist in a modern way. Serving home-made traditional foods – chicken liver in bacon (*pileća jetrica u slanini*); black pudding (*krvavice*); roast duck (*domaća pečena patka*). The terrace is covered with wisteria which is wonderful when in bloom.

VARAŽDIN Zlatne Ruke

Ivana Kukuljevića 13. **Tel** *(042) 320 065* — **Map** *D1*

This restaurant consists of three different sections: a beautifully decorated basement area with white stone walls, a terrace and a lounge bar. The menu is a mix of local specialities enlivened with a modern touch; if you're feeling hungry try boar meat in minced lard or the goulash.

VELIKI TABOR Grešna Gorica

Taborgradska Klet, Desinić. **Tel** *(049) 343 001* — **Map** *C1*

This farmhouse on a hill facing the town of Veliki Tabor, near Miljana castle, offers simple Croatian dishes. It has an orchard with tables and a rustic interior. There's a menagerie for the kids with peacocks, chickens, turkeys and deer wandering about – most of whom feature on the menu. Hearty food – grilled/roasted chicken, turkey and venison.

ZABOK Dvorac Gjalski

Gredice Zabočke 7, Zabok (near Bedekovčina). **Tel** *(049) 201 100*

This excellent restaurant is in a hotel of the same name (*see p233*), which is located in a splendid castle set in the gentle hills of Hrvatsko zagorje and a medieval theme is apparent. The extensive menu includes a wide variety of Croatian cuisine. The restaurant is elegantly decorated and the service is attentive and professional.

SHOPPING IN CROATIA

Croatia does its best to encourage its visitors to go shopping (indeed it is a significant factor in local economies) and there is a range of traditional and typical crafts, which are excellent souvenirs. The prices are by and large very reasonable too. Shoppers can choose from a variety of products from works of creative handicraft such as handmade lace or hand-painted ceramics to jewellery.

Doll in Costume, Osijek

On the island of Pag, exquisite lace is made and in Osijek, where beautiful embroidery is a proud tradition, you can also buy pretty costume dolls. Ties and fountain pens, both of which originated in Croatia, also make good purchases. In some resorts, local artists make a living by selling their watercolours. Visitors can also buy all sorts of delicious Croatian consumables from honey to plum brandy.

Jars of various types of honey, a speciality on the island of Šolta

OPENING HOURS

Shops and department stores are usually open from 8am to 8pm from Monday to Friday (but some stores may open at 7am and close at 9pm) and from 8am to 2 or 3pm on Saturdays. However, remember that sometimes small shops in the smaller towns close at lunchtime, usually from noon to 4pm in summer. Shops are generally closed on Sundays and holidays but in the high season in the tourist resorts many shops stay open for business as usual.

PRICES

The prices are fixed in the shops and it is not generally done to haggle over prices. This is also the case in the markets and at the street stalls where prices are also fixed and it is not common practice to negotiate. The prices are

often displayed in the markets, but it should be remembered that at times the prices displayed are not always the same as those applied to the local people. The spending power of foreign visitors is frequently much greater than that of the local Croats and can occasionally result in pricing variations for locals.

PAYING

In department stores, shopping centres and the major chain stores, it is only possible to pay in local currency or by using one of the main international credit cards. In the smaller shops and in places such as markets, payments should be made in cash, in kuna.

VAT REFUNDS

Tourists in Croatia who spend more than 500 kuna on a single item are entitled to a refund of the Value Added Tax (VAT), which is called PDV in Croatia. When making your purchase, you should ask the sales assistant for the appropriate form (PDV–P), which should be properly filled in and stamped, on the spot.
  This document should be handed to the customs authorities on departure from Croatia, thus verifying that the item bought is genuinely destined for export.
  A PDV refund in kuna can be obtained within six

months, either at the same shop where the goods were purchased (in which case the tax is refunded immediately), or by posting the verified receipt back to the shop, together with the number of the bank account into which the refund should be paid. In this case the refund is dealt with within 15 days of receipt of the claim.

MARKETS

The street markets of Croatia are colourful, lively places to stroll around.
  In Zagreb, the Dolac *(see p153)* is a daily market where food is sold under colourful red umbrellas. There is also an underground area here where other products such as meat, dairy products and food are sold.
  In Split there is a morning market which is held every

Fruit and vegetables on sale at the Dolac market in Zagreb

day on Pazar, just east of the palace walls. This market sells absolutely everything: fruit, vegetables, flowers, shoes, clothes and a vast assortment of souvenirs. There is a local saying which has it that if you cannot find what you are looking for at this market, it probably does not exist (at least not in Split).

SHOPPING CENTRES

Large shopping centres can also be found in Croatia, mainly in the larger towns and cities. Here you will find a number of shops selling assorted merchandise under one roof, usually including a large department store or supermarket.

In Zagreb one of the busiest and best-known department stores is **Nama**, which is right in the centre of the city. Another useful shopping centre, also in the city centre, is **Importanne**. The **Importanne Galerija** is only open on weekdays.

Avenue Mall is another huge shopping centre which has over 130 shops, including international names such as Benetton, Calvin Klein and Marks & Spencer. **Westgate Shopping City** is a huge shopping centre just outside Zagreb.

TRADITIONAL HANDICRAFTS

There are plenty of opportunities for the visitor to buy a variety of typical Croatian handicrafts and produce, which make very tempting souvenirs.

The country has a long tradition of skilled production of a rich range of handicrafts and typical produce. Production of these crafts is encouraged and supported by the local authorities, who see it as a good way of preserving the cultural heritage and the ancient traditions and crafts of the country.

In Zagreb, you can buy handicrafts, embroidered articles, dolls in traditional costume, terracotta, ceramics, wooden objects and many other similar items at **Rukotvorine**.

Decorated ceramic objects on display in a shop

In Split you can find a large assortment of souvenirs, including objects clearly inspired by maritime themes. You can also buy good reproductions of objects from the era of Roman rule in the underground area of Diocletian's Palace *(see p120)*.

In Osijek, many shops in the centre of the city sell typical locally made handicrafts. Here you can also find dolls dressed in beautifully made costumes, packages of special lace and in particular fabrics finely embroidered with gold and silver thread.

EMBROIDERY AND LACE

One important typical Croatian craft is the art of embroidery, which is carried out more or less everywhere.

Gold thread embroidery produced in the town of Osijek

A characteristic design is a red geometric pattern stitched onto a white background. This design is used to decorate table linen, pillowcases and blouses.

In 2009 lace making in Croatia was inscribed on the UNESCO Intangible Cultural Heritage of Humanity list. This includes three different traditions of lace making, namely Pag needlepoint lace, Lepoglava bobbin lace and Hvar aloe lace.

The lace of Pag is justly famous and widely admired. The origins of the lace date back to the Renaissance period, when it was used to decorate the blouses of the ladies of the island of Pag.

However, it was not until the beginning of the 20th century that this particular handiwork assumed its well-deserved fame, thanks to a beautifully decorated blouse given by a noblewoman to the Archduchess of Austria Marie Josephine. This gift was so greatly appreciated and admired that the archduchess went to Pag in person to order more items of clothing. At that time, the Austrian court set trends for others to follow, and this was enough to guarantee the future success for the production of this lace.

The lace is made on a long cylindrical cushion by lacemakers of great skill and tremendous patience. The lace patterns produced are the lacemaker's interpretation of patterns and designs which

Lacemaker working on a piece of Pag lace

have been passed down from generation to generation. In this way, the pieces of lace that are produced can often be very different from one another. However, all the patterns originate with the same geometric structure which forms the base.

Pag lace is surprisingly light but at the same time strong. If at all possible, pieces of the lace should be bought in Pag itself. Not only can you be sure of paying a better price than elsewhere but you will be helping to keep alive a tradition which is over a century old.

Prices vary according to the size of the piece you buy, but if you consider that a table centrepiece measuring 10 cm (4 in) in diameter takes a good 24 hours to make, you will have some idea of the labour involved.

The only place to buy lace in Pag is at the **Lace gallery and shop** in the old part of town.

LUCKY JEWELLERY

There is one item of jewellery which can only be found in Croatia or, more precisely, only in Rijeka. This is the *morčić* or small Moorish figure. The figurine, in the form of a black character wearing a turban, was originally produced as earrings but today you can also find tie-pins and brooches. The *morčić* has become the symbol of the city and, in 1991, it was proclaimed the mascot of

Rijeka. A legend dates the origins of the figurine to the city's unexpected liberation from a Turkish siege during the 16th century. It was shown that a determining factor in the victory was the contribution of the women of Rijeka and it is said that their men decided to give them a gift of special earrings made to represent the invaders who had been forced to flee for their lives.

In fact, it seems more likely that the *morčić* originated in the 17th and 18th centuries as a local reproduction, made from decidedly poor materials, of a figurine set with stones which was very popular with the Venetians. The figurine represented the connections between Venice and the East and the mystery that this part of the world symbolized

for them at the time. The figure soon became a symbol of good luck among the Istrian people and since that time it has become more lavish and elaborate, so much so that its production has become the preserve of goldsmiths. The body of the figure is traditionally glazed ceramic. On request, precious stones may be used to decorate this figure. The best place to buy a *morčić* in Rijeka is the **Mala Galerija**.

CURIOSITIES

Croatia can claim to have invented one of the most well-known of men's accessories, the tie, or cravat. The tie actually originates from a type of scarf worn by Croatian cavalrymen to distinguish them from other soldiers during the bloody 30-year war which devastated Europe in the 17th century. The French took to referring to this particular way of tying the scarf as *"à la cravate"*, meaning "in the Croatian way". Since that time the tie, or cravat, has become a standard symbol of smart, elegant dressing for hundreds of millions of men in the world.

An earring with the *morčić* of Rijeka

The production of ties in Croatia today is still of a very high standard, and a tie would make a highly appropriate choice for a souvenir of your visit.

There are some very good clothes shops in the centre of Zagreb where you can buy an

One of many jeweller's shops in Croatia

assortment of ties, and these include **Boutique Croata** and **Heruc Galeria.**

Another little-known fact is that the inventor of the fountain pen was an engineer from Zagreb. In 1906, one Eduard Slavoljub Penkala patented a mechanical pencil and a year later a pen with a reservoir of ink, called the "mechanical pen", which revolutionized the way people wrote.

The inventor opened the first factory for the production of fountain pens in Zagreb in 1911. Within a short space of time it became an enormous success and developed into one of the most important manufacturing centres for writing instruments, producing fountain pens which were exported all over the world. There could not be a more appropriate place to buy this everyday item than Zagreb itself.

Elegant ties on display in a shop in the centre of Zagreb

LOCAL PRODUCE

The gastronomic specialities and local produce of Croatia are as varied as the landscape of Croatia.

Among the country's best-known natural products, one of the most important is lavender. Lavender is sold dried in small bags or as essence in bottles. It can be found more or less all over the country but is particularly linked with the island of Hvar *(see pp126–7)*, where its colour and scent can nearly

***Paški sir,* the sheep's cheese of Pag, sold on the island**

overwhelm the senses when the shrubs are in flower. The scent is particularly pungent when you browse the lavender stalls near the port, where you can buy any number of cosmetic products made with lavender.

The gastronomic specialities of Croatia also make excellent souvenirs. Many places have their own particular speciality. Among many items worthy of mention are the mustard (in traditional containers) made in Samobor, near Zagreb, the honey from Grohote, on the island of Šolta, and cukarini biscuits from Korčula.

Another unmissable delicacy is the delicious truffle found around Buzet, overlooking the Mirna valley in Istria (although these are only available in season). Other delicacies include *pršut* (a type of smoked ham) and *kulen* (a type of smoked sausage) found in Slavonia.

However, the most highly valued product is cheese. Croatia produces a range of its own cheeses, and the most well-known is *paški sir,* a mature cheese made from sheep's milk, produced on the island of Pag *(see pp102–3)*. It is still made according to traditional methods and the grazing pasture for the sheep, full of aromatic herbs, is said to give it a distinctive flavour.

To buy the cheese on the island just look for signs with the name of the cheese, "paški sir" outside the farmhouses.

DIRECTORY

SHOPPING CENTRES

Avenue Mall
Avenija Dubrovnik 16, Zagreb.
Tel (062) 283 683. ◯
9am–10pm Mon–Sat; 10am–9pm Sun (cafés, restaurants and cinema stay open longer).

Importanne Centar
Starčevićev trg bb, Zagreb.
Tel (01) 457 70 76.
◯ *9am–9pm Mon–Sat.*

Importanne Galerija
Iblerov trg, Zagreb.
Tel (01) 461 95 03.
◯ *9am–9pm Mon–Sat.*

Nama
Ilica near Trg bana Jelačića, Zagreb.
Tel (01) 480 31 11.

Westgate Shopping City
Zaprešićka 2, Jablanovec, Donja Bistra (free bus service from Zagreb).
Tel (01) 555 33 33.

SHOPS

Boutique Croata
Prolaz Oktogon, Ilica 5, Zagreb.
Tel (01) 481 27 26.

Heruc Galeria
Ilica 26, Zagreb.
Tel (01) 365 08 19.

Lace gallery and shop
Vela Ulica 14, Pag.

Mala Galerija
Užarska 25, Rijeka.
Tel (051) 335 403.

Rukotvorine
Trg bana Jelačića 7, Zagreb.

Seller of essence and lavender bags on the island of Hvar

ENTERTAINMENT IN CROATIA

Although Croatians speak a language which is most likely completely unknown to the average visitor, the country still manages to offer a surprisingly varied range of accessible and engaging entertainment for visitors of all age groups. A choice of opera, ballet, folk music festivals, disco nightclubs, cinemas, casinos, tennis, football and basketball matches should be sufficient to satisfy

Classical ballet, Croatian National Theatre in Zagreb

anyone. The settings for many of these entertainments are often memorably spectacular, too. Performance details are readily available from weekly or monthly magazines of events and from tourist offices and websites. Tickets are usually easy to come by, and can be bought at venue ticket desks or often in advance from local tourist offices. Read ahead to see what's on and where to go.

The ornate interior of the Croatian National Theatre in Zagreb

INFORMATION AND TICKETS

For information concerning dates, times, prices and booking details of the various festivals, shows, theatre performances and musicals, it is best to get in touch with the relevant local tourist information office in Croatia. All these offices can provide details about the cultural events happening in their part of the country. Another good source of information can be the Internet. The Croatian National Tourist Board's website is www.croatia.hr.

Posters announcing forthcoming events are often displayed all over the cities and towns and these are often useful for finding out about the more important or more popular shows.

For information concerning theatre performances, you can also go to the theatre box office itself, where you can usually buy tickets on the spot.

THEATRE AND DANCE

Plays are generally performed in the Croatian language which, unless you speak it, can marginalise the theatre as an evening's entertainment for all but the most ardent thespians. There is, however, an important reason why you should nonetheless check out what's on at the theatre in any town you happen to be in. High-class performances of opera and ballet, for which not knowing the language is not a barrier to enjoyment, are put on by Zagreb's **Croatian National Theatre,** Zadar's **Croatian National Theatre,** Rijeka's **Croatian National Theatre Ivan pl Zajc** and Split's **Croatian National Theatre**.

For a more unusual form of drama which also has the advantage of being accessible to visitors, especially families with younger children, consider a visit to the unique Zagreb puppet theatre, the

Zagrebačko Kazalište Lutaka. They put on performances almost every weekend.

Croatia's many traditional festivals not only have particular dishes associated with them, but dances too. The most famous of these is undoubtedly Korčula's sword dance, traditionally enacted in the town centre on the evening of St Theodore's Day, July 29th. Such is the attraction of the *moreška*, as it is known, that this costumed 15th-century dance is now performed outside of that holiday date – every Monday and Thursday at 9pm throughout July and August, sometimes even in June and September as well. Tickets at the event, or in advance from an agency, are not terribly expensive. It is obviously touristy, but still worth seeing as they really do swing those swords around. At any festive occasion in Croatia, there are several famous folk dances you may well come across: the *poskočica*, where couples weave themselves into intricate configurations; the *kolo,* a pan-Slavic circular dance and the *drmeš,* a type of speeded-up polka.

Costume drama in Dubrovnik, at the Rector's Palace

Musicians playing traditional Croatian music

MUSIC

Whilst Croatia has nurtured classical composers and does have many aspiring rock bands, unfortunately few people outside of Croatia have ever heard of them. But don't let that put you off.

Croatia does have a rich tradition of folk music and these bands play all along the Adriatic at summer open-air concerts, on holiday festivals and even in hotel lobbies to entertain tourists after dinner.

Unusual instruments to look out for are the *tamburica*, a sort of Turkish mandolin, in Slavonia and the *citra*, a poignant-sounding type of zither (a horizontal stringed instrument). You will also come across variations on the folk theme, such as *klapa* – five- to ten-part harmony singing, mainly by males – or lively *lindo* dance music from the Dubrovnik region accompanied by the *lijerica*, which is a three-stringed instrument. The traditional songs of the Međimurje in the north of Croatia are very beautiful.

For a wide range of musical styles, global, local and avante-garde, the **Aquarius Club** in Zagreb is one of the top places in Croatia. Otherwise, be sure not to miss the music and pyrotechnics of **Dubrovnik's Summer Festival**, held over five weeks between July and August, and anything

at all going on in the evening at Pula's ancient and stunning **Roman Amphitheatre**.

NIGHTCLUBS

Cafés, bars and pubs all over Croatia often put on live music, especially at weekends. But if, after a few drinks, you want to party on into the night, then the capital or the coast in summer are the places to be. Entrance prices vary within between 50–100 kuna and venues open around 10pm, although most people arrive fashionably late, towards midnight or later.

Winter closing times are 11pm from Sunday to Thursday and midnight on Friday and Saturday, but in the summer clubs go on into the early hours of the morning. Open-air bars on the Adriatic coast will serve until 3am; open-air discos stop at 5am.

Younger Croats simply don't have the cash to go out as often as they would like – but if there's a Croatian band on and it's a weekend they'll be out in force, dressed-up and fully made-up. Weekday parties in the coastal resorts are therefore going to be predominantly for holiday-makers. Where you will find plenty of locals almost anytime are the multipurpose entertainment complexes in Zagreb or Split, where all their café-bars, cinemas, discos etc are usually crowded with youngsters.

Zagreb, Rijeka, Split, Pula and Dubrovnik all have well known discos and nightclubs, though times and conditions change so frequently that they should be checked out locally beforehand.

Zagreb has the ever-popular **Aquarius Club** which although 4 km (over 2 miles) from the city centre has dancing to commercial, techno and Croatian bands on a terrace overlooking Lake Jarun. **Saloon** is more sophisticated, with an older crowd dancing to well-known hits and paparazzi lurking in the wings as local celebrities are liable to pitch up. **Boogaloo Club**, a popular place for young people, always tries to be up-to-date in the Croatian and world music scene and hosts international DJs. **Močvara**, in a disused factory on the banks of the river Sava, is a trendy place, home to gigs, exhibitions and performances of an alternative, off-beat kind.

Down a side street in Rijeka is a cult venue which over the years has seen the

The amphitheatre in Pula, summer venue for spectacular concerts

A late-night bar in Dubrovnik

birth of many new bands. It's called **Club Palach**, after the Czech student who set fire to himself in 1968 to protest at the Soviet invasion, and is easily the top place in town. If you prefer a big, techno party house teeming with teenagers, the **Colosseum** in otherwise staid and stately Opatija is the place to go.

Split boasts several clubs with open-air terraces looking out to sea, the best of which are the two-storey **O'Hara** and the palm-filled **Tropic Club Ecuador**. The **Hemingway Bar** offers a wide selection of drinks, especially cocktails, good music and occasional live performances.

Rock Club Uljanik has Pula's liveliest alternative concerts in a vacant building above the shipyards. Out of town are two classics: **Aruba Club**, a lounge bar and disco, and **Aquarius**, one of the largest outdoor nightclubs in Croatia.

Dubrovnik is diverse in what it offers: **Gil's** is a more expensive, up-market fusion of food, dancing and spectacle; **Latino Club Fuego** is casual, relaxed and plays a range of music. **Club Lazareti** is popular and holds concerts, parties and events.

On the islands, Hvar has become a fashionable centre for night life and developed a bit of a reputation as a party island. Early evening activity centres around the harbour, in bar-cum-clubs like **Carpe Diem** where the dancers warm up before heading up the tree-covered hillside to a big old Venetian fort that has been converted into an open-air nightclub, **Veneranda**. **Papaya Club**, on the beach in Pag, hosts the world's leading djs. Less fashionable but just as much fun is the **Faces Club**, on the island of Brač, near Bol.

CASINOS

As you would expect, the capital Zagreb has the most casinos and as with the rest of Croatia they are found in the more upmarket hotels. (There are "casinos" in lesser hotels but they are usually not worth visiting.) Try those at the **Hotel International, Hotel Esplanade** and the Golden Sun Casino in the **Hotel Antunović**. Any casino will have an array of slot machines along with a number of card tables where stakes are relatively low. Normally you can wear just smart casual clothing and walk straight in. However, it might be worth calling ahead beforehand – the most upmarket casinos may ask to see your passport before you can enter.

CINEMA

Most large towns in Croatia have a cinema. Zagreb has several multiplexes, such as **Cinestar** in Avenue Mall and Branimir Centar and **Movieplex** in Kaptol Centar. **Kinoteka** shows cult and art films. Tickets cost from 20 to 40 kuna and films are shown in their original languages with Croatian subtitles. You can expect to see the latest Hollywood hits. Conditions can be more basic in smaller towns where you may come across rows of wooden chairs, rather like being back at school. Neither will things be so luxurious in the summer open-air cinemas which are more atmospheric: the films too might not be your first choice but the experience is worth trying.

SPECTATOR SPORTS

Tito's post-war Yugoslavia, of which Croatia was a part, consistently put out strong teams in handball, football (soccer), basketball and water polo. Since 1991, when Croatia broke away to become an independent nation, this small country of only 4.5 million people continues to excel in those sports and has added tennis to its sporting repertoire. If you love tennis then go to www.croatiaopen.hr to find out the latest news on the ATP Croatia Open Championships, held at Umag in July.

Croats, just like so many other Europeans, love their football. The 1990s saw now legendary Croatian players

The Hotel Esplanade in Zagreb, home to a casino

like Štimac, Boban and Šuker rise as international stars as Croatia for the first time became a serious footballing nation: quarter-finalists in the 1996 European Championships and, two years later, third at the World Cup, 1998. Although they haven't scaled those heights since. If you want to see a game during your stay, try either Dinamo Zagreb at the **Maksimir Stadium** on the capital's east side or Hajduk Split at the **Poljud Stadium**, Split. Matches are traditionally held on Sunday afternoons throughout most of the year, with only a short holiday break in the summer.

Like football, the country's top two basketball teams are in Split – KK Split who have been European Club Champions many times – and Zagreb – with rival contenders, Cibona. Those familiar with the game will know the names of the local stars on the international scene, such as Čosić, Petrović, Kukoč, Tabak and Rađa, and that Croatia was the third best team at the Toronto World Cup in 1994.

If you want to see a basketball game the Cibona team in Zagreb, hosts top quality matches at the **Dražen Petrović Basketball Centre** every Saturday evening from October to April – tickets are sold on the door.

The Cibona basketball team from Zagreb during a match

DIRECTORY

THEATRES

Croatian National Theatre
Trg Gaje Bulata 1, Split.
Tel (021) 344 999.

Croatian National Theatre
Široka ulica 8,
Zadar.
Tel (023) 314 552.

Croatian National Theatre
Trg Maršala Tita 15,
Zagreb.
Tel (01) 488 84 18.

Croatian National Theatre Ivan pl. Zajc
Uljarska 1, Rijeka.
Tel (051) 355 900.

Zagrebačko Kazalište Lutaka
Ulica Baruna Trenka 3,
Zagreb.
Tel (01) 4878 444.

MUSIC

Dubrovnik Summer Festival
Placa,
Dubrovnik (ticket office).
Tel (020) 321 509.

Roman Amphitheatre
Tourist office: Forum 3,
Pula.
ℹ *(052) 212 987,
212 987.*

NIGHTCLUBS

Aquarius Club
Aleja Matije Ljubeka bb,
Jarun, Zagreb.
Tel (01) 364 02 31.

Aquarius
Medulin, Pula.

Aruba Club
Šijanska cesta 1a, Pula.

Boogaloo Club
Ulica grada Vukovara 68,
Zagreb.
Tel (01) 631 30 22.

Carpe Diem
Riva, Hvar.

Club Lazareti
Frana Supila 8, Dubrovnik.

Club Palach
Kružna 6,
Rijeka.
Tel (099) 3158 522.

Colosseum
On the Lido,
Opatija.

Faces Club
near Bol, Brač.

Gil's
Svetog Dominika bb,
Dubrovnik.

Hemingway Bar
8 Mediteranskih igara 5,
Split.
Tel (099) 211 99 93.

Latino Club Fuego
Brsalje 11, Near Pile Gate,
Dubrovnik.

Močvara
Trnjanski Nasip bb, Zagreb.
Tel (01) 615 96 68.

O'Hara
Uvala Zenta 3, Split.
Tel (098) 364 262.

Papaya Club
Zrće Beach, Novalja,
Pag.

Rock Club Uljanik
Dobrilina 2,
Pula.

Saloon
Tuškanac 1a, Zagreb.
Tel (01) 481 07 33.

Tropic Club Ecuador
Kupalište Bačvice 11,
Split.
Tel (021) 323 571.

Veneranda
On the hill behind the
Delphin Hotel, Hvar.

CASINOS

Hotel Antunović
Zagrebačka Avenija 100a,
Zagreb.
Tel (01) 387 05 30.

Hotel Esplanade
Mihanovićeva 1,
Zagreb.
Tel (01) 456 66 66.

Hotel International
Miramarska 24, Zagreb.
Tel (01) 610 88 00.

CINEMA

Cinestar Avenue Mall
Avenija Dubrovnik 16,
Zagreb.
Tel (062) 283 683.

Cinestar Branimir Centar
Kneza Branimira 29,
Zagreb.
Tel (01) 4699 031.

Movieplex
Kaptol Centar, Nova Ves 17, Zagreb.
Tel (01) 486 07 77.

SPECTATOR SPORTS

Dražen Petrović Basketball Centre
Savska cesta 30,
Zagreb.
Tel (01) 48 43 333.

Maksimir Stadium
Maksimirska 128,
Zagreb.
Tel (01) 23 86 111.
www.nk-dinamo.hr

Poljud Stadium
8 Mediteranskih igara 2,
21000 Split.
Tel (021) 323 650
www.hajduk.hr

OUTDOOR ACTIVITIES

One of the keys to Croatia's tourist success is that it is blessed with such bountiful natural resources – waterfalls, islands, hills, rivers, lakes, canyons, mountains, pine woods and verdant parks – all soaked in dependable Mediterranean sunshine. To its credit, Croatia has responded well by providing a good infrastructure backed by a multitude of organizations to get visitors

Sailing school along the coast

climbing and rafting, sailing and surfing, hiking and biking throughout its wonderfully diverse topography. There are also less energetic activities to be enjoyed. Croatia has several thermal spa centres that can be a bit utilitarian but are getting better as retreats for unwinding after some activity. Finally, of course, the coastline and myriad islands have a glittering choice of beaches for sunworshippers.

Sailing along the Croatian coast

SAILING

The Croatian coastline has many natural harbours, ports and marinas, making it a real haven for sailors. As a result, the best way to fully appreciate the rugged beauty of Croatia's Adriatic coastline is not by car but by yacht or motorboat. With clean, clear sea; steady, moderate winds; waters in which it is easy to anchor and well-equipped marinas open all year-round, a sailor's life is made easy in Croatia. If possible, avoid July to August, unless you really want to spend the time with every weekend admiral in Europe. May to June or September to October are more peaceful, cost less and what is more the weather is still good.

The **Croatian National Tourist Board** (www.croatia.hr) lists over 140 companies with some 2,700 boats available for hire, typically rented out on a weekly basis from 5pm Saturday to Saturday next at 9am. The most important decision for the holiday maker is whether to go

"bareboat" or "skippered". The former requires that you show a valid licence with at least 2 years' experience on it and register the crew. You are then free to sail off on your own. "Skippered" means that for about another 130 euros per day, plus food, you'll have a local in charge who knows exactly what he's doing. Prices vary depending on the size of boat and time of year. The British company **Nautilus Yachting**, for example, will arrange a week "bareboat" on an 11-metre (36 ft) boat sleeping six for around 2,200 euros, whilst the Croatian company **Club Adriatic** have a few 4-berth 10-metre (33 ft) craft for around 1,800 euros, again for seven days.

Anyone sailing to Croatia in their own boat must report to the nearest Harbour Master's Office on arrival if it is over 3 m (10 ft) in length and has an engine over 4 kW.

From Umag to Dubrovnik, Croatia has 50 marinas with everything a sailor could want: refuelling and repair services, water and electrical

hook-ups, medical assistance and surveillance, cafes, bars and restaurants. Marinas are classified according to the level of service they offer and charge accordingly. The **Adriatic Croatia International Club**, known as **ACI**, runs a chain of 21 marinas to which you can take out a yearly contract for use of all facilities and discounted berth fees. In addition there are plenty of temporary moorings available. Or you could simply overnight in a deserted bay.

Another way to experience the combination of sailing and Croatia's unique coastline is to enroll on a special holiday to learn how to sail. **Adriatica.net** offer holidays for sailors of all different levels of experience, although there are plenty of other similar companies.

Coastal radio stations give weather updates in both Croatian and English. Useful radio stations include Radio

Mooring in the harbour at Makarska

Rijeka UKW channel 24, Radio Split UKW channels 07, 21, 23, 81 and Radio Dubrovnik UKW channels 07 and 04.

WINDSURFING

Most coastal resorts offer windsurfing courses and boards for hire, but serious surfers will enjoy two places in particular: Bol, on the island of Brač, and Viganj on the Pelješac Peninsular, close to Orebić. Both resorts have many renowned windsurfing clubs, offering kit and courses from beginner to expert. Also, note, both places play annual host to international championship events in July.

The windsurfing season runs from early April to late October and the westerly winds are at their peak in the early afternoon. Conditions

Windsurfing, a very popular sport along the Croatian coast

are ideal in late May/early June and in late July/early August – though the latter, of course, is in the high season.

DIVING

Although Croatia may not be the Caribbean or the Red Sea, it nonetheless has its fair share of interesting dive sites. Nature has fashioned plenty of underwater caves from the porous karstic limestone along the coast, to which you can add the further attractions of sea walls and shoals of fish and, at greater depths, shipwrecks and corals. Lošinj Island has all the above features and is probably the most comprehensive dive site

The clear waters off Croatia, rich in marine life and coral

in Croatia. If fish are your interest, try Vis – thanks to its military background the island was never commercially fished and consequently, has the richest marine life. The best underwater caves are around the beautiful Kornati Islands, while interesting shipwrecks can be found near Rovinj (Baron Gautsch,1914 passenger ferry), Dubrovnik (Taranto, 1943 merchant ship) and the Pelješac Peninsular (S57, another merchant casualty of war, from 1944).

There are, however, rules and regulations about who can dive where. To dive at all, you will need to show a current diver's card issued by an internationally recognized diving organisation. For a small fee, this is then given a year-long validation by the **Croatian Diving Federation** or any of its agents – which could be an authorised tourist agency or the nearest diving

club to your hotel. Diving clubs abound in the Adriatic and are useful not only for hiring equipment but also for going on guided tours with English-speaking instructors.

Areas off-limits to divers are around military installations, protected cultural monuments and some, but not all, nature reserves. Diving is forbidden in Krka and Brijuni parks for example but, with a permit, is allowed in the Kornati National Park and the islands of Mljet. Check beforehand if you intend to be adventurous.

FISHING

The Adriatic Sea is one of the richest in Europe and draws all kinds of fishermen. In order to go fishing you will need a licence. These are issued by tourist offices, authorised agencies and diving centres and clubs which have an arrangement with the Ministry of Agriculture and Forestry. The cost of a licence is not terribly great and depends on its duration – you can purchase licences valid for 1 day, 3 days, a week or 30 days. The licences permit fishing with a rod and line or a spear gun and it is possible to fish everywhere except in the protected areas of the marine parks (that is, Kornati, the Brijuni islands, Krka and Mljet). Along with the licence you will receive a list of the areas which are off-limits and indications of the number of each fish species that you are allowed to catch.

Locals showing the wide variety of fish and shellfish in the Croatian sea

HIKING IN THE MOUNTAINS

Croatia is criss-crossed with countless hiking paths and trekking trails – marked by a white dot within a red circle painted onto a tree or rock. Contact the **HPS (Croatian Mountaineering Association)** for information about the many local walking clubs, maps and the national whereabouts of mountain huts for simple overnight accommodation. The best time of year for hiking is between April and October. However, be aware that the removal of unexploded mines is still taking place in the conflict zones of the 1991–95 war and don't wander off established trails. See the Croatian Mine Action Centre website (www.hcr.hr) for specific information.

Top trails would have to include the Premužić ridge path, heading for 50 km (31 miles) at around 914 meters (3,000 ft) through the Velebit massif, a short distance east of the central Dalmatian coast, and offering breathtaking views both into continental Croatia and way out to sea;

the gorges and beech forests of Paklenica National Park, 40 km (19 miles) northeast of Zadar; Mt Ilija above Orebić for superb mountain coastal scenery; the fortified hill-towns of the Istrian interior; Samobor and the Risnjak National Park in central Croatia and the Zagorje Castles district in the northern counties.

FREE CLIMBING

As with hiking, climbing is also best pursued from April to October – after which there's the prospect of a sudden snowfall or being blasted by the *bura,* a strong cold wind from the northeast. Croats may not be thought of as Alpinists but they have scaled the Himalayas many times, have their own **Croatian Mountaineering Association** and plenty of home mountain ranges in which to practice their sport. Again, the Paklenica National Park is popular, having more than 400 climbing routes to choose from. Cetina Valley near Omiš in central Dalmatia is another prime destination for climbers. Should you want to climb and spend time

Abseiling down a rock face in summer

at the beach as well, consider heading for the peaks on the islands of Brač, Vis, Mljet, Krk, Hvar, Cres and Lošinj plus those on the peninsulars of both Istria and Pelješac.

CYCLING

Cyclists, like hikers, get the full benefit of the outdoor fragrances, riotous bird-song and chance encounters with the locals that their sport brings. Regional tourist boards in Croatia have worked hard to promote a sensible series of designated bike routes. The national parks and nature reserves lead the way with clearly marked bike trails taking you in a circular tour back to where you began. The Plitvice Lakes provide scenic cycling at its European best. Similarly circuitous routes exist on the islands of Rab, Hvar and Mljet where out-of-the-way beaches and restaurants come into the picture, too. Istria tourist board has also been prominent in looking after cyclists by running rural trails out of and back into Rovinj, Labin and Novigrad. You can find more details at www.istra.hr. Hiring bikes can be the best way to get around the island and find secluded bays. Expect to pay around 10–15 euros a day for bike hire.

Hikers on one of the paths in Paklenica National Park

Clay court tennis, a popular sport in Croatia

TENNIS

After football, tennis is Croatia's most popular sport. Almost every town, holiday hotel and camping site will have the necessary facilities – usually plenty of excellent clay courts. Two of the best-equipped clubs are the **Tennis Club Pećine** in Rijeka and the **Tennis Club Smrikve** in Pula. If you enjoy watching tennis, the ATP Croatia Open Championships are held at Umag in July. At any tennis club in Croatia you're likely to be reminded of the achievements of their best-known sportsman: Goran Ivanišević, who is perhaps most famous internationally for winning the Men's Singles at Wimbledon in 2001.

GOLF

Golf is becoming increasingly popular in Croatia. There are five major courses: **Golf & Country Club Zagreb**, **Golf Centre Novi Dvori** near Zagreb, **Golf & Country Club Dolina Kardinala**, near Karlovac, **Kempinski Golf Adriatic** near Umag and **Spa & Golf Resort Sveti Martin** near Čacovec, as well as several smaller locations with golf facilities.

To play at a Croatian golf club you may need to show a membership card issued by the national federation from your home country. This will indicate your handicap, which may be required prior to

you tee-ing off. It's a good idea to check what identification you'll need in advance.

WHITEWATER RAFTING

This most accessible of the extreme sports began in Croatia around the late 1980s, opening up remote canyons and rivers known before only to kayakers and fishermen. The most rewarding places to raft through wild scenery on greenish waters clear down to the riverbed itself – and innocent of vicious rapids or huge waves – are the Dalmatian rivers of Zrmanja, near Zadar and Cetina, near Omiš and the rivers Dobra and Kupa, near Karlovac in central Croatia. Agencies like **Kompas** in Zagreb organise trips with guides and all the gear. Otherwise try the website www.activeholidays-croatia.com

RELAXATION

Several spa resorts offer natural thermal springs and treatments. They emphasise the relaxation aspect more than the treatment but have excellent sporting facilities (*see Thermal Spas Tour pp212–13*).

A golfer on a practice course

DIRECTORY

SAILING

ACI Marinas
M.Tita 151, Opatija. **Tel** *(051) 271 288.* **www**.aci-club.hr

Adriatica.net
Heinzelova 62a, Zagreb.
www.adriatica.net

Club Adriatic
www.clubadriatic.com

Nautilus Yachting
www.nautilus.hr

WINDSURFING

www.croatia.hr

DIVING

Croatian Diving Federation
Dalmatinska 12, Zagreb.
Tel *(01) 484 87 65.*
www.diving-hrs.hr

HIKING & CLIMBING

Croatian Mountaineering Association
Kozarčeva 22, Zagreb. **Tel** *(01) 482 41 42.* **www**.plsavez.hr

CYCLING

www.istra.hr
www.croatia.hr

WHITEWATER RAFTING

Kompas
www.kompas.hr

TENNIS

Tennis Club Pecine
Šetalište XIII Divizije 33, Rijeka.
Tel *(051) 421 782.*

Tennis Club Smrikve
Stinjanska cesta 91, Pula.
Tel *(052) 517 011.*

GOLF

Dolina Kardinala
Tel *(091) 173 11 00.*

Golf & Country Club Zagreb
Tel *(01) 653 11 77.*

Golf Centre Novi Dvori
Tel *(01) 334 07 77.*

Kempinski Golf Adriatic
Tel *(052) 707 371 111.*

Spa & Golf Resort Sveti Martin

SURVIVAL GUIDE

PRACTICAL INFORMATION

In Croatia, tourism is an important source of revenue (accounting for approximately 20 per cent of the GDP in 2011) and every

Logo of the Croatian National Tourist Board

effort is being made to foster the growth and development of the industry. Since independence in 1991, a number of measures have been taken to encourage visitors, including simplifying border formalities and introducing tax reductions on items destined for export. Hotels and historic buildings damaged in the war have been rebuilt and modernized, and road and maritime links have been improved, both internally and with neighbouring countries. The country is rapidly reaffirming itself as a popular holiday destination, able to offer tourist facilities of international standard at competitive prices. Croatia is set to join the European Union in 2013, though many of its regulations and practices already fall in line with EU standards.

WHEN TO GO

The busiest, most popular time to visit the Croatian coastline are the summer months of July and August. With its crystal clear seas, combined with thousands of islands and bays for exploring and swimming, the coast is a major attraction. In addition, the summer weather is reliably sunny, another important aspect for many.

In the peak season, hotels and resorts are at their busiest, so if a quieter holiday is preferred, it would be better to choose the months of May, June or September, when the weather is still fine but resorts are not so crowded. Another advantage of travelling out of peak season are the low prices on offer. Spring and autumn are the best months for hiking, climbing and mountain biking.

Inland Croatia is home to a number of thermal spas, and it is possible to combine a few days of therapeutic treatment or relaxation *(see pp212–3)* with visits to cities and towns with their rich historical and artistic heritage.

Unlike nearby Slovenia, Croatia's facilities for winter tourism are not yet well-developed, although there are a few ski slopes, such as in Platak, the Medvednica and the Bjelolasica mountains.

Zagreb, the capital, offers numerous attractions and is a great destination the entire year round.

VISAS AND PASSPORTS

To enter Croatia, visitors need to have a valid passport. People from countries in the European Union, the US, Canada, Australia and New Zealand do not need a visa and may stay for up to 90 days. Croatian authorities have signed a bilateral agreement with EU countries, according to which EU citizens need only carry an identity card to enter Croatia.

To check whether you require a visa, visit the website of the Croatian Ministry of Foreign Affairs (www.mvp.hr) for a list of countries whose citizens require visas. If you do need one, seek advice from the Croatian Embassy in your home country.

All foreign citizens must register with the local police within 48 hours of arrival in the country. Failure to do so may result in a fine or even expulsion from the country. In practice, if you are staying in a hotel, the reception staff will take care of this procedure for you.

People travelling with pets must ensure that their pets have been microchipped and carry an International Pet Passport as well as all the necessary documents verifying that their pets' vaccinations are complete and up to date, particularly with regard to rabies.

Bottle of Croatian wine

CUSTOMS INFORMATION

There are no restrictions on personal effects brought into Croatia by travellers and customs regulations are harmonized with the standards of EU member states. It is also possible to carry into or out of Croatia, 200 cigarettes or 50 cigars, 1 litre of spirits, 2 litres of wine, and 50 millilitres (one bottle) of perfume or essence.

On entering the country, all major, high-value items such as radio equipment, computers, photographic equipment, video cameras and other recording equipment and portable televisions must be declared.

Arrival in the country by boat must be reported to the Harbour Master's Office along with the number of people on board and all equipment.

Local currency worth only 15,000 kn can be imported or exported but no such limit is imposed on foreign currency.

TOURIST INFORMATION

Every town and city has a tourist office, called Turistički Ured, Turistička Zajednica or Turistički Informativni Centar. These state-run offices provide information on sightseeing, excursions and transport and will often help visitors to find accommodation in hotels or private rooms *(see pp218–9)*.

However, in smaller cities and towns, these offices are open during summer only.

Additionally, there are county and regional tourist offices, managed by the Ministry of Tourism.

Alternatively, you can contact the **Croatian National Tourist Board** in your home country before leaving. The Croatian Ministry of Tourism has set up information offices in all major countries to publicize the attractions Croatia has to offer. The website of the Croatian National Tourist Board is particularly helpful.

Tourist asking for help and directions

ADMISSION PRICES

Most state-run museums and historical sites charge an entrance fee between 10 kn and 70 kn. Children are normally entitled to a 50 per cent reduction in admission prices. Churches are usually free, though if there is an adjoining bell-tower or treasury, you may have to pay to visit them.

OPENING HOURS

Public offices open from 8am to 4pm or 9am to 5pm on weekdays. While most other office businesses more or less follow these standard opening times, these hours may vary for other businesses. For example pharmacies *(see pp268–9)*, banks *(see pp270–71)* and post offices *(see pp272–3)*, the bigger ones of which are also open on Saturdays. Shops are usually open

8am–8pm *(see p250)*, while cafés tend to open quite early.

Note that many museums and other cultural attractions are closed on Mondays. During summer, most have extended daily opening hours, and in coastal resorts, some close in the afternoon (when visitors are most likely to go to the beach) but open in the evening.

LANGUAGE

Croatia is called Hrvatska in the national language, Croatian (hrvatski). It is a Slavic language and is written in the Latin script. Croatian is not an easy tongue to learn, but since most people in the country have studied at least one other foreign language, visitors should be able to make themselves understood in most circumstances. Italian, German and English are widely spoken while French is less common. Young Croatians generally speak very good English.

ETIQUETTE AND SMOKING

Smoking is very common in Croatia (an estimated 30 per cent of the population smokes), but is officially banned in all enclosed public spaces, except for cafés that have approved air conditioning systems. While most establishments in Zagreb adhere to this law, it is frequently ignored in the south of the country. All the same, in summer, you can sit at the outdoor tables to avoid the smoke in closed spaces.

TAXES AND TIPPING

The practice of tipping, usually calculated at 10 per cent, is widespread in Croatia, even in restaurants, where a service charge is normally included in the price. When paying in bars or in taxis it is expected that at least the sum will be rounded up. It is also customary to tip the tourist or museum guides after a tour has ended.

In department stores, supermarkets and shops, the prices for goods are fixed but elsewhere, particularly in the street markets, it is still possible to bargain.

TRAVELLERS WITH SPECIAL NEEDS

In Croatia there is a great awareness of the problems faced by the disabled particularly because of the war of independence which left many people with disabilities. Stations, airports, larger hotels and restaurants above a certain standard, and the main public offices in larger towns are accessible to those in wheelchairs. However, facilities at the ports are not so good.

Disabled visitors are entitled to a 50 per cent reduction in ticket prices at most state-run museums. For further information, contact the **Hrvatski Savez Udruga Tjelesnih Invalida** (HSUTI), the Croatian organization for the disabled, which has its headquarters in Zagreb. Also useful is the **HUPT** website, which provides information on accessible beaches and accommodation.

Pedestrians walking on a stone bridge in Ploce Gate, Dubrovnik

TRAVELLING WITH CHILDREN

Tourist complexes such as large hotels and resorts, usually provide facilities for children, such as playgrounds, pools and baby-sitting services. However, these may be harder to find in smaller towns and inland regions less visited by tourists.

When travelling with Croatia Airlines on domestic flights, children under 2 years of age go free, while those between 2–12 years of age get a 50 per cent discount. Children are also entitled to a 50 per cent reduction in tickets prices for most state-run museums.

GAY AND LESBIAN TRAVELLERS

Homosexuality is still rather taboo in Croatia. Same-sex couples should refrain from public displays of affection so as not to cause offence. You can find out more at www.friendlycroatia.com.

TRAVELLING ON A BUDGET

Low-cost accommodation is available in most destinations in the form of youth hostels and private rooms to rent. Decent youth hostels can be found in the cities of Zagreb, Split, Dubrovnik, Rijeka, Pula, Zadar and Šibenik, as well as on the island of Hvar and Lošinj. Some, but not all, come under the Croatian Youth Hostel Association (www. hfhs.hr) umbrella group. Many hostels are part of the

Conventional clothing in the church for both men and woman

A secluded beach on the Dalmatian coast

Hostelling International group (www.hihostels.com)and if you plan to stay in these it is worth joining and acquiring a membership card before setting off.

An International Student Identity Card (www.isic.org) entitles you to discounts on travel expenses such as 25 per cent off train tickets.

WHAT TO TAKE/WEAR

In summer you will need light cotton clothing with a jacket or pullover for the evenings, plus swimwear. In winter you will need woollen jumpers and a warm coat. Also be sure to pack at least one pair of decent walking shoes as some of the medieval towns have unevenly paved or cobbled streets.

Although it is rarely neces sary to dress in formal clothes, clothes which are neat and tidy will be appreciated. For example, trainers are not suitable for dining in an up-market restaurant.

Croatia is quite a religious country. So, when visiting churches make sure you have your thighs and shoulders covered (that goes for both men and women).

FORMS OF GREETING

Croatians tend to be quite reserved with strangers. Attempting a few words in the local language will be appreciated. The forms used vary according to the person you are addressing: he or she may be a *gospodin* (a man), a

gospoda (a married woman) or a *gospodica* (a young single woman).

Greetings vary for the different times of the day: *dobro jutro* (good morning), *dobar dan* (good afternoon or good day), *dobra večer* (good evening), *laku noć* (good night). *Bok* (hi) and *ciao* are informal greetings. *Dovidenja* is commonly used to say goodbye to people you are not familiar with.

For polite requests use *molim* (please) and *hvala* (thank you). For more vocabulary, see the Phrase Book *(pp295–6)*.

NATURISM

Croatia is a popular country for naturism, where it is practised freely at designated places and resorts that are outstanding for their quality and high standards. Naturism has a very long tradition in Croatia. In fact, the first vacation resort for naturists was opened in Rajska plaža (Paradise beach) on the island of Rab in 1934.

Today there are many nudist beaches that are marked "FKK" (German for "free body culture"). There are about 20 official naturist resorts offering accommodation along the Croatian coast (mainly in the form of camping). The majority are in Istria and some even have Blue Flag (clean beach) status. These places are appropriately screened, allowing guests to enjoy the absolute freedom and peace the surrounding nature has to offer.

British tour operators offering naturist holidays in Croatia include **Away with Dune** (formerly Dune Leisure) and **Peng Travel**.

TIME

Croatia is one hour ahead of Greenwich Mean Time (GMT) in winter, and two hours ahead in summer.

ELECTRICITY

The electric current supplied is 220V, 50Hz all over the country. The standard European two-pin plugs are used throughout Croatia.

RESPONSIBLE TOURISM

Visitors can support local communities by shopping for local seasonal produce at markets such as the daily covered markets in Zagreb, Rijeka and Pula, the vast open-air market in Split, and many other smaller markets in towns and villages.

Visitors can buy local specialities direct from producers in various destinations, such

as *paški sir* (sheep's cheese) on the island of Pag, lavender oil and dried lavender on the island of Hvar, *pršut* (prosciutto), dried figs throughout Dalmatia, *tartufi* (truffles) in Istria, and wine in all the major wine-producing regions (you can visit vineyards and taste their wine before purchasing).

Visitors can take part in eco-friendly activities such as hiking, mountain biking, sailing and rafting – a greener alternative to fuel-guzzling motorboats for example.

Croatian ethical tour operators include the Makarska-based **Biokovo Active Holidays**, who organize outdoor adventures sports including hiking and mountain biking on Mount Biokovo, and rafting down the River Cetina near Omiš, and the Dubrovnik-based **Adria Adventure**, who specialize in sea kayaking and hiking holidays. The UK-based ethical tour operators arranging holidays in Croatia include **Responsible Travel** and **Swim Trek**.

Trogir market, Dalmatia

DIRECTORY

Personal Security and Health

Croatian public health services meet the standards of those elsewhere in Europe, and in general, tourists run no serious health risks. There are no endemic diseases but tourists should take care against insect bites and over-exposure to the sun. Tap water is drinkable all over the country. In inland regions, de-mining along former lines of confrontation is not complete. Therefore, travellers should not stray from known safe routes in these zones. Crime rate is comparatively low, and there is little street crime, although visitors should take the usual precautions in busy places to protect valuables.

A Croatian policeman with a police car

POLICE

Regular Croatian police (*policija*) officers wear dark blue uniforms and keep a relatively low-profile presence. In addition, there are the seldom seen Intervention Police (who wear blue military-style uniforms) and the Special Police or SWAT (who wear khaki military-style uniforms). If you are a victim of crime, you should report this to the local police station and obtain a police statement.

WHAT TO BE AWARE OF

The level of safety on the roads and in public places is good, and the police are deemed responsible for the protection and safety of the country's visitors as well as its citizens. Croatia has a relatively low crime rate, and violent crime is comparatively rare. If a petty theft occurs, it is more likely to happen in crowded areas such as bus and railway stations.

It is highly unlikely that the police will create any problems for foreign visitors on holiday in Croatia unless, of course, the law is broken in some way. However, it is advisable to carry your identification documents, such as a passport, with you as the police have the right to ask for identification.

According to an inter-national agreement, if a tourist is held for questioning or detained for whatever reason, he or she has the right to contact a diplomatic representative of his or her country (an embassy or consulate) and receive assistance in appointing a local lawyer, preferably English-speaking *(see p265)*.

Any eventual costs and the lawyer's fee are the respon-sibility of the accused.

IN AN EMERGENCY

In case of emergencies, the appropriate services to call are listed in the directory opposite. For accidents or other medical emergencies, go to casualty *(hitna pomoć)*.

There are general hospitals in all the main cities while rural towns and the islands are served by local doctors. People can be transferred by ambulance or helicopter to the nearest hospital in case of any emergency.

LOST AND STOLEN PROPERTY

Precautions for avoiding theft and loss of documents and personal belongings are the same as in any other country, so use your common sense. You should avoid leaving objects of value and money unattended and keep an eye on your luggage and bags, particularly in crowded areas. Do not wear showy, expensive jewellery that could attract the wrong kind of attention.

When you travel, it is always a good idea to make a photocopy of your personal documents and keep them in a separate place; in this way it will be much easier to obtain a duplicate. In the event of loss, report the circumstances to the police as soon as possible.

HOSPITALS AND PHARMACIES

All the main cities have a hospital, and the standard of health care is on par with most European Union countries. For less serious problems, visit a pharmacy *(ljekarna)*, which can be identified by the green cross above the door. Croatian pharmacists are highly qualified and can dispense medication not usually

An ambulance driving past a hospital

Aerial view of people sunbathing on a Dalmatian beach

available over the counter back home. Although it is easy to find all the more common over-the-counter medicines in pharmacies without too much difficulty, it is best to carry an adequate supply of any prescription medicines you may need.

Some medicines are not known by the commercial names given to them in their country of origin, but by the active ingredients contained in them. This may cause difficulty for a pharmacist trying to comply with the request of a foreign visitor. In any event, it is useful if you can produce a legible prescription written by your own doctor as proof that you are authorized to take a particular medicine.

Pharmacies are usually open all day (8am to 8pm) or in the morning or afternoon, depending on the day.

MINOR HAZARDS

Most of the problems that visitors suffer from in Croatia are those common to tourists anywhere else.

To prevent sunstroke, you should drink lots of liquids and avoid strenuous sports or activities at the hottest time of the day. Make sure to use sunscreen creams with a high sun protection factor.

A change in diet can cause stomach upsets, which are often a nuisance but can usually be treated quickly. In Croatia there is no risk of

dysentery or similar illnesses.

On the beaches and near the coast, the most common problem is probably irritating insect bites, particularly from mosquitoes and it is a good idea to take some anti-histamine cream and insect repellent with you.

Tick-born diseases can be a problem in rural areas in late spring and throughout the summer. Anyone spending a lot of time outdoors should take precautions, such as wearing long-sleeved tops and using insect repellant. Seek medical advice if bitten.

For hikers and climbers venturing inland, there is the possibility of encountering snakes, so take the appropriate serum with you if you are planning such a trip. However, most minor ailments and disturbances can usually be avoided with a little care and common sense.

Boat travel is a common means of transport for connections between the coastal towns and cities and obviously the only means of getting to virtually all the islands. Unfortunately many people suffer from seasickness and people who are susceptible should take some kind of travel sickness pill before embarking on a sea journey. It is advisable to keep to the central areas of the boat where any pitching and rolling is felt less and go on deck where fresh air and a visible horizon may help.

TRAVEL AND HEALTH INSURANCE

Foreign tourists do not pay for emergency medical services if the Health Care Convention has been signed between Croatia and the country they come from. This applies to all countries in the European Union including the UK, Ireland and Italy. All EU citizens should carry a European Health Insurance Card (EHIC), available from the UK Department of Health or from a main post office. If you come from a country that has not signed the Convention, you have to pay for health services according to a standardized price list.

It is, however, advisable to take out an insurance policy to cover medical assistance. The policy should also include repatriation by air-ambulance, as well as the refunding of any medical expenses that are necessary. All visitors have a right to emergency medical assistance, but certain medical services must be paid for.

Activities such as diving, rock climbing and in some cases, even hiking or motor-cycling, are often not included in travel insurance cover, as they are regarded as dangerous activities. Check the insurance policy details; it may be necessary to pay a surcharge to cover these kinds of sports.

DIRECTORY

EMERGENCY SERVICES

Police
Tel 192.

Fire
Tel 193.

Ambulance
Tel 194.

General Emergency
Tel 112.

Breakdown Service (Automobile Club)
Tel 1987 www.hak.hr.

Rescue at Sea
Tel 9155.

Information
Tel 981.

Banking and Currency

The Croatian currency is the kuna, which in May 1994 took the place of the dinar. It is in fact a very old currency; coins displaying the kuna were known to be in use in Slavonia in 1256. It is not difficult to change money into kuna at bureaux de change and banks throughout the country. Visitors need to pay for everything in Croatian kuna, even though hotel room prices are (confusingly) almost always posted in euros. Although Croatia will join the European Union in 2013, it will take several years before it officially adopts the euro, if indeed it adopts it at all.

BANKS AND BUREAUX DE CHANGE

Money can be changed from one currency to the other in banks and authorized bureaux de change or exchange offices. Banks are usually open from Monday to Friday from 8am to 7pm and on Saturday from 8am to 1pm but times can vary, so always check in advance if possible. However, in the smaller towns, some banks may close in the middle of the day from noon to 3pm and on Saturdays a little earlier, at noon.

Exchange offices have more flexible timings and are open until late in the evening in tourist areas. A commission is charged on the exchange, which varies from 1 to 1.5 per cent at the exchange offices. These charges are lesser or almost non-existent if you change money at a bank.

You can also change foreign currency in post offices and tourist agencies. If at all possible, avoid changing money at hotels or camping sites where the exchange rates are decidedly less favourable. Do not be tempted to change money at stations

One of the many ATMs found in all main towns and cities

and ports or along the roads with people who are not authorized. Finally, if you hold on to your original receipts you can re-convert any unused kuna banknotes back to the orignal currency at the end of your stay. However, only banks offer this kind of service.

ATMs

Automated Teller Machines (ATM) are now widespread throughout the country, even in remote villages on the islands. Not every ATM accepts all forms of credit and debit cards, so it is best to check that the logo of the card you want to use is on the machine *(bankomat)* before making a withdrawal. Remember to always shield the ATM machine from strangers when feeding your PIN into it.

TRAVELLER'S CHEQUES

Traveller's cheques are not accepted anywhere in Croatia.

CREDIT AND DEBIT CARDS

The most commonly accepted credit cards are MasterCard, American Express, Visa and Diners. Credit cards can be used in almost every shop, resort, hotel and restaurant. Of course, there are always exceptions, so check the signs on the door of the establishment to see which cards they accept. If there is no sign, ask in advance to avoid unpleasant surprises.

In the event of the loss or theft of your credit card, it is extremely important to report it immediately so that the card can be blocked. This can be done by calling the relevant card's emergency number

DIRECTORY

BANKS, EXCHANGE OFFICES AND ATMS

Zagrebačka banka
www.zaba.hr

Hrvatska narodna banka
www.hnb.hr

LOST OR STOLEN CREDIT CARDS

American Express
Tel 1 905 474 0870
(collect call). **www.**
americanexpress.com

Diners Club
Tel 1 702 797 5532 (collect call).
www.diners.com.hr

Eurocard–MasterCard
Tel 1 636 722 7111 (collect call).

Visa
Tel 0 800 220 111 (wait for the second dial tone, then enter 866 654 0125).

The Zagrebačka Banka, with offices in Zagreb

(which is usually a number providing a 24-hour service, seven days a week). Inform your bank that you are travelling so that they do not block your card due to unusual activity.

CURRENCY

The kuna is divided into 100 lipa (the word "lipa" means a linden tree). The Central Bank issues banknotes of 1000, 500, 200, 100, 50, 20 and 10 kuna, featuring Croatian heroes. Coins come in denominations of 5, 2 and 1 kuna, and 50, 20, 10, 5, 2 and 1 lipa. The local abbreviation for kuna is kn, but the international abbreviation is HRK.

The Croatian currency was formerly closely linked to the German mark and until 31 December 2001, prices for accommodation, especially private rooms, were always quoted in marks. However, the mark was replaced by the euro in January 2002 when it became the common currency of the European Union. The government tries to keep rates of exchange steady, which helps travellers and also helps to present an overall image of stability to potential foreign investors.

The euro is now accepted in all banks and bureaux de change.

Banknotes

The Central Bank issues banknotes of 1000, 500, 200, 100, 50, 20 and 10 kuna. Notes bear the portraits of famous Croats such as Stjepan Radić and Josip Jelačić.

20 kuna

50 kuna

100 kuna

200 kuna

Coins

The kuna is divided into 100 lipa. The coin denominations are 5, 2 and 1 kuna and 50, 20, 10, 5, 2 and 1 lipa. The 20 and 50 lipa coins are silver-coloured and the 10 and 5 lipa coins are bronze-coloured.

1 kuna

2 kuna

5 kuna

1 lipa

2 lipa

5 lipa

10 lipa

20 lipa

50 lipa

Communications and Media

A Croatian postbox

Croatia has good communication systems and well-functioning public services such as the post and telecommunications. The news and information network is well-organized, although most visitors (unless they speak Croatian) will face the obvious language barrier. However, foreign television programmes can be received via satellite and it is also easy to find foreign newspapers and magazines with newsagents, although they might be available a little later than they would be at home. Internet use is also widespread in Croatia.

Using a mobile phone on the streets of Dubrovnik

INTERNATIONAL AND LOCAL TELEPHONE CALLS

Calling Croatia from abroad is very easy: after dialling the international code (00 world-wide), dial the international country code (385), followed by the area code without the initial zero (Croatia is divided administratively into counties, each with a corresponding code) and finally the number of the subscriber. To telephone abroad from Croatia, dial the international code (again 00), followed by the international code of the country (for the UK it is 44), then the area code (omitting the initial zero) and finally the subscriber's number. The international codes for other English-speaking countries are as follows: the US and Canada, 1, Australia, 61, New Zealand, 64 and Ireland, 353.

When making local calls from a landline within Croatia, you need to include the area code when dialling,

unless you are calling from within that area. There is a list of Croatian area codes in the directory on p273.

Numbers beginning with the code 060 are information services. These services can be dialled up from anywhere within Croatia, using the same code.

MOBILE PHONES

In Croatia several companies offer mobile phone services (GSM network): Tele 2, with the code 095; T-Mobile, with the code 098 and 099; and Vipnet, with the codes 091 and 092. The HT GSM network covers approximately 98 per cent of the country.

Check with your mobile phone service provider before you leave to see whether they have a roaming agreement with the Croatian networks.

If you expect to be in Croatia for more than a week, purchasing a local SIM card to use in your mobile phone may be worthwhile. You will need your phone to be unlocked in order to use the new SIM card.

Keep in mind that it is illegal to use a mobile phone while you are driving.

PUBLIC TELEPHONES

There are fewer public telephones in Croatia now, but they do still exist. Pay phones in Croatia are operated by telephone cards *(telefonska kartica)* that are available in units of 15, 30, 50 and 100 (1 unit = 1 kuna) and can be purchased from tobacconists, newsagents and news kiosks.

It is cheaper to call from a public phone rather than from your hotel, as hotels generally apply a supplement to any calls which are made from their rooms.

INTERNET

Internet and email facilities are widely available in Croatia, and it is easy to find Internet cafés with speedy connections in most places, even on the islands.

If you want to use a laptop computer, you will find that many hotels and hostels offer free Wi-Fi to their guests. Some cities (such as Rijeka and Osijek) also have 'Hot Spots' with free Wi-Fi in public spaces. Ask at the relevant local tourist offices for the exact location of these zones.

POSTAL SERVICES

The Croatian national postal company HP operates a network of post offices, with branches in all towns, and offers a wide range of services, including the sale of stamps and telephone cards, fax

Surfing the net at an Internet café in Dubrovnik

Typical newspaper kiosk in Valpovo

facilities and postal services of all kinds. If you are sending ordinary post, stamps *(marke)* can also be bought at news-agents *(kiosk)*. Note that unless airmail is specifically requested, postcards and letters will be sent overland.

Letters and cards can be posted at post offices or the roadside yellow post boxes. The costs vary according to the type of correspondence and the destination. Post offices are open 7am–7pm Monday–Friday, and 7am–1pm on Saturday. During summers, the post offices in the tourist resorts extend their opening times until 10pm.

A practical and straight-forward way to receive post while on holiday is to use the *poste restante* service. Any correspondence sent to the following addresses will be held until it is collected by the addressee. In Zagreb, the address is Poste Restante, 10000 Zagreb, Croatia and in Split, Poste Restante, Main Post Office, 21000 Split, Croatia.

Entrance to the Post Office (HP) in Dubrovnik

NEWSPAPERS AND MAGAZINES

The top-selling national daily newspapers are *24 Sata*, *Jutarnji List*, *Večernji List* and *Slobodna Dalmacija*, all in Croatian. British, Italian and German newspapers and magazines are usually readily available at newsstands in all the major resorts and cities. Also look out for the very informative English-language *In Your Pocket* bi-monthly guides, available for various destinations including Split, Dubrovnik, Rijeka, Zadar and Zagreb.

TELEVISION AND RADIO

The main Croatian radio and television company is *Hrvatski radiotelevizija* (HRT). There are two national TV channels: HRT1 and HRT2, both of which broad-cast foreign and domestic programmes. Other television stations are RTL and Nova TV, as well as about 20 private regional channels. Almost all programmes including films and other foreign productions are broadcast in their original language, with Croatian sub-titles. The radio has daily news in both English and German.

Many hotels have satellite television and hotel guests will have access to a wide range of European stations.

Croatian radio stations broadcast in Croatian only, apart from some traffic reports. On the Second Channel (at RDS-HRT2), reports on news in general are given in English, German and Italian.

TRAVEL INFORMATION

Most visitors take a direct flight from the UK to Zagreb, Split or Dubrovnik and there are useful internal flights between the three main airports. During the summer months, numerous charter flights operate and the smaller airports in Croatia open. Many tourists visiting the country come from nearby Germany, Italy and Austria, which are all well connected by road or sea.

Signage indicating Customs

These visitors often use their own transport, usually car or motorbike. A great deal has been done to develop and improve all means of transport and the country now has good connections to the rest of Europe and the world. It is also possible to get to Croatia by train, for those who prefer this form of transport – this is a much slower method, although the network is being modernized.

ARRIVING BY AIR

The national airline company, **Croatia Airlines**, links Croatia's main airports with the rest of Europe. The major European destinations are Amsterdam, Athens, Barcelona, Frankfurt, Berlin, Brussels, Copenhagen, London, Munich, Paris, Rome, Podgorica, Tel Aviv, Istanbul, Skopje, Zurich, Sarajevo, Venice and Vienna.

Other European airlines offering scheduled services to Croatia include **British Airways** (which operates both a summer and a winter service between London Gatwick and Dubrovnik, making Dubrovnik a year-round city break destination), and Star Alliance members Lufthansa, Austrian Airlines, Brussels Airlines, Air France, TAP Portugal, Turkish Airlines, SAS Scandinavian Airlines, Swiss International Airlines and British Midland. Flying time from London is 2 hours 10 minutes and from Frankfurt 1 hour 30 minutes.

The no-frills airline **EasyJet** flies to Dubrovnik from London Gatwick and Stansted; to Split from Bristol, London Gatwick and Stansted; and to Zagreb from London Gatwick. **Jet2.com** flies to Dubrovnik from Belfast, Edinburgh, Leeds, Manchester and Newcastle; and to Pula and Split from Manchester. **Monarch** flies to Dubrovnik from London Gatwick, Birmingham and Manchester. **Wizz Air** flies to Dubrovnik and Split from Luton airport; and **Ryanair** flies to the cities of Pula and Rijeka from Stansted; and to Zadar from Stansted and East Midlands airport.

From Dublin, **Aer Lingus** flies direct to Dubrovnik. Since there are no direct flights from the US or Canada to Croatia, travellers will need to change at one of the main European hubs such as London, Rome or Frankfurt, and then take a further connecting flight to Croatia. There is a daily flight to Zagreb from Rome Fiumicino, for example, as well as five flights a week to and from Split, and two flights a week to and from Dubrovnik.

There are also flights to Zagreb from Australia and New Zealand that have stopovers at major Asian and European airports.

AIR FARES

The air fares on scheduled flights to Croatia vary according to the airline and the time of year. Fares tend to be higher in the summer. From the UK there are regular scheduled flights from Gatwick and Heathrow to Zagreb, with connections to Pula, Dubrovnik, Rijeka and Split, as well as direct flights from Gatwick to Dubrovnik. There are charter flights to Croatia from a wide range of UK regional airports during the summer months (May–September). Note that it is possible to get discounts on ticket prices by booking them through price comparison websites such as Kayak, Zugu, Momondo and Skyscanner.

TRANSPORT FROM AIRPORT TO TOWN

Croatia has three main airports. Zagreb airport is 17 km (10 miles) from the centre of the city and is connected by a bus service to the central bus station in Držićeva; the journey takes about 25 minutes and runs from the city to the airport from 4:30 or 5am to 8pm and in the opposite direction from 7am to 8pm

A Croatia Airlines plane at Split airport

(or before and after Croatia Airlines flight departures and arrivals). The airport at Split is 24 km (15 miles) from the centre of the city and is also connected by a regular bus service, which runs to the seafront promenade, in front of the ferry port. The journey takes about 30 minutes. Dubrovnik airport is 18 km (11 miles) from the city and is connected by a regular bus service, running to the main bus station, with a stop at Pile Gate which is just outside the fortified old town. The journey time for this service is about 20 minutes.

Driving along the Magistrala coastal road

PACKAGE DEALS

A number of tour operators offer package holidays where the price includes flights (usually charter flights) and accommodation. There are also several UK tour operators offering package holidays such as **Light Blue Travel**, **Balkan Holidays** and **Thomson Holidays**. **Saga Holidays** organizes tours for the 50-plus age group. **Adriatic Holidays** offer sailing holidays including 7- and 14-day trips along the Dalmatian coast, taking in a number of the surrounding islands and Dubrovnik, Split, Zadar and Pula.

ARRIVING BY TRAIN

You can travel from London to Zagreb by train, via Paris, Milan and Venice a trip of around 30 hours. An alternative route goes via Brussels and Ljubljana in Slovenia. You can also travel from London to Paris, then take an overnight train from Paris to Bologna, followed by a train to the Italian port of Ancona, from where there are regular overnight ferries to Split. **Rail Europe** and **European Rail** can supply information.

Connections from other European cities include the Intercity Munich–Zagreb (which takes 9 hours); the Eurocity "Mimara" which covers the Frankfurt-Munich–Salzburg–Ljubljana–Zagreb route (12 hours) and the Intercity "Croatia" takes the

route Vienna–Maribor–Zagreb (6 hours 30 minutes). Vienna–Rijeka takes 8 hours.

There are rail connections from Italy too. From Venice, there is a direct sleeper train daily to Zagreb. There are regular trains to Zagreb from Belgrade (four a day; 6 hours 15 minutes) and Budapest (two a day; 6 hours).

The headquarters of the **Croatian Railways** (Hrvatske Željeznice) is in Zagreb.

Road signage at the Slovenian border

ARRIVING BY COACH

Croatia is also accessible to other countries by coach. International coaches connect Croatia with the bordering states and also with France, Switzerland, Germany, Austria, Slovakia, Bosnia Herzegovina and Montenegro.

From Germany there are almost daily services from Berlin, Cologne, Dortmund, Frankfurt, Mannheim, Munich and Stuttgart to Zagreb and the coastal cities, covering the stretch from Rijeka to Split.

Many Italian cities such as Bologna, Florence, Milan, Rome and Trieste are also connected to Zagreb by coach. The main bus station is **Autobusni Kolodvor Zagreb** in the capital.

The SAF Autoservizio Friuli Venezia Giulia runs services four times a day in the summer and twice in winter from Trieste to Pula in Istria. From Trieste you can also get to Rijeka by coach which runs four times a day.

Eurolines run a service from the UK to Croatia. Buses depart from London's Victoria station to arrive in Zagreb 32 hours later, with a change in Frankfurt, Germany.

ARRIVING BY ROAD

Travelling to Croatia by car (or by motorbike) is popular with tourists coming from the neighbouring countries. There are six main border crossings between Croatia and Hungary, 23 frontier points between Croatia and Bosnia-Herzegovina, eight frontier points between Croatia and Serbia and two between Croatia and Montenegro.

Traffic coming overland from Italy enters Croatia via border crossings with Slovenia, all classified as international and open 24 hours a day, all year round. Rabuiese-Muggia, towards Savudrija, is the crossing point for Istria; Basovizza-Pesek, for Rijeka and Dalmatia; Fernetti-Villa Opicina, for those going towards Zagreb.

People driving to Croatia need to carry a valid driving licence, the car's log book (if appropriate) and a green card. For insurance purposes, on entering the country, any prior damage to the car which has not yet been repaired must be declared.

ARRIVING BY SEA

Croatia's main international ferry connections are with Italy via the ports of Ancona, Bari, Venice and Trieste. The main Croatian maritime company is **Jadrolinija** which runs services between Ancona and Split (three times a week). The crossing takes nine hours. Ancona–Zadar runs three times a week, an 8-hour journey, and Bari–Dubrovnik runs three times a week in winter and six times a week in summer (taking 10 hours by night; 7 and a half hours by day for the journey). In peak season (mid-July to mid-August) the Ancona–Split ferry also makes a stop at Stari Grad on the island of Hvar. **Blue Line** is another Croatian company running regular 10-hour ferry services between Ancona and Split, and seasonal ferry services between Ancona and Hvar, and Ancona and Vis. Ferries are well equipped with restaurants, bars and duty free shops.

One of the ships that connect Croatian ports with the rest of the Adriatic

Venezia Lines operate in the Northern Adriatic and link the northern Adriatic coasts of Italy and Croatia, though they run in summer only (April–September). Regular catamaran lines run between Venice and the Istrian towns of Poreč, Rovinj, Pula and Rabac, and also between Venice and Mali Lošinj on the island of Lošinj.

JADROLINIJA

Symbol of the maritime company, Jadrolinija

Trieste Lines also run a fast catamaran in the Northern Adriatic, connecting Trieste, Rovinj and Pula, from late-June to mid-September. The Italian ferry company **SNAV** runs a fast daily Croatia Jet catamaran service between the cities of Ancona and Split from mid-June to late September (the journey time being 5 hours).

DIRECTORY

CROATIAN NATIONAL TOURIST BOARD

2 The Lanchesters, 162–64 Fulham Palace Road, London W6 9ER.
Tel (020) 8563 7979.
www.croatia.hr

AIRLINES

Aer Lingus
Tel 0871 718 2020 (from UK). **www**.aerlingus.com

British Airways
Tel 0844 493 0787 (from UK). **www**.britishairways.com

Croatia Airlines
Tel 0844 371 0310 (UK); (01) 667 6555 and (062) 500 505 (Cro).
www.croatiaairlines.com

EasyJet
Tel 0843 104 5000 (from UK). **www**.easyjet.com

Jet2.com
Tel 0901 230 0230 (from UK). **www**.jet2.com

Monarch
Tel 0871 940 5040 (from UK). **www**.monarch.co.uk

Ryanair
Tel 0871 246 0000 (from UK). **www**.ryanair.com

Wizz Air
Tel 0906 959 00 02 (from UK). **www**.wizzair.com

PACKAGE HOLIDAYS

Adriatic Holidays
Tel 01865 339 481 (UK).
www.adriaticholidays online.com

Balkan Holidays
Tel 0845 130 1114 (UK).
www.balkanholidays.co.uk

Light Blue Travel
Tel 01223 568 904 (UK).
www.lightbluetravel.co.uk

Saga Holidays
Tel 0800 096 0074.
http://travel.saga.co.uk

Thomson Holidays
Tel 0871 231 4691 (UK).
www.thomson.co.uk

COACHES

Dubrovnik bus station
Tel (060) 305 070.
http://libertasdubrovnik.hr

Eurolines
Tel 0044 871 781 8178.
www.eurolines.com

Split bus station
Tel (060) 327 777.
www.ak-split.hr

Trieste bus station
Tel 0039 040 425 020.
www.autostazionetrieste.it

Zagreb bus station
Tel (060) 313 333 and (01) 611 2789. **www**.akz.hr

RAILWAYS

Croatian Railways
Tel (060) 333 444 (Cro).
www.hznet.hr

European Rail
Unit 25, Tileyard Studios, Tileyard Road, London N7 9AH. **Tel** 020 7619 1083.
www.europeanrail.com

Rail Europe

193 Piccadilly, London W1J 9EU.
Tel 0844 848 4064.
www.raileurope.co.uk

FERRY SERVICES

Blue Line
Tel (0045) 3672 2001.
www.blueline-ferries.com

Jadrolinija
Riva 16, Rijeka.
Tel (051) 666 111.
www.jadrolinija.hr

SNAV
Ancona, Italy.
Tel 0039 071 207 6116.
www.snav.it

Trieste Lines
Viale Miramarer 9, Trieste, Italy.
Tel 0039 0923 873 813.
www.triestelines.it

Venezia Lines
Trg Matije Gupca 11, Poreč. **Tel** (052) 422 896.
www.venezialines.com

Getting Around Croatia

The transport system within Croatia is reasonably efficient, particularly if you are travelling by road or by sea. Connections between the mainland and the islands are excellent, and thanks to an extensive bus network, even smaller, lesser known towns can be easily reached. Although using air travel to get around the country is not that common, domestic flights link the major towns. Travelling by train is fine only if you have plenty of time as the rail network is small due to the mountainous terrain, and is in need of modernization. Train travel takes much longer than the time it takes to cover the same distance by road.

Biking in the mountainous terrain of Croatia

GREEN TRAVEL

In Croatia, when it comes to green travel, the most positive moves have been seen in Zagreb where as of 2007, the ZET (Zagreb Municipal Transit System) started using bio-fuels in public transport vehicles. Zagreb has a taxi company, called Eko Taxi, which markets itself as "low-emissions", and there are now marked cycle lanes in parts of the city, making it a bicycle-friendly destination.

Cycling in rural areas is growing in popularity, and cycling holidays are now available in Istria and parts of Dalmatia (mountain biking in the latter case). Hiking is also popular, both with Croatians and foreign visitors. The best seasons for hiking are spring and autumn. Organized hiking holidays are also available.

Last but not least, sailing is one of the most environmentally friendly ways of exploring the Croatian coast, using the power of wind as opposed to that of a motor.

DOMESTIC FLIGHTS

Croatia Airlines runs regular connections between the three major airports in the country – Zagreb, Split and Dubrovnik. There are also connections between these airports and other secondary airports, such as the airport of Osijek, Zadar, Rijeka (on the island of Krk), Pula and Brač, which is open only in the summer months.

TRAVELLING BY CAR

Cars drive on the right in Croatia and safety belts should be worn in both the front and back seats. Children under 12 must sit in the back.

The speed limits are 50 km/h (30 mph) in towns, 80 km/h (50 mph) outside built-up areas, and 130 km/h (80 mph) on the motorways. Cars towing caravans must not exceed 80 km/h (50 mph).

Road signs are generally more or less identical to those found in the rest of Europe.

Note that it is illegal to drive when drunk over the 0.5 per cent limit.

Service stations are open daily from 7am to 7 or 8pm, but in summer they are open till 10pm. On the main roads in the larger towns and cities and on major international routes service stations are open 24 hours a day. All the usual petrol types are available: Eurosuper 95, Eurosuper 98 and Eurodiesel.

ROADS AND TOLLS

As part of a vast programme of improvements to the country's infrastructure, the national motorway *(autocesta)* network is being extended, necessitating the building of several impressive viaducts and tunnels. Croatia's motorways are now regarded as among the most modern and safest in Europe. The new A1 motorway connecting Zagreb and Split opened in 2007, and a section from Split to Ploče in 2012, with an eventual extension planned all the way down the coast to Dubrovnik for 2015.

On certain stretches of motorway drivers pay a toll (by either cash or credit card): Zagreb–Karlovac, Zaprešić, Krapina, Varaždin-Goričan, Zagreb–Oprisavci, Rijeka–Delnice, Zagreb–Split. There is also a toll to pay for the bridge to the island of Krk and the Učka Tunnel.

PARKING

As elsewhere in Europe, car parking is an ever-increasing problem in most cities. Some hotels have parking spaces reserved for guests. If you are travelling by car it is worth checking this in advance. Likewise, in many smaller coastal towns, the seafront promenades are closed to traffic through the summer season, severely reducing parking spaces.

Where indicated, a parking ticket must be clearly displayed inside the windscreen. If you park in a no-parking area, your vehicle can be forcibly removed by officials.

Town traffic in the charming city of Osijek

BREAKDOWN ASSISTANCE AND TRAFFIC INFORMATION

Emergency road services are provided by the local **Automobile Club, HAK,** which can be reached 24 hours a day all year round by dialling 1987 (preceded by 003851 for calls from outside Croatia). The service provides repairs (a charge will apply) on the spot or in a garage (subject to transport), the removal of damaged cars and transport up to 100 km (62 miles) distance.

The HAK also provides useful information on road and maritime traffic, motor way tolls, any temporary diversions, the prices of petrol, ferry times, possible alternative routes and general assistance for those travelling by car. Their website – www.hak.hr – provides useful information and links.

ROAD CONDITIONS/ HAZARDS

Croatian roads are of a decent standard, comparable to those in most EU countries, while the newly constructed motorways are superior to most. However, the picturesque Magistrala (coastal highway), which runs down the Adriatic from Rijeka to Dubrovnik, twists and turns and can be extremely slippery when wet. On the islands and in rural areas, the roads may be narrow and poorly surfaced.

CAR HIRE

Car rental agencies can be found in all the main towns and cities, airports and holiday resorts. A valid driving licence is required and the driver must be at least 21 years old. Besides the well-known large multinational rent-a-car companies such as **Avis** and **Hertz**, there are many local independent companies as well.

The larger companies, however, offer the option of leaving the car in a different town from the collection point. Not all rental companies are able to offer this flexibility and there is always an extra charge for this service.

Entrance to a large railway station in Zagreb

TRAINS

Although the railway network in Croatia is slowly being modernized, travelling by train is not very popular except for the area around Zagreb. However, all the main Croatian towns and cities are linked by rail with the exception of Dubrovnik, where there is no railway station at all.

The main railway station is in the capital city (*Glavni Kolodvor Zagreb*). There are trains to Rijeka with connections to the Istrian towns; to Split, with a branch line for Zadar and Šibenik, serving the Dalmatian coast; to Osijek, to the east and Varaždin, to the north.

The following journey times can be expected: 4 hours for Zagreb to Rijeka, 6 hours from Zagreb to Split (or 8 hours 30 min by night), 2 hours for Zagreb–Varaždin, and 4 hours 30 minutes for Zagreb–Osijek. Express services operate on some routes. Croatian Railways (Hrvatske Željeznice) has its main office in Zagreb.

Travelling by coach in the city of Dubrovnik

BUSES

Buses are a convenient means of transport for visitors. The national bus service covers an extensive network across the country with numerous connections and destinations, although the tickets will be more expensive than on equivalent trains.

Suitcases and larger rucksacks will need to go into the luggage storage compartments below the bus and incur a surcharge.

Services are divided into "intercity" (direct connections between the larger cities) and the regional services (with connections between the smaller towns and the main cities).

There are daily connections between the towns and cities of Croatia and night buses cover the longer routes.

For information, go to the local bus station (*Autobusni Kolodvor*) and consult the timetable. *Vozi svaki dan* indicates the daily services, while *ne vozi nedjeljom ni praznikom* shows which services do not run on Sundays and public holidays. The main bus station in the country is the *Autobusni Kolodvor Zagreb* in Zagreb.

COACH TOURS

The travel agency **Atlas** offers a choice of coach tours, such as the 8-day escorted "Highlights of Croatia" which includes Dubrovnik, Split, Trogir, Zadar, Zagreb and Plitvice and the 10-day

"UNESCO Heritage Sites and National Parks of Croatia". Atlas also runs regular 1-day trips from Dubrovnik to nearby destinations such as Ston and Korčula, Mostar (in Bosnia Herzegovina) and the River Tara (in Montenegro).

ISLAND FERRIES

The majority of ferries and catamarans connecting the mainland and the islands are run by the state-owned company, **Jadrolinija**. These ferries can transport both passengers and vehicles.

The Croatian ferry network is divided into five districts. In the Rijeka district, Cres and Lošinj are connected to the mainland by the Valbiska–Merag and Brestova–Porozina routes. There is also a ferry running from Rijeka to Mali Lošinj, with stops at Cres, Unije and Susak en-route. The island of Rab is connected to the coast by the Jablanac–Mišnjak route and with the island of Krk by the Lopar–Valbiska route. Finally, the island of Pag is connected to the coast by the Prizna– Žigljen route, while Novalja on Pag is connected to Rijeka with a stop at Rab Town en-route.

In the district of Zadar, there are connections to the cities of Preko, on the island of Ugljan, Bribinj and Zaglav, on the island of Dugi Otok and from Biograd to Tkon on the island of Pašman.

In the district of Šibenik, the town is connected to the islands of Zlarin and Prvić.

In the Split district there are connections between Split and the islands of Brač (Supetar), Korčula (Vela Luka), Hvar (to Starigrad), Šolta (Rogač), Vis (to the port of the same name) and Lastovo (to Ubli). There are also connections between Makarska and Sumartin (island of Brač), between Ploče and Trpanj on the Pelješac peninsula, between Orebić and Dominče (on the island of Korčula) and between Drvenik and Sućuraj (island of Hvar).

Finally, in the district of Dubrovnik, the main connection is between Dubrovnik and the island of Mljet (Sobra), while there are also small ferries running between Dubrovnik and the Elaphiti islands of Koločep, Lopud and Šipan.

FERRY FREQUENCY

Ferry services run frequently in the high season (July and August), but are significantly reduced outside the summer months. On some short routes, such as Jablanac–Mišnjak and Drvenik–Sućuraj, ferries sail non-stop so as to cope with the long queues that tend to form in the middle of the day.

For those travelling without a car or motorbike, high-speed catamarans connect Split to the surrounding islands of Brač, Hvar, Vis, Korčula and Lastovo with the most frequent services from June to September. The crossing times range from 45 minutes to Hvar to 2 hours 30 mins to Lastovo.

In addition to Jadrolinija, there are several small private companies that operate certain routes. **G & V Line** runs catamarans from Dubrovnik to Mljet and from Zadar to several small nearby islands. **Linijska Nacionalna Plovidba** runs catamarans from Split to Brač and Šolta, and from Pula to Zadar (summer only), as well as ferries from Valbiska (on Krk) to Lopar (on Rab) and from Drvenik (on the mainland) to Dominča (on Korčula). **Miatours** runs hydrofoils from Zadar to the nearby islands, while **Rapska Plovidba** runs ferries from Jablanac (on the mainland) to Mišnjak (on Pag), and from Rab Town (on Rab) to Lun (on Pag).

DIRECTORY

AIRPORTS

Brač
Tel (021) 559 711.
www.airport-brac.hr

Dubrovnik
Tel (020) 773 100.
www.airport-dubrovnik.hr

Osijek
Tel (031) 514 400.
www.osijek-airport.hr

Pula
Tel (052) 530 105.
www.airport-pula.hr

Rijeka
Tel (060) 300 301.
www.rijeka-airport.hr

Split
Tel (021) 203 555.
www.split-airport.hr

Zadar
Tel (023) 205 800.
www.zadar-airport.hr

Zagreb
Tel (060) 320 320.
www.zagreb-airport.hr

DRIVING

Automobile Club, HAK
Tel 1987.
Tel (062) 777 777
(traffic information).

CAR RENTAL

Avis
Tel (01) 467 36 03.
www.avis.com.hr

Budget
Tel (062) 300 331.
www.budget.hr

Hertz
Tel (01) 484 67 77.
www.hertz.hr

BUSES

Autobusni Kolodvor Zagreb
Information
Tel (060) 313 333.
http://akz.hr

Autobusni Kolodvor Split
Information
Tel (060) 327 777.
www.ak-split.hr

COACH TOURS

Atlas
Vukovarska 19, Dubrovnik.
Tel (020) 442 222.
www.atlas-croatia.com

FERRIES

Jadrolinija
Tel (051) 666 111.
www.jadrolinija.hr

G & V Line
Tel (020) 313 119
(Dubrovnik) and
(023) 250 733 (Zadar).
www.gv-line.hr

Linijska Nacionalna Plovidba
Tel (021) 338 310.
www.lnp.hr

Miatours
Tel (023) 254 300.
www.miatours.hr

Rapska Plovidba
Tel (051) 724 122.
www.rapska-plovidba.hr

Getting Around Zagreb

The city of Zagreb has developed a good, efficient transport network which, by means of trams, buses and a funicular railway connecting the Lower and Upper Towns, ensures good connections between all the central and suburban districts. Trams run at regular intervals and there are some night services also. Gradec, the old town, has many areas which are pedestrianized and closed to ordinary traffic, making this a pleasant, pollution-free zone to stroll around in. There is no underground system in Zagreb.

White facade of St. Catherine's Church, Upper Town, Zagreb

WALKING

Zagreb is a very large city and visitors will need to use some form of public transport to get around. However, the best way to visit the centre, that is the areas of Kaptol and Gradec (together these are known as Gornji Grad or Upper Town), is to walk there. Walking is especially rewarding in the old centre of Zagreb with its venerable churches and imposing buildings.

It is a good idea to get a map of the city before setting off. Maps can be obtained from any tourist office. If you are lost and need assistance, you can always ask the locals for directions. They are generally friendly and helpful to tourists, although there may be a barrier to understanding if you are not familiar with the Croatian language.

TRAMS

The company that runs the capital's public transport is the Zagrebački Električni Tramvaj, known as **ZET**. The network of electric trams is efficient, with frequent services covering a wide area.

A total of 15 tram routes run during the day (starting at around 4am and ending at midnight) and four lines run at night (midnight to 4am).

The routes operating during the day are:
1 Zapadni kolodvor–Borongaj;
2 Črnomerec–Savišće;
3 Ljubljanica–Žitnjak;
4 Savski most–Dubec;
5 Jarun– Kvaternikov trg;
6 Črnomerec–Sopot;
7 Savski most–Dubrava;
8 Mihaljevac– Zapruđe;
9 Ljubljanica– Borongaj;
11 Črnomerec–Dubec;
12 Ljubljanica–Dubrava,
13 Žitnjak– Kvaternikov trg;
14 Mihaljevac–Zapruđe;
15 Mihaljevac–Dolje;
17 Prečko–Borongaj.

All the lines run frequently during the day with intervals of 6 to 10 minutes between trams, depending on whether it is a weekday or public holiday. On Sundays and other holidays tram numbers 3 and 8 do not run.

The four tram lines which run at night pass every 20 to 40 minutes on the following useful routes:
31 Črnomerec–Savski most,
32 Prečko–Borongaj;
33 Dolje–Savišće and
34 Ljubljanica–Dubec.

The main hub for tram stops is Trg bana Jelačića, where seven different tram routes intersect.

BUSES

There is an intricate network of bus connections with numerous routes branching out to the various termini: Britanski trg, Jandrićeva, Jankomir, Savski most, Ljubljanica, trg Mažuranića, Črnomerec, Mandaličina, Zaprešić, Kaptol, Petrova, Svetice, Dubrava, Kvaternikov trg, Glavni kolodvor, Žitnjak, Sesvete, Borongaj, Mihaljevac and Velika Gorica.

TICKETS

Tickets for trams and buses can be bought on board, from newsagents or kiosks (where they are slightly cheaper). The basic ticket is for a single journey. It must be punched in the machine as soon as you get on board and is valid for 90 minutes from that time. Tickets cost 12 kuna each (or 15 kuna from the driver on the bus or tram). There is also a one-day ticket that costs 40 kuna, a good idea if you intend to make various trips during the day (these

One of many tram lines serving the entire city

tickets are valid until 4am on the following day). Monthly season tickets are also available. A useful website is www.zagreb-touristinfo.hr. Travelling without a ticket is punishable by a fine of 210 kuna.

FUNICULAR RAILWAY

An interesting method of transport is the *uspinjača*, a steep funicular railway that has been in operation since 1890. At 66 m (216 ft), this is one of the shortest climbs in the world and takes a little less than a minute to climb up from the Lower Town to the Upper Town, arriving close to the Lotrščak tower. Departures are from Tomićeva street, right in the centre, and the cable cars leave every 10 minutes from 6.30am to 10pm (midnight in summer). The price of a single ticket is 5 kuna.

Funicular railway connecting the Lower and Upper Towns

CABLE CAR

The Žičara is a cable car that connects Zagreb with Sljeme, the highest peak in the Mount Medvednica range, in a journey time of 20 minutes. The system has been in operation since 1963, however it is currently closed for renovation as a new cable car is planned. Until this has been completed buses will connect Zagreb with Sljeme.

Taxis readily available in all the big cities of Croatia

TAXIS

In Zagreb, as in any other large city, taxis can be found readily. There are several small private companies, such as **Eko Taxi**, **Radio Taxi Zagreb** and **Taxi Cammeo**, all operating taxis with metres on board. Taxi fares vary from company to company, but you can expect to pay 15 kuna as the basic starting rate and then 6 kuna for every kilometre of your journey. Journeys made on Sundays, public holidays and at night can incur a surcharge, as can luggage.

CAR RENTAL

In the capital, it is also possible to rent a car by contacting one of the main car rental companies such as **Budget**, **Hertz** and **Avis**. Assistance while you are on the road is provided by the Croatian Automobile Club, which can also offer advice on routes (*see pp278–9*).

CYCLE HIRE/BIKE SCHEMES

Being fairly flat and even, Zagreb is a bicycle-friendly city. There is a network of clearly marked bicycle lanes connecting most of the main attractions, except for the medieval quarter of Gornji Grad. There are several companies offering bikes for hire in the city centre, and some companies, such as **Zagreb by Bike**, also arrange guided tours by bicycle.

(see pp278–9).

DIRECTORY

USEFUL NUMBERS

ZET
Tel (01) 365 15 55, 060 100 001.
www.zet.hr

TAXIS

Eko Taxi
Tel 1414 and (060) 77 77.
www.ekotaxi.hr

Radio Taxi Zagreb
Tel 1777, (060) 800 800.
www.radio-taksi-zagreb.hr

Taxi Cammeo Zagreb
Tel (060) 7100.
www.taxi-cammeo.hr

CAR RENTAL

Avis
Oreskoviceva 21, Zagreb.
Tel (01) 467 36 03.
www.avis.com.hr

Budget
c/o Hotel Sheraton,
Kneza Borne 2, Zagreb.
Tel (01) 467 61 11.
www.budget.hr

Kompas Hertz
Vukotinoviceva 4, Zagreb.
Tel (01) 484 67 77.
www.hertz.hr

CYCLE HIRE

Zagreb by Bike
Trg Franklin Roosevelt 5, Zagreb.
Tel (01) 370 77 92.
www.zagrebbybike.com

General Index

Acknowledgments

Fabio Ratti Editoria would like to thank the following staff at Dorling Kindersley:

Map Coordinator
Dave Pugh.

Senior DTP Manager
Jason Little.

Publishing Manager
Anna Streiffert.

Managing Art Editor
Marisa Renzullo.

Publisher
Douglas Amrine.

Dorling Kindersley would also like to thank all those whose contribution and assistance have made the preparation of this book possible.

Principal Author
Leandro Zoppè was born in Venice and graduated in Political Science from Padua University. At present he lives in Milan where, as a historian, he works as a freelance journalist and writer of tour guides and historical, artistic or naturalistic books.

Contributors
Božidarka Boza Gligorijević, Public Relations Manager for the Croatian National Tourist Board in Milan; Graeme Harwood, author and gourmand.

Text Revision
Sanja Rojić (University professor),
Iva Grgic (University professor).

Checking of Practical Information
Lucia Čutura, Viktor Jovanović Marušić, Jane Foster.

Senior Editor, UK Edition
Jacky Jackson.

Proof Reader
Alessandra Lombardi, Stewart J Wild.

Indexer
Helen Peters.

Fact Checker
Katarina Bulic.

Revisions Team
Claire Baranowski, Marta Bescos, Sonal Bhatt, Nadia Bonomally, Louise Cleghorn, Karen DSouza, Anna Fischel, Anna Freiberger, Prerna Gupta, Kaberi Hazarika, Juliet Kenny, Sumita Khatwani, Carly Madden, Sam Merrell, Nataša Novakovic, Ellen Root, Julie Thompson, Ajay Verma, Dora Whitaker.

Special Thanks
Croatian National Tourist Board, Zagreb, in particular the director Niko Bulić; Croatian National Tourist Board, Milan, in particular the director Klaudio Stojnic and the public relations manager Božidarka Boza Gligorijević; the regional and local tourist boards of Croatia; Vinko Bakija (director of the tourist office, Supetar, island of Brač); Zdravko Banović (tourist office, Split); Daniela Barac (tourist guide in Crikvenica); Nikša Bender (marketing manager of the tourist office of Dubrovnik); Maja Boban (tourist guide of the environs of Zagreb); Ankita Boksic Franchini (tourist office, Split); Tanja Bunjevac (tourist office, Varaždin) Rujana Bušić (tourist guide in Vinkovci); Vanja Dadić (tourist guide in Šibenik); Mirjana Darrer (public relations manager of the tourist office in Dubrovnik); Marchese Doimo Frangipane di Aiello del Friuli; Danijela Duić (tourist guide in Karlovac); Jurica Dužević (director of the tourist office in Stari Grad, island of Hvar); Daniela Fanikutić (tourist office, Poreč); Ennio Forlani (director of the tourist office of Vodnjan); Vesna Gamulin (tourist guide in Dubrovnik); Miljenko Gašparac (guard of the Risnjak National Park); Boris Gržina (front office manager of the Hotel Esplanade in Zagreb); Vesna Habazin and Snježana Hrupelj (tourist guides in the area of the thermal spas); Mladenka Jarac-Rončević (Croatian Consul in Italy); Zoran Jelaska (tourist guide in Split); Vesna Jovičić (tourist guide in Pula); Darko Kovačić (tourist guide in the Lonjsko Polje Nature Park); Darko Kovačić (director of the tourist office, Omiš); Stanka Kraljević (director of the tourist office in the town of Korčula); Vlasta Krklec (Museum of Krapina); Tonči Lalić (tourist guide in Makarska); Damir Macanić (director of the tourist office in Osijek); Damir Mihalić (tourist office, Varaždinske Toplice); Josip Mikolčić (tourist office, Virovitica); Danijela Miletić (tourist office, Zagreb); Smiljan Mitrović (tourist guide in Zadar); Franjo Mrzljak (director of the National Museum of Naive Art, Zagreb); Andro Krstulović Opara (former Croatian Consul in Italy); Ottone Novosel (tourist guide in Križevci); Ankica Pandzic (director of the Museum of Croatian History in Zagreb); Danika Plazibat (Meštrović Gallery, Zagreb); Gordana Perić (tourist office, Zadar); Ante Rendić-Miočević (director of the Archaeological Museum, Zagreb); Mladen Radić (Director of the Museum of Slavonia, Osijek); Ljubica Ramušćak (Civic Museum of Medimurje, Cakovec); Ljiljana Sever (tourist guide in Varaždin); Josipa Šipek (director of Hotel Coning in Trakošćan); Doris Staničić (tourist guide in Osijek); Alka Starac (Archaeological Museum of Istria, Pula); Branka Tropp (director of the tourist office in Varaždin); Duro Vandura (director of the Gallery of Ancient Masters, Zagreb); Klara Vedriš (Gallery of Modern Art, Zagreb); Vjenceslav Vlahov (tourist guide in Zagreb); Igor Zidić (director of the Gallery of Modern Art, Zagreb); Marko Zoričić (director of the tourist office in Opatija).

DK wishes to thank Lady Beresford-Peirse of the International Trust for Croatian Monuments for her time and invaluable suggestions.

Photography Permissions

The publisher would like to thank all the museums, the local corporations and associations, hotels, restaurants, shops and other places of interest for their co-operation and their kind permission in allowing their establishments to be photographed.

Additional Photography

Adriano Bacchella, Nataša Novakovic, Aldo Pavan, Lucio Rossi, Rough Guides/Tim Draper, Tony Souter, Leandro Zoppé

Picture Credits

Key to positions: a=above, b=below/bottom, c=centre, f=far, l=left, r=right, t=top.

The publisher would like to thank the following individuals, associations and photograpic agencies for permission to reproduce their photographs:

ALAMY IMAGES: Comstock Images: 15c; Europe/ Peter Forsberg 281tr; Jason Wallengren Photography 237tl; Jon Arnold Images/Alan Copson 11cl; Peter Adams Photography/Peter Adams 10bl; toto 237c; ALDO PAVAN, AURA AGENCY, MILAN: 15tc, 24cl, 46cb, 68br, 97crb, 112cla, 132cl, 132cr, 134tl, 135b, 136cl, 136cr, 137clb, 239cl, 250cl, 254tc, 254cl, 255tl, 256tl; ARCHAEOLOGICAL MUSEUM, Zagreb: 31tc, 31br, 164c, 165c, 169c, 190c; THE ART ARCHIVE: 35br.

CORBIS: Ruggero Vanni: 144b; Reuters/Matko Bijlak 238cl; Seth Joel 272br; CROATIA AIRLINES: 274bl; THE CROATIAN NATIONAL TOURIST BOARD ARCHIVES, MILAN: 1c, 2–3, 19bl, 20bc, 21tc, 19cl, 23cl, 24tc, 24br, 25tl, 26–27 (all), 28, 32t, 33bc, 34bc, 38tc, 46tr, 67t, 98crb, 99tl, 106cla, 107cr, 112br, 113tl, 115cl, 124 (all), 130t, 131tr, 131br, 133 (all), 134cr, 134bl, 135tl, 135c, 136tr, 136bl, 137tl, 137cra, 137br, 138–139, 140cr, 143ca, 146c, 146br, 147 (all), 152bl, 158tl, 175bl, 180, 186tl, 194br, 200cl, 201br, 202cl, 212c, 213tr, 221tl, 234tc, 252tl, 253tc, 255br, 257tr, 258tc, 259cl, 2591br, 261bc, 264tc, Dubrovnik-Jesuit monastery/Sergio Gobbo 266bl, 273 (all), 276cl, Luka Tambaca 277cl, 278bc, 281cl; CROATIAN RAILWAYS: Dragutin Staničić 278tr.

DK IMAGES: 12bl, 238cr, 270bc; DOIMO FRANGIPANE:

177cla, 177cr; DREAMSTIME.COM: Photoinsel 270bl.

GALLERY OF MODERN ART, Zagreb: 8–9, 162b; GALLERY OF OLD MASTERS, Zagreb: 164–165 (all).

ILOK CIVIC MUSEUM: 187br; IMAGE BANK, MILAN: 56br, 67br, 86cl, 87tr, 91tl, 145br, 151crb, 160tl. MARCO LISSONI: 20br, 70cr, 106tl, 114cl, 132tl, 253br, 254br; LONELY PLANET IMAGES: Wayne Walton 13tr. MEŠTROVIĆ GALLERY, Zagreb: 20tr, 154tl, 157cr, 157bl, 157br; MONDADORI ARCHIVES: 9 (frame), 18bcl, 21cr, 30tl, 31tr, 31bc, 37 (all), 38cr, 38bc, 39 (all), 40tl, 40bl, 40br, 41bc, 42tl, 45 (frame), 121tl, 157tc, 157cl, 177ca, 192tl, 194tr, 195cra, 195crb, 195bl, 206br, 217 (frame), 239tlc, 259tc, 263 (frame); MUSEUM OF CROATIAN HISTORY, Zagreb: 40cb, 41tc, 41clb, 42cb, 154cl.

NATIONAL MUSEUM OF NAIVE ART, Zagreb: 21bl, 154bl, 159tl.

OFFICE OF THE PRESIDENT OF THE REPUBLIC OF CROATIA: 43tc.

PAKLENICA NATIONAL PARK: 18cl, 101c, 101b, 101tr, 260 (all); ANDREA PISTOLESI: 111tr.

T-COM CROATIA: 270bc; THE REGENT ESPLANADE ZAGREB: 219, Niall Clutton 235br; THE STROSSMAYER GALLERY: 164cb; TOURIST BOARD OF KRAPINA-ZAGORJE COUNTY: 212bc, 212bl; TOURIST BOARD OF PAG: 103tl.

VALSABBION: 234cl.

WESTERN ZAGREB HOTEL: 219br.

ZAGREB MUNICIPAL TRANSIT SYSTEM (ZET): Goran Kekic 280bc.

JACKET

Front – PHOTOLIBRARY: Ellen Rooney.
Back – AWL IMAGES: Travel Pix Collection tl; DORLING KINDERSLEY: Lucio Rossi bl; Tony Souter clb; Leandro Zoppe cla.
Spine – PHOTOLIBRARY: Ellen Rooney t.

All other images © Dorling Kindersley.
For further information: www.dkimages.com

Road Map of Croatia

Phrase Book

Pronounciation

c – "ts" as in rats
č – "chi" as in church
ć – "t" is a soft t
đ – "d" is a soft d
g – "g" is a hard g as in get
j – "y" as in yes
š – sh
Ž – shown here as "zh", sounds like the "J" in the French name, Jacques
"aj" – shown here as "igh", sounds like "I" or the "igh" in night.

In Emergency

Help!	Pomoć!	pomoch
Stop!	Stani!	stahnee
Call a doctor!	Zovite doktora!	zoveetey doktorah
Call an ambulance!	Zovite hitnu pomoć!	zoveetey heetnoo pomoch
Call the police!	Zovite policiju!	zoveetey poleetseeyoo
Call the fire brigade!	Zovite vatrogasce!	zoveetey vatrohgastsay
Where is the nearest telephone?	Gdje je najbliži telefon?	gdyey yey n-igh-bleezhee telefon
Where is the nearest hospital?	Gdje je najbliža bolnica?	gdyey yey n-igh-bleezhah bolnitsa

Communication Essentials

Yes	da	dah
No	ne	ney
Please	molim vas	moleem vas
Thank you	hvala	hvahlah
Excuse me	oprostite	oprosteetey
Hello	dobar dan	dobar dan
Goodbye	dovidenja	doveedjenya
Good night	laku noc	lakoo noch
Morning	jutro	yootroh
Afternoon	popodne	popodney
Evening	večer	vecher
Yesterday	jučer	yoocher
Today	danas	danas
Tomorrow	sutra	sootrah
Here	tu	too
There	tamo	tahmoh
What?	što?	shtoh
When?	kada?	kada
Why?	zašto?	zashtoh
Where?	gdje?	gdyey

Useful Phrases

How are you?	Kako ste?	kakoh stey
Very well, thank you	Dobro, hvala	dobroh, hvahlah
Pleased to meet you	Drago mi je!	dragoh mee yey
See you soon	Vidimo se	veedeemoh sey
That's fine	U redu	oo redoo
Where is/are...?	Gdje je/su?	gdyey yey/soo
How far is it to...?	Koliko je daleko do...?	kolikoh yey dalekoh doh...
How can I get to...?	Kako mogu doći do...?	kakoh mogoo dochee doh...
Do you speak English?	Govorite li engleski?	govoreetey lee engleskee
I don't understand	Ne razumijem	nay razoomeeyem
Could you speak more slowly please?	Molim vas, možete li govoriti sporije?	moleem vas, mozhetey lee govoreetee sporiyey
I'm sorry	Žao mi je	zhaoh mee yey

Useful Words

big	veliko	veleekoh
small	malo	mahloh
hot	vruć	vrooch
cold	hladan	hlahdan
good	dobar	dobar
bad	loš	losh
enough	dosta	dostah
well	dobro	dobroh
open	otvoreno	otvohrenoh
closed	zatvoreno	zatvohrenoh
left	lijevo	leeyevoh
right	desno	desnoh
straight on	ravno	ravnoh
near	blizu	bleezoo
far	daleko	dalekoh
up	gore	gorey
down	dolje	dolyey
early	rano	ranoh
late	kasno	kasnoh
entrance	ulaz	oolaz
exit	izlaz	eezlaz
toilet	WC	Vey tsey
more	više	veeshey
less	manje	manyey

Shopping

How much does this cost?	Koliko ovo košta?	kolikoh ovoh koshta
I would like...	Volio bih...	volioh bee...
Do you have...?	Imate li...?	eematey lee...
I'm just looking	Samo gledam	Samoh gledam
Do you take credit cards?	Primate li kreditne kartice?	preematey lee credeetney carteetsey
What time do you open?	Kad otvarate?	kad otvaratey
What time do you close?	Kad zatvarate?	kad zatvaratey
This one	Ovaj	ov-igh
That one	Onaj	on-igh
expensive	skupo	skoopoh
cheap	jeftino	yefteenoh
size (clothes)	veličina	veleechinah
size (shoes)	broj	broy
white	bijelo	beeyeloh
black	crno	tsrnoh
red	crveno	tsrvenoh
yellow	žuto	zhootoh
green	zeleno	zelenoh
blue	plavo	plavoh
bakery	pekara	pekarah
bank	banka	bankah
book shop	knjižara	knyeezharah
butcher's	mesnica	mesnitsah
cake shop	slastičarna	slasteecharnah
chemist's	apoteka	apohtekah
fishmonger's	ribarnica	reebarnitsah
market	tržnica	trzhneetsah
hairdresser's	frizer	freezer
newsagent's/ tobacconist	trafika	trafeekah
post office	pošta	poshtah
shoe shop	prodavaonica cipela	prodavaonitsa tseepelah
supermarket	supermarket	soopermarket
travel agent	putnička agencija	pootneechka agentseeyah

Sightseeing

art gallery	galerija umjetnina	galereeyah oomyetneenah
cathedral	katedrala	katedralah
church	crkva	tsrkvah
garden	vrt	vurt
library	knjižnica	knyeezhneetsah
museum	muzej	moozey
tourist information centre	turistički ured	tooreesteechkey oored
town hall	gradska vijećnica	gradskah veeyechneetsa
closed for holiday	zatvoreno zbog praznika	zatvorenoh zbog prazneekah
bus station	autobusni kolodvor	aootoboosnee kolodvor
railway station	željeznički kolodvor	zhelyeznichkih kolodvor

Staying in a Hotel

Do you have a vacant room?	Imate li sobu?	eematey lee soboo
double room	dvokrevetna soba	dvokrevetnah sobah
single room	jednokrevetna soba	yednokrevetnah sobah
room with a bath	soba sa kupatilom	sobah sah koopateelom
shower	tuš	toosh

porter	portir	portir
key	ključ	klyooch
I have a reservation	Imam rezervaciju	eemam rezervatseeyoo

Eating Out

Have you got a table for...?	Imate li stol za...?	eematey lee stol zah
I want to reserve a table	Želim rezervirati stol	Zheleem rezerveeratee stol
The bill please	Molim vas, račun	moleem vas, rachoon
I am a vegetarian	Ja sam vegeterijanac	yah sam vegetereeyanats
waiter/waitress	konobar/ konobarica	konobar/ konobaritsah
menu	jelovnik	yelovneek
wine list	vinska karta	veenskah kartah
glass	čaša	chashah
bottle	boca	botsah
knife	nož	nozh
fork	viljuška	veelyooshkah
spoon	žlica	zhleetsah
breakfast	doručak	doroochak
lunch	ručak	roochak
dinner	večera	vecherah
main course	glavno jelo	glavnoh yeloh
starters	predjela	predyelah

Menu Decoder

bijela riba	beeyelah reebah	"white" fish
blitva	bleetvah	Swiss chard
brudet	broodet	fish stew
čevapčići	chevapcheechee	meatballs
crni rižot	tsrnee reezhot	black risotto (prepared with cuttlefish ink)
desert	desert	dessert
glavno jelo	glavnoh yeloh	main course
grah	grah	beans
gulaš	goolash	goulash
jastog	yastog	lobster
juha	yoohah	soup
kuhano	koohanoh	cooked
maslinovo ulje	masleenovoh oolyey	olive oil
meso na žaru	mesoh nah zharoo	barbecued meat
miješano meso	meeyeshanoh mesoh	mixed grilled meats
na žaru	nah zharoo	barbecued
ocat	otsat	vinegar
palačinke	palacheenkay	pancakes
papar	papar	pepper
paški sir	pashkih seer	sheep's cheese from Pag
pečeno	pechenoh	baked
piletina	peeleteenah	chicken
plava riba	plavah reebah	"blue" fish
predjelo	predyeloh	starters
prilog	preelog	side dish
pršut	prshoot	smoked ham
pržene lignje	przhene leegnyey	fried squid
prženo	przhenoh	fried
ramsteak	ramsteyk	rump steak
ražnjići	razhnyeechee	pork kebabs
riba na žaru	reebah nah zharoo	barbecued fish
rižot frutti di mare	reezhot frootee dee marey	seafood risotto
rižot sa škampima	reezhot sah shkampeemah	scampi risotto
salata	salatah	salad
salata od hobotnice	salatah od hobotneetsey	octopus salad
sarma	sarmah	cabbage leaves
sir	seer	cheese
sladoled	sladoled	ice cream
slana srdela	slanah srdelah	salted sardines
škampi na buzaru	shkampee nah boozaroo	scampi in tomato and onion
školjke na buzaru	shkolkay nah boozaroo	shellfish in tomato and onion

špageti frutti di mare	shpagetee frootee dee marey	spaghetti with seafood
sol	sol	salt
tjestenina	tjesteneenah	pasta stuffed with meat and rice
ulje	oolyey	oil
varivo	vareevoh	boiled vegetables

Drinks

bijelo vino	beeyeloh veenoh	white wine
čaj	ch-igh	tea
crno vino	tsrnoh veenoh	red wine
gazirana mineralna voda	gazeeranah meeneralnah vodah	sparkling mineral water
kava	kavah	coffee
negazirana mineralna voda	neygazeeranah meeneralnah vodah	still mineral water
pivo	peevoh	beer
rakija	rakeeyah	spirit
tamno pivo	tamnoh peevoh	stout (dark beer)
travarica	travareetsah	spirit flavoured with herbs
voda	vodah	water

Numbers

0	nula	noolah
1	jedan	yedan
2	dva	dvah
3	tri	tree
4	četiri	cheteeree
5	pet	pet
6	šest	shest
7	sedam	sedam
8	osam	osam
9	devet	devet
10	deset	deset
11	jedanaest	yedanest
12	dvanaest	dvahnest
13	trinaest	treenest
14	četrnaest	chetrnest
15	petnaest	petnest
16	šestnaest	shestnest
17	sedamnaest	sedamnest
18	osamnaest	osamnest
19	devetnaest	devetnest
20	dvadeset	dvahdeset
21	dvadeset i jedan	dvahdeset ee yedan
22	dvadeset i dva	dvahdeset ee dvah
30	trideset	treedeset
31	trideset i jedan	treedeset ee yedan
40	četrdeset	chetrdeset
50	pedeset	pedeset
60	šezdeset	shezdeset
70	sedamdeset	sedamdeset
80	osamdeset	osamdeset
90	devedeset	devedeset
100	sto	stoh
101	sto i jedan	stoh ee yedan
102	sto i dva	stoh ee dvah
200	dvjesto	dveestoh
500	petsto	petstoh
700	sedamsto	sedamstoh
900	devetsto	devetstoh
1,000	tisuću	teesoochoo
1,001	tisuću i jedan	teesoochoo ee yedan

Time

One minute	jedna minuta	yedna meenootah
One hour	jedan sat	yedan saht
Half an hour	pola sata	polah sahtah
Monday	ponedjeljak	ponedyelyak
Tuesday	utorak	ootorak
Wednesday	srijeda	sreejedah
Thursday	četvrtak	chetvrtak
Friday	petak	petak
Saturday	subota	soobotah
Sunday	nedjelja	nedyelyah

Phrase Book

Pronounciation

c – "ts" as in rats
č – "chi" as in church
ć – "t" is a soft t
đ – "d" is a soft d
g – "g" is a hard g as in get
j – "y" as in yes
š – sh
Ž – shown here as "zh", sounds like the "J" in the French name, Jacques
"aj" – shown here as "igh", sounds like "I" or the "igh" in night.

In Emergency

Help!	Pomoć!	pomoch
Stop!	Stani!	stahnee
Call a doctor!	Zovite doktora!	zoveetey doktorah
Call an ambulance!	Zovite hitnu pomoć!	zoveetey heetnoo pomoch
Call the police!	Zovite policiju!	zoveetey poleetseeyoo
Call the fire brigade!	Zovite vatrogasce!	zoveetey vatrohgastsay
Where is the nearest telephone?	Gdje je najbliži telefon?	gdyey yey n-igh-bleezhee telefon
Where is the nearest hospital?	Gdje je najbliža bolnica?	gdyey yey n-igh-bleezhah bolnitsa

Communication Essentials

Yes	da	dah
No	ne	ney
Please	molim vas	moleem vas
Thank you	hvala	hvahlah
Excuse me	oprostite	oprosteetey
Hello	dobar dan	dobar dan
Goodbye	dovidenja	doveedjenya
Good night	laku noc	lakoo noch
Morning	jutro	yootroh
Afternoon	popodne	popodney
Evening	večer	vecher
Yesterday	jučer	yoocher
Today	danas	danas
Tomorrow	sutra	sootrah
Here	tu	too
There	tamo	tahmoh
What?	što?	shtoh
When?	kada?	kada
Why?	zašto?	zashtoh
Where?	gdje?	gdyey

Useful Phrases

How are you?	Kako ste?	kakoh stey
Very well, thank you	Dobro, hvala	dobroh, hvahlah
Pleased to meet you	Drago mi je!	dragoh mee yey
See you soon	Vidimo se	veedeemoh sey
That's fine	U redu	oo redoo
Where is/are…?	Gdje je/su?	gdyey yey/soo
How far is it to…?	Koliko je daleko do…?	kolikoh yey dalekoh doh…
How can I get to…?	Kako mogu doći do…?	kakoh mogoo dochee doh…
Do you speak English?	Govorite li engleski?	govoreetey lee engleskee
I don't understand	Ne razumijem	nay razoomeeyem
Could you speak more slowly please?	Molim vas, možete li govoriti sporije?	moleem vas, mozhetey lee govoreetee sporiyey
I'm sorry	Žao mi je	zhaoh mee yey

Useful Words

big	veliko	veleekoh
small	malo	mahloh
hot	vruć	vrooch
cold	hladan	hlahdan
good	dobar	dobar
bad	loš	losh
enough	dosta	dostah
well	dobro	dobroh
open	otvoreno	otvohrenoh
closed	zatvoreno	zatvohrenoh
left	lijevo	leeyevoh

right	desno	desnoh
straight on	ravno	ravnoh
near	blizu	bleezoo
far	daleko	dalekoh
up	gore	gorey
down	dolje	dolyey
early	rano	ranoh
late	kasno	kasnoh
entrance	ulaz	oolaz
exit	izlaz	eezlaz
toilet	WC	Vey tsey
more	više	veeshey
less	manje	manyey

Shopping

How much does this cost?	Koliko ovo košta?	kolikoh ovoh koshta
I would like…	Volio bih…	volioh bee…
Do you have…?	Imate li…?	eematey lee…
I'm just looking	Samo gledam	Samoh gledam
Do you take credit cards?	Primate li kreditne kartice?	preematey lee credeetney carteetsey
What time do you open?	Kad otvarate?	kad otvaratey
What time do you close?	Kad zatvarate?	kad zatvaratey
This one	Ovaj	ov-igh
That one	Onaj	on-igh
expensive	skupo	skoopoh
cheap	jeftino	yefteenoh
size (clothes)	veličina	veleechInah
size (shoes)	broj	broy
white	bijelo	beeyeloh
black	crno	tsrnoh
red	crveno	tsrvenoh
yellow	žuto	zhootoh
green	zeleno	zelenoh
blue	plavo	plavoh
bakery	pekara	pekarah
bank	banka	bankah
book shop	knjižara	knyeezharah
butcher's	mesnica	mesnitsah
cake shop	slastičarna	slasteecharnah
chemist's	apoteka	apohtekah
fishmonger's	ribarnica	reebarnitsah
market	tržnica	trzhneetsah
hairdresser's	frizer	freezer
newsagent's/ tobacconist	trafika	trafeekah
post office	pošta	poshtah
shoe shop	prodavaonica cipela	prodavaonitsa tseepelah
supermarket	supermarket	soopermarket
travel agent	putnička agencija	pootneechka agentseeyah

Sightseeing

art gallery	galerija umjetnina	galereeyah oomyetneenah
cathedral	katedrala	katedralah
church	crkva	tsrkvah
garden	vrt	vurt
library	knjižnica	knyeezhneetsah
museum	muzej	moozey
tourist information centre	turistički ured	tooreesteechkey oored
town hall	gradska vijećnica	gradskah veeyechneetsa
closed for holiday	zatvoreno zbog praznika	zatvorenoh zbog prazneekah
bus station	autobusni kolodvor	aootoboosnee kolodvor
railway station	željeznički kolodvor	zhelyeznichkih kolodvor

Staying in a Hotel

Do you have a vacant room?	Imate li sobu?	eematey lee soboo
double room	dvokrevetna soba	dvokrevetnah sobah
single room	jednokrevetna soba	yednokrevetnah sobah
room with a bath	soba sa kupatilom	sobah sah koopateeloom
shower	tuš	toosh

porter	portir	portir
key	ključ	klyooch
I have a reservation	Imam	eemam
	rezervaciju	rezervatseeyoo

Eating Out

Have you got a table for...?	Imate li stol za...?	eematey lee stol zah
I want to reserve a table	Želim rezervirati stol	Zheleem rezerveeratee stol
The bill please	Molim vas, račun	moleem vas, rachoon
I am a vegetarian	Ja sam vegeterijanac	yah sam vegetereeyanats
waiter/waitress	konobar/ konobarica	konobar/ konobaritsah
menu	jelovnik	yelovneek
wine list	vinska karta	veenskah kartah
glass	čaša	chashah
bottle	boca	botsah
knife	nož	nozh
fork	viljuška	veelyooshkah
spoon	žlica	zhleetsah
breakfast	doručak	doroochak
lunch	ručak	roochak
dinner	večera	vecherah
main course	glavno jelo	glavnoh yeloh
starters	predjela	predyelah

Menu Decoder

bijela riba	beeyelah reebah	"white" fish
blitva	bleetvah	Swiss chard
brudet	broodet	fish stew
ćevapčići	chevapcheechee	meatballs
crni rižot	tsrnee reezhot	black risotto (prepared with cuttlefish ink)
desert	desert	dessert
glavno jelo	glavnoh yeloh	main course
grah	grah	beans
gulaš	goolash	goulash
jastog	yastog	lobster
juha	yoohah	soup
kuhano	koohanoh	cooked
maslinovo ulje	masleenovoh oolyey	olive oil
meso na žaru	mesoh nah zharoo	barbecued meat
miješano meso	meejeshanoh mesoh	mixed grilled meats
na žaru	nah zharoo	barbecued
ocat	otsat	vinegar
palačinke	palacheenkay	pancakes
papar	papar	pepper
paški sir	pashkih seer	sheep's cheese from Pag
pečeno	pechenoh	baked
piletina	peeleteenah	chicken
plava riba	plavah reebah	"blue" fish
predjelo	predyeloh	starters
prilog	preelog	side dish
pršut	prshoot	smoked ham
pržene lignje	przhene leegnyey	fried squid
prženo	przhenoh	fried
ramsteak	ramsteyk	rump steak
ražnjići	razhnyeechee	pork kebabs
riba na žaru	reebah nah zharoo	barbecued fish
rižot frutti di mare	reezhot frootee dee marey	seafood risotto
rižot sa škampima	reezhot sah shkampeemah	scampi risotto
salata	salatah	salad
salata od hobotnice	salatah od hobotneetsey	octopus salad
sarma	sarmah	cabbage leaves
sir	seer	cheese
sladoled	sladoled	ice cream
slana srdela	slanah srdelah	salted sardines
škampi na buzaru	shkampee nah boozaroo	scampi in tomato and onion
školjke na buzaru	shkolkay nah boozaroo	shellfish in tomato and onion

špageti frutti di mare	shpagetee frootee dee marey	spaghetti with seafood
sol	sol	salt
tjestenina	tjesteneenah	pasta stuffed with meat and rice
ulje	oolyey	oil
varivo	vareevoh	boiled vegetables

Drinks

bijelo vino	beeyeloh veenoh	white wine
čaj	ch-igh	tea
crno vino	tsrnoh veenoh	red wine
gazirana mineralna voda	gazeeranah meeneralnah vodah	sparkling mineral water
kava	kavah	coffee
negazirana mineralna voda	neygazeeranah meeneralnah vodah	still mineral water
pivo	peevoh	beer
rakija	rakeeyah	spirit
tamno pivo	tamnoh peevoh	stout (dark beer)
travarica	travareetsah	spirit flavoured with herbs
voda	vodah	water

Numbers

0	nula	noolah
1	jedan	yedan
2	dva	dvah
3	tri	tree
4	četiri	cheteeree
5	pet	pet
6	šest	shest
7	sedam	sedam
8	osam	osam
9	devet	devet
10	deset	deset
11	jedanaest	yedanest
12	dvanaest	dvahnest
13	trinaest	treenest
14	četrnaest	chetrnest
15	petnaest	petnest
16	šestnaest	shestnest
17	sedamnaest	sedamnest
18	osamnaest	osamnest
19	devetnaest	devetnest
20	dvadeset	dvahdeset
21	dvadeset i jedan	dvahdeset ee yedan
22	dvadeset i dva	dvahdeset ee dvah
30	trideset	treedeset
31	trideset i jedan	treedeset ee yedan
40	četrdeset	chetrdeset
50	pedeset	pedeset
60	šezdeset	shezdeset
70	sedamdeset	sedamdeset
80	osamdeset	osamdeset
90	devedeset	devedeset
100	sto	stoh
101	sto i jedan	stoh ee yedan
102	sto i dva	stoh ee dvah
200	dvjesto	dveestoh
500	petsto	petstoh
700	sedamsto	sedamstoh
900	devetsto	devetstoh
1,000	tisuću	teesoochoo
1,001	tisuću i jedan	teesoochoo ee yedan

Time

One minute	jedna minuta	yedna meenootah
One hour	jedan sat	yedan saht
Half an hour	pola sata	polah sahtah
Monday	ponedjeljak	ponedyelyak
Tuesday	utorak	ootorak
Wednesday	srijeda	sreejedah
Thursday	četvrtak	chetvrtak
Friday	petak	petak
Saturday	subota	soobotah
Sunday	nedjelja	nedyelyah